Politics, Globalization and Insurgency

By the same Author

- Development Issues in Contemporary India
- Rural Development Under Decentralised Governance
- Rural Development Governance and Participation

About the Editor

Dr. M.R. Biju, (b. 1965) Editor of South Asian Journal of Socio-Political Studies (SAJOSPS) is a prolific writer on socio-political and developmental issues. He has published 24 books and 115 research papers in the prestigious journals published from India and abroad. He is also working as Member, Associate Board of the renowned Management Journal Economics and Management (E+M) published by the Technical University of Liberce, Czech Republic. He is also serving as Member Editorial Advisory Board of the International Journal of Business and Innovation. He has reviewed over Seven Hundred books for South Asian Journal of Socio-Political Studies.

He was conferred with Post Doctoral Research Award by the University Grants Commission in 2004-2007. He has successfully completed three major research projects on Panchayati Raj funded by Ministry of Panchayati Raj, Government of India and University Grants Commission.

Dr. Biju has successfully guided doctoral students of University of Kerala and also been serving with over a dozen of professional, academic organizations of national and global repute. He has presented papers and chaired sessions of a number of national and international seminars and conferences. He is also working as Director and Member Secretary of the Asian Institute of Development Research (AIDR) since 2007. Dr. Biju is currently working as Associate Professor, PG & Research and Department of Political Science, Sree Narayana College. Kollam affiliated to University of Kerala. He is a Member in the PG Board of Studies in Political Science and Public Administration, University of Kerala.

Politics, Globalization and Insurgency

Trends and Challenges

Edited by

M.R. Biju

CONCEPT PUBLISHING COMPANY PVT. LTD.
NEW DELHI-110059

ISBN-13: 978-93-5125-155-2

First Published 2015

Published and Printed by

Concept
Since 1974

Concept Publishing Company Pvt. Ltd.
A/15-16, Commercial Block, Mohan Garden
New Delhi-110059 (India)
T: 25351460, 25351794, *F*: 091-11-25357109
E: publishing@conceptpub.com, W: www.conceptpub.com
Editorial Office: H-13, Bali Nagar, New Delhi-110 015, India.

Cataloging in Publication Data--Courtesy: D.K. Agencies (P) Ltd. <docinfo@dkagencies.com>

Politics, globalization and insurgency : trends and challenges / edited by M.R. Biju.
pages cm
Includes bibliographical references and index.
ISBN 9789351251552

1. India--Politics and government--21st century. 2. Globalization--Economic aspects--India. 3. Insurgency--India. I. Biju, M. R., 1965-, editor.

DDC 320.954 23

Dedicated

to

the everloving and everlasting

memory of my beloved wife

JAYA BIJU

(7th September, 1969–31st August, 2012)

Acknowledgements

I would like to express my gratitude to those who have been kind enough to help me in the preparation of this volume. I wish to express a deep sense of gratitude to the esteemed contributors to this anthology of articles. The views and opinions expressed by the contributors are of immense value for researchers and academics and administrators for framing policies and strategies on Indian Polity and Governance. I am extremely thankful to Shri Ashok Kumar Mittal of Concept Publishing Company Pvt. Ltd., New Delhi, who brought out the volume in an elegant form. I also wish to express my sincere thanks to Dr. K.B. Manoj, Principal, Sree Narayana College, Kollam for his support.

I also express my deep sense of affection, love and gratitude to my beloved wife for her support, care and exceptional sincerity. I lost her on 31st August 2012 at an age of 42. Whatever little academic activity I had undertaken hitherto was due to her solid support. Jaya came to my life on 14th November 1993. From that day onwards she supported me like a friend and motivator. She inspired me a lot giving a new meaning and dimension to my life. All the prefaces to the volumes I have published up to 2012 have been concluded by showering petals of love and affection for Jaya and our kids. From the previous volume onwards, she turned a fragrant memory. My onward journey and academic mission were in a standstill after the painful departure. From the previous issue onwards, I am making an attempt to carry forward the unfulfilled mission. If not, I may be doing an injustice to Jaya. Moreover, I pray to the Almighty to give her soul eternal peace and guide us—Aishwarya, Ananthapadmanabha and me—to face the days to come.

Finally, I am also grateful to Paul Ambrose, JoySoft Computers, Kollam, for the data entry services.

Gandhi Jayanthi Day, 2014.

M.R. Biju
Associate Professor
PG & Research Department of Political Science,
Sree Narayana College, Kollam, Kerala, India.

Contents

List of Contributors

Dr. D. Rajasenan, Dean, Faculty of Social Sciences, Cochin University of Science and Technology, Kochi, Kerala, India.

Dr. Dasarathi Bhuiyan, Lecturer, P.G. Department of Political Science, Berhampur University, Berhampur, Odisha.

Dr. J. Prabhash, Professor and Head, Department of Political Science, University of Kerala, Thiruvananthapuram.

Dr. Kalpana S. Agrahari, Associate Professor, Department of Political Science, Kumaun University, Nainital.

Dr. Kartick Das, Assistant Professor in Political Science, Mathabhanga College, Mathabhanga, West Bengal.

Dr. M.R. Biju, Associate Professor, P.G. and Research Department of Political Science, Sree Narayana College, Kollam, University of Kerala.

Dr. Manju Singh, Assistant Professor, Department of Political Science, University of Rajasthan, Jaipur.

Dr. Midatala Rani, Professor, Department of Studies in Political Science, Manasagangotri, University of Mysore, Mysore.

Dr. Neelima Deshmukh, Professor and Head, Department of Public Administration and Local Government and Director, Centre for Women's Studies and Development, RTM Nagpur University, Nagpur.

Prof. Niranjan Pani, Department of Public Administration, Utkal University, Vanivihar, Bhubaneswar, Odisha.

Dr. Padmalaya Mahapatra, Associate Professor and Head, Department of Public Administration, Utkal University, Vanivihar, Bhubaneswar, Odisha.

R. Mahesh, Senior Urban Economist, Ministry of Housing, Kingdom of Bahrain.

Raj Kishor Pradhan, Assistant Superintendent, Sample Survey Office, Field Operations Division, Ministry of Statistics, Government of India, Sambalpur, Odisha.

Dr. Roopa Sharma, Associate Professor, CPJ College, IP University, Delhi.

Dr. Swami Prakash Srivastava, Head, Department of Economics, Faculty of Social Sciences, Dayalbagh Deemed University, Agra, Uttar Pradesh.

Vijayaraj Kumar Charles, IAS, Managing Director, Tamil Nadu Water Supply and Drainage Board (TWAD), Chennai.

Introduction

Sir Winston Churchill, while addressing the House of Commons, (11 November, 1947) stated "Many forms of Government have been tried, and will be tried in this world of sin and woe. No one pretends that democracy is perfect or all-wise. Indeed it has been said that democracy is the worst form of Government except for all those other forms that have been tried from time to time...." Democracy is not a finished product rather it is a dynamic process. A perfect form of democracy has never existed anywhere in the world. The founding fathers of Constitution of India adopted for us the system of parliamentary democracy. Under it, Parliament enjoys a place of primacy and pre-eminence in the governance of the state.

India after Sixty-Seven years of independence exist as the most vibrant democracy in the world and it presents diverse amalgamation of historical legacy, the experiences of the national movement and endeavours to combine best from cross nations experiences to design the Constitution of the country catering to the democratic necessities of the nation. The legacy of the national movement in terms of liberal, socialist and Gandhian ideals continues to shape and deepen India's democratic process and structure. The Indian democratic experiment envisioned and operationalised by our forefathers constitutional experts and leaders have worked successfully and have evolved and devolved strengthening the very foundations of the democratic system. But the long march to democracy to prove its worth has not been without constraints and hurdles. Its struggle to achieve national unity and political integration by democratic means is threatened by unlawful and centrifugal tendencies of many kinds.

Every time during the sixteen general elections for Lok Sabha and the few hundred for State Assemblies, the people have exercised their franchise to elect the legislatures and the governments of their choice and given ample evidence for their inherent and innate democratic qualities. By now, there have been several instances of peaceful, constitutional transfer of power between political parties or alliances and societal classes both at the Union and State levels. Moreover, Indian democracy has been widely hailed as the most stable in South Asia—the only one where the democratic system and the Constitution have stood the test of times and have endured and functioned. Despite once being labelled as a 'soft state' or a 'functioning anarchy' by Galbraith and Myrdal, the performance of India's democratic institutions has been widely acknowledged as the best in what continues to be called 'the third world'.

In the recently concluded Lok Sabha elections, after a full quarter century, the electorate, who never trusted any party with majority seats since 1984, has given majority seats to the BJP now. Moreover, the BJP has decimated the Congress and effectively taken its place as the principal national party, not in terms of just seats but also in popular votes. In all elections till now, the BJP's share of popular votes was less than that of the Congress. Now, its share is more. The BJP's vote share is estimated at more than 50 per cent in North and West India. Because it has secured less than a tenth of the total seats, the Congress has lost its claim to be the recognised opposition party. The misery of the Congress and the Gandhis seems unmitigated.

The results of the Sixteenth General Elections 2014 came out causing a veritable political earthquake in secular democratic India. It was a massive anti-Congress wave, and an inevitable fallout of the disastrous economic policies of Manmohan Singh and P. Chidambaram, that was capitalized by Narendra Modi (who, over a period of nine months travelled 3 lakhs km. to attend 5187 events and address 477 election rallies) who must be credited with having consequently choreographed by his party's spectacular success without parallel at the hustings, winning as many as 282 (and the NDA with 336 seats), whereas the Congress had to suffer its most humiliating defeat in the post-independent India. The landslide victory of the BJP and the most ignominious defeat of the Congress were basically due to the fragmentation of the secular anti or non-BJP votes. In a sense it is quite bizarre that BJP who is ruling the nation which has managed to garner a mere 31 per cent votes when across the nation—the lowest vote share till today by any party that has won a majority of seats in the Lok Sabha, whereas the Congress with a 19.3 per cent vote share could get only 44 seats.

Another important aspect of the 2014 general elections has been the enormous role of money power to the extent that it has become a very serious threat to democracy. True, these trends of ever-increasing role of money were noticed in all recent elections. But in the 2014 general elections we may have arrived at the critical stage where democratic processes and aspirations can get over powered by massive as well as cleverly calculated use of money power.

A leading Hindi newspaper, the *Navbharat Times* (from *The Times of India* group), published a special report on the funding of elections (May 8, 2014). This report said that election expenses have been increased rapidly from Rs. 2500 crore in 1996 to well over Rs. 30,000 crores in 2014, or Rs. 50 to 55 crore per Lok Sabha seat. This massive increase of election expenses has been met most prominently by corporate sources this report said, with coal mining interests in the first row. Most big corporates now keep a separate election fund, the report said. Elections are also fed by lots of black money and *hawala* transactions. In Andhra Pradesh about Rs. 120 crore worth of cash was seized by the Election Commission, followed by significant seizures in Tamil Nadu, Maharashtra, Punjab, Madhya Pradesh and elsewhere.

Yet another curious aspect to which this report drew attention was that the expenses of the BJP were about 75 per cent higher than those of the Congress. Normally it is the ruling party which is considered to have the highest capacity to raise funds, but in the 2014 election, it was the main opposition party which was able to generate much larger funds, as was evident also from the more obvious spending patterns such as those relating to media advertising. In print as well as electronic media, advertisement space was grabbed on a massive scale by the BJP. The media has grown rapidly and now its influence in even interior areas is well established. In the urban areas its influence can be very dominating. The BJP and its friends were able to use this media space to their advantage to an unprecedented extent in legal and illegal, ethical and unethical ways.

The sensational sweep and scale of the Bharatiya Janata Party's electoral victory was unquestionably the direct result of the strong upsurge in the popularity of its prime ministerial candidate, Narendra Modi. He was the star campaigner and the massive "Modi wave" that has caught the imagination of large sections of India's voters has given the BJP-led National Democratic Alliance an unprecedented and historic mandate. With the BJP winning a majority on its own, a remarkable paradigm shift has taken place in the trajectory of India's parliamentary politics. Breaking the trend of the last few decades in which no party was able to pull off a runaway victory of this kind, the BJP will come to power, free from the pressures of coalition politics, giving it unfettered space and scope to govern. This election marked the entry of 100 million new voters, young Indians impatient for change and extremely aspirational in their focus. The voter turnout—66.38 per cent—was the highest ever in India's post-Independence electoral history, beating the record of 1984 when 64.01 per cent of Indians voted in the aftermath of Indira Gandhi's assassination.

This landmark election has also seen the incumbent United Progressive Alliance crash to an ignominious defeat with the Congress party, already on a downward spiral in several elections, now humiliatingly reduced to a double-digit figure in Parliament, its worst electoral tally since Independence. An indefensibly uninspiring campaign led by Rahul Gandhi failed to rally a young and impatient electorate. The BJP's landslide victory, almost entirely attributable to the sweeping effect of the Modi wave across India, reflects the intensity of the desire for more effective governance. The rising public anger as a result of the UPA's policy paralysis, stalled economic growth and worst of all, the series of corruption scandals, created a hunger for change especially among young Indians who see Modi as a leader symbolizing their expectations of fast economic growth unshackled from red tape and corruption. It is indeed an ironic twist of history that the former Gujarat Chief Minister—whose governing record is shadowed by the disquieting facts that have not really gone away, relating to his moral and political responsibility for the Gujarat pogrom of 2002—has adroitly become the beneficiary of the increasing eagerness for a higher growth trajectory. It is also discomfiting that the election campaign that Modi conducted in the Hindi heartland States, especially Uttar Pradesh, drew heavily upon Hindu cultural nationalism, invoking as he did Hindu sacred geography in Varanasi and using Hindu cultural idioms, not really imagery suitable to the public space in democratic India.

Besides its ideological underpinning, this election also marks a tectonic shift in the electoral side of Indian politics, which is incredible in more ways than one. After a full quarter century, the electorate, who never trusted any party with majority seats since 1984, has given majority seats to the BJP now. Moreover, the BJP has decimated the Congress and effectively taken its place as the principal national party, not in terms of just seats but also in popular votes. In all elections till now, the BJP's share of popular votes was less than that of the Congress. Now, its share is more. The BJP's vote share is estimated at more than 50 per cent in North and West India. Because, it has secured less than a tenth of the total seats, the Congress has lost its claim to be the recognised opposition party. The misery of the Congress and the Gandhis seems unmitigated. The BJP has wiped out or handed the worst defeat to the Congress in most of India—particularly in North, East and West—including where the Congress is in power like Himachal Pradesh, Uttarakhand, Haryana, Maharashtra, Assam and Karnataka or where it was the strongest five years ago like Andhra Pradesh. In contrast, the BJP has wiped out the Congress where the BJP is in power, be it Gujarat, Madhya Pradesh, Rajasthan, or Chhattisgarh. A desperate Congress created Telangana and got decimated in Andhra Pradesh. Yet, it could not get Telangana Rashtra Samiti to ally with it and lost Telangana to TRS. But the BJP, despite voting to create Telangana, allied with the Telugu Desam Party that is opposed to Telangana and won in AP, both in Assembly and Lok Sabha. The responsibility for this dire state of the Congress squarely falls on the Gandhi family which directly controlled the party and remote-controlled the UPA government. The 2014 election has thrown up a national leader of unprecedented popularity with mass backing, ideological conviction and political courage unseen since Indira Gandhi, but with a vital, very vital, difference. Inheriting Gandhiji's name and Nehru's lineage, Indira became Prime Minister and then acquired popularity through power. Modi became popular by hard work overcoming social and economic backwardness, supported by the RSS and the BJP he is part of.

In short, the most important factor in the verdict that gave the BJP 282 seats was the return of single-party majority in the Lok Sabha after a gap of 30 years. It became the first non-Congress party to achieve this feat and also led the National Democratic Alliance (NDA) to a creditable 336 seats. The other tangible elements were the unprecedented rout of the Congress, the rise of an imposing personality cult in the form of Narendra Modi, and the near-total marginalisation of caste-region-and identity-based small parties from the power structure at the Centre. At the social level, the verdict marked an unparalleled non-representation of the country's largest minority community, Muslims, who account for approximately 16 per cent of the population, in the treasury benches. There is only one Muslim MP in the NDA, and none in the BJP.

Three decades later, the lessons of 1984 and 1989 are still relevant. The magnitude of the BJP's victory was also through the hyperbolic image of Modi as the messiah who would bring about deliverance from Congress' misrule, boosted by his own high-flown rhetoric, might well be the BJP's undoing. The conflict between the sectarian communal agenda represented by the RSS and its associates and the pressures from the corporate sector's drive to enhance its own gains and profits could be important factors in this social and political churning. Maintaining the superman image in this country of paradoxes and ironies can happen only at a considerable cost to democracy, a fact perhaps not known to the post-Emergency generation of India.

Against this backdrop, the present volume address the issues pertaining to Indian politics, electoral politics, women's participation, transnational terrorism, gender and poverty issues, agrarian crisis, public private partnership, sustainable energy generation and insurgency. The volume contains fourteen research papers contributed by senior academics, administrators and development practitioners on the core areas of the subject. In their submissions, the authors have tried to explore the constraints faced by Indian polity and present innovative solutions to revamp the system.

CONTENT OF THE VOLUME

In the inaugural paper, the volume editor traces the political process of India in the context of the recently held Sixteenth Lok Sabha Polls. According to him, riding a nationwide wave created substantially by his campaign, Narendra Modi won an unprecedented victory for the BJP, matched in its intensity and sweep only by the crushing defeat of the Congress in the 16th General Elections. The BJP returns to power at the Centre after 10 years. Allies will also be part of the government, though the BJP is not dependent on any for numbers. "Good days are ahead," tweeted Modi as soon as trends became clear, reiterating the words of his campaign jingle '*Acche din aanewale hain*' that had inspired hope among people and created a hype around his persona. The BJP won a simple majority for the first time, only the second time a non-Congress party has done so. The BJP also be came the first party since 1984 to get a majority on its own.

The author further states that, in its worst performance, the Congress won less than one-third of its 1977 tally of 154, when a massive anti-Congress wave swept India after the Emergency. The BJP consolidated its hold in Gujarat, Rajasthan, Madhya Pradesh, Maharashtra and Chhattisgarh, leaving only a handful of seats to its opponents. It also engineered a decisive turnaround in Uttar Pradesh and Bihar, made inroads into Assam and West Bengal, won the southern most seat in India, Kanyakumari in Tamil Nadu, and came a close second in nearby Thiruvananthapuram in Kerala.

According to M.R. Biju, the Congress failed to hold ground in any state except Kerala where its alliance won a majority of the seats, and Karnataka. In its unrivalled march, the BJP managed to break barriers of caste, decimating parties such as the BSP, the SP and the RJD in Uttar Pradesh and Bihar. While the Left fell to its lowest tally in history, three regional parties outside the BJP alliance, the Trimool Congress in West Bengal, AIADMK in Tamil Nadu and the Biju Janata Dal in Odisha, held their ground. With most senior leaders of the Congress routed, and no regional heavyweight other than Mulayam Singh in the new Lok Sabha, the opposition appears weak against the overwhelming of the BJP. BJP had put hardcore *Hindutva* agenda on the backburner when it began alliance building in 1996, but with absolute numbers on its side, the demand from within to bring these up may rise. But Modi sought to reassure the country, stating that he would "take the entire 125 crore people of India along."

The author is also of the firm opinion that besides its ideological underpinning, 2014 polls marked a tectonic shift in the electoral side of Indian politics, which is incredible in more ways than one. After a full quarter century, the electorate, who never trusted any party with majority seats since 1984, has given majority seats to the BJP now. Moreover, the BJP has decimated the Congress and effectively taken its place as the principal national party, not in terms of just seats but also in popular votes. In all elections till now, the BJP's share of popular votes was less than that of the Congress. Now, its share is more. The BJP's vote share is estimated at more than 50 per cent in North and West India. Because it has secured less than a tenth of the total seats, the Congress has lost its claim to be the recognised opposition party. The misery of the Congress and the Gandhis seems unmitigated. The BJP has wiped out or handed the worst defeat to the Congress in most of India particularly in North, East and West—including where the Congress is in power like Himachal Pradesh, Uttarakhand, Haryana, Maharashtra, Assam and Karnataka or where it was the strongest five years ago like Andhra Pradesh. In contrast, the BJP has wiped out the Congress where the BJP is in power, be it Gujarat, Madhya Pradesh, Rajasthan, or Chhattisgarh. A desperate Congress created Telangana and got decimated in AP. Yet, it could not get Telangana Rashtra Samiti to ally with it and lost Telangana to TRS. But the BJP, despite voting to create Telangana, allied with the Telugu Desam Party that is opposed to Telangana and won in AP, both in Assembly and Lok Sabha. The responsibility for this dire state of the Congress squarely falls on the Gandhi family which directly controlled the party and remote-controlled the UPA government.

Biju concludes his study by saying that, the 2014 election has thrown up a national leader of unprecedented popularity with mass backing, ideological conviction and political courage unseen since Indira Gandhi, but with a vital, very vital, difference. Inheriting Gandhiji's name and Nehru's lineage, Indira became Prime Minister and then acquired popularity through power. Modi became popular by hard work overcoming social and economic backwardness, supported by the RSS and the BJP he is part of.

After making a detailed escavation on national politics, the same author presents a detailed study on how Kerala has voted in the General Elections of 2014. To him, compared with national level political scenario, the Electoral politics of Kerala since 2006, undoubtedly shows that the CPI(M) led LDF had not won a single major election in the state. The LDF's victory even in 2006 was built almost entirely on the faults of the then Congress led coalition rather than on its own merits. Thereafter, the Lok Sabha Polls in 2009, Local body polls in 2010 and the Assembly polls in 2011 and two significant by elections at Piravam and Neyyattinkara that followed, electoral fortune was in favour of the UDF. Some of the key reasons responsible for the debacle of the Left include:

(1) the factional feud within the CPI(M) and individualistic adventures of some of its top leaders;
(2) the arrogant and autocratic style of functioning of party leaders from top to bottom;
(3) irrational and unethical electoral pact of the left with some communal forces with alleged extremist links;
(4) estrangement coalition partners for a variety of decisions taken by the CPI(M) leadership;
(5) alienation of some communities on issues of Government policy on self-financing education;
(6) CPI(M)'s indulgence in political violence and murder and futile attempts of the party to defend and protect party comrades who had direct involvement with the offences;
(7) loosing public interest in the agitations organized or sponsored by the CPI(M); and
(8) absence of a dynamic social movement for worthy causes that were once the hallmark of the left etc.

The author further reveals that, despite of these electoral setbacks, the Left parties could retain their vote share. For example, in the Lok Sabha Polls in 2009, though the Left secured only four seats out of 20, they could capture 41.89 per cent of the votes as compared to 47.73 per cent won by the UDF. In the 2001 assembly polls the Left won 44.94 per cent of votes, when the UDF which replaced it in Government got 45.83 per cent of votes. Within the LDF, the CPI(M)'s vote share in the elections in 2009 and 2011 was 30.48 per cent and 28.18 per cent respectively and that of the CPI was only 7.44 per cent and 8.72 per cent respectively. But in the 2014 polls the vote share of the CPM came down to 21.6 per cent and the share of the CPI to 7.6 per cent.

M.R. Biju concludes his study by cautioning that the rout of the CPM in West Bengal and the less impressive performance in Kerala mark the beginning of the end for the CPM as a key player in the national politics. Though a debacle in West Bengal was not unexpected, the CPM leadership cannot give any explanation for its humiliating defeat in Bengal, a state considered as a Left fiefdom till recently. In Kerala, the defeat of M.A. Baby, the PB member A. Vijayaraghavan Central Committee member has put the fellow travellers of the CPM into a quandry. The only solace for the CPM in Kerala was its victory of Kannur, Aalathur, Palaghat and Attingal. However, P. Karunakaran, another Central Committee member escaped with a thin margin of 6921 votes in Kasaragod. In this juncture the party headed to make a serious introspection and take remedial measures if it wanted to survive as an entity of any political relevance.

J. Prabhash's paper is captioned "Propaganda and the Changing Chemistry of Indian Elections". To quote his own words: "Another notable trend seen in the electoral campaign was the personal indictment and hate speeches resorted to by all major political actors exceeding all cannons of decency and ethical conduct. A few excerpts from such hate speeches would prove this point. There were frequent references about pan-Pakistan disposition by the Muslim population of the country ('those who oppose Modi will have a place in Pakistan'); the need for dispossessing them of their property ('Muslim property in Hindu areas should be encroached upon'); and reminding one of the foreign origin of Rahul Gandhi and Sonia Gandhi ('Sonia Gandhi and Rahul Gandhi should be stripped off of their clothes and sent back to Italy') (Naqvi, 2014:36-37).

On the reverse side, Narendra Modi was described as a barbarian ('Modi is a butcher/*narahantaka*') having even illicit relationship with Mayavati ('Mayavati sat on Modi's lap), and threats were also issued against voting for BJP/Congress and CPM ('Do not allow even a single person to vote for the BJP/Congress or CPM) (Ramachandran, 2014). The sole purpose of these invectives was to terrify thc opposition and consolidate one's core constituency. As could be inferred, the campaign simply bypassed the quotidian life concerns of the population and steered clear of other vital issues of national significance except making some isolated references about development, that too during the early stages of the electioneering."

According to the author, it was the personal rather than the social/ political that has dominated the election campaign and the same was further reflected the way in which it was conducted by political parties, BJP in particular. Despite, the fact that it has a long array of senior leaders, the entire burden of crafting the party's electoral success was borne by one single individual, Narendra Modi. The importance of the leadership of the coalition partners of the NDA also paled into insignificance before his single handed, aggressive and expensive campaign. So relentless has been his campaign that he has converted a complex parliamentary system into a presidential style referendum on himself (Pradhan and Mahurkar, 2014:23). It was plainly a plebiscite on Modi, and BJP, as a party, was only the backdrop to this main script (Palshikar, 2014). This is the most thoroughly planned and organized campaign in India and has changed the chemistry of electioneering in the country.

Prof. Prabhash further adds that, through all these propaganda the central message that was conveyed was clear and simple: 'either you accept Modi or reject him.' Every other leader and party, including his own, was rendered inconsequential. In the end, he sounded more efficient than everybody and managed to appropriate not just secularism but also nationalism (Pradhan and Mahurkar, 2014:25). Looking back one is, therefore, compelled to state that election 2014 has changed, beyond recognition, the electoral landscape and the nature of Indian party system.

Kalpana Agrahari discusses indepth on the issues and challenges of women's participation in Indian context. According to her, it is important to stress that participation and representation in legislative bodies may not itself be enough for women's political empowerment or to remedy the problems of discrimination faced by women in Indian society. Equality with equity is a goal which may not easily be achieved only by high representation of women in legislatures and other public bodies but has to be buttressed by other supportive measures. Even so, the demand for reservation of seats for women in political bodies to rectify the imbalance has gained strength in India in the light of persisting gender gaps in various spheres of development. In the absence of any serious political self-correction so far, the demand for reservation of seats in legislatures and party structures has been stressed in India aiming at such an equitable representation. While the steady increase in the electoral participation and mobilization of women in India has increased the visibility of women in the legislative politics this has not happened in the exercise of executive power due to their lack of presence in the decision-making structures. From this perspective, the important question is 'what are the benefits of democracy for women'.

She further adds that women's equality in power sharing and active participation in decision-making, including decision-making in political process at all levels must be ensured for the achievement of the goals of empowerment. All measures must be taken to guarantee women equal access to and full participation in decision-making bodies at every level, including the legislative, executive, judicial, corporate, statutory bodies, as also the advisory Commissions, Committees, Boards, Trusts, etc. Affirmative action such as reservations/quotas, including in higher legislative bodies, must be considered whenever necessary on a time bound basis. Women-friendly personnel policies must also be drawn up to encourage women to participate effectively in the developmental process.

Kalpana concludes her meaningful enquiry by stating that there is a general view that only electoral quotas are not the final solution. Electoral participation and quotas through affirmative action alone are not enough to result in gender equality. The focus should be on creating such conditions, wherein women could prefer to join the politics on their own terms and participate in the decisions of their destiny. For the purpose, we are strongly needed a mechanism which could provide the full training of legislative process, can make them aware towards their rights and duties as elected member and gender sensitisation of every elected member.

Followed by Kalpana, **Dasarathi Bhuiyan** has made an enquiry on the same area focusing Odisha. To him, the Indian state of Odisha is also not free from this low tempo of political participation. There was also a big gap between men and women in Odisha in electoral field during the pre-independent era. Odisha formed its first government when it became a separate province on 1st April, 1936 by an act of the Central Government. This can be inferred from the fact that none of the three ministries, of Odisha during the Pre-Independence Assembly period, i.e. from 1936 to 1947 included any woman, although Sarala Devi and Punya Prabha Devi were elected from the Cuttack town constituency (Ghosh, 1979). But in the link assembly from 1947 to 1952 among the women legislators A. Laxmi Bai was the Deputy Speaker of the Odisha Legislative Assembly from 29-5-1946 to 20-2-1952 and Basant Manjari Devi, queen of Ranpur—a small kingdom du Manjarng the British-Odisha, was the Deputy Minister of Health in the Harekrushna Mahatab Ministry, who assumed the charge of office of Prime-Ministership on 23rd April, 1946 (Rout, 2006).

According to him, women empowerment in a general sense, it refers to empowering women to be self-dependent by providing them access to all the freedoms and opportunities, which they were denied in the past only because of their being women. In a specific sense, women empowerment refers to enhancing their position in the power structure of the society. The words "women empowerment" essentially means that the women have the power or capacity to regulate their day-to-day lives in the social, political and economic terms—a power which enables them to move from the periphery to the centre stage (Bhuiyan, 2006). Moreover, within the framework of democratic polity, our laws, developmental policies, plans and programmes are aimed at women's advancement in different spheres. India has also ratified various international conventions to secure rights of women. Women of India are now uplifted and emancipated and granted equal status with men in all walks of life—political, social, domestic and educational. Their voice is now as forceful and important as that of men. They are becoming equal partners in making or dismissing of a government (Bhuiyan, 2006).

He further adds that, Women Empowerment is still an illusion of reality. Notwithstanding, the remarkable changes in the position of women in free India, there is still a great divergence between the constitutional position and stark reality of deprivation and degradation. There still exists a wide gulf between the goals enunciated in the Constitution, legislations, policies, plans, programmes and related mechanisms on the one hand and the situational reality on the status of women in India, on the other.

There is a strong relationship between access to economic resources and participation in the political sphere. As such, they did not have their own resources to enter or participate in the political process. One major finding was that education and household income of women leaders have significant positive relationship with their political status, modernisation and role performance. The lack of access to economic resources results in low representation of women as elected members at all levels of governance. Similarly, lack of access to information, results in women members not being taken seriously. The most effective way to provide women with information is through training and capacity building.

He also observes that restricting women's participation in trade unions and cooperative movements has resulted in denying women the opportunity to gain similar experience like men, which enables them to participate in mainstream political activities. The cultural norms operate both as a restriction on a woman's mobility as well as an impediment for her participation in the public sphere. These cultural norms are perpetuated and sustained by powerful institutions of family, caste and religion.

Women in the family are viewed as liabilities because of which gender-based discrimination in all dimensions of their lives prevails. This is reflected in the alarming proportions of violence against women within the family—female foeticide, infanticide, malnourishment, school dropouts, neglect and deprivation through limited access to resources, dowry violence, torture, etc. Women having a new born baby in the family do not have the support system that can free them to participate in the political activities outside the home. Younger women and unmarried women have more restrictions placed on their participation because of the control exercised on their sexuality.

To him, women receive minimal support from their families. The nature of this support tends to be in the form of encouragement to run for elections but rarely does it extend to helping them fulfil their responsibilities as elected representatives by taking the burden of domestic work off them. Usually women elected officials get help from their husbands in the form of their initial contacts and encouragement to join politics. But in some cases resistance from in-laws proves to be another major detriment for women participating in political activities. Sometimes, support from in-laws is purely for the women getting elected but not to carry out her duties. Even if there is family support if the community does not accept the women they are faced with difficulties. Support of the community is as important as that of the family and the two needs to go together, and this support ideally should be there from the beginning. Patriarchal values relegate women to the home. By the very nature of this value system, any woman bold enough to come out in the open and into politics is viewed with suspicion. It is natural that she is particularly targeted for slander and character assassination.

Dasarathi concludes his study by pinpointing that—

- Women's decision-making is prevented due to party interference. Political parties do not want to transfer control to women and are reluctant to invest in women as candidates fearing that they do not have the capacity to draw votes, and finally they do not see women as having financial credibility to compete with male contestants. In such circumstances, women who do occupy positions in politics, either through support from political parties or through reservation, do not find the space to participate fully without interference.

- It is probably most useful to look at challenges by sphere, notably socio-cultural, economic and political. Compulsory gender quotas to be applied in the elections should be legalized. Women's branches of political parties should be granted an autonomous status in order to protect them from being kept under tutelage by the party administration. The political parties should undertake necessary alterations in their administrative system in order to facilitate women's participation and representation in the decision-making bodies and executive boards of the party. Women's branches should be organized in the way that endows their members with necessary political skills and experience. The nomination process of candidates in the political parties should be carried out in a non-arbitrary and transparent manner. The establishment of equality committees, which would monitor the observation of the principle of gender equality in political parties, should be encouraged.
- For true equality to become a reality for women, the sharing of power on equal terms with men is essential. The government has acknowledged the need to increase the number of women in decision-making processes at all levels, as early as in 1976. As a first step to facilitate women's participation in politics, in 1993, it introduced 33 per cent reservation for women in institutions of local governance through the 73rd and 74th Constitutional Amendments. While the government has succeeded in facilitating women's participation by providing for reservation at the lower levels of governance, it has failed to do so in passing the Reservation Bill for women in the higher echelons of political institutions, i.e. in the State Assemblies and the Parliament.
- The government has attempted to introduce reservation for women at the legislature and parliament levels on three occasions in the years 1996, 1999 and 2000, which have lapsed. Further, women, being in insignificant numbers, are often pressurised to align with men along their caste, class, religion and ethnic identities rather than on the basis of gender. This has resulted in

dividing women on the one hand from centre-staging gender issues and concerns and on the other their solidarity.

In her paper on Transnational Terrorism, **Miditala Rani** observes that, the relationship between globalisation and transnational terrorism is a paradoxical one. Transnational terrorism is an authentic product of the globalised world and yet in fundamental conflict with it. While it aims to repel US led globalisation transnational terrorism has harnessed globalisation features in three ways, viz. exploitation of new technologies, global financial networks and reduced barriers to cross border interactions. Globally connected networks facilitate the recourse to asymmetric attacks and are thus key enablers of transnational terrorism. Modern transnational terrorism is very dangerous as it derives its power from globalisation.

According to Rani, globalisation has enabled transnational terrorism through the exploitation of new technologies. The information revolution has speeded up computing, telecommunications and data transference capabilities. The use of internet, mobile phones and satellite telecommunications has increased terrorist related activities and extended the global reach of terrorist groups. The global information age enhanced terrorist planning and coordination of operations, recruitment of members, communication among adherents, attraction of supporters across national borders. Terrorist activities are no longer confined to defined regions but enjoy expanded range and impact of operations. The internet is also used clandestinely for passing encrypted messages in graphic codes. The reliance on advanced telecommunication networks has defined the organisational structures of transnational terrorist groups. Networks have enabled terrorist groups across regions to rely on one another for technology, expertise and resources. Thus the level of inter-connectivity between terrorist groups has increased even between those of different aims or ideologies.

She further adds that, integrated global financial networks are a key supporting mechanism for funding the operations of transnational terrorist groups. Integrated financial markets are exploited and adapted by terrorist organisations and "digitization of money" facilitates instantaneous transfer of funds across the borders. Also financial globalisation limits the level of control that governments have over financial matters as huge volume of transactions occurs on daily basis. This makes tracing terrorist funds extremely difficult. The integrated global economy provides transnational terrorist groups the chance to accumulate wealth and ability to redistribute it quickly under garb of anonymity.

Miditala concludes her detailed enquiry by stressing—

- Terrorism emerging along with globalisation process is a major challenge to the nation states in contemporary period. One of the paradoxes of globalisation is it engenders terrorism with the wish to protect traditional cultures. Clearly globalisation changed the nature of terrorism and is a key motivator and enabler of transnational terrorism. The 9/11 terror attack has forced the nation states to adopt a new kind of conception and idea of security. It has also brought into focus as to whether safety and risk should be first taken care of instead of security and what kind of discourses and practices are to be found related to the notion of security in the world of the current threat of terrorism.
- The discourse on the war on terrorism is slowly beginning to consolidate. It is very important to develop a strategy for countering the growth of terrorist groups based on law and morality rather than war. Perhaps it may never be possible to eliminate terrorist groups but it is possible to reduce their recruiting power and minimise the damage they are able to inflict. Apart from a global agenda for progressive governance, more specific policies are needed to tackle transnational terrorism. First the strategy to protect civilians against all forms of illegal violence. Second is to counter the ideology of terrorist groups through grassroots political mobilisation by involving civil society groups. Third is the strategy to counter the sophisticated organisational infrastructure of the terrorist groups. Four factors including education, media, welfare and jobs are part of this strategy to reduce global insecurity.
- Just as globalisation facilitates transnational terrorism it can also be used as a weapon against terrorism. Transnational terrorism is inherently global and a clearly unified global response is required. The multifaceted transnational terrorism must be comprehended through other perspectives like history, politics, psychology and religion. A comprehensive approach is to be applied to defeat transnational terrorism. Transnational terrorism and globalisation are although paradoxical are connected with the present international security system. As such they cannot be viewed separately. A wholistic approach instead of nationally autonomous approach is the only preferable solution to rid off global terrorism for a peaceful secure world.

P. Mahapatra and **Niranjan Pani** have presented a paper on Gender, Poverty in the context of Globalization. According to the authors, globalization has been described as the gradual elimination of economic borders and concomitant increase in international exchange and transnational interaction. It has been identified with economic reform, structural adjustment programmes, New World Trade order and the opening up of the commercial markets and the global communication village. Anthony Giddens in his book '*The Edge: Living with Global Capitalism*' identifies multiple meaning of Globalization. To it he refers the worldwide communication revolution, for instance (this is not only air travel, but the opening up of worldwide, e-mail, internet). Secondly, he refers to what he terms the 'weightless economy'. By this he means the new 'Knowledge Economy' with financial markets at its leading edge. Financial markets today are stunning in their scope, their instantaneous nature and their enormous turnover.

The authors further states that,

- In the contemporary scenario development issues are intertwined with globalization and structural adjustment in India. With the economic climate altering drastically, a contradictory situation is developing. On the one hand, there is a developed India that has got the benefits of globalization. On the other, there is an undeveloped India which is very backward and remains poor. After 67 years of independence, large scale poverty remains a reality in India. The poor can be defined as those who are deprived of basic human needs. But there are differences on what exactly constitutes these basic needs. Most national governments associate poverty with deprivation of basic needs required for physical survival such as food, nutrition, clothing, shelter, water and education.
- The rhetoric of globalization promises to remove backwardness through a worldwide exchange of information and skills in order to establish a truly cosmopolitan culture. There is an underlying belief that mutual cooperation and concern for social justice is automatically cared for under this system. In actual practice since the global order is based on unequal power relations these concerns are put on hold. Globalization seems to increase choices but only for those with money and access to the market. Women in the informal sector continue to bear the brunt of gender and class inequalities, experience increasing marginalization and

pauperization. These growth-oriented policies have taken away whatever control women had over traditional occupations and denied those better avenues of employment. In the shift from welfare development to economic development women have been the worst affected, because a large number of them are in the informal sector.

- Yet it cannot be denied that there is an irreversibility of the reform process that has already been initiated. There is a need to make a collective and concentrated effort to accommodate the strategic gender needs. Moreover, in this period of transition social safety nets are created for the women—the vulnerable sections of society. Also there is a need of policy, action and research to protect the interests of especially women, the marginalized sections, in the informal sector, so that they have better access and control on resources.

Agrarian crisis of Vidharbha is the topic of discussion in the paper presented by **Neelima Deshmukh**. According to her, Agriculture is a largest economic sector and plays a very significant role in the socio-economic development of our country, which is now in crises. The farmers of various states particularly in Maharashtra are in distress due to multiple factors ending in suicide in large scale. Agriculture Farmer's suicides in growing numbers throughout the states of Maharashtra, Karnataka, Andhra Pradesh, and Punjab is the most crucial problem and calls for the topmost priority in the agenda of rulers and policy makers. The suicidal trend set in 1991 by the farmers of Andhra Pradesh has spread to Maharashtra in 2000-01 and has been continued even today. Vidarbha is more suicide-prone danger zone of the state. In Vidarbha region alone till the date about 2932 farmers have committed suicide to overcome the miseries due to non-production of crops, bad debts, drought, lack of markets, marketing and irrigation facilities exploitation by private money lenders and other social and family causes arising out of the combination of various factors, and no one particular reason could be attributed to this saddest event of the mankind in the Indian history.

Neelima further adds that, the New Economic Policy (NEP) and Economic Reforms were formally adopted and made operational in 1991. These invited various changes in the institutional set up suiting to the need of hour. Ever since the period of last 2 decades lot of debates has been invoked about the gap between the results expected and delivered. These reforms has not been proved effective rather it has created many obstacles in the way of industrialization undercutting the industrial development particularly in the agro based industries located in rural areas units which were contributing to the rural economy to a great extent. Vidarbha region of the Maharashtra State comprising 11 districts is known for fine cotton which is a raw material for cotton yarn required by the textile mills which are in quite large numbers scattered all over the state. Further the cloth from textile mills is in great demand for the readymade cotton garments being exported in huge quantity earning the profits made by textile mills. Those rich businessmen in exports business are becoming more and more rich but the poor farmer the cotton grower, producer of the raw material is becoming poor to the extent to commit suicide. Obviously, the reform had devastating impact and there is an acute need for coming out of it. Cotton was not included in the list till very recent past.

Neelima concludes her innovative enquiry by stating that,

- The cotton farmers in India are paying more prices for the inputs like seeds, pesticides, fertilizers, electricity, water, and labour whereas the price of cotton has gone down, along with the diseased productivity. In contrast to this picture in India, US government is giving USD 4.0 billion to cotton farmers and asking for further liberalisation of cotton trade in USA.
- The provided Prime Ministers relief packages are the amalgamation of existing schemes. Apart from the helpline and direct financial assistance there was hardly anything new being offered. Pumping extra funds into additional schemes shows that no new idea was applied to overcome the grave situation, where existing measures have obviously failed. Farmers helpline did not give them any substantial help to them. Also the basis of selection of beneficiaries under the assistance scheme was not well defined. Further the type of assistance to be given to given led to the problems like a farmer needing pair of bullock cart got pump set and *vice versa*. Awareness regarding this package is also pretty low.
- We are strong in economic reforms as a result of which GDP has been raised. India's ranking as 127 in the year 2000 has gone up to 103 in 2004 is indicative of improved aspect of development. Challenges ahead in with regard to management of economic situation are for market places. Imperial evidences suggests that liberalisation has to be in terms of economic policies and governance. As the lower societies have gone much beyond their

capacities to bear with the globalisation. We should have gone in for internal reforms first rather than external directly. The reforms *vis-à-vis* changes in the policy have not been conducive to the changing economic scenario in the global perspective and has failed to bring out the desired result at local level. As a result of this rich have become more richer and poor have became more poorer widening the gap between the rich and poor.

- In order to meet the challenges of WTO, GATT various facilities, finances, subsidies and incentives have been provided by the Maharashtra Government to encourage direct foreign investment, and industrialisation all over the state but again due to regional disparities Vidarbha region remains neglected. Further these facilities are given to ginning factories, textile mills, garments manufacturers, and exporters but the poor cotton producer remains deprived of all the basic inputs, including the credit facilities from the banks and other financial institutions.
- Due to encouraged privatisation policy more and more private parties have entered the market and captured most of the business. Due to the various lapses and inefficiency of State Cotton Federation the farmers prefer to sell their crops to private parties at a lower rate than that of the federation as they have lost their faith in its working. Inefficient, corrupt, opaque administrative practices of the federation have been supporting factors to the rich and powerful persons to manipulate the business in their own vested interest which everyone cannot do.
- As a impact of globalisation countries like Sudan, Israel, Egypt have also entered into domestic market, selling their quality crops at much cheaper rates to local factories leaving no scope for the son of the soil neither in domestic nor international markets.
- Further looking at the intricacies of rural life and the agro based business the farmers have started converting the agricultural land into non-agriculture for the urban usage, selling the same lands and migrating to cities, living much substandard life than what they were leading in the village. Decreased farming, and increased migration resulting in burden on urban local bodies.
- Maharashtra's cotton monopoly scheme has failed to render the expected desired results in cotton procurement particularly in Vidarbha region which is being implemented through Maharashtra State Cotton Federation and calls for further administrative reforms.

Vijayaraj Kumar Charles has made a study on Public Private Partnership (PPP). According to him, despite becoming the second fastest growing and the fourth largest economy of the world, India continues to face large gaps in the demand and supply of essential social and economic infrastructure and services. Rapidly growing economy, increased industrial activity, burgeoning population pressure, and all-round economic and social development have led to greater demand for better quality and coverage of water and sanitation services, sewerage and drainage systems, solid-waste management, roads and seaports, and power supply. Increased demand has put the existing infrastructure under tremendous pressure and far outstripped its supply.

He further adds that, many analysts argue that the best way to improve service provision is to change the way in which governments administer them in India. For those who believe in neo liberal ideology, privatization is the only way to solve this problem. According to the World Bank, the key task is to 'manage infrastructure like a business, and not like a bureaucracy' (World Bank, 1994: 2). The neo-liberals call for 'reinventing government' by inspiring a new entrepreneurial spirit (Osbome and Gaebler, 1992; Hammer and Champy, 1993). They propose a lean state and lean government and advocate a greater role for private sector in service provision and they argue that 'market type management approaches could be effectively applied to the public sector' (Hood, 1991; Osbome and Gaebler, 1992). The proponents of New Public Management emphasize the need for 'speed and flexibility and touted the advantages of markets for both greater private sector engagement and consumer voice for citizens' (Savas, 1987). The New Public Management Reform is focused on competition and entrepreneurialism (Warner, 2008). The belief is that the market would make government service provision self-correcting in three ways: efficiency, cost minimization and quality delivery.

To him, one very striking and important outcome from the analysis of data related to perceived corruption levels and cost of regulation in states that the states which have been rated as better investment climate states need not necessarily to have low level of corruption and regulation. The top five states which have attracted more per capita investment in PPP projects are Karnataka, Kerala, Gujarat, Maharashtra and Andhra Pradesh. All these states except Kerala have been rated as states having better investment climate, which shows a positive correlation between perceived investment climate and investment in PPPs. However, when we compare the perceived corruption levels in these states, to our surprise these states have been perceived by investors as having high level of corruption. Same way if we compare the proxies for cost of regulation, again these states give a different picture than normally expected, that they have attracted more PPP investment in spite of having high cost of regulation. Therefore, we can conclude that, when it comes to investment in infrastructure particularly in PPP mode, if the overall cost benefit of the project in the entire concession period is higher, and if the cost benefit can absorb the cost of corruption and cost of regulation, than the states still tend to attract more investment in PPP in spite of high costs of corruption and high cost of regulation. There is no doubt that, to make these states even more attractive for investment, the states have to minimize the cost of corruption and regulation.

Vijay Kumar concludes his study by stating that,

- Availability and enforcement of Legal and Institutional frameworks that are conducive for PPP investment are no doubt important factors, for the investors while deciding about investment in PPP projects, but it is not a prerequisite for any PPP investment flow into any states. To some extent they exhibit the government's commitment and willingness for collaborating with private partners in infrastructure projects, but that alone is not sufficient. In fact the investors look for Independent regulatory authorities to enforce the tariff and performance standards agreed upon in a concession contract. If Indian states want to attract more investment in infrastructure projects through PPP mode they should give up the *ad hoc* approaches they were following so far and develop a robust legal and institutional framework required for attracting more investment in infrastructure sector.
- Though the analysis shows that the investment flow in PPP projects in infrastructure into a state is based on the overall estimated actual net cost benefits by private sector investors, it indicates that if the cost of corruption and the cost of regulation are less, then the state's investment climate make it more attractive for PPP projects in infrastructure, as it will reduce the project cost and make it more viable.
- The availability of infrastructure like power supply and transport facilities in a state shows a positive correlation with the high performance in attracting more investment in PPP projects as it will reduce the project cost and make it more viable in long term. Similarly, the states which have high demand for such

infrastructural services like power supply and transportation facilities have the capacity to attract more such projects in PPP.

R. Mahesh and **D. Rajasenan** have presented a chapter captioned Income Inequality among Small-Scale Fishery Households: A case study in a Coastal village of Kerala. According to the authors in Kerala, the open acccss marine fishery is unregulated and is characterized by dualism in the form of co-existence of a small-scale sector side by side with a large-scale sector; but their activities are largely concentrated in the inshore areas. In the last two decades there has been enormous increase in fishing pressure as a result of increase in the number of fishing crafts, particularly in the number of motorised crafts in the small-scale sector. In spite of this increase in the number of fishing crafts the annual fish production remains stagnant around 5.9 lakh tonnes, against the optimal sustainable yield of 5.7 lakh tonnes, thus leading to resource depletion crisis (GOK, 2002). Under the open access regime, larger and faster vessels meant larger share of the common wealth of marine fishery. The official statistics of fish landing show a declining share to the small-scale sector, especially to the non-motorised sector. Within the traditional sector itself, the introduction of motorisation and ring seine brought new appropriation and technological dilemmas for the non-motorised and non-ring seine using segment (Paul, 2003). With about 50 per cent of the fish output cornered by the large-scale sector and another 40 per cent by operators of large seines in the motorised sector, the traditional fishermen especially those in the non-motorised sector find themselves to be marginalized (Yohannan *et al.*, 1999).

The authors further feels that,

- The socio-economic condition of the fishing community in the small-scale sector has to be seen in the context of modernization of fishing technology, over fishing and consequent degradation of marine fishery resources. While households possessing fishing assets are financially in a better position, households depending solely on fishing labour and other fish related activities face insecurity due to fluctuating and often uncertain daily income. This situation is reflected in the low average income, wide income inequality and severe poverty of households in the small-scale fishery sector. The inequality of income in the small-scale fishery sector as measured by the Gini coefficient worked out to 0.33; and considering the low levels of consumer expenditure that has been obtained from the survey data it must be judged to signal substantial inequality. Within the community, the inequality, of income was found to be higher for the subgroup of the fisher population 'without fishing assets' (0.24 for the subgroups 'with fishing assets' and 0.35 for the subgroups 'without fishing assets'). At the same time the income level of this sub-group is lower than the sub-group 'with fishing assets'. That is to say, 'without fishing assets' group has a lower mean income and a higher level of inequality. In economic terms the households depending only on fishing labour occupy the lower stratum compared to those with fishing crafts.

- The lower income inequality of the 'with fishing asset' group suggests that income inequality of the population may have some relation with asset possession. In order to verify this, using the Theil index, the overall income inequality was decomposed as the sum of inequalities between and within the subgroups. However, this exercise showed that only less than 10 per cent of the overall inequality could be explained by the inequality between the two subgroups, suggesting that possession of fishing assets does not have a major contribution in explaining income inequality. The cause of income inequality has, therefore, to be sought elsewhere.
- The comparatively better economic condition of the households owning fishing assets can be traced to the pattern of sharing sale value of catch prevailing in the coastal area. If the owner along with the fishing vessel goes for fishing, he gets a share as wage for the labour in addition to the share as rent. Usually the owner and often other members of the household go for fishing. This has the effect of enhancing household income and also of smoothing inequality of income. As a result the group of households 'with fishing assets' is seen to have a higher average income and lower income inequality as compared to 'without fishing assets' who are really the fishery labour households. In spite of this difference in income pattern, it cannot be said that households 'with fishing assets' and 'without fishing assets' are two isolated independent groups; on the contrary the two are closely related to each other by an exploitation linkage rooted in technology and the socio-cultural system prevailing in the community which perceives the fishery resources as common property.

Swami Prakash Srivastava's paper is on Municipal Solid Waste Management and its future Impact on sustainable Energy Generation in India. To him, solid waste is the unwanted or useless solid materials generated from combined residential, industrial and commercial activities in a given area. Municipal Solid Waste (MSW) originates in homes, businesses, and other urban areas. It may be categorized according to its origin (domestic, industrial, commercial, construction or institutional); according to its contents (organic material, glass, metal, plastic paper etc.); or according to hazard potential (toxic, non-toxin, flammable, radioactive, infectious etc.). Management of solid waste reduces or eliminates adverse impacts on the environment and human health and supports economic development and improved quality of life. A number of processes are involved in effectively managing waste for a municipality. These include monitoring, collection, transport, processing, recycling and disposal.

According to him Swami Prakash, solid-waste management has become an important issue in the Asia-Pacific region, and it needs to be resolved through an integrated community, private sector, and policy-based approach. Solid-waste management is a major challenge in urban areas throughout the world. Without an effective and efficient solid-waste management programme, the waste generated from various human activities, both industrial and domestic, can result in health hazards and have a negative impact on the environment. Understanding the waste generated, the availability of resources, and the environmental conditions of a particular society are important to developing an appropriate waste-management system.

Swami further adds that, a number of key statistics, such as the value of recyclables, the amount of environmental pollution from waste sources, and the quantity of industrial waste generated, need to be computed to gain a better understanding of this sector. In terms of research related to waste to energy, detailed analysis of costs and available funding is needed.

Kartick Das's paper is on Naxalbari to Today's Naxalite Movement. To him, Naxalite or Naxalism is an informal name given to Communist groups that were born out of the Sino-Soviet split in the Communist movement in India. Ideologically they belong to various trends of Maoism. Initially the movement had its centre in West Bengal. In recent years, they have spread into less developed areas of rural central and eastern India, such as Chhattisgarh and Andhra Pradesh through the activities of underground groups like the Communist Party of India (Maoist). They are conducting an insurgency, typically called the Naxalite-Maoist insurgency. Naxals hold sway in about 180 districts across ten states of India, accounting for about 40 per cent of India's geographical area. They are especially concentrated in an area known as the 'Red Corridor', where they control 92,000 square kilometres. According to India's intelligence agency, the Research and Analysis Wing, 20,000 Naxalites were in April 2006 in operation and their growing influence prompted Indian Prime Minister Manmohan Singh to declare them as the most serious threat to India's national security.

According to Das, the rule of law, one of the pillars of a democratic polity and society, is based on an element of trust and reciprocity. It is not farfetched to assume that those who expect protection under the rule of law are also upholders of it and respect it in their politics and in their daily lives. Terrorists and Maoists do not fall into this category since they believe that political and socio-economic grievances entitle them to kill innocent people and those they consider to be their enemies. They have no respect for the rule of law and therefore, logically, they cannot expect any protection from it. All such rebels always have a specific and clear agenda, but here the Maoists' agenda is not clear. What Maoists are doing is just anarchism against Parliamentary democracy and the Constitution of India.

Das concludes his study by stating that the Centre, in consultation with the state governments, must formulate a multidimensional strategy to end the Maoist terror. There is a false opposition between security and development in our public discourse. These paradigms can, and ought to, coexist in the government's vision of the battle against Maoists. That, by no means, is an impossible task.

Raj Kishor Pradhan, in his paper examines the economic issues related to Naxal Problem in Indian context. According to Raj Kishor, the complexity of the causes of the Naxalite problem as well as its implications both for internal and external security reflect a solution that is multi-dimensional and calls for a synergy between the Central Government and the States. In order to comprehensively dissolve the Naxalite threat, the government has to address its root causes. Socio-economic alienation and the dissatisfaction with the widening economic and political inequality will not be solved by military force alone, which seems to be the main instrument employed by the government. The problem calls for a three-pronged solution: social and economic development, multi-lateral dialogue and military force.

He further adds that,

- As the Naxalites are fuelled by discontent from the marginalised and the poor, a larger percentage of the national budget must be allocated to addressing the needs of these regions. More of the national expenditure needs to be focused on developing these poorer regions through initiatives regarding health, education, social welfare and rural and urban development. Government service delivery should be improved in these tribal areas. Both State and Central Government must ensure that things such as statutory minimum wages, access to land and water sources initiatives are implemented. In coming up with strategies for national economic growth, the government must always bear in mind the possible effects of fast growth for all socio-economic groups in a country as large and diverse as India. If the social needs of these marginalised people are addressed, there will be no discontent to fuel the Naxalite's movements.
- The growing Naxalite insurgency also reflects a flaw in the federal structure. Because law and order is seen as a state responsibility, the Central Government is unable to be implementing a coherent national strategy to address the threat. Ganguly notes that "in the absence of a near complete breakdown of public order or without the express request of the afflicted state, the Central Government cannot... [Intervene]." The Government has the overall responsibility of mobilising development, but it cannot do so without the support of the States. The Central Government and the States need to cooperate together to solve the internal security threats and coordinate the implementation of this multi-dimensional approach.

In the fourteenth chapter, **Manju Singh** traces the evolution and emergence of United Liberation Front of Assam (ULFA). ULFA is a separatist group in Assam, among many other such groups in North East India. It seeks to establish a sovereign state of Assam. The Government of India banned the organization in 1990 and classified it as a terrorist group, while the U.S. State Department lists it under 'other groups of concern'. ULFA was formed on April 7, 1979 by Bhimkanta Buragohain, Arbindo Rajkhowa, Anup Chetia, Pradip Gogoi, Bhadreshwar Gohain and Paresh Barua at Rang Ghar, the 17th century amphitheatre of the Ahom Royalty in Sibsagar to establish a 'Sovereign Socialist Assam' through an armed struggle.

According to Manju, the Government of India has classified ULFA as a terrorist organization and has banned it under the Unlawful Activities (Prevention) Act in 1990. The Government of India accuses ULFA of maintaining links with the Inter Services Intelligence (ISI) of Pakistan and Directorate General of Forces Intelligence (DGFI) of Bangladesh and waging a proxy war on their behalf against India. The outlawed group is said to be looking to China for shelter following mounting pressure from both Myanmar and Bangladesh which in turn are pressured by India.

To her, ULFA is reportedly commanding three active armed battalions and is in possession of sophisticated weapons. It is running training camps in neighbouring countries with the help of ISI and other insurgent groups. In the last quarter of 2004 Government of Bhutan took a tough stand against ULFA. The King of Bhutan personally commanded his army and demolished all the ULFA camps from his territory. Even though ULFA lost its credibility to a great extent due to 'lumpenisation' of its cadres and killing of innocent civilians, it continues its militancy in the state in association with other terrorist groups and is still a force to reckon with.

The author further adds that

- The separatist violence of ULFA has shed the blood of thousands of people including innocent civilians during last twenty-five years but instead of reducing the danger against which it has been fighting, it has only aggravated it. It has now joined hands with the same forces, which are responsible for adding to the plight of Assamese. Its compromise with Bangladesh and Pakistan in encouraging Islamic militancy and abatement to Illegal migration, therefore, eroded its popularity to a great extent but ethnic Assamese are still not ready to fully disown it. Underlying sympathy for ULFA among the ethnic Assamese are still the unresolved key issues and its main strength.
- The Union Government made several efforts to make contacts with the ULFA leaders but nothing fruitful came out. The Centre extended ban on ULFA on February 7, 2003 under the Unlawful Activities Prevention Act, 1967 for two years. ULFA was declared an Unlawful Organization on 27th November, 1996 and the ban has been extended every two years ever since. The U.S. State Department in its 2004 country report on terrorism released on 28th April, 2005, added ULFA to the Other Selected Terrorist Organizations (OSTO) list.
- ULFA was born like a cub to protect its territory from the

poachers of Bangladesh. Ironically, it jumped into the circus ring of Islamic expansionists jointly managed by Pakistan and Bangladesh, which occasionally release and command it only for creating devastating disorder in Assam. It wants secession from India without realizing the ground reality that how the various ethnic groups, who hardly have anything in common with ethnic Assamese, would react if the State is separated from India. Will it again seek help from ISI or other agencies inimical to India for maintaining its hegemony over them? Or will it prefer to become their colony?

- In view of the changing historical reality of the country, ULFA's dream for political destiny of Assam being separate from India, which disappeared following the reconstitution of its colonial geography on the eve of partition—may not come true. Perhaps only the people of Assam could convince the ULFA leaders to join the national political current and save the aggravated crisis of their identity from the threat of Islamisation and socio-economic degeneration of their motherland. The flip side is that the Government of India is not paying required attention to the North East. Instead of looking at problems from the vote bank politics, there is need to understand the genuine grievances of the Assamese and redress the past wrongs. Assam may be geographically too far away but the Assamese are great people with a sense of history and belonging to proud cultural milieu. They need understanding and respect.
- If the ULFA were to rethink on its demand for sovereignty and the Union Government about suspending army operations in the State, then peace is possible. Furthermore, the ULFA must be sincere and respond positively to a negotiated political settlement. The vicious terror that the ULFA has unleashed is being perceived as self-serving and it has lost considerable support from the masses. The process of peace can be expected only when direct talks are held and ceasefire prevails in the State.

In the concluding chapter Roopa Sharma examines the significance of Corporate Social Responsibility in the Indian context. According to her, CSR is basically a concept whereby companies decide voluntarily to take social responsibility. Roopa broadly classifies here study under four broad parts. Part I unfolds the CSR in India, Part II examines environmental compliance status of Indian industries, Part III evaluates economic incentives and policy initiatives by the government and part IV reveals local initiatives and movements against pollution.

Before concluding I would like to express my gratitude to those who have been kind enough to help me in the preparation of this volume. I wish to express a deep sense of gratitude to the esteemed contributors to this anthology of articles. The views and opinions expressed by the contributors are of immense value for researchers and academics and administrators for framing policies and strategies on Indian Polity and Governance. I am extremely thankful to Shri Ashok Kumar Mittal of Concept Publishing Co. Pvt. Ltd., New Delhi, who brought out the volume in an elegant form. I also wish to express my sincere thanks to Dr. M.B. Manoj, Principal, Sree Narayana College, Kollam for his support.

I also express my deep sense of affection, love and gratitude to my beloved wife for her support, care and exceptional sincerity. I lost her on 31st August 2012 at an age of 42. Whatever little academic activity I had undertaken hitherto was due to her solid support. Jaya came to my life on 14th November 1993. From that day onwards she supported me like a friend and motivator. She inspired me a lot giving a new meaning and dimension to my life. All the prefaces to the volumes I have published up to 2012 have been concluded by showering petals of love and affection for Jaya and our kids. From the previous volume onwards, she turned a fragrant memory. My onward journey and academic mission were in a standstill after the painful departure. From the previous issue onwards, I am making an attempt to carry forward the unfulfilled mission. If not, I may be doing an injustice to Jaya. Moreover, I pray to the Almighty to give her soul eternal peace and guide us—Aishwarya, Ananthapadmanabha and me—to face the days to come.

Finally, I am also grateful to Paul Ambrose, JoySoft Computers, Kollam, for the data entry services.

Gandhi Jayanthi Day, 2014. **M.R. Biju**

References

Atul Kohli, *Democracy and Discontent: India's Growing Crisis of Governability*, Cambridge University Press, 1990.

Atul Kohli, *Poverty Amid Plenty in the New India*, Cambridge University Press, 2012.

Atul Kohli, *State—Direct Development: Political Power and Industrialisation in the Global Periphery*, Cambridge University Press, 2004.

Frontline, Various volumes.
Jansatta, 10 May, 2014.
Jha, P.K., Indian Politics in Comparative Perspective, Pearson, New Delhi, 2012.
Mainstream, Various issues.
Sudha Pai, *Handbook of Politics in Indian State*, Oxford University Press, 2013.
The Hindu, 17 May, 2014.
The *New Indian Express*, 17 May, 2014.

1

...ificance of the Sixteenth ...Sabha Elections 2014 in India

1

Political Significance of the Sixteenth Lok Sabha Elections 2014 in India

M.R. Biju

The Indian General Election of 2014 was held to constitute the 16th Lok Sabha, electing members of Parliament for all 543 parliamentary constituencies of India. Running in nine phases from 7 April to 12 May, 2014, this was the longest election in the country's history. According to the Election Commission of India, 814.5 million people were eligible to vote, with an increase of 100 million voters since the last general election in 2009, making this the largest-ever election in the world. Around 23.1 million or 2.7 per cent of the total eligible voters were aged 18-19 years. A total of 8,251 candidates contested for the 543 Lok Sabha seats. The average election turnout over all nine phases was around 66.38 per cent, the highest ever in the history of Indian general elections. The results were declared on 16 May, fifteen days before the 15th Lok Sabha completes its constitutional mandate on 31 May, 2014. The counting exercise was held at 989 counting centres. The National Democratic Alliance, led by the Bharatiya Janata Party, won a sweeping victory, taking 336 seats. The BJP itself won 31.0 per cent of all votes and 282 (51.9%) of all seats. It is the first time since the 1984 Indian general elections that a party has won enough seats to govern without the support of other parties. http://en.wikipedia.org/wiki/Indian_general_election,_2014 - cite_note-10. The United Progressive Alliance, led by the Indian National Congress, won 58 seats, 44 (8.1%) of which were won by the Congress, that won 19.3 per cent of all votes. It was the Congress party's worst defeat in a general election. BJP and its allies won the right to form the largest majority government since the 1984 general election.

I. PRE POLL SCENE

Since the last general election in 2009, the anti-corruption movement by Anna Hazare, and other similar moves by Baba Ramdev and Arvind Kejriwal (founder of Aam Aadmi Party), gathered momentum and political interest. Kejriwal went on to form a separate political party, Aam Aadmi Party in November 2012. The 2012 presidential election, resulted in Pranab Mukherjee of Indian National Congress becoming the President. The Telangana movement for a separate Telangana state from Andhra Pradesh also continued with agitations, including the initial Central Government decision to grant statehood and then rescind it after counter-protests. Andhra politics was further shaken following the death of its Chief Minister, Y.S.R. Reddy. His son, Y.S. Jaganmohan Reddy, then broke from the INC and founded the YSR Congress taking several politicians with him. The final session of Parliament started on 6 February and ended on 21 February. Amongst the agenda in the final session was passing The Lokpal and Lokayuktas Bill, 2013 in tackling corruption and the creation of Telangana.

Major Campaign Issues

Important issues during the campaign included high inflation, lack of jobs, economic slow down, corruption, security and terrorism, religious division and communalism, and infrastructure such as roads, electricity and water. Other major campaign issues include:

On Economy: Bloomberg highlighted India's slowing economy amidst a record high current account deficit and a falling rupee in summer 2013. It pointed out to a lack of infrastructure investment and a government increasingly likely to give subsidies that the national finances cannot afford just before the election. Other points it mentioned were stagnant policy-making and an inefficient bureaucracy. The economy was the main issue in the campaign. The lack of a clear mandate as a result of the election could lead to an increase in the price of gold in the country. Modi also brought up the issue of farmer suicides that resulted from high debt and poor yield on their crops. Former Finance Minister Yashwant Sinha criticised the incumbent Chidambaram in saying that he had a "habit that he will get a strong economy, and he will ruin it before he leaves. Shri Chidambaram will be remembered in history as a spoiler, as someone who specialises in sub-five per cent growth rate, for his hubris, arrogance."

On Corruption: During the UPA-2, a number of scams came to public domain deteriorating the image of the government among the common man: These scams included coal scam, 2G scam and CWG scam.

On Price rise: The price of onions, a staple in Indian cuisine, faced a dramatic increase. In the lead up to the election, consumer price inflation increased more than expected while, paradoxically, industrial production fell by more than expected causing a dilemma amid slowing growth. The price of salt was also indicative of general food inflation.

On Telangana: On 30 July, 2013, the Congress Working Committee unanimously passed a resolution for the creation of Telangana. Telangana Rashtra Samiti (TRS) welcomed the decision. YSR Congress party leader Jaganmohan Reddy, however, opposed the decision and in agitation against it, all its MLAs resigned over the issue. The BJP national spokesperson Prakash Javadekar suggested that the INC's move was under pressure and that BJP "will watch till Telangana is formed." In February, Chief Minister of Andhra Pradesh Kiran Kumar Reddy resigned over the proposal to partition the region. The conflicting views of the political parties thus made the Telangana issue a crucial one in the elections.

II. VOTING PATTERN

According to the Election Commission of India, 814.5 million people were eligible to vote, with an increase of 100 million voters since the last general election in 2009, making this the largest-ever election in the world. Around 23.1 million or 2.7 per cent of the total eligible voters were aged 18-19 years.

In total there were 1.4 million electronic voting machines in 930,000 voting centres. The Voter-verified Paper Audit Trail (VVPAT) system which enables EVM to record each vote cast by generating the EVM slip, was introduced in 8 constituencies of Lucknow, Gandhinagar, Bangalore South, Chennai Central, Jadavpur, Raipur, Patna Sahib and Mizoram as a pilot project. Also, Braille ballot sheets for the blind were arranged at polling stations. The scale of the election required 1.1 million of civil servants and 5.5 million civilian employees to handle the election. It was the first election that had the "none of the above" option and allowed Non-Resident Indians to vote; though only in India. Security was increased during the election, particularly as the Communist Party of India (Maoist) [CPI (Maoist)] called for a boycott of the election. On 12 April, even though there was no voting this day, a vehicle in Chhattisgarh hit a CPI (Maoist) landmine resulting in the deaths of two bus drivers and five election officials, with four more injured, while travelling from Kutru to Bijapur in preparation for the fifth phase of voting. On the same day, within an hour, they also ambushed a vehicle resulting in the deaths of five paramilitary soldiers in the Darbha forest. The election was the longest and the most expensive general election in the history of the country, with the Election Commission of India estimating that the election did cost the exchequer Rupees 3500 crore (US$577 million), excluding the expenses incurred for security and by the individual political parties. Parties were expected to spend Rupees 30,500 crore (US$5 billion) in the election, according to the Centre for Media Studies. This was three times the amount spent in the previous election in 2009, and was then the world's second highest after the US$7 billion spent on the 2012 US presidential election.

The election reportedly boosted the hospitality sector as, according to ASSOCHAM, tourist arrivals from the countries such as the US, UK, France, Singapore and the UAE have gone up by 10-15, while the movement of domestic tourists jumped by 62 per cent.

III. PHASES OF POLL

Phase 1: 7 April: Turnout was 75 per cent in Assam and 84 per cent in Tripura. Assam's INC Chief Minister Tarun Gogoi said that "there is no Narendra Modi magic in Assam. The Congress has been winning every form of elections since 2001 in Assam, and we are going to repeat the performance this time." Additionally, the borders with Bangladesh and Bhutan were closed for security reasons.

Phase 2: 9 and 11 April: The turnouts were recorded at 82.5 per cent in Nagaland, 71 per cent in Arunachal Pradesh, 66 per cent in Meghalaya and 70 per cent in Manipur. Mizoram's voting was deferred to 11 April, where the turnout was 60 per cent.

Phase 3: 10 April: About 110 million of people were eligible to vote for 91 seats. The turnout was 76 per cent in Kerala, 64 per cent in Delhi, 55.98 per cent in Madhya Pradesh, 54.13 per cent in Maharashtra, 65 per cent in Uttar Pradesh and 66.29 per cent in Jammu. Kerala and Chandigarh set new voter turnout records. A higher proportion of eligible electors voted in 2014 than in 2009.

Phase 4: 12 April: Voter turnout set new records or were near record levels with 75 per cent in Goa, 75 per cent in Assam, 81.8 per cent in Tripura and 80.97 per cent in Sikkim (including the Sikkim Legislative Assembly election, 2014). West Bengal Chief Minister Mamata Banerjee nearly cancelled the polls in her region after initially refusing to changes to the appointments of civil service departments, but was forced to constitutionally do so.

Phase 5: 17 April: The largest voting day involved nearly 200 million eligible voters, 1,769 candidates for 121 seat. The voting turnout in Uttar

Pradesh was 62 per cent, West Bengal was 80 per cent, over 70 per cent in Odisha, 69 per cent in Jammu and Kashmir, 54 per cent in Madhya Pradesh and 62 per cent in Jharkhand. Manipur had 74 per cent and Maharashtra had a 61.7 per cent turnout. In Karnataka, the average voting was up on 65 per cent against 58 per cent in the previous election, though urban voters were lower. In Chhattisgarh, the voter turnout was 63.44 per cent compared to 57.6 per cent in 2009, while Rajasthan recorded a 63.25 per cent voter turnout, compared to 48.09 per cent in 2009. In Bihar's seven constituencies, the turnout was 56 per cent, compared to 39 per cent in 2009. http://en.wikipedia.org/wiki/Indian_general_election,_2014 - cite_note-223. In one of six constituencies from Jammu and Kashmir, Udhämpur, the turnout of 70 per cent was significantly higher than the 2009 figure of 45 per cent. Overall across India, the turnout on the day was over 65 per cent and nearly all constituencies had a higher voter turnout than 2009.

Phase 6: 24 April: The second largest voting day entailed 180 million eligible voters across 201,735 voting centres to elect 117 members of parliament from 2,098 candidates. Tamil Nadu set a new voter turnout record for Lok Sabha elections with 73 per cent, while West Bengal experienced the highest voter turnout for the day at 82 per cent. As compared to that, urban centres such as Mumbai and Chennai saw lower voter turnouts, but bettered their figures from previous years. Mumbai witnessed a 53 per cent turnout, compared to 41 per cent in 2009. The rural areas of Maharashtra saw over 60 per cent turnout, Madhya Pradesh had 64 per cent, Uttar Pradesh had over 60 per cent, Chhattisgarh had about 66 per cent, Assam had over 70 per cent, Bihar has about 60 per cent, Jharkhand had 63.4 per cent, Rajasthan had about 60 per cent and Pudhucherry had about 82 per cent. One of six constituencies from Jammu and Kashmir, Anantnag, had the lowest turnout of 28 per cent, after a boycott call by separatists, an attack on 22 April that killed three people, and with thousands of Kashmiri Pandits protesting in the afternoon that their names were missing from the electoral roll. As with previous phases, the overall voter turnout for the day was higher than 2009. In both Madhya Pradesh and Rajasthan, the turnout was about 9 per cent higher, while Uttar Pradesh saw a 13 per cent increase.

Phase 7: 30 April: The 7th phase of voting entailed about 140 million eligible voters to elect 89 members of parliament from 1,295 candidates in 7 states and 2 Union Territories. Punjab set a new record in its voter turnout for general elections with 73 per cent. Gujarat saw the highest jump in voter turnout for the day with 62 per cent turnout compared to 48 per cent turnout in 2009 Lok Sabha elections. The nine constituencies in West Bengal reported over 81 per cent turnout. Uttar Pradesh witnessed 57 per cent turnout compared to 48 per cent in 2009, while Bihar saw 60 per cent compared to 52 per cent in 2009. One of six constituencies from Jammu and Kashmir, eligible to vote in this phase, had the lowest turnout for the day at 26 per cent compared to 25.55 per cent in 2009, after a boycott call by separatists. Telangana region of Andhra Pradesh, which will become India's new state on 2 June, 2014, saw nearly 72 per cent turnout to elect Lok Sabha members as well as its first state government. The aggregate turnout so far in the first 7 phases for 438 parliamentary seats has been 66.20 per cent, significantly more than 57.41 per cent figure in 2009 general elections.

Phase 8: 7 May: The 8th phase saw voting for 64 Lok Sabha seats in 7 states with 897 candidates competing. Along with the general elections, polls were also held for the first Legislative Assembly of Andhra Pradesh excluding Telangana region. The voter turnout was high, with West Bengal, Andhra Pradesh and Himachal Pradesh each setting their respective general election voter turnout records. West Bengal recorded 81 per cent polling compared to 78 per cent for 2009. Andhra Pradesh recorded nearly 76 per cent voter turnout. Himachal Pradesh saw about 66 per cent turnout compared to 58 per cent for 2009. Uttarakhand also set a new voter turnout record with 62 per cent compared to 53 per cent in 2009. The 2 constituencies of J&K that voted witnessed a 49.9 per cent turnout, while constituencies of Bihar saw 58 per cent compared to 45 per cent in 2009. Uttar Pradesh experienced a 55.5 per cent turnout compared to 43.4 per cent in 2009.

Phase 9: 12 May: The 9th and last phase of voting entailed over 90 million eligible voters to elect 41 members of parliament from 606 candidates in 3 states. The 6 seats in Bihar saw a voter turnout of 58 per cent, compared to 46 per cent in 2009. Uttar Pradesh's 18 constituencies witnessed a 55.3 per cent turnout, compared to 46.6 per cent in 2009. In West Bengal, the 17 constituencies that voted, saw a turnout of about 80 per cent compared to 82 per cent in 2009. The 2014 general elections, according to the Election Commission of India, recorded a cumulative total of 66.38 per cent voter turnout, or 551.3 million out of 814 million eligible people casting their vote, according to provisional figures. The 2014 turnout surpassed India's previous highest voter turnout record of 64 per cent in 1984 general elections. The voter turnout in 2009 general elections was 58.19 per cent, while 2004 general elections saw a voter turnout of 56.98 per cent. http://en.wikipedia.org/wiki/Indian_general_election,_2014 - cite_note-busi12 May-247. The 2014 general elections entailed 8,202 candidates competing for 543 seats.

IV. VOTER TURNOUT

State/UT-wise Voter Turnout Details Based on Data from Election Commission of India

State/UT	*Male Electors*	*Male Voters*	*Male Turnout*	*Female Electors*	*Female Voters*	*Female Turnout*	*Total Electors*	*Total Voters*	*Total Turnout*	*Total Seats*
Andaman & Nicobar Islands (UT)	142,782	101,178	70.86%	126,578	89,150	70.43%	269,360	190,328	70.66%	1
Andhra Pradesh	32,670,930	24,352,913	74.54%	32,267,820	24,005,632	74.39%	64,938,750	48,358,545	74.47%	42
Arunachal Pradesh	379,627	289,291	76.2%	379,760	307,665	81.02%	759,387	596,956	78.61%	2
Assam	9,787,209	7,876,763	80.48%	9,098,065	7,209,120	79.24%	18,885,274	15,085,883	79.88%	14
Bihar	34,092,938	18,779,230	55.08%	29,668,858	17,106,136	57.66%	63,761,796	35,885,366	56.28%	40
Chandigarh (UT)	333,621	244,956	73.42%	281,593	208,499	74.04%	615,214	453,455	73.71%	1
Chhattisgarh	8,915,783	6,320,693	70.89%	8,707,266	5,934,886	68.16%	17,623,049	12,255,579	69.54%	11
Dadra & Nagar Haveli (UT)	106,215	87,800	82.66%	90,402	77,486	85.71%	196,617	165,286	84.06%	1
Daman & Diu (UT)	57,011	42,378	74.33%	54,816	44,855	81.83%	111,827	87,233	78.01%	1
Goa	528,308	395,766	74.91%	532,469	421,234	79.11%	1,060,777	817,000	77.02%	2
Gujarat	21,229,092	14,259,115	67.17%	19,374,012	11,564,888	59.69%	40,603,104	25,824,003	63.6%	26
Haryana	8,716,612	6,351,584	72.87%	7,381,137	5,143,566	69.69%	16,097,749	11,495,150	71.41%	10
Himachal Pradesh	2,474,430	1,569,632	63.43%	2,335,641	1,528,869	65.46%	4,810,071	3,098,501	64.42%	4
Jammu & Kashmir	3,802,021	1,927,584	50.7%	3,400,142	1,639,279	48.21%	7,202,163	3,566,863	49.52%	6
Jharkhand	10,685,149	6,860,476	64.21%	9,641,594	6,122,464	63.5%	20,326,743	12,982,940	63.87%	14

(*Contd.*)

(*Contd.*)

State/UT	Male Electors	Male Voters	Male Turnout	Female Electors	Female Voters	Female Turnout	Total Electors	Total Voters	Total Turnout	Total Seats
Karnataka	23,586,223	16,165,832	68.54%	22,625,886	14,873,056	65.73%	46,212,109	31,038,888	67.17%	28
Kerala	11,734,258	8,678,185	73.96%	12,592,391	9,297,708	73.84%	24,326,649	17,975,893	73.89%	20
Lakshadweep (UT)	25,433	21,585	84.87%	24,489	21,654	88.42%	49,922	43,239	86.61%	1
Madhya Pradesh	25,309,830	16,734,556	66.12%	22,808,210	12,905,240	56.58%	48,118,040	29,639,796	61.6%	29
Maharashtra	42,743,156	26,714,578	62.5%	37,974,127	22,004,266	57.95%	80,717,283	48,718,844	60.36%	48
Manipur	871,431	685,427	78.66%	902,894	727,210	80.54%	1,774,325	1,412,637	79.62%	2
Meghalaya	777,639	524,774	67.48%	789,602	553,284	70.07%	1,567,241	1,078,058	68.79%	2
Mizoram	346,219	216,167	62.44%	355,951	217,034	60.97%	702,170	433,201	61.69%	1
Nagaland	600,490	529,325	88.15%	582,458	509,585	87.49%	1,182,948	1,038,910	87.82%	1
NCT of Delhi	7,051,098	4,653,522	66.00%	5,660,138	3,618,244	63.93%	12,711,236	8,271,766	65.07%	7
Orissa	15,194,309	11,032,523	72.61%	14,001,732	10,499,752	74.99%	29,196,041	21,532,275	73.75%	21
Puducherry (UT)	432,048	351,360	81.32%	469,309	388,657	82.81%	901,357	740,017	82.1%	1
Punjab	10,327,116	7,262,625	70.33%	9,280,892	6.582,507	70.93%	19,608,008	13,845,132.	70.61%	13
Rajasthan	22,638,323	14,627,976	64.62%	20,331,124	12,482,068	61.39%	42,969,447	27,110,044	63.09%	25
Sikkim	190,886	158,222	82.89%	179,725	150,745	83.88%	370,611	308,967	83.37%	1
Tamil Nadu	27,571,785	20,249,949	73.44%	27,542,720	20,370,491	73.96%	55,114,505	40,620,440	73.70%	39
Tripura	1,217,575	1,035,722	85.06%	1,171,244	988,137	84.37%	2,388,819	2,023,859	84.72%	2
Uttar Pradesh	76,071,444	44,979,619	59.13%	62,894,376	36,112,683	57.42%	138,965,820	81,092,302	58.35%	80
Uttarakhand	3,751,098	2,268,767	60.48%	3,378,841	2,123,123	62.84%	7,129,939	4,391,890	61.6%	5
West Bengal	32,689,449	26,886,706	82.25%	30,143,679	24,735,849	82.06%	62,833,128	51,622,555	82.16%	42
India	437,051,538	293,236,779	67.09%	397,049,941	260,565,022	65.63%	834,101,479	553,801,801	66.40%	543

V. PEOPLE'S VERDICT

The BJP secured 39 per cent support from first time voters, while Congress received 19 per cent of the first time votes. Of the 87 Lok Sabha seats in the country identified by the Centre for the Study of Developing Societies (CSDS) as having a high percentage of Muslim voters, the BJP won 45. These seats included 27 in Uttar Pradesh, 19 in West Bengal, 8 each in Assam and Kerala, 6 each in Bihar and Jammu and Kashmir, 4 in Maharashtra, 2 in Andhra Pradesh and Delhi, and one each in Haryana, Tripura, Lakshwadeep, Jharkhand and Uttarakhand. The BJP also won 47 seats in the 102 constituencies where at least one in five voters is a Muslim, higher than the 24 such seats they had won in the 2009 election.

The BJP had no success among the 19 Muslim-dominated constituencies in West Bengal. Most of these seats were won by the Congress and the Trinamool Congress. The BJP was also unable to win any seats in the 10 such constituencies in the southern states of Kerala and Andhra Pradesh. *India Today* reported that data released by the office of the Delhi Chief Electoral Officer indicated "a reversal in the Muslim community's support for the Aam Aadmi Party" in the capital. *India Today* noted that BJP had won all 7 seats in Delhi, with their candidates receiving a larger vote share. A large section of the Muslim population in the Union Territory celebrated the BJP's victory on 16 May, and stated that they felt no fear in voting for the party.

The NDA won 39 of 74 seats where Muslim voters make up between 21 to 95 per cent of the total electorate. The BJP won all 16 seats, where the Muslim electorate is between 21 and 50 per cent, in Uttar Pradesh. It also secured 5 out of 9 such seats in Bihar. Analyst Saeed Naqvi believes that Amit Shah managed to convince Dalits and OBC voters to elect the BJP by focusing on Mayawati and Mulayam Singh as "Muslim appeasers in an atmosphere of perpetual communal tension". The BJP won all 26 seats in Gujarat, marking the first time a single party won all seats in the state. The previous record was held by the Congress which won 25 of the 26 seats in the 1984 general election.

Results in Nutshell

BJP	*Congress*	*AIDMK*	*TMC*	*BJD*	*Siva Sena*	*TDP*
171,637,684 (31.0%)	906,935,311 (19.3%)	181,15,825 (3.3%)	21,25,96,81 (3.8%)	94,91,497 (1.7%)	10,262,982 (1.9%)	14,09,45,45 (2.5%)

RESULTS 2014 IN DETAILS

Partywise Vote Share

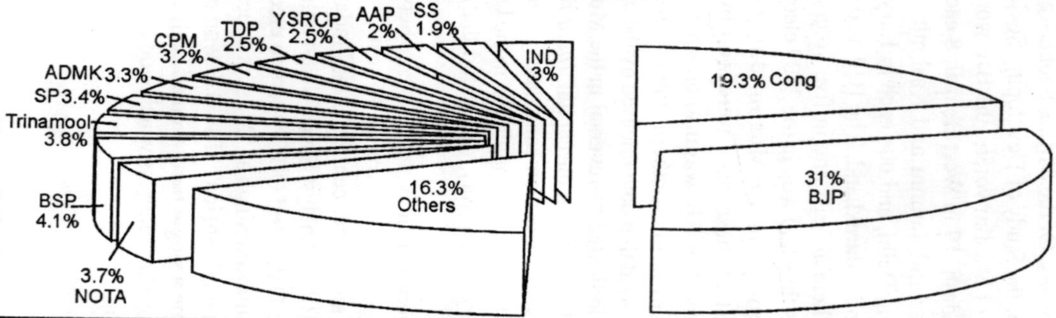

NDA (336)	*UPA (60)*	*Left (10)*	*Others (137)*
BJP-282	Congress-44	CPI(M)-9	AIDMK-37
Siva Sena-18	NCP-6	CPI-1	Trinamool Congress-34
Telugu Desam-16	RJD-4		Biju Janata Dal-20
Lok Jan Shakti Party-6	IUML-2		TRS-11
Shiromani Akali Dal-4	JMM-2		YSR Congress-9
Rashtriya Lok Samta Party-3	Kerala Congress (M)-1		Samajwadi Party-5
Apna Dal-2	RSP-1		AAP-4
All India NR Congress-1			AIUDF-3
Naga People's Front-1			JKPDP-3
National Peoples Party-1			INL-2
Pattalli Makkal Katchi-1			Janata Dal(S)-2
Swabhimani Paksha-1			Janata Dal(U)-2
			SDF-1
			AIMIM-1
			Independents-3 (2 independents were supported by the left in Kerala)

As per the Election Commission figures, the BJP came out with flying colours in the poll by winning 282 seats on its own, while it got nearly 17.16 crore votes accounting for 31 per cent vote share. The Indian National Congress, which has been left with just 44 seats, has managed to get 10.7 crore votes or about 19.3 per cent share. On the vote share front, Bahujan Samaj Party (BSP) has interestingly come third with 4.1 per cent vote share or 2.3 crore votes, but it has got zero seats in its kitty. Its candidates came second on 34 seats.

The poll results further show that parties like Mayawati-led BSP and Tamil Nadu's DMK managed to corner a large number of votes but failed to convert them into seats, while parties with lesser vote share have got seats to show in their kitty. Even among those having won some seats, given a large majority being cornered by the BJP, the number of seats is not in proportion with their respective vote shares. The Samajwadi Party is also not far behind with 3.4 per cent vote share, although Mulayam Singh Yadav-led party could manage to win only five seats. On the other hand, Mamata Banerjee-led Trinamool Congress (TMC) has got 34 seats with about 3.8 per cent vote share. The number of seats won by Jayalalitha-led AIADMK is even larger at 37, although vote share stands at 3.3 per cent. At the same time, CPM with a similar 3.3 per cent vote share has managed to win just nine seats. Biju Janta Dal, the fifth largest party in terms of seats after the BJP, Congress, AIADMK and TMC, has got 20 seats although it stands much lower on the vote share tally at 14th position with 1.7 per cent share.

The DMK has also got 1.7 per cent vote share, but has no seat to show in its kitty. Shiv Sena has got 1.9 per cent vote share with 18 seats, while the Aam Aadmi Party has 2 per cent votes and four seats. Nationalist Congress Party has managed six seats with 1.6 per cent votes.

The result also shows that a total of 18 parties have managed to win one per cent or more vote share in these elections, while those getting less than one per cent of total votes include CPI (0.8%), Janta Dal Secular (0.7%), Shiromani Akali Dal (0.7%) and Indian National Lok Dal (0.5%). Others with lesser vote shares include AIUDF, Ram Vilas Paswan-led LJSP, DMDK, PMK (0.4%), RSP, Jharkhand Mukti Morcha, JVM, MDMK, AIFB, SWP, IUML, BLSP, CPI(ML)(L), Naga Peoples Front, Apna Dal and BMUP.

A vote share comparison with past Lok Sabha elections shows that the BJP's vote share: has gone up from 18.8 per cent in 2009, while that of Congress has fallen sharply from 28.55 per cent at that time. The BSP's vote share has also come down from 6.17 per cent in 2009. The BSP was third largest in terms of vote share in 2009 elections also, but it had won as many as 21 seats at that time. During 2004 Lok Sabha elections, the Bahujan Samaj Party got 5.33 per cent votes and bagged 19 seats, while the party's tally in 1999 polls stood at, 14 seats and 4.16 per cent votes. During 1998 Lok Sabha elections, the BSP won five seats with 4.67 per cent votes.

BJP'S ENTRY INTO NEW AREAS

What the party has accomplished in Uttar Pradesh, Rajasthan and Madhya Pradesh is not as its performance in States such as Tamil Nadu (5% of votes polled), Odisha (21%), Jammu and Kashmir (32%), Assam (36%), and West Bengal (16%). By winning Ladakh in Jammu and Kashmir for the first time, it has also stormed into the Congress and the National Conference bastion. This improved performance in areas that were not BJP strongholds is being attributed to the acceptance of Narendra Modi as a national leader and Prime Minister.

The BJP's revised election strategy in the Lok Sabha polls had been to cover the last mile. Extensive campaigns were undertaken in distant parts of the country and people were promised employment, development, security and growth. Separate manifestos were drafted for each of the North-Eastern States and at rallies in the region Modi focused on development, protection of border areas; illegal immigration and even the ecology. For instance, in Manipur, where the party has a vote share of 11 per cent, construction of arterial roads has been promised, the contentious issue of the Armed Forces (Special Powers) Act, 1958 has been touched upon and decentralisation of administration has been spoken of. In West Bengal, between the Left and the Trinamool, it has managed to carve out a space for itself. Here again, the promise is of growth and a better economy. The BJP may not have bagged seats, but by securing 16 per cent of the votes it has made, a beginning. Similarly, with a vote share of 10 per cent in Kerala, 32 per cent in Jammu and Kashmir, 36 per cent in Assam, 21 per cent in Odisha, eight per cent in Meghalaya and 11 per cent in Manipur, the BJP is no longer confined to the North, West and Central India and is staking its claim as a true national party.

IMPRESSIVE INCREASE IN BJP'S VOTE SHARE IN KERALA

A seat in Kerala might still remain a dream for the BJP in Kerala. But the saffron party and the NDA could boast of being only party and alliance which could increase their vote share in all the assembly segments in the state. Both the UDF and the LDF lost a considerable number of votes in most assembly segments. Even though they shared the 20 Lok Sabha seats between them.

The BJP could increase its votes in all the 126 assembly segments in 18 Lok Sabha seats, the highest rise being in Nemom constituency (Trivandrum-36511 votes) and lowest in Idukki which saw an increase of just 17 votes. In 73 Assembly segments, the party's vote share increased between 4000 and 10000 in the last 5 years. However, the party's experience to forge and alliance in the last minutes looks failed as it could record only a marginal increase in all the 14 assembly segments in Alappuzha and Kottayam. Alappuzha is the constituency where the NDA got the least votes in the States followed Kottayam. The NDA candidates in both seats had contested on symbols other than BJP's lotus.

The BJP could increase as many as 30,000 votes in three assembly segments in Thiruvananthapuram District—Kazhakkoottam, Vattiyoorkavu and Nemom, a feat which could not be achieved by the other two fronts in any of the segments. The party could also add 20,000 votes in two assembly segments—Parassala and Kovalam, while it failed to do that well in Neyyattinkara. With 50,685 votes, Nemom is the only assembly segments in the state where the BJP got more than 50,000 votes, while the UDF got this much votes in 93 segments and LDF in 84 segments. While the UDF votes dipped in all segments in Wayanad and Pathanamthitta even though the front one these seats. The LDF did the same in Chalakkudy, even when it wrested the seats.

Vote increase	*BJP*	*NDA*	*UDF*	*LDF*
Below 1000	2	3	10	4
1000-4000	29	10	28	21
4000-10000	73	1	26	43
10000-20000	16		3	10
20000-30000	3			2
30000-40000	3			
Assembly total	140		67	80

Performance of AIADMK, BJD and TMC

The Ail India Anna Dravida Munnetra Kazhagam (AIADMK), the Biju Janata Dal (BJD) and the Trinamool Congress are truly in an all-dressed-up-but-nowhere-to-go situation. All the three parties chose to contest the elections on their own in the hope of bettering their numbers and increasing their bargaining power in a coalition government at the Centre. The first part of the gamble has paid off handsomely for all three: the AIADMK has picked up 37 of the 39 seats in Tamil Nadu, the BJD 20 of the 21 seats in Odisha, and the Trinamool Congress 34 of 42 in West Bengal.

While the Samajwadi Party (SP) and the Bahujan Samaj Party (BSP), which had hoped to stop the BJP juggernaut in Uttar Pradesh, have been swept aside as has the Dravida Munnetta Kazhagam in Tamil Nadu, the Telangana Rashtra Samithi and the YSR Congress have done fairly well in the maze that Andhra Pradesh politics had become after the creation of Telangana. But like all other regional parties, they have been rendered also—rans in this election which brings the curtains down on the 25-year run of coalitions.

LOWEST REPRESENTATION OF MUSLIMS

The number of Muslim MPs in the 16th Lok Sabha will be the lowest in 50 years. The Poll analysis of the 2014 election results has found that just 22 Muslims have been elected to the new Lok Sabha, seven fewer than the earlier House. Muslims now make up just over four per cent of parliamentarians despite accounting for over 13.4 per cent of the population as of 2001. There were over 30 Muslim MPs for the past 15 years, over 25 for the 20 years before that and over 40 for the 10 years between 1980 and 1989.

With the Bharatiya Janata Party sweeping the election but nominating fewer than five Muslim candidates across the country, the likelihood of a Muslim from the party making it to Parliament fell substantially. None of the BJP's five candidates won, but its ally, the Lok Jan Shakti Party (LJSP), had one Muslim candidate who won in Khagaria (Bihar). Eight of the Muslims who won were UPA candidates—four from the Congress, one from the Rashtriya Janata Dal (RJD) and two from the Nationalist Congress Party (NCP).

ELECTORAL DISASTER OF THE CONGRESS PARTY

Facing its worst moment in its 128-year-old history, not even winning enough seats to secure the position of the Leader of the Opposition in the Lok Sabha, a stunned Congress stared into a bleak future, its leaders recognising that this was not ordinary defeat without a massive course correction. There is a clear realisation inside the party that it stands at the crossroads, that there is an urgent need to change the narrative, Congress leaders acknowledged. But they were all unanimous that the party's fate—for better or worse—is inextricably entwined with that of the Gandhi-Nehru family: choosing a new leader is out of the question.

The Congress Party's defeat in the 2014 Lok Sabha elections reflected not just its failure to retain its vote shares of the previous polls in 2004 and 2009, but also the lack of a clear social profile of its voters. Most social sections had deserted the party (barring the Muslims) as its long-term decline from being India's grand old party was evident in these elections. The lack of adequate leadership and confusion in its ranks played an important role, but there were other systemic reasons for the Congress's defeat. This was, of course, not the first time that the Congress Party has been defeated at the parliamentary elections. Starting with 1977, it experienced setbacks in 1989 and 1996. In fact, the 1996 defeat ensured its subsequent inability to wrest power in two more elections. It must also be borne in mind that the 1977 and 1989 defeats took place under the leadership of much stronger leaders who were themselves leading the government. While it is commonplace to mark the 1989 defeat as the beginning of the post-Congress polity, the 1977 defeat itself marked the sharp decline in the ability of the party to continue its hegemonic hold over the polity. The two defeats of 1977 and 1989 brought about structural changes in the arena of competitive politics in India. In both 1977 and 1989, various non-Congress parties came together to ensure that the Congress was defeated within the framework of the simple plurality system. During the 1990s, along with structural changes in the system of competition, the process of social reconfiguration occasioned by major churning in terms of social blocs getting redefined and tending to realign also began to take shape. In that sense, the rout of the Congress in 2014 could be seen only as a continuation of that trend.

Gravity of the Debacle

In terms of both seats and votes, the parliamentary elections of 2014 witnessed the Congress dip to a new low-under 20 per cent vote share at the all-India level, and only 44 seats (which account for a little over 8 per cent of the total seats in Lok Sabha). In this sense, the 2014 defeat is the party's worst ever defeat so far. In 2009, the party polled 29 per cent of the votes; so within five years, it lost more than 9 per cent votes. The following table depicts performance of the Congress since its decline began in 1989.

Year	Total Seats	Turnout	Congress	
			Won	Vote
1984	542	64.07	415	48.01
1989	529	61.95	197	39.53
1991	537	55.88	244	36.64
1996	543	57.94	140	28.80
1998	543	61.97	141	25.82
1999	543	59.99	114	28.30
2004	543	58.07	145	26.53
2009	543	58.20	206	28.55
2014	543	66.44	44	19.31

Source: *EPW*, 27 September, 2014.

It is clear from the above table that in the entire period of last 25 years, the Congress was never able to recover from its downslide except in 2009. Since the 1996 elections, Congress vote share hovered in the range of 26 per cent and 29 per cent. In fact, it is possible to argue that 2009 was a slight exception because not only did the Congress come close to polling 29 per cent of the votes, it also recorded its best performance in terms of seats since 1996. The party could not build on that 'recovery', in fact, the recovery of the Congress actually takes place between 2004 and 2009 and post-2009, the party begins to stagnate and lose momentum.

Congress Performance—Region-wise

If one look at the Congress's performance in different regions, this political inability becomes clearer. The following table shows the Congress's performance in the different regions and it has two striking features. One is that in the region where the Congress polled highest vote share (central region), it could win only three seats. In the entire Hindi belt, the Congress won only eight seats and its remaining seats all came from the non-Hindi speaking belt. This is partly because of the Congress's historical inability to re-establish itself in the Hindi-speaking region. But this is also because of the nature of competition. In direct confrontation with the Bharatiya Janata Party, the Congress fared dismally. In bipolar contests, most of which were with BJP, the Congress polled almost 34 per cent of the votes but could win barely 5 per cent of the seats (six out of 113). In contrast, in multipolar contests, the Congress polled only a little over 15 per cent of the votes but bagged 9 per cent of the seats (38 out of 430).

Regions	*Total Seats*	*Turnout*	*Congress*	
			Won	*Vote*
East	117	69.3	6	12.3
North East	25	79.7	8	29.8
North	151	61.4	6	17.2
Central	40	63.7	3	35.9
West	78	62.0	2	23.7
South	132	72.5	19	18.6
Overall	543	66.5	44	19.3

Source: *EPW*, 27 September, 2014.

Thus, in terms of electoral calculations, one could say that the defeat of the Congress party could have been made somewhat moderate if the Congress Party had ensured many more multi-cornered contests. However, one must remember that in key states, such as Rajasthan, Gujarat, Madhya Pradesh, and Chhattisgarh, the party competition has already stabilised around only two players and there was little the Congress could have done to alter that.

In broader terms, two vital factors were responsible for the debacle of the Congress party in 2014, viz. performance of the UPA government and the issue of leadership in the Congress party. Close to the general elections, all parties opposed the UPA about the non-performance of the Government and various corruption scandals involving coalition partners. Besides, the downslide in the economy and resulting inflation could easily be blamed on the Government. The cumulative effect of these factors was that the popular dissatisfaction with the Government only increased. The Congress could not run away from the blame since it was seen as the main party in the ruling UPA. Moreover, the general impression of the common man was that the UPA was not able to handle the economy and the issues of governance. Further, Rahul Gandhi was not seen majority of voters as an equal to Narendra Modi both in terms of experience and ability to resolve issues. In short, what happed to the Congress in 2014 has the features of an electoral disaster rather than a defeat (Suhas Palshikar, 2014).

62 WOMEN MPs

The 16th Lok Sabha will be under-represented by women as usual, though it is likely to have the highest ever number of them. Of the 543 MPs, only

62, or a little more than 11 per cent, are women. This is a negligible improvement, from 2009, when 61 women candidates were elected to the Lower House. However, the Bharatiya Janata Party scores when it comes to the highest number of women MPs—out of the 58, 28 are from the BJP. The party had fielded 35 women candidates. The Trinamool Congress comes second with 11 of its 24 candidates emerging victorious. While none of the AAP's four victorious candidates are women, the Congress will send three women MPs to Parliament.

Out of a total number of 8,163 candidates, 636 women contested elections across the country. In 2009, 556 (6.9%) women candidates had contested out of a total of 8,070. While many among the winners are expected faces such as Congress's Sonia Gandhi, BJP's Sushma Swaraj and PDP's Mehbooba Mufti, the results also sprang surprises. Heena Gavit, 26, a first-timer from the BJP, defeated nine-time MP Manikrao Gavit from the Nandurbar constituency in Maharashtra, a place from where the Congress has never lost. Other first-timers include Hema Malini of tbe BJP from Mathura.

OVER 57 LAKHS VOTES FOR NOTA

Over 57 lakh 'None Of The Above' (NOTA) votes were cast in the 16th Lok Sabha elections, the first time that this option was given, Election Commission data shows. This accounts for 1.1 per cent of all the votes cast. The disproportionately high use of NOTA in reserved constituencies continues after the 2013 Assembly elections.

The poll results further indicated that the high use of NOTA in reserved constituencies could be on account of upper caste candidates preferring to vote for no one rather than vote for a Dalit or a tribal candidate. On an average, over 10,000 votes were cast in every constituency. In 46 constituencies, over 20,000 NOTA votes were cast. All but one of the ten constituencies in which the most NOTA votes were cast were reserved constituencies, eight of them for Scheduled Tribes (STs) and one for Scheduled Castes (SCs).

Over twice as many NOTA votes were cast in ST constituencies than in 'General' constituencies. It is found nearly 20,000 votes were cast on average in ST constituencies. While more NOTA votes were cast in SC constituencies too as compared to General constituencies, the difference was less.

The proportion of the negative votes was higher than the national average in Chhattisgarh (1.9%), Gujarat (1.8%), Jharkhand (1.5%), with the highest of all in the two ST constituencies in Meghalaya. The number of NOTA votes was highest of all in the SC constituency of Nilgiris in Tamil Nadu (over 46,000 votes), where the margin of victory between the AIADMK candidate and the DMK's A. Raja was 1 lakh votes. In Nilgiris, NOTA got more votes than the Congress candidate. In South Bangalore, NOTA votes cast were more than the votes received by the hardline right-winger Pramod Muthalik, who contested as an Independent. Despite being widely seen as an option that will empower the educated voter, the proportion of NOTA was lower than the national average in States and UTs such as Chandigarh, Delhi, Karnataka, Maharashtra and Himachal Pradesh, and only slightly above the national average in Kerala (1.2%).

HUMILIATING DEFEAT OF THE CPI(M)

With just nine seats in its kitty from three States, the CPI(M) is two short of the criteria that has afforded it national party status for years now. One of the various benchmarks set by the Election Commission for according national party status to a political party is 11 seats in the Lok Sabha from at least three States.

Now, the CPI(M) is hoping to use the two Independents—who contested the elections in Kerala as part of the Left Democratic Front—to build a case for retaining the national party status. The near decimation of the Left comes at a time when the Left in general and the CPI(M) in particular is extremely demoralised and still nursing the body blows delivered by the Trinamool Congress in successive elections from 2008. What has been particularly disappointing is that the Left had hoped to make some gains in West Bengal this time round when the field had opened from a direct fight with the TMC to a multi-cornered battle, with the Bharatiya Janata Party emerging as a strong contender in the State, courtesy the Modi factor.

Not only has the TMC managed to further push the Left out, ironically the two seats that the CPI(M) won in West Bengal—Murshidabad and Raiganj—were both from traditional Congress strongholds. Even veteran Basudeb Acharia—who had withstood the 2009 onslaught of the TMC which was then in coalition with the Congress—has been defeated this time in Bankura.

Needless to say, the CPI(M) insists that the verdict does not reflect the state of the Left in West Bengal as the verdict was "distorted" by "widespread rigging, violence and intimidation" targeting the Left Front.

"The Election Commission failed to intervene to rectify the situation from the third to the fifth round of polling in West Bengal," the CPI(M) Polit Bureau said in a statement. While the party has retained its hold over Tripura, the CPI(M) bettered its performance in Kerala by a seat; holding on to existing seats. Though the party had drawn flak for fielding nearly half-a-dozen independent candidates to reach out to the Christian community of Kerala, this strategy has borne fruit with two of them winning.

CPM (1971-2014)

1971	25	West Bengal 20, Kerala-2, Tripura-2, AP-1
1977	22	West Bengal-17, Maharashtra-3, Orissa-1, Punjab-1
1980	37	West Bengal-28, Kerala-7, Tripura-2
1984	22	West Bengal-18, Tripura-2, AP-1, Kerala-1
1989	33	West Bengal-27, Kerala-2, Bihar-1, Orissa-1, Rajasthan-1, UP-1
1991	35	West Bengal-27, Kerala-3, Assam-1, Bihar-1, Maharashtra-1, Orissa-1
1996	32	West Bengal-23, Kerala-5, Tripura-2, Assam-1, AP-1
1999	33	West Bengal-21, Kerala-8, Tripura-2, Bihar-1, Tamil Nadu-1
2004	43	West Bengal-26, Kerala-12, Tripura-2, TN-2, AP-1
2009	16	West Bengal-9, Kerala-4, Tripura-2, TN-1
2014	9	Kerala-5, West Bengal-2, Tripura-2

THE LANDSLIDE VICTORY OF BJP ACROSS THE NATION

The landslide victory of the Narendra Damodardas Modi-led BJP all across the country is a historic mandate. First, in terms of sheer numbers, both seats and percentage votes, the Modi wave is unprecedented. Second, geographically, the spread is the widest all across the country. Third, sociologically, it encompasses all identities, cutting across all castes, tribes and communities. Fourth, the present wave has made the BJP independent and autonomous of its coalition partners. Fifth, the Modi wave is distinct from the Ram Janmabhoomi agenda since it includes a richer mix of the development slogan with jobs for all, revival of economic growth, with a reinvention of the Mandal wave in the northern states and a subtle subterranean play of religion.

Percentagewise and Numberwise Growth: First, the numbers game: BJP alone has grabbed 283 seats out of 336 that the NDA has won in May 2014. This is the highest seats the BJP has ever won, a sharp increase from the 85 seats that the Jan Sangh had won as part of the

Janata Party pre-poll coalition in 1977. In 1998 and 1999, the Vajpayee-led NDA coalition had secured 179 and 182 seats respectively. The Modi wave is almost 102 seats more than the largest Vajpayee wave of 1999. In terms of vote percentage, the BJP has won 32 per cent votes, almost one-third of votes polled all across the country. This is 13 per cent positive swing compared to its 19 per cent votes that the BJP secured in 2009. This is the sharpest increase by a national party: between two consecutive polls in the history of Indian elections.

Cutting Across Geographical Barriers: Second, as BJP president Rajnath Singh declared, the Modi wave is "comprehensive in its geographical spread." The BJP has swept the western states, its stronghold and the Hindi heartland but with a greater intensity and penetration. But it has also grabbed newer regions; the north-eastern states such as Assam, where the BJP won 7 out of 14 seats, one out of two Lok Sabha seats in Arunachal (the BJP has also won 10 assembly seats in Arunachal, eight more than in 2009), one Lok Sabha seat in both Meghalaya and Nagaland each. In the north, all by itself the BJP has won three out of six seats in Jammu and Kashmir, wiping out the Congress and the National Conference for the first time. The PDP has won independently three seats from the state. In Punjab and Odisha, the party maintained its previous strength with a slight increase.

Improved Status in the South: In the key southern states, the NDA alliance has won two seats in Tamil Nadu for the first time. In Karnataka, the BJP rejuvenated with the return of Yeddyurappa who won 17 out of 28 seats (two seats less than in 2009). In Andhra Pradesh, the TDP-BJP alliance won 15 seats out of 25, 11 seats more than in 2009.

Cutting Across Communities: Fourth, cutting across identities, the Modi wave attracted the votes of all communities. The best example is the scale of its sweep in the largest and rnost caste-divided state of Uttar Pradesh where it grabbed 71 out of 80 seats thanks to the electoral ingenuity and sharp booth management skills of Amit Shah. As a result, the Bahujan Samaj Party (BSP) has been completely wiped off from the map of India's largest state without winning any seat. The BSP's core votes of Dalits majorly shifted towards the BJP. The Samajwadi Party (SP) is reduced to six seats having lost 17 seats in UP. Large sections of the OBC and the MBC voters of SP shifted towards the BJP. The Congress was reduced to two seats. In Bihar, the NDA won 30 out of 40 seats, 18 seats more than 2009 when the BJP had won 12 having a tie up with JD(U). The Rashtriya Janata Dal-Congress alliance won 8 seats and the Nitish Kumar-led Janata Dal (United) scraped the bottom with two seats.

Nitish's anti-pichra (MBCs) shifted to the BJP as did the Dalits *via* an alliance with Ram Vilas Paswan's LJSP.

Such is the intensity of the Modi wave that in several states the BJP won all seats. In Gujarat, Modi's home state, the BJP won 26 seats out of 26, an unprecedented feat. Similarly, in Rajasthan, the BJP won 25 out of 25. In Delhi, the BJP won seven out of seven. In Himachal, four out of four. In some key battleground states, the BJP almost won all seats. In Maharashtra, for the first time in history, the BJP-Shiv Sena alliance tore down the Congress-NCP alliance winning 44 seats out of 48. In Chhattisgarh, the BJP again won 10 out of 11, the same as in 2009. In Madhya Pradesh, the saffron camp won 27 out of 29 seats, 11 seats more than in 2009.

Stability becomes a Major Plank: Fifth, after three long decades, this is for the first time that the BJP victory has announced the end of an era—the era of coalition politics. Stability becomes a major plank under Modi. This provides the Modi government autonomy of decision-making, no relying on external and regional players who play pivotal politics. In this respect, the 2014 mandate is a repeat of 1984 without the sympathy wave. History has repeated itself after three decades although in the reverse direction. Tired of endless instability, constant political volatility, bickering among coalition partners and governmental indecision and political paralysis, the peeved voters have voted overwhelmingly for a politically stable option after 30 long years.

CONCLUSION

Riding a nationwide wave created substantially by his campaign, Narendra Modi won an unprecedented victory for the BJP, matched in its intensity and sweep only by the crushing defeat of the Congress in the 16th general elections. The BJP returns to power at the Centre after 10 years. Allies will also be part of the government, though the BJP is not dependent on any for numbers. "Good days are ahead," tweeted Modi as soon as trends became clear, reiterating the words of his campaign jingle '*Acche din aanewale hain*' that had inspired hope among people and created a hype around his persona. The BJP won a simple majority for the first time, only the second time a non-Congress party has done so. The BJP also became the first party since 1984 to get a majority on its own.

In its worst performance, the Congress won less than one-third of its 1977 tally of 154, when a massive anti-Congress wave swept India after the Emergency. The BJP consolidated its hold in Gujarat, Rajasthan,

Madhya Pradesh, Maharashtra and Chhattisgarh, leaving only a handful seats to its opponents. It also engineered a decisive turnaround in Uttar Pradesh and Bihar, made inroads into Assam and West Bengal, won the southern most seat in India, Kanyakumari in Tamil Nadu, and came a close second in nearby Thiruvananthapuram in Kerala.

The Congress failed to hold ground in any state except Kerala where its alliance won a majority of the seats, and Karnataka. In its unrivalled march, the BJP managed to break barriers of caste, decimating parties such as the BSP, SP and the RJD in Uttar Pradesh and Bihar. While the Left fell to its lowest tally in history, three regional parties outside the BJP alliance, the Trinamool Congress in West Bengal, AIADMK in Tamil Nadu and the Biju Janata Dal in Odisha, held their ground. With most senior leaders of the Congress routed, and no regional heavyweight other than Mulayam Singh in the new Lok Sabha, the opposition appears weak against the overwhelming of the BJP. BJP had put hardcore Hindutva agenda on the backburner when it began alliance building in 1996, but with absolute numbers on its side, the demand from within to bring these up may rise. But Modi sought to reassure the country, stating that he would "take the entire 125 crore people of India along."

Besides its ideological underpinning, 2014 polls marked a tectonic shift in the electoral side of Indian politics, which is incredible in more ways than one. After a full quarter century, the electorate, who never trusted any party with majority seats since 1984, has given majority seats to the BJP now. Moreover, the BJP has decimated the Congress and effectively taken its place as the principal national party, not in terms of just seats but also in popular votes. In all elections till now, the BJP's share of popular votes was less than that of the Congress. Now, its share is more. The BJP's vote share is estimated at more than 50 per cent in North and West India. Because it has secured less than a tenth of the total seats, the Congress has lost its claim to be the recognised opposition party. The misery of the Congress and the Gandhis seems unmitigated. The BJP has wiped out or handed the worst defeat to the Congress in most of India particularly in North, East and West—including where the Congress is in power like Himachal Pradesh, Uttarakhand, Haryana, Maharashtra, Assam and Karnataka or where it was the strongest five years ago like Andhra Pradesh. In contrast, the BJP has wiped out the Congress where the BJP is in power, be it Gujarat, Madhya Pradesh, Rajasthan, or Chhattisgarh. A desperate Congress created Telangana and got decimated in AP. Yet, it could not get Telangana Rashtra Samiti to ally with it and lost Telangana to TRS. But the BJP, despite voting to create Telangana, allied with the Telugu Desam Party that is opposed to Telangana and won in AP, both in Assembly and Lok Sabha. The responsibility for this dire state of the Congress squarely falls on the Gandhi family which directly controlled the party and remote-controlled the UPA government.

Finally, the 2014 election has thrown up a national leader of unprecedented popularity with mass backing, ideological conviction and political courage unseen since Indira Gandhi, but with a vital, very vital, difference. Inheriting Gandhiji's name and Nehru's lineage, Indira became Prime Minister and then acquired popularity through power. Modi became popular by hard work overcoming social and economic backwardness, supported by the RSS and the BJP he is part of.

References

1. Santwana Bhattacharya, 'NaMo Turns India Right', *The New Indian Express*, 17 May, 2014.
2. Varghese K. George, Prime Minister Modi, *The Hindu*, 17 May, 2014.
3. S.K. Ramachandran, 'BJP makes inroads into new areas', *The Hindu*, 17 May, 2014.
4. Smitha Gupta, 'Time for Congress to introspect', *Hindu*, 17, May 2014.
5. Anitha Joshua, 'CPI(M) two Seats short of EC', *Hindu*, 17 May, 2014.
6. Gargi Parsai, 'What Next for AAP?' *Hindu*, 17 May, 2014.
7. Chandrakant Vishwanath, 'Impressive Increase in BJP vote share', *The New Indian Express*, 19 May 2014.
8. Ajit Kumar Jha, 'Multiple Meanings of the Saffron Wave Set it Apart', *The New Indian Express*, 19 May, 2014.
9. Sumit Chakravartty, 'Behind Modi-led BJP's Spectacular Performance', *Mainstream*, 29 May, 2014.
10. S.G. Vombatkere, 'BJP: The People's Choice, but....' *Mainstream*, 29 May, 2014.
11. Kuldip Nayar, 'The Idea of India', *Mainstream*, 29, May, 2014.
12. Bharat Dogra, 'Elections Give BJP Historic Victory...', *Mainstream*, 29 May, 2014.
13. D.Bandyopadhyay, 'The Strength of Indian Democracy', *Mainstream*, June 7, 2014.
14. Sumi Chakravartty, 'Need for Vigilance', *Mainstream*, June 7, 2014.
15. Venkitesh Ramakrishnan, 'Right at the Centre', *Frontline*, June 13, 2014.
16. Prabhat Patnaik, 'Social Counter-Revolution', *Frontline*, June 13, 2014.
17. Subash Palshikar, 'The defeat of the Congress', *EPW*, 27 September 2014.
18. *The Hindu*, Thiruvananthapuram.

19. *The New Indian Express*, Thiruvananthapuram.
20. *Deccan Chronicle*, Kochi.
21. *The Malayala Manorama*, Kollam.
22. *The Mathrubhumi*, Kollam.
23. *The Kerala Kaumudi*, Kollam.
24. *The Kerala Sabdam*, Kollam.
25. *EPW*.
26. *Mainstream*.
27. *Samakalika* Malayalam.
28. *Kala Kaumudi*.
29. *Frontline*.
30. www.mapsofindia.com.
31. www.aljazeera.com.
32. www.eci.nic.in.
33. www.wikipedia.org.

2

Lok Sabha Polls 2014 in Kerala

Retrospect and Prospect

M.R. Biju

The Sixteenth Lok Sabha Elections were held in 9 phases from 7th April to 12th May, 2014. According to the Election Commission of India, the electoral population of the country was 814.5 million, an increase of 100 million since the 2009 general elections. The 2014 elections was the longest and most expensive poll in the electoral history of the nation. The poll cost Rs. 135 billion excluding the expenses of political parties. Parties were expected to spent Rs. 30500 crore in this elections.

Since the general elections in 2009, the national politics witnessed a series of developments. Notable among them include, anti-corruption movement led by Anna Hazara, formation of Aam-Admi party by Aravind Kejriwal, election of Pranab Kumar Mukherjee as the President, passing of Lok Pal, Lokayuktas and Food Security Bills, Communal riots at Muzaffar Nagar in UP, etc. This period also witnessed as number of scams and scandals. It include, Coal, 2 G Spectrum, Satyam, Cash for votes, Adarsh, Commonwealth Games, Tatra Trunk, Chopper etc.

Coming to the state of Kerala, it is one of the highly politicised states of India. The political sensibility of the state is the outcome of decades of political struggles, social reform movements and the massive participation of the people in the electoral process. The first general elections in the state of Kerala was held in 1951 in which the Indian National Congress made a spectacular performance. The Left dominated the state in the second, fourth and seventh Lok Sabha Polls held in 1957, 1967 and 1980 respectively. The Congress party secured majority either individually or through coalition in 1962, 1971, 1977, 1984, 1989, 1991 and 2009. (In the 1996 polls both the fronts shared equal number of seats).

I. PRE-POLL SCENE

A. Section of Candidates—Element of Caste Factor

Through caste based seat sharing in the Lok Sabha Polls was not as intense when compared with the assembly polls. But it is an open secret that, both the UDF and the LDF always try to follow a specific pattern to satisfy the various caste and religious outfits of the state. While the congress makes a caste based division considering the state as a single unit whereas the CPI (M) plays its communal card specifically on each constituency. The winning equation of the UDF is considered as "5E-4N-4M-5C-2S". It denotes five for Ezhavas, four for Nairs, four for Muslims, five for Christians and two for SCs/STs. However, in 2014 the Congress had to cut out Ezhava candidate to accommodate SJ(D)'s M.P. Veerendrakumar. In 2009, the UDF followed this equation and emerged victorious in 16 seats, but faced poorly when the Ezhava-Nair ratio of candidates was reversed in 2004 polls. Moreover, whenever the UDF fails to make the Ezhava equation correct, it affects the Front's chances. For instance, in the 2011 Assembly elections, despite the anti-incumbency factor against the CPI(M), the Congress fared poorly, especially in Ezhava dominated districts like Kozhikode, Alappuzha, Kollam and Idukki.

The CPM though, never followed such a specific equation, it has always respected the Ezhava/Thiyya domination in Malabar. It also boasts of creating upset victories by tweaking the caste card effectively. This time too, the party has played a new caste card in Vadakara and Kozhikode. The CPM has fielded a Muslim candidate A.N. Shamseer in Vadakara, where it had fielded only an Ezhava candidate, whenever it contested in its own symbol. For the first time, the CPM has tried an Ezhava candidate in Kozhikode seat against M.K. Raghavan of the Congress. Though the constituency has around 40 per cent Ezhava/Thiyya population, Kozhikode is branded as a seat of forward communities since 1984.

The CPM employed a similar strategy to win Alappuzha constituency way back in 1991. Though an Ezhava dominant constituency, the CPM fielded T.J. Anjalose of Latin Community against sitting M.P. Vakkom Purushothaman, who was contesting for the third consecutive time. Anjalose defeated Vakkom by a margin of 14,075 votes, sabotaging the caste equations of Alappuzha.

In 1987 elections, EMS took a bold step against religious and communal outfits. In 2014, the CPM has been disgraced to such a level, with the parry state secretary asking its ally Janata Dal (S) to field a Nair candidate in Kottayam seat. But JD(S) fielded Mathew T. Thomas. Similarly, the CPM has been courting K.M. Mani only to woo the Church. Now, if the UDF is the 'A' team of the Church, the LDF has emerged as its 'B' team.

While the IUML always fielded Muslim candidates in Malappuram and Ponnani, the Congress never tried a non-Latin Catholic candidate in Ernakulam seat since 1977. Though the CPM challenged with Hindu candidate V. Viswanatha Menon, who represented the constituency in 1967, and P. Subramanian Potti it did not payoff.

Idukki is another constituency in which both the Fronts never fielded a non-Christian candidate. On the contrary, placing the correct caste equation need not ensure a win, especially when both candidates hail from the same community.

Attingal is an Ezhava dominant seat, but since 1977, no Congress had won whenever both fielded Ezhava candidates. However, Congress leader Thalekkunnil Basheer had won twice. In 2009, UDF's Balachandran was defeated by CPM's A. Sampath.

Similarly, Nadar/Christian and Nair communities decide the results in Thiruvananthapuram constituency. With a record margin of over one lakh votes, Neela Lohitadasan Nadar upset CPI's M.N. Govindan Nair in 1980. In a major surprise, noted poet O.N.V. Kurup, who contested as LDF-backed independent candidate, was defeated by A. Charles of the Congress in 1989 with a margin exceeding 50,000 votes. In the 2014 Polls, the CPI fielded Dr. Bennet Abraham to woo the Nadar converted Christian communities, which form a major vote bank. Apart from serving as a member of the state PSC, as a CPI nominee, he has hardly any link with the party.

Without going for much experiment, both Fronts tried a forward caste candidate in Kollam constituency in the majority of the elections whereas Nair or Christian candidates are usually fielded by both fronts in Kottayam constituency.

As far as Congress is concerned, they have been pampering the communities, including the NSS and the SNDP outfits, after the liberation struggle of 1959. Later, K. Karunakaran effectively played the caste card to gain the power and expand the UDF.

Caste Composition 2014 in Kerala

Caste	*UDF*	*LDF*	*MPs (2009)*
Ezhava/Thiyya	4	5	5
Nair	2	3	5
Syrian X'an	3	2	3
Latin Catholic	1	2	1
Marthoma	—	2	—
Jacobite	1	—	1
CSI (Nadar)	—	1	—
Muslim	4	3	3
Jain	1	—	—
SC	2	2	2

B. Electoral Sex Ratio

With 1,178 women voters for every 1,000 men voters, the Attingal Lok Sabha constituency has the highest sex ratio of electors in Kerala, according to the final figures published by the Chief Electoral Officer. Of the total electorate of 12,46,554 in Attingal, 6,74,264 voters are women and 5,72,290 men. The second highest sex ratio of 1,140 women per 1,000 men has been registered in the Kannur constituency, where there are 6,19,738 female voters and 5,43,299 males. The lowest ratio (1,002 females to 1,000 males) is in Idukki which has 5,79,474 women to 5,77,94 men, followed by Malappuram (1,003 females to 1,000 males) where there are 6,00,031 women and 5,97,687 men voters. The female-male ratio for the State is 1.076 (1,25,70,439 women and 1,16,81,503 men). The female-male ratio of electors in the other constituencies is: Kasaragod; 1.093 (6,47,805 women and 5,92,658 men); Vadakara: 1.110 (6,20,367 women and 5,58,521 men); Wayanad 1.033 (6,34,015 women and 6,13,311 men); Kozhikode: 1.072 (6,09,626 women and 5,68,593 men); Ponnani: 1.057 (6,06,415 women and 5,73,616 men); Palackad: 1.060 (6,20,471 women and 5,85,32.7 men); Alathur: 1056 (6,23,519 women and 5,90,012 men); Thrissur: 1.103 (6,68,357 women and 6,05,724 men); Chalakudy: 1.036 (5,85,039 women and 5,64,335 men); Ernakulam: 1.044 (5,90,195 women and 5,65,023 men); Kottayam: 1.026 (5,87,055 women and 5,71,962 men); Alappuzha:1.085 (6,56,829 women and 6,04,910 men); Mavelikara: 1.122 (6,57,426 women and 5,85,812 men); Pathanamthitta: 1.101 (6,90,648 women and 6,27,203 men); Kollam:

I.122 (6,42,425 women and 5,72,559 men) and Thiruvananthapuram: 1.075 (6,56,740 women and 6,10,716 men).

Pathanamthitta has the largest electorate of 13,17,851 including the largest number of women voters in any constituency (690,648) and 6,27,203 men. Thrissur with 12,74,081 (6,68,357 women and 6,05,724 men) constitutes the second largest electorate, followed by Thiruvananthapuram with 12,67,456 (6,56,740 women and 6,10,716 men). Chalakudy has the smallest electorate of 11,49,374.

Voter Sex Ratio

Ratio of Women Voters to Men Voters

Constituency	*Ratio*	*Women voters*	*Men voters*
Kasargod	1.093	6,47,808	5,92,658
Kannur	1.140	6,19,738	5,43,299
Vadakara	1.110	6,20,367	5,58,521
Wayanad	1.033	6,34,015	6,13,311
Kozhikode	1.072	6,09,626	5,68,593
Malappuram	1.003	6,00,031	5,97,687
Ponnani	1.057	6,06,415	6,73,616
Palakad	1.060	6,20,471	5,85,327
Alathur	1.056	6,23,519	5,90,012
Thrissur	1.103	6,68,357	6,05,724
Chalakudy	1.036	5,85,039	5,64,335
Ernakulam	1.044	5,90,195	5,65,023
Idukki	1.002	5,79,474	5,77,945
Kottayam	1.026	5,87,055	5,71,962
Alappuzha	1.085	6,56,829	6,04,910
Mavelikara	1.122	6,57,426	5,85,812
Pathanamthitta	1.101	6,90,648	6,27,203
Kollam	1.122	6,42,425	5,72,559
Attingal	1.178	6,74,264	5,72,290
Thiruvananthaouram	1.075	6,56,740	6,10,716

Independent Sample t-test

Women voters	*Men voters*	
628,522.10	589,075.15	mean
32,398.16	28,935.02	std. dev.
5.15%	4.91%	C.V.
20	20	n
4.06		t
.0002		P Value
Significant		Result

From the above table it is clear that the average number of female electors in 20 Lok Sabha constituencies in Kerala is 6,28,522 and that of men voters are 5,89,075. Since, the Coefficient Value for men voters is less than female voters, it can be concluded that the average number of men voters are more stable and consistent. Now it is imperative to know whether there is significant difference between the number of female voters and that of men voters, independent sample t-test was done. Since the CVTS (t-test for Equality of Means) is 4.06 and P Value is 0.0002, ($P<0.05$), Ho formulated in this regard is rejected. That means there is significant difference between the number of female voters and that of men voters. This shows that in Kerala the number of female voters is more when compared with men voters.

C. Poll Campaign

The campaigning for the Lok Sabha elections in the 20 constituencies in the State came to a close on 8th April evening.

The Congress-led United Democratic Front (UDF), which had a 16-4 advantage in 2009, was up against the challenge of the Left Democratic Front (LDF) led by the Communist Party of India (Marxist) in the State, where the Bharatiya Janata Party (BJP) had not succeeded in opening its account so far.

The campaign this time was full of the unpredictable, with developments before and after its start fuelling its progress.

The State unit of the Revolutionary Socialist Party (RSP) left the LDF rankled by the CPI(M) not conceding the Kollam seat to it and its leader N.K. Premachandran was the UDF candidate against-CPI (M) Polit Bureau member M.A. Baby there. The campaign saw some fiery attack and counter-attack on this development, turning the Kollam fight into a prestigious one.

Leader of the Opposition V.S. Achuthanandan "choosing to end his confrontationist stand" in the CPI(M) was another development that provided grist to the campaign. While this was interpreted as a "big let down" by one section, it no doubt injected a new enthusiasm among the party cadre.

The Janadhipathya Samrakshana Samithi (JSS) of veteran leader K.R. Gouri then left the UDF to campaign for the LDF and a section of the Communist Marxist Party (CMP) of M.V. Raghavan also did the same, irked by lack of recognition of its worth in the UDF setup.

The campaign period witnessed an adverse comment on Chief

Minister Oommen Chandy by the High Court of Kerala in a land-grab case involving-his former gunman and the LDF immediately grabbed it to demand Chandy's resignation and embarrass the UDF.

The UDF managed to extricate itself from the issue with the government going in appeal before a Division Bench of the High Court and getting part of the damaging observation in the verdict of the single judge stayed. The 'solar scam' too had its reverberations throughout the campaign.

The T.P. Chandrashekharan murder case had a niggling presence as a caste-specific issue in the campaign against the CPI(M). While the LDF focused a great deal of attention in turning to its advantage the fears of the people of the high range areas of the State over the implementation of the K. Kasthoorirangan panel recommendations for the conservation of Western Ghats and those of the coastal fishermen over the implementation of the coastal zone regulations.

Though such State-specific issues figured in the campaign, the key issue put before the electorate was whether the state should back the Congress-led coalition to form the next government at the Centre against the "*Hindutva* threat" of the BJP, or whether it should bank on the assurance of the Left parties that "a non-BJP, non-Congress alliance is a viable possibility".

Corruption under the Congress-led regime at the Centre, price rise, and the economic policies of the government in general, were issues projected by the LDF throughout the campaign. On the other hand, the BJP was making a strong bid to open its account in Kerala using the Modi factor and the Aam Aadmi Party (AAP) was in the fray in 15 constituencies, testing their fortune.

National leaders who campaigned in the State include Congress president Sonia Gandhi, vice-president Rahul Gandhi and Union Defence Minister A.K. Antony; BJP's prime ministerial candidate Narendra Modi and senior leader L.K. Advani, CPI(M) general secretary, Prakash Karat and Polit Bureau members Sitaram Yechuri, Brinda Karat and S. Ramachandran Pillai; and Communist Party of India's senior leader A.B. Bardhan.

Communal and Caste Polarisation

The fortnight long campaigning was in fact a battle largely involving two equally placed political forces—the UDF and the LDF. 'Equal' in the sense that both are faced with possible shrinkage. In their electoral space at the national level; and must, therefore, garner as many seats as possible.

For the Congress, this meant hitting the double digit, as it did in 2009, sending as many as 13 MPs on its own and three through its allies to New Delhi. Given its difficulties in West Bengal and elsewhere, the CPI (M) and its Left allies too had the same ambitious goal. But, as the campaign entered in the final phase, neither the Congress nor the CPI(M) could say with confidence if they would be able to touch the double digit.

The BJP, a distant third in the fray, was hoping to put up a strong contest in two constituencies and appeared set to improve its vote share. However, the possibility of its opening its account in Kerala was still in the realm of conjecture. Questions relating to economic policies, corruption and price management have been key discussion points during the campaign. But the most important factor was communal and caste polarisation

The State witnessed the spectacle of top functionaries of the Catholic Church giving the Congress a good shake-up over the Kasturirangan Committee recommendations on protection of the Western Ghats. It appeared as if the Church, which has traditionally stood behind the Congress, was telling the party not to take it for granted. But the Congress did some quick fire-fighting, and later the Church appeared by and large ready to back the Congress.

While the Church-Congress sparring was on, the Muslim minority was quiet, unlike in past elections when every Muslim outfit worth its name was trying to make itself heard. The powerful Sunni factions are particularly silent and the usually articulate Jamaat-e-Islami has decided to back its own Welfare Party of India nominees and those contesting on an alternative platform.

The Abdul Nasir Maudany led People's Democratic Party has called for a 'conscience vote', perhaps indicating that nobody wishes to take a chance and the gainer could be the Congress.

The Church-Congress row has given the CPI(M)-led Left Democratic Front an opportunity to reach out to the predominantly Christian settler farmer community. The LDF has also tried to cut into traditional Congress votes by fielding a record five independents.

II. POLLING

Barring minor incidents, voting for the 16th Lok Sabha elections was largely incident-free. On 10th April, 2014. One incident of damaging an electronic voting machine was reported from Kolanthayil at Sreekantapuram. Tension prevailed at Malappattam in Sreekantapuram following skirmishes between Congress and CPI (M) activists. A similar incident took place at Chepath at Pathanapuram in Kollam District. Four Congress workers were hacked at Kizhakkancherry in Alathur. Four persons were reported to have collapsed and died in separate incidents in the State. Technical snag in EVMs affected the pace of polling at a number of places. One such instance was in Kollam where United Democratic Front (UDF) candidate N.K. Premachandran had to wait for a while to exercise his franchise. Rain affected polling at a number of places. Heavy rain disrupted polling at different places. Power outages also affected the pace of voting at many in the evening. Heavy rain, around 4 pm affected polling at Kothamangalam, Muvattupuzha, Thodupuzha and Cheruthoni in the Idukki Lok Sabha segment and Pala in Kottayam, among other places.

Polling Figures

A marginal increase of 1.67 per cent point in voter turnout over the 73.37 per cent polling in 2009 was registered in the state.

The highest voter turnout of 81.61 per cent in the State was recorded in the Vadakara parliamentary constituency, while Pathanamthitta registered the lowest, 66.01 per cent. According to the Election Commission, the polling percentage in the constituencies is as follows (the 2009 turnout in brackets): Kasaragod: 78.49 per cent (76.15%), Kannur: 81.32 (80.94), Vadakara: 81.61 (80.4), Wayanad: 73.28 (74.71), Kozhikode: 79.80 (75.65), Malappuraram: 71.27 (76.67), Ponnani: 73.83 (77.12), Palakkad: 75.39 (73.51), Alathur: 76.45 (75.28), Thrissur: 72.15 (69.43), Chalakudy: 76.94 (73.63), Ernakulam: 73.56 (72.89), Idukki: 70.66 (73.89), Kottayam: 71.78 (73.69), Alappuzha: 78.78 (79.37), Mavelikara: 71.35 (70.56), Pathanamthitta: 66.01 (65.86), Kollam: 72.12 (67.78), Attingal: 68.77 (66.25), and Thiruvananthapuram: 68.69 (65.74).

Polling Percentage in Kerala

Constituency	*2014*	*2009*
Kasargod	78.49	76.15
Kannur	81.32	80.94
Vadakara	81.60	80.40
Wayanad	73.28	74.71
Kozhikode	79.80	75.65

(*Contd.*)

(*Contd.*)

Constituency	*2014*	*2009*
Malappuram	71.27	76.67
Ponnani	73.83	77.12
Palakkad	75.39	73.51
Alathur	76.45	75.28
Thrissur	72.15	69.43
Chalakudy	76.94	73.63
Ernakulam	73.56	72.89
Idukki	70.66	73.89
Kottayam	71.78	73.69
Alappuzha	78.78	79.37
Mavelikara	71.35	70.56
Pathanamthitta	66.01	65.86
Kollam	72.12	67.78
Attingal	68.77	66.25
Thiruvananthapuram	68.69	65.74

Independent Sample t-test

Polling Percentage in 2014	*Polling Percentage in 2009*	
74.11	73.47	mean
4.36	4.63	std. dev.
5.88%	6.30%	C.V.
20	20	n
0.45		***t***
0.6582		**P Value**
Not Significant		**Result**

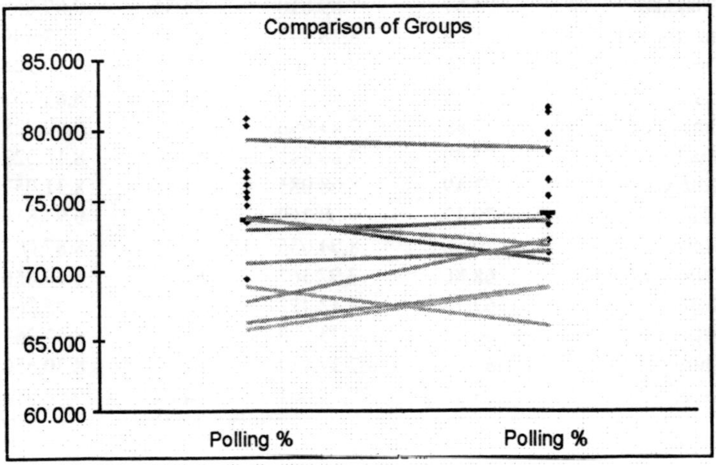

From the above table it is clear that the average percentage of votes polled in 2014 Lok Sabha election of Kerala is 74.11 per cent and that of 2009 Lok Sabha election of Kerala was 73.47 per cent. Since the Coefficient Value for 2014 Lok Sabha election of Kerala is less than that of 2009 Lok Sabha election, it can be concluded that the average percentage of votes polled in 2014 Lok Sabha election of Kerala is more stable and consistent. Now it is imperative to know whether there is significant difference between average percentage of votes polled in 2014 Lok Sabha election and that of 2009 Lok Sabha election of Kerala, independent sample *t*-test was done. Since the CVTS (*t*-test for Equality of Means) is 0.45 and P Value is 0.6582, (P > 0.05), Ho formulated in this regard is accepted. That means there is no significant difference between average percentage of votes polled in 2014 Lok Sabha election and that of 2009 Lok Sabha election of Kerala.

Voting Pattern in Kerala in 2009 and 2014

Constituency	*2009*		*2014*	
	Polling %	*Votes polled*	*Polling %*	*Votes polled*
Kasargode	76.15	8,47,491	78.49	9,73,592
Kannur	80.94	8,63,947	81.32	9,45,802
Vadakara	80.40	8,63,136	81.60	9,57,895
Wayanad	74.71	8,23,891	73.28	9,14,015
Kozhikode	75.65	7,98,060	79.80	9,40,220
Malappuram	76.67	7,83,548	71.27	8,53,662
Ponnani	77.12	7,69,587	73.83	8,71,239
Palakkad	73.51	7,89,810	75.35	9,09,060
Aalathur	75.25	8,28,797	76.45	9,27,389
Thrissur	69.43	8,15,868	72.15	9,19,244
Chalakudy	73.63	7,92,910	76.94	8,84,369
Ernakulam	72.89	7,44,996	73.56	8,49,828
Idukki	73.89	7,86,041	70.66	8,18,023
Kottayam	73.69	8,08,085	71.78	8,31,057
Alappuzha	79.37	9,08,360	78.78	9,94,819
Mavelikara	70.56	8,04,035	71.35	8,87,063
Pathanamthitta	68.86	7,97,367	66.01	8,69,856
Kollam	67.78	7,42,422	72.12	8,75,764
Attingal	66.25	7,23,233	68.77	8,57,263
Thiruvananthapuram	65.74	7,37,917	68.69	8,70,650
Kerala-Total	73.37	1,60,29,501	74.04	1,79,50,810

Independent Sample t-test

Women voters	Men voters	
628,522.10	589,075.15	mean
32,398.16	28,935.02	std. dev.
5.15%	4.91%	C.V.
20	20	*n*
	4.06	*t*
	.0002	P Value
	Significant	Result

From the above table it is clear that the average number of female electors in 20 Lok Sabha constituencies in Kerala is 6,28,522 and that of men voters are 5,89,075. Since the Coefficient Value for men voters is less than female voters, it can be concluded that the average number of men voters are more stable and consistent. Now it is imperative to know whether there is significant difference between the number of female voters and that of men voters, independent sample *t*-test was done. Since, the CVTS (*t*-test for Equality of Means) is 4.06 and P Value is 0.0002, (P <0.05). Ho formulated in this regard is rejected. That means there is significant difference between the number of female voters and that of men voters. This shows that in Kerala the number of female voters is more when compared with men voters.

In the Assembly constituencies, the highest turnout of 86.61 per cent was recorded in the Kuttiyadi segment in the Vadakara parliamentary constituency and the lowest of 63.04 per cent in the Thiruvananthapuram Assembly segment in the Thiruvananthapuram parliamentary constituency.

The failure to achieve a significant increase in voter turnout in the politically conscious state despite a month long intense campaign by political parties, mobilisation of young voters, and a host of initiatives by the Election Commission has surprised the parties and the Election Commission alike. The scorching summer heat and the rain that lashed parts of the State on the polling day also kept a section of voters away.

Intensive Campaign in the North Converted into Votes

The high voter turnout in Vadakara could largely be attributed to the robust campaigns by the Congress-led United Democratic Front (UDF) and the Communist Party of India (Marxist)-led Left-Democratic Front (LDF) in the constituency.

The keen contest between Congress nominee Mullappally Ramachandran and CPI(M) candidate A.N. Shamseer was a major factor. The presence of Bharatiya Janata Party (BJP) and smaller parties such as the Revolutionary Marxist Party (RMP), Aam Aadmi Party (AAP), Social Democratic Party of India (SDPI), and the Communist Party of India (Marxist-Leninist) in prompted heavy polling.

Voter enthusiasm was not new to the politically conscious electorate of Vadakara. The turnout was 81.61 per cent this time. It was 80.40 per cent in 2009. Last time, the constituency also came second, behind Kannur (80.94%), in the list of constituencies with highest polling. An increase of more than one percentage point revealed that the fight between the main contestants—Mullappally Ramachandran and Shamseer, has been tough in Vadakara. Long queues of voters were seen in booths identified as critical and sensitive.

This was the first major election after RMP leader T.P. Chandrashekaran was murdered on May 4, 2012. The Congress candidate won from this traditional Communist bastion after the candidature of T.P. Chandrasekharan cut into the vote share of the CPI(M) last time. This time, the CPI(M) marshalled all its resources to recapture the seat. This was evident when Polit Bureau member Kodiyeri Balakrishnan devotedly campaigned in the constituency.

The electorate principally comprised those in the Thiyya and Muslim communities. The impressive turnout in Nadaparam and Kuttiyadi showed that key rivals vigorously campaigned in these regions with sizable Muslim population. Towards the end of the electioneering, political parties overtly or covertly did not mind even canvassing votes in the name of religion. Muslim voters had always reportedly rallied behind the Congress–Indian Union Muslim League (IUML) combine in the elections. But, the time, their votes appeared to be divided after the CPI(M) too fielded a Muslim candidate. The poll outcome will tell whether the CPI (M) top leadership's gamble in nominating a Muslim candidate Vadakara really paid off. The electorate confronted several issues from the Kasturirangan report to communal disharmony to political violence. However, which way the electorate turned is still hazy.

III. THE VERDICT: KERALA BUCKED THE NATIONAL TREND

Kerala has bucked the national trend of the Congress and CPI(M) suffered humiliating routs in their strongholds, alliances led by them shared the spoils more or less equally even while suffered shock losses. While the

Congress-led United Democratic Front (UDF) secured 12 seats, down four from 2009, the CPI(M) led Left Democratic Front (LDF) was able to double its 2009 tally, securing eight seats.

Good news for the UDF came from Thiruvnanthapuram, Kollam, Pathanamthitta, Mavelikara, Alappuzha, Kottayam, Kochi, Ponnani, Malappuram, Kozhikode, Wayanad, and Vadaltara, The LDF's victory were in Attingal, Idukki, Chalkudy, Thrissur, Alathur, Palakkad, Kannur and Kasaragod. In the UDF, Congress won eight seats. Indian Union Muslim League (IUML) two, Kerala Congress (Mani) and RSP one each. In the UDF, the CPI(M) secured seven seats (two party supported Independents) and CPI one. The LDF wrested Idukki, Chaiakudy, Thrissur, and Kannur from the UDF.

The BJP came closest to opening its account in Parliament from Kerala this time with its nominee O. Rajagopal maintaining a steady lead over his Congress rival Shashi Tharoor till the very last round, only to lose by 15,470 votes. The LDF had a humiliating outing here with its nominee, Bennet Abraham got relegated to a distant third position, the only constituency where the Opposition alliance suffered such an ignominy in the State.

The biggest shock for the Congress was in Chalakudy where its senior leader P.C. Chacko tasted defeat at the hands of actor and LDF-backed independent candidate, Innocent. For the CPI(M), the biggest loss was in Kollam where party Polit Bureau member M.A. Baby was trounced by RSP's N.K. Premachandran by a whopping margin of 37,649 votes. The RSP had quit the LDF on election-eve and moved into the UDF almost immediately.

People's Verdict in Statitistical Terms

While the UDF garnered 42.08 per cent votes, the LDF was close behind with 40.23 per cent votes, with the BJP-led National Democratic Alliance (NDA) claiming 10.84 per cent and others (including the smaller parties, independents, and NOTA) cornering 6.85 per cent of the votes.

Votes in Numbers

In absolute numbers, the UDF's tally was 75,46,827 votes, 3,35,570 votes more than the LDF's share of 72,11,257 votes. The NDA secured 19,44,158 votes. The Socialist Democratic Party of India (SDPI) came next with 2,73,847 votes, followed by the Aam Aadmi Party (AAP) with

2,56,662. The BSP's share was 71,262 votes. The Welfare Party of India, the political outfit of the Jama-at-e-Islami could secure only 68,332 votes, far below the share of NOTA, which stood at 2,10,561 votes. The difference of votes between the UDF and the LDF was 1.85 per cent.

The share of the unattached independents was 3,34,936 votes. On its own, the BJP was able to secure 10.30 per cent of the total 1,79,17,942 votes polled across the State. The percentage share of the SDPI and AAP were 1.50 per cent and 1.40 per cent respectively. The share of NOTA came to 1.71 per cent.

Vote Share of the Congress Came Down

At a time when the Congress received a blow nationally due to the BJP, the party in the state which secured 55,68,130 votes of the total votes polled, was able to get a major portion of the vote share in the state. In 2009, when the Congress was able to win 13 seats, it got a vote share of 40.13 per cent while the CPM was able to get 30.48 per cent of the votes when four of its candidates won the polls.

This time around when the Congress got nine seats on its own, it was able to get 31.1 per cent of the total votes. The CPM was able to get 21.6 per cent of the total vote share or 38,78,110 votes. Details of the party-wise election results are given under:

Party	*Votes in per cent*	*Total votes*
INC	31.1%	55,88,130
CPM	21.6%	37,78,110
IND	11.4%	20,42,193
BJP	10.3%	18,56,623
CPI	7.6%	13,64,010
IUML	4.5%	8,16,226
KCM	2.4%	4,24,194
RSP	2.3%	4,085,28
SJD	1.7%	3,07.597
JDS	1.7%	3,03.595
SDPI	1.5%	2,73,831
AAP	1.4%	2,56,635
NOTA	1.2%	2,10,530
BSP	0.4%	71,350
WPOI	0.4%	68,332
RSPK(B)	0.2%	43,051

Mandate 2014—Kerala in Numbers

Party/Alliance	*Vote share*	*Percentage*
UDF	75,46,827	42.08
LDF	72,11,257	40.23
NDA	19,44,158	10.84
Others/Inds/NOTA	12,15,700	6.85
Total	1,79,17,942	100.00

Independents

The poll figures show that though the LDF was not able to ensure victory of three of its five independent candidates, the ploy helped it to garner precious votes. Thus, while Joice George in Idukki brought in 3,82,019 votes, Innocent (Chalakudy) secured 3,58,440 votes, V. Abdurahiman (Ponnani) 3,53,093 votes, Peelipose Thomas (Pathanamthitta) 3,02,651 votes and Christy Fernandez (Ernakulam) 2,66,794 votes.

A detailed analysis of the polling trends in the various Assembly segments show that in 48 of them, the incumbent MLAs may have a tough time winning back their alienated voters. In these constituencies, a higher number of voters have opted for candidates put up by the rival combination. The worst hit were the LDF legislators as there are 27 of them who will face such a situation. In comparison, only 21 UDF legislators face a similar situation.

Women Polled 10 per cent of Votes

Women constituted 10 per cent of the candidates (27 out of 269 candidates) in the Lok Sabha polls in Kerala. Interestingly, their combined vote share was also near 10 per cent. P.K. Sreemathi of the CPM (Kannur) got the highest number of votes among women candidates—4.28 lakh constituting more than 45 per cent of votes polled in the constituency. Next came K.A. Sheeba of the Congress who could not make it to the Lok Sabha from Alathur. She polled 3.75 lakh votes (about 40% of votes polled).

Bindu Krishna (INC, Attingal) and P.K. Sainabha (CPI-M, Malappuram) got only 37.6 per cent and 28.5 per cent votes respectively in their constituencies. Shobha Surendran of the BJP won about 15 per cent of the votes in Palakkad. S. Girijakumari, who had defected from the CPI(M) to the BJP, won 10.5 per cent of votes as the BJP candidate in Attingal.

The Aam Aadmi Party (AAP) candidates came next with Anita Pratap winning about six per cent of the votes in Ernakulam and Sara Joseph getting 4.9 per cent of the votes in Thrissur. Silvi Sunil of the AAP had to be satisfied with just 1.4 per cent of the votes in Idukki. Ramlath Mampad (Welfare Party of India), Wayanad, and Seleena Prakkanam (BSP), Pathanamthitta are the other two women who won more than one per cent votes. The lowest number of votes (292) was polled by R. Chandrika Kattakkada in Thiruvananthapuram.

IV. FACETS OF THE VERDICT

A. Voting Pattern of the Minorities

(a) ***Christians***: The voting pattern in the six Lok Sabha Constituencies in Central Kerala are generally watched with keen political interest due to the numerical strength of the Christian community. This Christian belt had always decided the political destiny of both the fronts in Kerala. This time the LDF fielded four independents—all of them Christians-Innocent in Chalakkudy, Christie Fernandez in Ernakulam, Peelipose Thomas in Pathnamthitta and Joice George in Idukki. Out of the four, Innocent and Joice came out victoriously, Kottayam and Ernakulam stood with the UDF.

(b) ***Muslims***: The Poll results did not lend much credence to the idea of possible consolidation of Muslim votes in favour of the UDF. The result throughout the state especially the Northern Districts show that there was no massive consolidation of Muslim votes in favour of the UDF. While the IUML candidate E. Ahammed won Malappuram seat by a huge margin of 194739 votes whereas E.T. Muhammed Basher retained his Ponnani seat with a thin margin of 25,410. In 2009 he had a margin of 82,684 votes.

B. LDF Doubled Tally yet...

Opposition Left Democratic Front (LDF) has doubled its tally from 2009, but the alliance has emerged all bruised from the electoral battle. The Front has taken a massive hit in Kollam where no less a person than CPI(M) Polit Bureau member M.A. Baby is the casualty. It could not win the politically sensitive Vadakara seat despite putting up a no-holds-barred fight. Its won in the traditional CPI(M) bastion of Kasaragod is by a margin that can only be termed measly.

In Thiruvananthapuram, the defeat is more than humiliating as the LDF nominee Bennet Abraham was relegated to a distant third position. In Kozhikode, CPI(M) Central committee member A. Vijayaraghavan had raised visions of victory, but could not use his impressive campaign to garner enough votes.

C. Claimants for Victory

The LDF's gains is likely to have many claimants, particularly in Thrissur and Idukki, which the CPI(M) has wrested from the Congress. Granting those claims may not be as difficult as answering why and how M.A. Baby lost in Kollam and how Bennet Abraham got such a bad drubbing. Both the CPI(M) and CPI will have to do much soul-searching on these questions when they get down to analyzing the results. The LDF strategy of fielding as many as five Independents has paid off only partially. Only two of the five, Joice George in Idukki and Innocent in Chalakudy, could make it.

While these wins do justify the move somewhat, the alliance would have to concede that it could have worked the other way if there was unity on the rival side. If it were not these two wins, the LDF tally would have been far less impressive. In Thrissur, it is a political victory, what with C.N. Jayadevan of the CPI, pipping a strong AAP candidate besides his UDF rival, to breast the tape.

D. Vadakara Scare

One major reason for the happiness for the LDF would be the massive victory M.B. Rajesh scored over M.P. Veerendrakumar of the Socialist Janata (Democratic) in Palakkad, by a margin of 1,05,300 votes. That the CPI(M) could give a scare to Union Minister Mullappally Ramachandran in Vadakara cannot also be taken lightly, the party's failure to take the constituency notwithstanding.

While in Idukki, the Kasturirangan row and aftermath came to LDF's aid, the same has not happened in Pathanamthitta where former DCC president Peelipose Thomas could not make it against his, UDF rival despite Anto Antony being bracketed with all those who stood for the controversial Aranmula green field airport project. In Wayanad, even the presence of a strong independent candidate could not help Sathyan Mokeri of the CPI emerge victorious.

It is clear from the verdict that the electorate has settled for choices on the basis of both regional and national factors. While, it is clear that there was popular disdain towards the UPA Government's policies in the state, the Oommen Chandy government's performance was also altered, as it was pegged as a campaign plank, going by the results.

Contrary to expectations, there was no serious consolidation of Muslim votes, which is the single largest vote pool among the state electorate, in favour of a particular candidate or front this time, despite the fierce anti-Modi campaign by opponents.

Though, history was set to be made while BJP's O. Rajagopal kept racing ahead in Thiruvananthapuram, the tide eventually turned in favour of Shashi Tharoor. The entire results in the state would have been eclipsed had he won, even by a thin margin.

The LDF strategy of fielding seven candidates from the Christian community didn't pay off as expected. CPM politburo member and sitting MLA M.A. Baby has faced an ignominious defeat in the bands of his former coalition mate N.K. Premachandran of the RSP in Kollam. The political message is clear from the reverses the CPM have received in Kollam and Vadakara, where the T.P. murder case was a keen factor. The experiment of roping in Independents as LDF candidates found desirable results only in two segments Chalakkudy and Idukki, while it flopped in Thiruvananthapuram and Pathanamthitta. P.C. Chacko, who has earned the rare distinction of being a 'migratory bird' in Kerala politics by changing constituencies in every election, tasted defeat handed out by a poll novice like Innocent. Those who have been viewed as performers like Jose K. Mani (KC-M), M.K. Raghavan (INC-Kozhikode), M.B. Rajesh (Palakkad), A. Sampath (Attingal) had a cakewalk this time.

Alathur MP P.K. Biju also clinched a remarkable victory. Except P. Karunakaran (Kasargod), all the other three sitting MP's of the CPM have improved their margin considerably. The Aranmula airport issue-rocked Pathanamtintta segment's verdict retaining Anto Antony as its representative may be a turning point itself on the issue.

Heavyweights like M.P. Veerendra Kumar would find it hard to digest the fact that the young M.B. Rajesh, who had scrapped through in the 2009 polls with a meagre 1,800 margin, has floored him now by more than one lakh votes.

The Kasthoorirangan factor, which had shaken the High Ranges, continued to cast its spell politically also, with Youth Congress state president Dean Kuriakose failing by the wayside. The Church backed High Range Samrakahsna Samithi's nominee Joice George, anointed as the LDF-backed Independent, has sprung a surprise which will go a long way in determining experiments of the ilk in future also.

Moreover, on a day when the Left parties tasted their worst-ever electoral debacle in its history, the CPM and the CPI are facing another nightmare. With the Left duo failing to garner sufficient votes, what's at stake is the national party status is of both parties. At the national-level, the Left parties also suffered major setback in the number of seats. The CPM came down to only nine seats (five from Kerala, two from West Bengal and two from Tripura) from its 2009 performance of 16 seats—nine from West Bengal, four from Kerala, two from Tripura and one from Tamil Nadu.

On the other hand, the CPI had a more pathetic performance. While it could win four seats in, 2009, this time the national party had to settle for a mere one seat Thrissur in Kerala.

E. The RSP Factor

The defeat of CPM Politburo member M.A. Baby in Kollam Lok Sabha constituency to erstwhile coalition partner RSP is a severe setback for the CPM for its arrogance and hegemony. It is a sweet revenge meted out to the CPM for forgetting the coalition *dharma*. Unlike in the past, the big brother CPM had been exhibiting increased amount of intolerance to minor coalition partners such as RSP, NCP and even the CPI.

Over the past few years, there had been many an occasion in which the relation between the major partners the CPM and the CPI—had soured for the CPM adopting a coercive stand towards its coalition partners. But the manner in which the RSP, a natural ally of the Left Democratic Front (LDF) for the past three decades, was belittled by the CPM could not have been expected just ahead of the elections. RSP leaders A.A. Aziz and N.K. Premachandran had stated that they had not been consulted before announcing the LDF candidate in Kollam. When they demanded that the Kollam seat should be given to them, they were told that their demand would be considered later.

But, when the election process got lacked off, instead of even convening an LDF meeting, the CPM unilaterally announced M.A. Baby as its candidate in Kollam. It was the last straw that broke the camle's back. The RSP had only two options—either to genuflect before the big brother in surrender or take the bold decision to move out of the Front. They chose the latter.

Now, the CPM leadership has to explain much within the party and to the public about its miscalculation. No matter how small a party is in a political front, it has certain relevance that adds to the total strength of the front. Moreover, the 'wreched comments' made by Pinarayi Vijayan on the eve of the poll against N.K. Premachandran had to pay heavy price in the poll. According to media reports, it is also a part of the game politics within the CPM state unit. With the defeat of M.A. Baby, Pinarayi could sabotage, Baby's chances to reach the higher echelon of the party as there has been a clamour from the West Bengal CPM that General Secretary Karat should step down. In such situation Baby would have been considered for the highest post in the CPM. In fact M.A. Baby was keen to give Pathanamthitta or Kottayam seat to N.K. Premachandran. It was reported that, Vijayan who was against such a move which resulted in the parting of the RSP from the LDF.

F. BJP's Vote Share Increased

The Modi wave has brushed through Kerala too but was not strong enough to lift any of its candidates to the Lok Sabha.

The wave increased the party's vote share; but performance is slightly weaker than in 2004 when it had contested the polls in alliance with IFDP's P.C. Thomas (now in Kerala Congress). However, compared to 2009, it has nearly doubled its votes—from just over 10 lakh to nearly 20 lakh. The vote share works out to be about 10 per cent against 6.3 in 2009 and 10.4 in 2004.

As prime ministerial candidate, Narendra Modi had taken some initiatives to rally the backward classes, especially the Ezhavas, Pulayas, and Dheevaras, behind him in Kerala. Even in Mavelikara, in SC constituency, where Congress candidate Kodikkunnil Suresh managed to woo back Pulayas, the party has been able to double its votes. The top performer for the BJP in the State was former Union Minister of State O. Rajagopal. He surpassed his earlier record, set in 2004, for any BJP candidate in the State. His score this time was 2.82 lakh votes against 2.28 lakh in 2004. Apparently, a Hindu consolidation has occurred in his favour beyond caste lines. There are also many voters who voted for him in regard to his performance as Minister of State in the Vajpayee government.

Another notable performance was that of K. Surendran who increased his votes from 1.25 lakh in 2009 to 1.72 lakh in Kasaragod. Perhaps, more lustrous is the performance of A.N. Radhakrishnan in Ernakulam, who increased his votes from about 53,000 to about 99,000.

BJP national council member Shobha Surendran, who contested from Palakkad, managed to double her party's vote in the constituency—from about 69,000 to 1.37 lakh. Local issues catapulted the party's votes in Pathanamthitta constituency—from about 56,000 to 1.39 lakh. The controversy over the Aranmula airport spearheaded by Vishwa Hindu Parishad had improved the BJP's stock there.

BJP candidate M.T. Ramesh just has to be there to benefit from long struggle by evictees and believers, though all those opposed to the project may not have voted for him. Similarly, the party more than doubled its performance in Wayanad owing to its growing influence among the tribal people. Increase in BJP votes was significant in Thrissur, Chalakudy, and Attingal also.

G. SDPI Expands its Vote Share

When the established political parties failed to deliver what they had promised, the Malabar region has witnessed Muslim vote polarisation. The Social Democratic Party of India (SDPI), which represents radical Islamic ideology, has expanded its vote base and the votes secured by its candidates are either above or just below the victory margin of the elected candidates.

The candidates fielded by the SDPI, most of them novices, came either fourth or fifth in the seven parliamentary constituencies in Malabar. Both the LDF and the UDF have suffered badly as many of their traditional Muslim voters sided with the SDPI. The success of SDPI in its maiden general election is also being seen as the failure of Muslim League, which hitherto has been acting as the champions of the Muslim community.

H. Fairly Well Performance of the AAP

Though the Aam Admi Party failed to make an impact in the wake of the Modi wave, the party did fairly well in the state. In fact, the votes polled by the AAP in three constituencies were higher than the margin of the winning candidates. It performed well in Ernakulam, Chalakkudy and Thrissur constituencies. The party got 2,55,076 votes which is 1.4 per cent of the total polled in the State. The same is higher than NOTA. AAP candidates in Thrissur, Ernakulam. Chalakkudy, Thiruvananthapuram and Kannur garnered respectable votes. Anitha Pratap got 51,517 in

Ernakukam while Sarah Joseph secured 44,638 in Thrissur. In Chalakkudy, K.M. Noordeen became a decisive factor in the tightly fought contest by getting 35,189 votes. Ajit Joy in Thiruvananthapuram also made his presence felt by collecting 14,153 votes. Anil Aikkara (Kottayam) gained 26,381 votes, K.P. Ratheesh (Kozhikode) 13,000, Silvi Sunil (Idukki) 11,215 and D. Mohanan (Alappuzha) 9,414.

The party had not fielded any candidate in Malappuram, Pathanamthitta, Attingal and Kollam constituencies.

I. NOTA Effect

In the first national elections since the NOTA option was introduced in voting machines, as many as 2,10,563 voters across the Stale exercised the right to reject all candidates in the fray. In the Kannur and Vadakara Lok Sabha constituencies, NOTA votes became a decisive factor in the electoral outcome by exceeding the winning margin.

As many as 7,026 NOTA votes were cast in Kannur where P.K. Sreemathy of the CPI(M) won by a margin of 6,566 votes over K. Sudhakaran of the Congress in a close match. In the Vadakara constituency where Union Minister Mullappally Ramachandran prevailed over A.M. Shamseer of the CPI(M), the number of NOTA votes was 6,107, almost twice the winning margin of 3,306.

The highest number of NOTA votes, 21,829, was polled in the Malappuram Lok Sabha constituency where Union Minister E. Ahamed of the IUML won by the highest margin of 1,94,739. Alathur recorded 21,417 NOTA votes and Pathanamathitta, 16,538. The other constituencies that registered five figure NOTA votes include Kottayam (14,024), Idukki (12,338), Alappuzha (11,338), Palakkad (11,291), Wayanad (10,735), Chalakudy (10,552), and Thrissur (10,050).

The lowest number of NOTA votes was polled in the Thiruvananthapuram constituency which witnessed a tough three-cornered electoral contest between Union Minister Shashi Tharoor, O. Rajagopal of the BJP and Bennet Abraham of the Communist Party of India.

J. Solar Failed to Shine for the Left

The solar scam that loomed large over the UDF during the election seems to have had little impact on the results, with UDF candidates who faced the 'solar heat' emerging victorious without any burns. The victory of sitting MP and Union Minister of State K.C. Venugopal in Alappuzha is a prime example of how people rejected the solar scam issue or his alleged involvement in the scam. The clear margin of 19,407 votes shows that even the allegations levelled from within the Congress camp failed to yield result.

K. Caste Factor

Failing to set the equations right, both the UDF and the LDF appear to have burnt their fingers in the 2014 Lok Sabha polls by playing the 'caste card'. It backlashed for the CPI in Thiruvananthapuram, while CPM's Muslim community card in Vadakara nearly fetched them a victory. Similarly, CPM's Ezhava card did not pay off in Alappuzha and Kozhikode, while the Congress had to pay heavy price for ignoring caste factors in Kasargod and Palakkad constituencies.

The Left's tango with caste politics in Thiruvananthapuram failed to keep step with changing times, with voters relegating CPI's Bennet Abraham to a highly-forgettable third spot. Never once did Bennet appear to be part of the battle as BJP's O. Rajagopal and the eventual winner Shashi Tharoor of the Congress converted it into a private duel. Bennet, who secured nearly 2.49 lakh votes, was a major factor in the fight, but never rose above that supporting role. The choice of Bennet Abraham, a director of the CSI Somerwell Memorial Medical College, Karakonam, as the Left candidate in Thiruvananthapuram had raised eyebrows since the college had been the object of fierce Left agitations. And, it was an open secret that his Nadar Christian identity had won him the candidature.

With an apparently weaker Tharoor and O. Rajagopal in the fray, the Left calculated that it could dip its finger freely into the nearly four lakh-strong Nadar vote pie by fielding the medical teacher. The choice, however, was frowned upon by hardcore Left workers in the district. The CPM's attempt to regain the prestigious Vadakara seat and to wipe out the stain caused due to TP murder case by fielding A.N. Shamseer against the incumbent Mullapally Ramachandran did not bear fruit till 2014, the CPM had only fielded an Ezhava candidate in Vadakara whenever it contested on its own symbol. The UDF had to compromise the 'Ezhava factor' in Palakkad to maintain coalition principles but suffered a body blow as CPM's M.B. Rajesh thrashed SJ(D) candidate M.P. Veerendrakumar by more than one lakh votes. Once again, the Congress has sacrificed Kasargod constituency. Despite the general demand for a Hindu candidate for the seat, the Congress went ahead with a Muslim leader. For the first time, CPM tried an Ezhava candidate in Kozhikode constituency to regain the seat, which is branded as a seat of forward communities since 1984. However, UDF's M.K. Raghavan improved his previous winning margin by more than 16,006 votes against CPM's A. Vijayaraghavan.

In Alappuzha, the CPM tried out district secretary C.B. Chandrababu against sitting MP K.C. Venugopal, who eventually won by a margin of 19000-plus votes. In a way, it was also caste that led to the defeat of CPM's M.A. Baby in Kollam. In the traditional Nair bastion, Baby was left behind even in his own Assembly constituency—Kundara.

K. Success Mantra of the 'Social Coalition'

The 2014 Polls undoubtedly shows the success mantra of the said coalition prevailing in the state. The X'an-Nair-Ezhava coalition (tieup) has been a time tested talisman of the Congress party in Kerala, starting with the first Congress ministry of Pattom Thanu Pillai in 1948, with T.M. Varghese and C. Kesavan being part of the government. Now the triangular line up nurtured by Oommen Chandy, Ramesh Chennithala—V.M. Sudheeran paved the way for the success of the Congress throughout the state.

V. CONCLUSION

(a) National

Besides its ideological underpinning, 2014 polls marked a tectonic shift in the electoral side of Indian politics, which is incredible in more ways than one. After a full quarter century, the electorate, who never trusted any party with majority seats since 1984, has given majority seats to the BJP now. Moreover, the BJP has decimated the Congress and effectively taken its place as the principal national party, not in terms of just seats but also in popular votes. In all elections till now, the BJP's share of popular votes was less than that of the Congress. Now, its share is more. The BJP's vote share is estimated at more than 50 per cent in North and West India. Because it has secured less than a tenth of the total seats, the Congress has lost its claim to be the recognised opposition party. The misery of the Congress and the Gandhis seems unmitigated. The BJP has wiped out or handed the worst defeat to the Congress in most of India particularly in North, East and West—including where the Congress is in power like Himachal Pradesh, Uttarakhand, Haryana, Maharashtra, Assam and Karnataka or where it was the strongest five years ago like Andhra

Pradesh. In contrast, the BJP has wiped out the Congress where the BJP is in power, be it Gujarat, Madhya Pradesh, Rajasthan, or Chhattisgarh. A desperate Congress created Telangana and got decimated in AP. Yet, it could not get Telangana Rashtra Samiti to ally with it and lost Telangana to TRS. But the BJP, despite voting to create Telangana, allied with the Telugu Desam Party that is opposed to Telangana and won in AP, both in Assembly and Lok Sabha. The responsibility for this dire state of the Congress squarely falls on the Gandhi family which directly controlled the party and remote-controlled the UPA government.

Finally, the 2014 election has thrown up a national leader of unprecedented popularity with mass backing, ideological conviction and political courage unseen since Indira Gandhi, but with a vital, very vital, difference. Inheriting Gandhiji's name and Nehru's lineage, Indira became Prime Minister and then acquired popularity through power. Modi became popular by hard work overcoming social and economic backwardness, supported by the RSS and the BJP he is part of.

(b) Kerala

Compared with national level political scenario, the Electoral politics of Kerala since 2006, undoubtedly shows that the CPI(M) led LDF had not won a single major election in the state. The LDF's victory even in 2006 was built almost entirely on the faults of the then Congress led coalition rather than on its own merits. Thereafter, the Lok Sabha Polls in 2009, Local body polls in 2010 and the Assembly polls in 2011 and two significant by elections at Piravam and Neyyattinkara that followed, electoral fortune was in favour of the UDF. Some of the key reasons responsible for the debacle of the Left include:

1. The factional feud within the CPI(M) and individualistic adventures of some of its top leaders;
2. The arrogant and autocratic style of functioning of party leaders from top to bottom;
3. Irrational and unethical electoral pact of the left with some communal forces with alleged extremist links;
4. Estrangement coalition partners for a variety of decisions taken by the CPI(M) leadership;
5. Alienation of some communities on issues of Government policy on self-financing education;
6. CPI(M)'s indulgence in political violence and murder and futile

attempts of the party to defend and protect party comrades who had direct involvement with the offences;
7. Loosing public interest in the agitations organized or sponsored by the CPI(M); and
8. Absence of a dynamic social movement for worthy causes that were once the hallmark of the left etc.

Despite of these electoral setbacks, the Left parties could retain their vote share. For example, in the Lok Sabha Polls in 2009, though the Left secured only four seats out of 20, they could capture 41.89 per cent of the votes as compared to 47.73 per cent won by the UDF. In the 2001 assembly polls the Left won 44.94 per cent of votes, when the UDF which replaced it in Government got 45.83 per cent of votes. WIthin the LDF, the CPI(M)'s vote share in the elections in 2009 and 2011 was 30.48 per cent and 28.18 per cent respectively and that of the CPI was only 7.44 per cent and 8.72 per cent respectively. But in the 2014 polls the vote share of the CPM came down to 21.6 per cent and the share of the CPI to 7.6 per cent.

Before conclude, it has to be stated that the rout of the CPM in West Bengal and the less impressive performance in Kerala mark the beginning of the end for the CPM as a key player in the national politics. Though a debacle in West Bengal was not unexpected, the CPM leadership cannot give any explanation for its humiliating defeat in Bengal, a state considered as a Left fiefdom till recently. In Kerala, the defeat of M.A. Baby, the PB member A. Vijayaraghavan Central Committee member has put the fellow travellers of the CPM into a quandry. The only solace for the CPM in Kerala was its victory of Kannur, Aalathur, Palaghat and Attingal. However, P. Karunakaran, another Central Committee member escaped with a thin margin of 6921 votes in Kasaragod. In this juncture the party headed to make a serious introspection and take remedial measures if it wanted to survive as an entity of any political relevance.

References

1. *The Hindu*, Thiruvananthapuram.
2. *The New Indian Express*, Thiruvananthapuram.
3. *Deccan Chronicle*, Kochi.
4. *The Malayala Manorama*, Kollam.
5. *The Mathrubhumi*, Kollam.

6. *The Kerala Kaumudi*, Kollam.
7. *The Kerala Sabdam*, Kollam.
8. *EPW*.
9. *Mainstream*.
10. *Samakalika Malayalam*.
11. *Kala Kaumudi*.
12. *Frontline*.
13. **The SNC Lavalin scandal**
    The SNC Lavalin scandal is financial scam related to the contracting of the Indian *government* with a *Canadian* company, *SNC-Lavalin* which resulted in an alleged *net loss* to the *exchequer* of 3745.0 million in the renovation and modernization works of the hydro-electric power stations at Pallivasal (37.5 mW), Sengulam (48 mW) and Panniar (30 mW)—also known as PSP project in short-installed between 1940 and 1964 at *Idukki* district in *Kerala* state of India Several politicians were involved and eventually charged, including former ministers *G. Karthikeyan* of Indian National Congress, *Pinarayi Vijayan*. the first Politbureau member in the CPI(M) history to be prosecuted in a corruption case. On 5 November 2013, Pinarayi Vijayan and 6 other accused were discharged from the list of accused by a CBI Special Court holding that the charge-sheet filed by CBI was not legally maintainable.
14. **Solar Panel Scam**
    "Solar scam" is related to the collection of huge amounts of money from customers for setting up panels for the production of solar power. The persons involved in it were alleged to have developed contacts with the higher-ups, including politicians, ministers, etc, and such contacts were said to have been cited to win customers for the fraudulent companies projected to be solar panel suppliers. In this connection, the accused are said to have approached even the Union Minister for non-conventional energy, Farooq Abdullah, for certain favours with a letter of introduction on the letterhead of the Chief Minister. Two staff members of the Chief Minister's office and his private secretary were at the centre of the storm. The Chief Minister, while vehemently denying any direct involvement, nevertheless admits that his policy of keeping his office easily accessible for all personnel who approached it with grievances has backfired and that he should have been cautious on such matters.
    The testimony by one individual that he had paid a sum of Rs. 40 lakh for booking solar panels after ascertaining from the Chief Minister the credentials of the suppliers, the decision of the state cabinet to make solar panels compulsory for all buildings with a base area of more than 2,500 square feet, the government's order to allocate land under the department of irrigation for setting up the solar panels. Before entering into the "business" of solar panels, they were involved in other fraudulent projects. That was during the LDF regime. There again the mainstay of the accused

was the connection with higher-ups including politicians and reportedly even a minister. The UDF, which is in power now, points out that the investigations into the complaints of having been cheated financially, lodged with the police as early as in 2007, are being investigated now, and that the LDF cannot claim innocence or non-involvement with the perpetrators of the crime.

15. **T.P. Murder Case**

The murder of T.P. Chandrasekharan in the month of May 2013 had made the CPI(M), unpopular as never before. It was not only the murder alone, but the series of what were conceived as half truths and untruths propagated in its aftermath as well that agitated the public minds. The revelations by some of the accused in the TP murder case that they were the real culprits in certain political murders committed by the CPI(M) in the past, and that as part of the understanding between the party leaders and the police, innocent persons had been implicated and even punished in some of them, also did immense damage to the image of the CPI(M).

3
Propaganda and the Changing Chemistry of Indian Elections

J. Prabhash

An important feature of elections in India in recent times is that they have ceased to be political contests—contests between political parties who have a distinct and clear understanding about social reality and hence alternative conceptions about public policies. Neither have they been contests between political parties having a distinct and rigid set of cadres and leadership. The implication is that the two important factors which distinguish political parties from each other are fast disappearing from Indian politics. To put the argument straight, an organization can call itself a political party even when it doesn't have any ideology and an exclusive cadre and leadership base. Indian political parties, with exceptions apart, are merely becoming a crowd of indiscrete individuals. They are neither political nor parties. The recently concluded Lok Sabha election offers the best testimony to this.

The election is noted for four important, but unhealthy, trends: galactic sums spent on propaganda, highly individualistic campaign, unprecedented degree of floor crossing by prominent political leaders including central ministers and top office bearers, and the smear campaign engaged by the party leaderships and candidates. All of these have made this election less political, public, secular and democratic.

Today the intensity of connection between politics and the business world has enhanced manifold. As could be conjectured, this cosy relationship between the two has produced a corresponding disconnect between the people and the parties. Thus the ratio of these two relationships is inversely proportionate. Interestingly, the terms of the relationship between the parties and the business is structured on a *quid pro quo* basis with the latter supporting the former in monetary terms during elections and at other times when such help is needed, and the former chipping in with public policies favourable to business, besides providing it subsidies of various sorts. As a result of this, elections are noted, contemporaneously, not for their pedagogic or educative value but for their pomp and splendour which, incidentally, are inversely proportionate to the money spent on electioneering. According to one estimate, a whopping of Rs. 30500 crore is spent on campaigning in the justly concluded Lok Sabha polls (Vishnu, 2014: 33). This is indicative of how big business is funding parties (Mukherjee, 2014: 12).

Table 3.1 indicates the major items of expenditure incurred by various political parties and candidates in this election. According to it, publicity is the single largest drain on party coffers (Rs. 8350 crore) followed by graft given to voters (Rs. 5500 crore), hospitality (Rs. 2300 crore), and food and liquor (Rs. 3000 crore). Even the lowest expenditure—booth management—is estimated at Rs. 300 crore. Further the value of cash and goods confiscated by the Election Commission since March 5, 2014 itself had come to Rs. 1100 crore which is estimated to be just 10 per cent of the total black money in circulation to buy votes (Vishnu, 2014: 33, Pillai, 2014: 137). All these show that in Indian democracy elections are contested on the strength of money rather than politics or policy alternatives.

Table 3.1: 2014 Election: Major Items of Campaign Expenditure

Item	*Estimated Expenditure (Rs. in crore)*
Publicity	8350
Graft for voters	5500
Hospitality/entertainment/liquor	6000
Travel	2700
Caps/flags/tea-shirts	2000
Rallies and event management	600
Booth management	300
Total	25450

Source: Arindam Mukherjee, 'Count Your Zeroes Before They Addle', *Outlook*, Vol. LVI, No. 20, 26 May, 2014, pp. 12-13.

In addition to money, what has drained election of its political content is the ease with which non-political individuals were fielded as candidates and the speed with which political functionaries changed sides with impunity and the legitimacy accorded to it by the political society. According to one estimate, in all 72 candidates with no previous experience in politics and social work were fielded by prominent political parties (Gandhi *et al.*, 2014:30). This included retired military men, IT professionals, former top bureaucrats (19 IAS and IPS officers, for instance), film stars, journalists and even magicians. The only factor that weighed with the political leadership in this regard was the winnablility of the candidates. Interestingly, no midnight oil was burnt to ascertain the ideological compatibility of these fortune seekers. Neither was an assessment made about their contribution to public life and understanding of the country's social reality.

Some of the utterances made by these charlatan politicians are themselves sufficient to convey their foolhardy perception about socio-political issues. Take for instance the statement made by P.C. Sorcar Jr. (a magician by profession, who contested from Barasat in West Bengal as a BJP candidate) that he had been making different things disappear, and that he would now make 'poverty, the wicked, bad businessmen and other things which cripple the society disappear' with his magic wand (Banerjee, 2014:22). Similarly, Moon Moon Sen (TMC candidate from Bankura in West Bengal) said that she had learnt about politics from Julius Caesar and that she wanted to bring that nobility back to politics (Gandhi *et al.*, 2014:27). To people like Sorcar and Sen, social reality is as simple as this.

Equally significant in this connection was the widespread occurrence of party-hopping made by the political class of all hues and shades on the eve of the election. Such hoppers included Union Ministers, MPs, MLAs, Leader of Opposition (Odisha), and even a former Chief Minister (Arunachal Pradesh). The party worst affected by this was obviously the Congress. In Seemandhra alone, about 50 per cent of the Party functionaries at various levels deserted it and migrated to other parties. This desertion drama was later repeated state after state and at the opposite end was invariably welcomed and such persons were rewarded with seats in the election. In just three states—Haryana, Uttar Pradesh and Gujarat—BJP fielded 39 (34.21%) such individuals. Incidentally, all of them were from the Congress Party. The number of such candidates will be substantial if statistics from other states are also collated. Viewed thus, one is forced to argue that the BJP which Narendra Modi has resurrected is a party with Congress DNA. This widespread cross-migration that took place among political parties in this election does not augur well for our democratic system as it adversely affects the architectural distinction between parties.

Another notable trend seen in the electoral campaign was the personal indictment and hate speeches resorted to by all major political actors exceeding all cannons of decency and ethical conduct. A few excerpts from such hate speeches would prove this point. There were frequent references about pan-Pakistan disposition by the Muslim population of the country ('those who oppose Modi will have a place in Pakistan); the need for dispossessing them of their property ('Muslim property in Hindu areas should be encroached upon'); and reminding one of the foreign origin of Rahul Gandhi and Sonia Gandhi ('Sonia Gandhi and Rahul Gandhi should be stripped off of their clothes and sent back to Italy) (Naqvi, 2014:36-37).

On the reverse side, Narendra Modi was described as a barbarian ('Modi is a butcher/*narāhantaka*') having even illicit relationship with Mayavati ('Mayavati sat on Modi's lap), and threats were also issued against voting for BJP/Congress and CPM ('Do not allow even a single person to vote for the BJP/Congress or CPM) (Ramachandran, 2014). The sole purpose of these invectives was to terrify the opposition and consolidate one's core constituency. As could be inferred, the campaign simply bypassed the quotidian life concerns of the population and steered clear of other vital issues of national significance except making some isolated references about development, that too during the early stages of the electioneering.

Thus, it was the personal rather than the social/political that has dominated the election campaign and the same was further reflected the way in which it was conducted by political parties, BJP in particular. Despite the fact that it has a long array of senior leaders, the entire burden of crafting the party's electoral success was borne by one single individual, Narendra Modi. The importance of the leadership of the coalition partners of the NDA also paled into insignificance before his single handed, aggressive and expensive campaign. So relentless has been his campaign that he has converted a complex parliamentary system into a presidential style referendum on himself (Pradhan and Mahurkar, 2014:23). It was plainly a plebiscite on Modi, and BJP, as a party, was only the backdrop to this main script (Palshikar, 2014). This is the most thoroughly planned and organized campaign in India and has changed the chemistry of electioneering in the country. Statistics has it that Modi has travelled 300000 kilometres, attended 5187 events, and addressed 477 rallies in 25 states (Pradhan and Mahurkar, 2014:23, Vajpai, 2014:72-73).

Through all these propaganda the central message that was conveyed was clear and simple: 'either you accept Modi or reject him.' Every other leader and party, including his own, was rendered inconsequential. In the end, he sounded more efficient than everybody and managed to appropriate not just secularism but also nationalism (Pradhan and Mahurkar, 2014:25). Looking back one is, therefore, compelled to state that election 2014 has changed, beyond recognition, the electoral landscape and the nature of Indian party system.

References

Banerjee, Rabi (2014), 'Starry fight', *The Week*, Vol. 32, No. 13, 30 March.

Gandhi, Jatin, Jayant Sriram and Kaushik Deka (2014), 'Parachute Politicians', *India Today*, Vol. XXXIX, No. 14, 7 April.

Mukherjee, Arindam (2014), 'Count Your Zeroes Before They Addle', *Outlook*, Vol. LIV, No. 20, 26 May.

Naqvi, Saba (2014), 'Be All End All', *Outlook*, Vol. LIV, No.17, 5 May.

Palshikar, Suhas (2014), 'A New Phase of the Polity', *The Hindu*, 22, May.

Pillai, Madhavankutty, 'The Uranium Itch and Other Maladies in Seemandhra', *Open*, Vol.6, Issue 18, 12 May.

Ramachandran, Manoj (2014), 'Poison Prose', *The Hindu*, 24 April.

Vajpai, Ananya (2014), 'Urgency of the Alternative', *Open*, Vol. 6, Issue 14, 14 April, 2014.

Vishnu, G. (2014), 'The Dirty Underbelly of Election 2014', *Tehelka*, Vol. II, Issue 19, 10 May.

4
Women's Participation in Indian Politics
Issues and Challenges

Kalpana S. Agrahari

Liberty, equality and justice are the *sine qua non* for every democratic society, thus the nature and level of political participation and its resultant empowerment can be evaluated only on the basis of the availability of the basic democratic values. The accessibility of democratic values in true sense is a prerequisite for the attainment of maximum extent of participation and empowerment. The International Encyclopaedia of Social Sciences defined political participation as the principal means by which consent is granted or withdrawn in a democracy and rulers are made accountable to the ruled.[1] Empowerment does not mean to achieving power to dominate others, but rather power to act with others for change. Women's equality in power sharing and active participation in decision-making in political process at all levels is a key question for achievement of the goal of empowerment.

The principle of gender equality is enshrined in the Constitution of India, in its Preamble, Fundamental Rights, Fundamental Duties and Directive Principles. The Constitution not only grants equality to women, but also empowers the State to adopt measures of positive discrimination in favour of women.[2] Although the Constitution of India did guarantee women equal rights, women continue to remain oppressed and struggle over everything from survival to resources in the country. Despite the fact that there exists a strong legal environment and a movement to protect women's rights; the social status of the majority of the women has been unchanged. While women have made considerable progress in some areas such as education and employment, they continue to be subjected to the influence of the existing patriarchal attitudes in Indian society. The dilemma for Indian women today is that despite the liberal provisions of the Constitution and various laws, serious inequalities remains. Gender disparity remains in various forms, the most obvious being the trend of continuously declining female ratio in the population in the last few decades; social stereotyping and violence at the domestic and societal levels are some of the other manifestations.

The causes of gender inequality are related to social, economic and political structure, which is based on informal and formal norms, and practices. The patriarchal society not only harbours a culture of violence against women in the form of dowry, domestic violence and female infanticide, it also manifests even in government policies towards women. This has been analyzed extensively in the Report of the Committee on the Status of Women in India, "Towards Equality", 1974.[3] Both men and women are equal citizens in the eyes of the law; but this is far from the reality. The comparative position of gender-related development index (GDI) reveals that among 177 countries, India ranks 113, indicating its very low gender-equity status and huge disparity in access of women to economic, political, educational and health care opportunities and their participation in such services.[4] In 2013 Global Gender Gap Index, released by World Economic Forum, India ranked a lowly 101st of 136 countries, while India has bettered it's rank by four positions from the previous year, it emerged at the near bottom of the heap. While none of the countries analysed have achieved gender equality. The Nordic countries of Iceland, Finland and Norway, set an example, which have consistently ranked at the first three positions, having closed over 80 per cent of their gender gaps across sectors.[5]

There still exists a wide gap between the goals enunciated in the Constitution, legislation, policies, plans, programmes, and related mechanisms on the one hand and the situational reality of the status of women in India, on the other. These factors has been highlighted in the National Perspective Plan for Women, 1988-2000.[6]

Women in Politics in Post-independent India

The Constitution of India guarantees all its citizens justice, liberty, equality, and dignity through several provisions like documents of fundamental rights and directive principles but also takes care of the disadvantaged and the minorities. Several articles are integrated in the Constitution in order to become visible the desired objective of equality and justice for the women in India. In addition to preamble, Articles 14, 15, 16 under Part III, Articles 39, 42, under Part IV, are striking.[7] India is a bicameral parliamentary democracy, with a strong multi-party political system. The lower house is called the Lok Sabha (Peoples' Assembly) and has 545 members. The upper house is called the Rajya Sabha (States' Assembly) with 250 members.[8] As the country debates the Women's Reservation Bill, data on parliaments across the world shows that India, the largest democracy, lags much behind other countries including its neighbours Pakistan and Bangladesh when it comes to participation of the fair sex in politics. With only 11 per cent of women representation in the Lok Sabha and nine per cent in the Rajya Sabha, India ranks 99 in the world, according to the comparative data by the Inter-Parliamentary Union, an international organisation that works for promoting democracy, peace and co-operation among people in the world.[9] With only 59 women representatives out of 545 members in Lok Sabha and 21 female MPs in the 245 member Rajya Sabha, India ranks 50 places below Pakistan which is placed at 49 in the list with 22 per cent women representation in its Lower House and 17 per cent in the Upper House.[10]

Table 4.1 portrays the low profile of women's representation in parliament between 1952 and 2009. The recently concluded 15th Lok Sabha elections have delivered a record 59 women as members of Parliament, the highest since independence, raising their parliamentary participation to 11 per cent from eight per cent (45 women MPs) in 2004. Women's Lower House participation in 2004 was lower than in 1999, which was nine per cent (49 women MPs). In 1998, women constituted eight per cent of the membership of the Lok Sabha. This was higher than the preceding 1996 and 1991 parliament with only seven per cent participation. The election results in 1989 showed a further decline in women's representation, women constituted mere five per cent of the membership of the Lok Sabha. This was lower than the preceding 1984 parliament, eight per cent of total membership. In 1977 only 19 women were elected for Lower House, only three per cent, which was the lowest participation data, even in first general election in 1952, the percentage was four (22 out of 499 members). In altogether women participation in Lok Sabha has varied from as low as three per cent to 11 per cent despite being the 50 per cent of the population.

The trend in the Rajya Sabha is also not very different than that of Lok Sabha. Table 4.2 depicts the representation of women in Rajya Sabha since 1952 to 2006. In Rajya Sabha, proportion of female members started with 7 per cent in 1952 and rose to 16 per cent in 1991 (the highest per cent of representation ever), but again declined to six per cent in 1998 and rose to 11 per cent in 2005, again slightly declined to nine per cent in

Table 4.1: Women's Representation in Lok Sabha, 1952-2009

Sl. No.	*Year*	*Total Seats*	*Women Members*	*Men Members*	*Percentage Women*
1.	1952	499	22	477	4.4
2.	1957	500	27	473	5.4
3.	1962	503	34	469	6.8
4.	1967	523	31	492	5.9
5.	1971	521	22	499	4.2
6.	1977	544	19	525	3.4
7.	1980	544	28	516	7.9
8.	1984	544	44	500	8.1
9.	1989	517	27	490	5.3
10.	1991	544	39	505	7.2
11.	1996	543	39	504	7.2
12.	1998	543	43	500	7.9
13.	1999	543	49	494	9.0
14.	2004	545	45	500	8.2
15.	2009	545	59	486	10.8

Source: 1. India, Ministry of Human Resource Development, Department of Women and Child Development (2004). Government of India, II and III Periodic Report on the Convention on the Elimination of All Forms of Discrimination against Women; CEDAW Periodic Report. New Delhi. p. 86

2. www.parlliamentofindia.nic.in

2006. In 2006 only 21 seats belonged to women out of 245 members Rajya Sabha. This representation was lower than that of 2004 account of 28 seats belonging to women. There has been not any consistent pattern in the women representation in Rajya Sabha also.

This trend is worrying given the recent state-led initiatives to ensure women's representation in political institutions. Thus, the representation of women in the Lok Sabha as well as Rajya Sabha is very low when compared with their voting strength. Their numerical strength is also marginal in decision-making bodies. Only a very limited number of women have succeeded in getting berths in the Council of Ministers. The following Table 4.3 provides a clear picture of women's representation in the Union Council of Ministers.

Though women have entered many male dominated professions, their representation in the higher echelons of society and in positions of decision-making is much below that of men. The Table 4.3 clearly shows that a very few women have succeeded in getting into the Union Cabinet. Only four per cent (mere 1 woman in the strength of 29 members) of

Table 4.2: Women's Representation in Rajya Sabha, 1952-2006

Sl. No.	*Year*	*Rajya Sabha (Upper House)*			
		Total Seats	*Women Members*	*Men Members*	*Percentage Women*
1.	1952	219	16	203	7.3
2.	1957	237	18	219	7.5
3.	1962	238	18	220	7.6
4.	1967	240	20	220	8.3
5.	1971	243	17	226	7.0
6.	1977	244	25	219	10.2
7.	1980	244	24	220	9.8
8.	1984	244	28	216	11.4
9.	1989	245	24	221	9.7
10.	1991	245	38	207	15.5
11.	1996	223	20	203	9.0
12.	1998	245	15	230	6.1
13.	1999	245	19	226	7.8
14.	2005	245	28	217	11.4
15.	2006	245	21	224	8.6

Source: 1. India, Ministry of Human Resource Development, Department of Women and Child Development (2004). Government of India, II and III Periodic Report on the Convention on the Elimination of All Forms of Discrimination against Women; CEDAW Periodic Report. New Delhi, p. 86.

2. www.parlliamentofindia.nic.in

Table 4.3: Representation of Women in the Central Council of Ministers, 2006 and 2009

S. No.	*Ministerial Rank*	*Central Council of Ministers*						*Percentage Female to Total*	
		Female		*Male*		*Total*			
		2006	2009#	2006	2009#	2006	2009#	2006	2009#
1.	Cabinet Minister	1	3	28	30	29	33	3.5	9.1
2.	Minister of State	6	5	33	40	39	45	15.4	11.1
	Total	7	8	61	70	68	78	10.3	10.3

Source: 1. www.parliamentofIndia.nic.in

2. India, Ministry of Statistics and Programme Implementation, Central Statistical Organisation (2007). *Women and Men in India* 2006. New Delhi, p.104.

3. # www.cabsec.nic.in/women.htm

cabinet ministers were women in the year 2006 and it rose to nine per cent (3 women members among the 33 cabinet ministers) in 2009. In 2006 among the minister of state positions there were 15 per cent women, which further declined to 11 per cent in 2009. In the central council of ministers women maintained a steady 10 per cent representation in 2006 (total 7 women among the 68 members) as well as in 2009 (meagre 8 women out of 78 ministers).

Thus it seems clear that the actual political power remained something of a male domain and only few crumbs are thrown to women. Women are unjustifiably rare in the decision-making bodies. Moreover, if anybody is elected to such bodies they will have to struggle hard to be counted for notable posts. This is the real situation that exists in India in terms of political participation of women. Throughout the world, one allegation is that women are treated as second class citizens. Often they are treated as subordinates to man almost in every place. As a result, the advancement of women seems constrained at all levels.[11]

Challenges and Issues for Political Empowerment

The Articles 325 and 326 of Constitution of India ensures the political participation for every citizen of India, but unfortunately women in India have not been the beneficiary of this article. They have been alienated in the Indian politics and their active participation in the politics has been restricted by many historical, cultural, geographical, sociological and economic reasons. There are so many causes which may be understood to be responsible for the lower participation of women in political process like the unavailability of resources and information, family responsibilities, organizational structural factors, cultural impediments, patriarchal values, insensitive laws and policies, rising criminalisation of politics and fears of character assassination etc.

Due to high illiteracy rate and lower level of education, access to information is quite difficult for women. Even understanding the language is not an easy job as India has the 34.6 per cent female illiteracy rate.[12] It restricts their mobility as they have very limited exposure towards public life. It affects the recognition and enjoyment of the right to women to vote, contest elections, and entertainment of social networks.

An average Indian woman has little control over her own fertility and reproductive health. Women are part of informal economy; they work for longer hours than men, carry the major share of household work,[13] and don't get the salary for their domestic work, even the recognition too. Fulfilment of family expectations and responsibilities are great challenge for female politicians. Ambitious women have to take departure from their political carrier for the sake of their family life. There is another option to take the extreme step of separation from family for the fulfilment of their uncertain political career, but the accomplishment in politics with the stigma of divorce and alienation from family, is very difficult for women without sound political background.

The nature of Indian party system is also one aspect, where the party structure is week at organizational level and local elites are dominant. The elections are fought generally either on single issue or upon some patriarchal issues, which is also responsible for the lack of gender sensitive politics. Sometimes, it is suggested that at least all the political parties must provide the 33 per cent tickets to women only within the framework of party to ensure the gender equity, but the multifarious structure of multi-party political system and compulsions of politics are also among the main obstacles against female participation. The goal of power attainment is ultimate for any political party. The factors like hung parliament, coalition government and slender majority are already the matters of their concern, and fielding the female candidate (except few exceptions) might be a great risk. Many times the political parties complains for the inappropriateness of the female candidates, even they are not the free voters, they have lack of political awareness, consciousness, and information, the decisions are taken by their husbands on behalf of them. This is a fact, the matter of gender participatory politics has been a *de jure* rather than a *de facto* subject. There is a gap between the formal idea of women's participation and their meaningful use of power.[14] Even though the awareness for women friendly politics has been increasing day by day, but there is a lack of the sensitivity and seriousness required for the issue. Though every political party has the women's wing,[15] but these are ancillary bodies only, it becomes quite difficult for women to reach on the top positions, like party president etc. Very few women politicians could have managed to reach the level of cabinet ministers, mostly women remain as deputy minister or minister of states and awarded with soft portfolios like social service sector of health, education, women and child development etc.[16]

The issue of women's participation was used to be understood as the social and economic participation rather than political till 1980s. The CSWI report (Committee on Status of Women in India), published in 1976, first time proposed for reservation policy to increase women's political share.[17] In the 1988 the proposal of 30 per cent reservation at all levels was introduced by NPPW (National Perspective Plan for Women).[18] Acceptance for women's reservation at local level through 73rd and 74th Constitutional Amendment Act was a milestone achievement for increase of women's share in political arena. In 1995 the issue of women's reservation at national level was raised for the first time. The proposed legislation to reserve 33.3 per cent seats in Parliament and State Legislatures for women was drafted first by the then H.D. Devegowda led United Front Government. The Bill was introduced in the Lok Sabha on September 12, 1996. Though it has been introduced in Parliament several times since then, the bill could not be passed because of lack of political consensus.[19] Even if it was a serious step towards women friendly political environment, it opened Pandora's Box. Initially, most political parties agreed to this proposal. But soon doubts surfaced. When the bill was introduced, several parties and groups raised objections. Differences on the matters of women's reservation policy have many folds. The first question is related with the class difference and the other one is related with caste or with the question of reservation within reservation. One can't ignore the fact, that despite the general identification of disadvantaged, it must not conclude all women in the same category, overlooking their class and caste differences. The opponents of this kind of reservation argue that the proposed common reservation bill only increase the social and political disparities of opportunity. It will smooth the political entry of only elite class women with sound political and economic background. They argue that only quantitative enhancement of females in parliament will not help in solving women's issues until the representation belongs to the real deprived section of women who could represent the real concerns. They see the solution in the sub-reservation of backward class women within the proposed general reservation.

Every political party has a different opinion on the issue. However, the supporters feel that undoubtedly any affirmative action like reservation for women in Parliament will strengthen the democratic process, with the help of woman reservation bill, the political sphere will be much representative and participation of women in decision-making process will not only strengthen the status of women in society, but also it will provide a feminist view in the matters of decision-making. The concerns of women's can't be taken seriously until the women themselves are not involved. The 73rd Constitutional Amendment has increased the participation of fair sex at local level to a record extent, which rose hope for 83rd Constitutional Bill. The quest for greater political representation of women is, therefore, still relevant.[20]

Conclusion

It is important to stress that participation and representation in legislative bodies may not itself be enough for women's political empowerment or to remedy the problems of discrimination faced by women in Indian society. Equality with equity is a goal which may not easily be achieved only by high representation of women in legislatures and other public bodies but has to be buttressed by other supportive measures. Even so, the demand for reservation of seats for women in political bodies to rectify the imbalance has gained strength in India in the light of persisting gender gaps in the various spheres of development. In the absence of any serious political self-correction so far, the demand for reservation of seats in legislatures and party structures has been stressed in India aiming at such an equitable representation. While the steady increase in the electoral participation and mobilization of women in India has increased the visibility of women in the legislative politics this has not happened in the exercise of executive power due to their lack of presence in the decision-making structures. From this perspective, the important question is 'what are the benefits of democracy for women'.

Women's equality in power sharing and active participation in decision-making, including decision-making in political process at all levels must be ensured for the achievement of the goals of empowerment. All measures must be taken to guarantee women equal access to and full participation in decision-making bodies at every level, including the legislative, executive, judicial, corporate, statutory bodies, as also the advisory Commissions, Committees, Boards, Trusts, etc. Affirmative action such as reservations/quotas, including in higher legislative bodies, must be considered whenever necessary on a time bound basis. Women-friendly personnel policies must also be drawn up to encourage women to participate effectively in the developmental process.

Finally, there is a general view that only electoral quotas are not the final solution. Electoral participation and quotas through affirmative action alone are not enough to result in gender equality.[21] The focus should be on creating such conditions, wherein women could prefer to join the politics on their own terms and participate in the decisions of their destiny. For the purpose, we are strongly needed a mechanism which could provide the full training of legislative process, can make them aware towards their rights and duties as elected member and gender sensitisation of every elected membe-.

References

1. *International Encyclopedia of Social Sciences*, Vol.12, New York, 1968, p. 253.
2. P.M. Bakshi, *The Constitution of India, with select comments,* Universal Law Publishing Co. Pvt. Ltd., p. 27.
3. *Report of the Committee on the Status of Women in India*, "Towards Equality", 1974. p. 102.
4. http://www.du.ac.in/fileadmin/DU/Academics/course_material/hrge_08.pdf
5. Madhavi Rajadhyaksha, (2013). "Ranked 101, India's gender gap among worst", *Sunday Times of India*, New Delhi, October 27, 2013, p. 9.
6. http://www.worldcat.org/title/national-perspective-plan-for-women-1988-000-ad/oclc/187410601
7. *Ibid., 2.*
8. D.D. Basu, An *Introduction to the Constitution of India*, p. 210.
9. *Ibid.*, p. 4.
10. *Ibid.*, p. 4.
11. Kaushik, Susheela, (1996), *Why Women in Legislatures?,* Paper presented at the meet of Parliamentarians, New Delhi.
12. http://www.indiaonlinepages.com/population/literacy-rate-in-india.html
13. Sen, Kalyani Menon, Shiva Kumar, A.K., (2001). *Women in India: How Free? How Equal?*, Report commissioned by the Office of the United Nations Resident Coordinator in India, New Delhi.
14. Kaushik Susheela, (1993). *Women's Participation in Politics*, Vikas, New Delhi.
15. Ranjana Kumari, (1994), *Women Parliamentarians*, Haranand Publications, New Delhi.
16. *Human Development Report* (HDR) (2007/08), UNDP, Palgrave Macmillan, New York, pp. 326-329.
17. http://www.iwraw-ap.org/aboutus/pdf/FPwomen_and_pol_pax.pdf
18. *Ibid., 5.*
19. http://news.rediff.com/special/2010/mar/08/whats-the-womens-reservation-bill-all-about.htm
20. Mehta, Aasha Kapur, Arora, Dolly and Kabra, Kamal Nayan, (2001), 'Parliamentary Debate on the Golden Jubilee of Independence: Equity and Social Justice', *Mainstream*, August 18, 2001.
21. Subhas C. Kashap, "Reservation for women and good governance", *South Asia Politics*, October 2009, Vol. 8, No. 6, pp. 6-8.

5

Women Politics in an Indian State of Odisha

Dasarathi Bhuiyan

Women in India constitute nearly half the population of the country, but they are poorly represented in the various governance and decision-making bodies. The position depicted through the 15 general elections so far reflects a low representation of women in Parliament, State Legislatures, in political parties and other decision-making bodies. Less than 8 per cent of Parliamentary seats, less than 6 per cent Cabinet positions, less than 4 per cent of seats in High Courts and the Supreme Court, have been occupied by women. Less than 3 per cent of the administrators and managers are women. The average percentage of women's representation in the Parliament, Assemblies and Council of Ministers taken together has been around 10 per cent (UNIFEM, 2000). The evolution of Indian democracy through the 15 general elections so far has reflected a low representation of women in Parliament, State Legislatures, in political parties and other decision-making bodies.

The Indian state of Odisha is also not free from this low tempo of political participation. There was also a big gap between men and women in Odisha in electoral field during the pre-independent era. Odisha formed its first government when it became a separate province on 1st April, 1936 by an Act of the Central Government. This can be inferred from the fact that none of the three ministries of Odisha during the Pre-Independence Assembly period, i.e. from 1936 to 1947 included any woman, although Sarala Devi and Punya Prabha Devi were elected from the Cuttack town constituency (Ghosh, 1979). But in the link assembly from 1947 to 1952 among the women legislators A. Laxmi Bai[1] was the Deputy Speaker of the Odisha Legislative Assembly from 29-5-1946 to 20-2-1952 and Basant Manjari Devi, queen of Ranpur—a small kingdom du Manjarng the British-Odisha, was the Deputy Minister of Health in the Harekrushna Mahatab Ministry, who assumed the charge of office of prime ministership[2] on 23rd April, 1946 (Rout, 2006).

After the Independence of India there had been a spectacular increase in the political participation of women in Odisha. A few of them have also appointed as ministers both at the Centre and in the States. But real powers continued to lie with the male politicians. Although Basant Manjari Devi (Orissa Reference Annual, 2004) was a prominent woman political personality during the post-independence, she lacked state-wide influence. Despite the fact that Basant Manjari Devi had been the Deputy Minister, she was, at best, a "decorative piece" of the cabinet of H.K. Mahatab and Nabakrishna Chaudhury from 1946 to 1959. Up to the end of 1960s the political scene of Odisha was dominated by male leaders (B.B. Jena, 1988).

In the mid-term election to the Odisha Assembly in 1961 Smt. Saraswati Pradhan, a Congress party candidate was (Ashalata Parija, 1988) elected from Bhatali constituency of Sambalpur district (Orissa Reference Annual, 2004). Saraswati Pradhan was installed as a Deputy Minister of Education in Biju Patnaik's Cabinet in 1961, also in Biren Mitra's government on 2nd October, 1963 and again in the Ministry of Sadasiv Tripathy as the same Deputy Minister of Education. But she was not promoted to the Minister of State or Cabinet rank. The fact that Smt. Saraswati Pradhan was appointed only to fill up the women quota in the Ministry (B.B. Jena, 1988).

Anang Manjari Devi, a Jana-Congress candidate from Sukinda constituency, Swaraswati Pradhan of the Congress Party from Bhatli constituency and Ratnaprabha Devi of Swatantra Party from Dhenkanal constituency were elected to the Odisha Assembly in the elections of 1967. Even the Swatantra-Jana Congress Ministry[3] did not include any elected woman from their respective parties. In the mid-term elections of 1971 although 12 women candidates contested, none of them were elected. But Nadini Satpathy[4], then a Union Minister of State became the Chief Minister of Odisha. Later on she was elected to the Assembly from Cuttack Constituency on 26 November, 1972 in a bye-election (Ghosh, 1979). In the 1974 mid-term elections of March 6, 1974 along with Nandini Satpathy, Sairindri Nayak, Subhansunalini Ray and V. Sugyan Kumari Deo[5] were elected to the Assembly. But none of them were included in the ministry of Smt. Satpathy. The succeeding Acharya Ministry also did not induct any woman minister. Even though, out of seven women legislators five were elected from Janata party, Routray Ministry of

June 26, 1977 did not include any woman minister. In the 1980 elections 5 women members were elected but J.B Patnaik inducted Saraswati Hembram, into his Ministry. In the 1985 election 7 women members were elected and Miss Fida Topno was inducted in the second Ministry of J.B. Patniak in 1985. J.B. Patnaik reshuffled his Ministry on 22nd July, 1986 and he inducted Smt. Parama Pujari and Smt. Saraswati Hembram as Deputy Ministers. Hemananda Biswal took over as Odisha's Chief Minister on 5th December, 1989. He included all the women ministers of J.B. Patnaik's cabinet. But all the three women ministers were inactive and without any substantive power and function (Harihara Das, 1990). In the March 1990 elections seven women members were elected. Except Nandini Satpathy, all others were elected from Janata Dal ticket. But Biju Patnaik inducted only Dr. Kamala Das into his Cabinet. In the 1995 elections eight women members were elected. But J.B. Patnaik inducted only Smt. Bijayalaxmi Sahoo, into his cabinet. On 9th February, 1999 his successor Giridhar Gomango inducted Usha Rani Panda, Parama Pujari, Swaraswti Hembram and Bijayalaxmi Sahoo in his cabinet in February 1999 (B.B. Jena, 1988). When Hemananda Biswal succeeded and he retained all the women ministers of the Gomango Ministry[6].

In 2000 election 14 women were elected to Odisha Assembly. This was the highest number of women members ever elected to the Assembly (Table 5.4). Naveen Patnaik inducted Kamala Das and Draupadi Murmu in his BJD-BJP coalition Ministry on 5th March, 2000. But in 2002 he dismissed Kamala Das from his Ministry and after the reshuffle on 6th August 2002 he included Bishnupriya Behera. He suspended Kumudini Patnaik, Member of Parliament from Aska constituency and wife of senior B.J.D. leader and former Finance Minister, Ramkrishna Patnaik on April, 2002 to avert a possible split in the Parliamentary Party. In order to prevent a split in the Parliamentary Party, Bishnu Priya Behera, wife of party M.P. Padmanav Behera were accommodated in the Ministry[7]. In the 2004 election 11 women members were elected. Naveen Patnaik inducted Pramila Mallick, Member of legislative from Binjarpur constituency of Cuttack district, as the Cabinet Minister of Women and Child Development and Smt. Surama Padhy as the Minister of State for Cooperation. The 2009 assembly election saw just six women candidates making it to the State Assembly and none to Lok Sabha. Pramila Mallick was made a Minister in the Naveen Patnaik cabinet as the Minister of Women and Child Development. But after a couple of days she was asked to resign from the state cabinet for her alleged involvement in pulses (*dal*) scam. In the last week of May 2012, while Naveen Patnaik was in

London, his long-time adviser and second power centre in the party, Rajya Sabha member Pyarimohan Mohapatra, along with a couple of his MLA supporters made an attempt to oust him from the chief ministerial *gaddi* in his absence. Naveen Patnaik dismissed Women and Child Development Minister Anjali Behera from the Ministry, because of her support for Pyarimohan Mohapatra.

In 2014 Assembly elections a total of 115 women candidates had participated in the Assembly polls this time, which works out to roughly 8 per cent of the total number of contestants. The ruling BJD, which keeps talking of 'women's empowerment' on every conceivable occasion, had no more than 14 women in its list of candidates for the 147 Assembly constituencies. Still, it was ahead of other parties—the Congress had nominated just eight women candidates and BJP, nine. The representation of Odisha women in the Lok Sabha presents an equally dismal picture. Only two women Rita Tarai from Jaipur and Sakuntala Laguri from Keonjhar (both from BJD) are representing the State in the Lower House this time. Out of the 11 women MLAs, eight are new faces while Sugnana Kumari Deo, Pramila Mallick and Usha Devi of BJD are old timers, and the last two have been ministers in the Naveen Patnaik government.

If we consider the issue of women representation in Odisha since 1936, then the Congress party has had the highest number of women representatives in the Odisha Assembly and the Swatantra Party has had lowest number of women representatives in the Odisha Assembly. A total number of 37 women members were elected on the Congress ticket (Table 5.3). Because it is the only party which has been contesting the Assembly elections since the creation of Odisha as a new province in 1936. But other political parties whether it was the regional or national party contested only for a particular time period and automatically withered away. Therefore, their women representation is less in comparison to Congress party.

The 12th Assembly has given highest number of women representation in Odisha because of the charismatic and embellishing the clean and secular image of Naveen Patnaik who led a regional political party Biju Janata Dal in the state by captivating the regional sentiment of the Odisha people and gave more nomination to women candidates in the electrons. A total number of 14 women candidates were elected in the 2000 assembly elections and the lowest was in 1971 elections. The assembly did not represent any woman candidate but after a bye-election it represented only one candidate. The percentage of women candidates in the 12th assembly elections of 2000 was 9.52 per cent (Table 5.1 and

Table 5.1: Number of Women Legislators with Percentage of Representation (1952-2009)

	1952	1957	1961	1967	1971	1974	1977	1980	1985	1990	1995	2000	2004	2009	2014
Total Assembly Seats	140	140	140	140	140	147	147	147	147	147	147	147	147	147	147
Women Representation	3	5	4	5	1	4	7	5	8	9	10	14	11	6	11
Percentage	2.14	3.57	2.85	3.57	0.71	2.72	4.76	3.40	5.44	6.12	6.80	9.52	7.48	4.08	7.48

Table 5.2: Caste-wise representation of Women Legislators

Year	*Brahmin*	*Kshatriya*	*Karan*	*Khandayat*	*Scheduled Caste*	*Scheduled Tribe*	*Others*	*Total*
1952		3						3
1957		5						5
1961		3		1				4
1967		4		1				5
1971	1							1
1974	1	2		1				4
1977	1	4	1			1		7
1980	1					4		5
1985	1	1			1	5		8
1990	2			5	1	1		9
1995	6	2				2		10
2000	2	3	1	1	3	3	1	14
2004	1	2	2	0	2	4		11
2009		2			3	1		6
2014	2	3	0	0	4	1	1	11
TOTAL	16	31	4	9	10	21	1	103

Chart 5.2). It is the highest percentage so far. Though the story was same between 1952 and 1967 with a little difference. But, there was a remarkable fall in women's representation in 1971 election. Again it went upward till 2000 assembly elections except in the 1980 elections. But since 2000 Assembly elections there is fall of women representation (Chart 5.3). If we make an assessment of all the elections of Odisha the following trends can be found with regard to the women representation in Odisha which are based on the observations of the author.

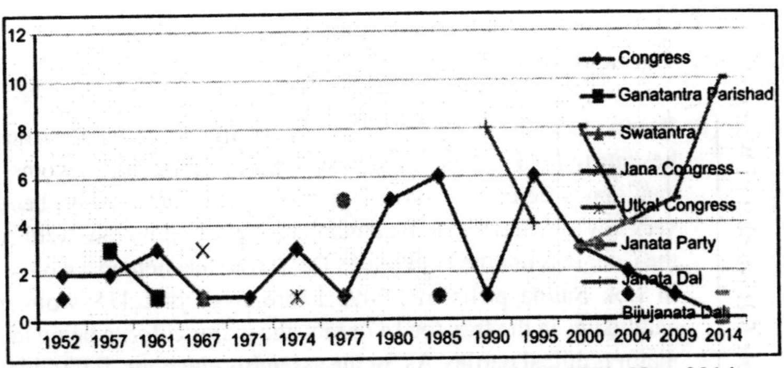

Chart 5.1: Party-wise representation of women from 1951-52 to 2014.

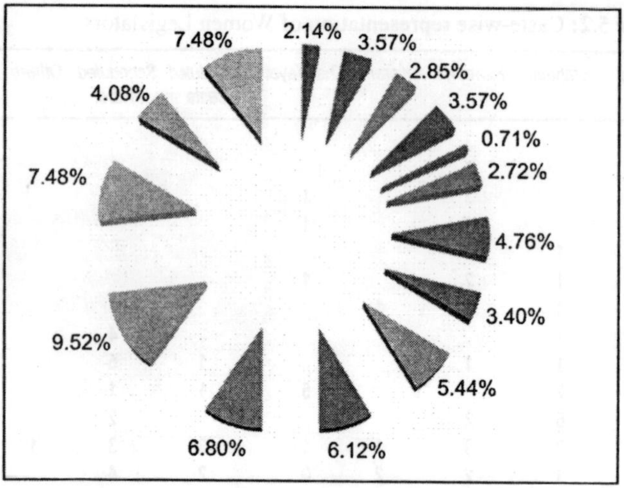

Chart 5.2: Percentage of Women Representation from 1951 to 2014

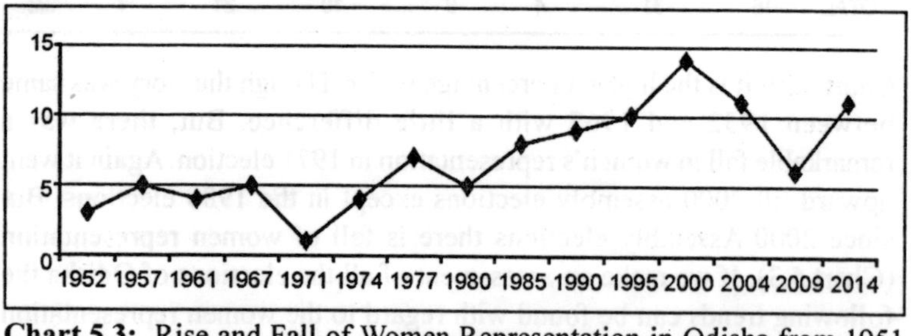

Chart 5.3: Rise and Fall of Women Representation in Odisha from 1951 to 2014

Trends of Women Politics in Odisha

(i) **Parties hesitate to field women candidates:** Almost all parties hesitate to field women candidates. Hence, the number of women candidates fielded by various political parties has always been very low as compared to their numbers in the population. Neither the Congress nor the Biju Janata Dal (BJD) has fielded a woman in Lok Sabha polls of 2009. There were just 118 women candidates in the fray for 147 seats, the major culprits being the major political parties. As for the assembly elections, BJD Chief

Naveen Patnaik, although he claims to be committed to the empowerment of women and tribals, fielded only eight women for the 130 assembly seats the party is contesting. Sonia Gandhi's Congress has not done much better: Only 15 out of its 147 candidates are women. None of the Left parties—CPI, CPI(M) and CPI(ML)—have fielded a woman candidate. Significantly, out of the total 140 women candidates in the assembly elections this time, 37—or roughly one-third—are contesting as Independents. The BJP nominated 14 too. The figure reflects the high level of frustration among women candidates at being denied party nominations. The trend of the 2009 Assembly Election in Odisha was the poor representation of women candidates. This election saw just six women candidates making it to the State Assembly and none to Lok Sabha. If compared to the 2004 polls, the scenario was on the reverse. In 2004, as many as 12 women candidates were elected to the Assembly, the share standing at an abysmal 8.1 per cent of the total. It has dropped to a mere four per cent this time. Similar was the state of affairs of Lok Sabha representation. The 14th Lok Sabha had just one member from Odisha and she was Sangeeta Kumari Singh Deo. But it has been blanked out this time. In fact, most political parties did not give enough representation in terms of nominating women candidates. It is ominous for the cause of women empowerment in Odisha. Talking about the issue does not make any sense if political parties do not practice what they say. Not nominating adequate number of women candidates is an indicator in itself (Chart 5.1).

(ii) **Less Important Portfolios:** Women are for the most part appointed and remain deputy ministers or ministers of state. When women reach the few ministerial positions, they are generally assigned portfolios in the social service sectors of Health, Education, Social Welfare, Women and Child Development etc. (B.B. Jena, 1988).

(iii) **Most parties resorted to tokenism and symbolism:** Another trend of women representation in Orissa reveals that most parties resorted to tokenism and symbolism when it came to representation of women. Women's issues were not taken up by parties in a serious manner nor translated into programmes, policies and legislation nor were they mandated specifically to address issues of women (B.B. Jena, 1988).

Table 5.3: Party-wise Women representation in Odisha since 1952

Party-wise representation of women from first general elections to fourteenth general elections Year	*Congress*	*Ganatantra Parishad*	*Swatantra*	*Jana Congress*	*Utkal Congress*	*Janata Party*	*Janata Dal*	*Biju Janata Dal*	*BJP*	*Others/ Independent*	*Total*
1952	2									1	3
1957	2	3									5
1961	3	1									4
1967	1		1	3							5
1971	1										1
1974	3				1						4
1977	1					5				1	7
1980	5										5
1985	6					1				1	8
1990	1						8				9
1995	6						4				10
2000	3							8	3		14
2004	2							4	4	1	11
2009	1							5			6
2014	0							10	1		11
Total	37	4	1	3	1	6	12	27	8	4	103

(iv) **Women Cells working as ancillary bodies:** Almost all political parties set up a women's cell or wing but they worked as ancillary bodies. Very few women were able to capture seats of power. The number of women in the legislatures remained very small. Very few women reached the position of party president or leader of legislative party.

(v) **Legacy of the Past:** The political mobilization and participation of women has been impressive in the Indian National Movement. They belong to the elitist groups and higher caste groups. It is worth noting that the political mobilization of women and their participation in elections has steadily increased since the first General Elections of 1952. Women like A. Laxmibai, Subhadra Mahtab, Kiran Lekha Mohanty, Sarala Devi, Saraswati Devi joined real politics after the during this period.

(vi) **Belong to the elite and high castes groups:** Women legislators elected from Odisha to State Assembly and Parliament so far, mostly belong to the elite and high castes groups. The Khatriyas (rulers of ex-princely states) have contributed the largest number of women legislators (J.K. Baral). The noticeable supremacy of Kshayatriya women over other women in the field of politics is mainly due to the feudal ruling backdrop and influential temperament. So far 31 Kshayatriya women have been represented. It is imperative to note that, up to 1971 not a single Brahmin woman could be elected as an MLA despite the fact that it is one of the "Dominant Castes" of the state. It was after only in 1972 the Brahmins, Karans and Khandayats entered into politics. The fate of OBC women representatives is also miserable (Table 5.2, and Chart 5.5). It can be said that the Brahmin and Karan women entered in the field of politics is mainly due to their better socio-economic status of family life.

(vii) **Representation through Reservation of seats for SCs and STs:** Up to now there is no reservation for women in the Parliamentary and Assembly elections. But due to the introduction of reservation in representation, some scheduled caste and scheduled tribe women are getting involved in politics where there are no male candidates available. Some of them have got elected as MLAs and MPs as a result of the reservation policy of the government. It is important to note that the election success of scheduled caste or scheduled tribe women is merely symbolic.

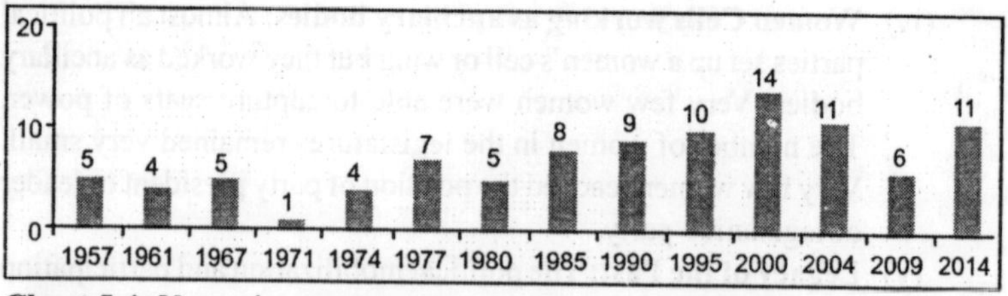

Chart 5.4: Year-wise women representation from 1952-2014

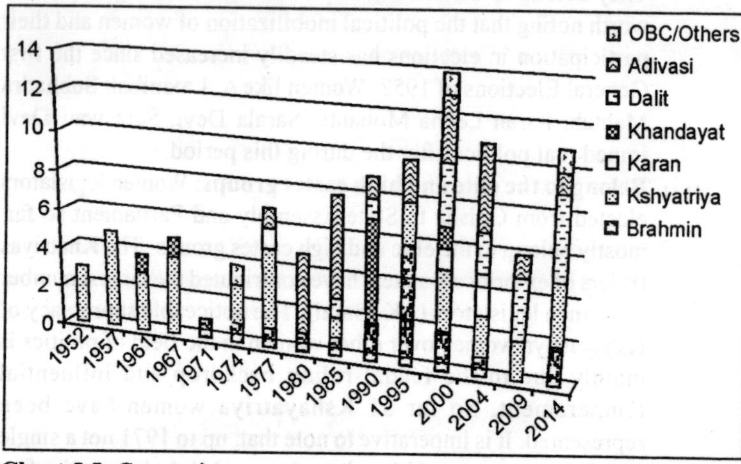

Chart 5.5: Caste-wise representation of Women from 1952-2014

(viii) **Mostly through family dynasties or through male political patronage:** Another trend can be easily noticed that it is the elite and politicized families from which there is a smooth entry for women in politics. Women playing supportive roles to males in the family and emerging from their shadows have also found easy entry.

(ix) **Through family legacy:** Another trend has been the entry of wives and daughters of prominent political figures into politics and positions of power. In other cases wife and daughters of influential leaders have also got party tickets for contesting the election. In Odisha some women legislators like Smt. Hema Gomang, wife of former Chief Minister, Smt. Patta Nayak wife of ex-minister Sri Trinath Nayak and their daughter Anjali Behera, Smt. Ratna Manjari Devi wife of Raja Sisir Kumar Narendra Deb, Shanti Devi wife of Shri Ananta Narayan Singh

Deo, ex-minister of Odisha, Subhadra Mahtab wife of Dr. Harekrushna Mahtab, Usha Devi, wife Shri Trigunateeta Deb of Chikiti, V. Sugnana Kumari Deo wife of Purna Chandra Mardaraj Deo and daughter-in-law of Ramchandra Mardaraj of Khallikote royal family, Smt. Bishnu Priya Behera wife of Shri Padmanav Behera, Jayanti Patnaik, wife of former Chief Minister, J.B. Patnaik, Kumudini Patnaik, wife of former minister Ramkrushna Patnaik, have entered politics through this family legacy.

(x) **Widows' succession—Entry of widows of prominent political figures:** Another trend has been the entry of widows of prominent political figures into politics and positions of power. Some widows of the departed MLAs have also got the party tickets in order to contest in the bye-elections. There is a long list in this regard where widows of the departed MLAs have got the party tickets. Gertzog (1980) (Irwin, New York) calls it "Widows succession," which refers to a female who is elected to her husband's elected office upon his death, has fascinated many Congressional scholars in USA since the first documented case of widows' succession in 1923. With a limited number of women serving in the parliament and state legislatures, Thomas suggests, researchers have tended to focus on women's participation in politics, rather than the reasons why they have entered the "political arena." Nuwer (Nuwer, September 2000) points out that as the data have become available to academia, scholars have been eager to analyze these factors as they influence who attains legislative office.

Bijayalaxmi Pattnaik wife of an Ex-M.L.A. Sri Arun Pattnaik, Mandakini Behera wife of ex-MLA Sri Bhagabat Behera, Smt. Patta Nayak wife of ex-minister Sri Trinath Nayak and their daughter Anjali Behera, Smt. Ratna Manjari Devi wife of Raja Sisir Kumar Narendra Deb, Shanti Devi wife of Shri Ananta Narayan Singh Deo, Usha Devi wife of Shri Trigunateeta Deb of Chikiti, V. Sugnana Kumari Deo wife of Purna Chandra Mardaraj Deo and daughter-in-law of Ramchandra Mardaraj of Khallikote royal family, Mandakini Behera wife of ex MLA Sri Bhagabat Behera have entered politics through widows' succession.

(xi) **No tribal representation outside reservation:** Orissa has 33 seats out of the 147 in the Legislative Assembly reserved for tribals. At the parliament level, five of the total 21 seats are reserved for ST candidates. As per 2001 Census, the Scheduled Tribe (ST) population of the State of Orissa (now Odisha) is 8,145,081. This constitutes 22.1 per cent of the total population of the State and 9.7 per cent of the total tribal population of the country. The state holds 3rd and 11th rank among the States/ UTs in terms of ST population and the proportion of ST population to total population of the State respectively. Historically, political parties have never fielded more than a significant number of women in these seats. But when women candidates have been given a chance, they have won—not just once, but twice and thrice—proving that they too can master the 'winability factor'. Saraswati Hembram, starting as a Sarpanch (village council head) and went on to represent the Congress Party from Kuliana in Mayurbhanj for three terms in the state assembly from 1980 to 2000. She was also the first tribal woman to be given ministerial office. Frida Topno, a gazetted state government officer, won the Lok Sabha seat in 1991 and again in 1996 from Sundargarh district. Sushila Tiriya, went to the Rajya Sabha twice (in 1994 and 2006) from Mayurbhanj and once to the Lok Sabha. Interestingly, Fida and Sushila, both graduates, are deeply committed to social work and have chosen to remain single. Two high profile women from tribal communities contested elections from Odisha in 2009 (LS and assembly elections in the state were held simultaneously in two phases on April 16 and 23) were Draupadi Murmu and Hema Gamang. Draupadi, a Santhal and a graduate, is a two-time Bharatiya Janata Party (BJP) MLA from Rairakhol, Mayurbhanj. In 2009 she contested the Lok Sabha seat from Mayurbhanj. She started her career as part of the government clerical staff, and went on to become a minister.

Hema Gamang, from the Saura tribe of Rayagada, was the youngest entrant in this lot. She was only 38 when she entered the Lok Sabha in 1999 from Koraput district on a Congress ticket. Although there were local politicians in her family, it was her husband, Giridhar Gamang, who was instrumental in opening the portals to mainstream politics to her. He was the Odisha Chief Minister at that time and had won in six consecutive Lok Sabha elections. He needed Hema to keep his Lok Sabha seat safe, while he dominated state politics. In 2004, she fought a furious and very public battle with her husband to retain her Koraput Lok Sabha seat, which her husband wanted back. The Congress sided with Giridhar and Hema had to settle for the Gunupur assembly seat in Rayagada. History repeated itself in 2009 as well. She gave up the Gunupur constituency, which she had nurtured because both her brother and son wanted to contest from there. Therefore, she fought from the Laxmipur assembly constituency in Rayagada.

What does it take for a woman from a tribal community to get a foothold in national politics? "Family political background, personal qualities, exposure to the world outside one's own community, education and adequate funds—in that order." In sharp contrast to Hema, Draupadi Murmu does not come from a political background. After eight years as a legislator and after heading two ministries, she has no house to her name, only a modest bank balance and some land. Although she was in the right place at the right time and had access to politics, she did not get her the Lok Sabha ticket in 2004, which she had badly desired. The selection committee of Jharkhand Mukti Morcha doubted whether a woman would be able to fight the election. This was the opinion of Jharkhand Mukti Morcha's strongman, Sudam Marandi. So Draupadi's male colleague, Bhagirathi Majhi, was fielded instead. He lost and this may have forced the party to do a re-think: Draupadi was pitted against Marandi in the last election. Women participate more in the election process in every way. But, they are given a raw deal at the time of ticket selection. Even the nomination of Padma Shri Tulasi Munda, to the Rajya Sabha in 2006, was blocked by the Adivasi Mahasabha comprising several tribal organisations. It was a surprising case of tribals pitting themselves against other tribals, but it reinforced the fact that when it comes to political power sharing, the deeply entrenched G-Factor, or gender factor, kicks in. If the status of women in these neglected tribal communities is to change for the better, political parties across the board in tribal-dominated states like Odisha will have to do a serious re-think about their ticket distribution strategies.

(xii) **Poor Representation in Parliament (Union Legislature):** The representation of Odia women in the Parliament election is very poor. It is pertinent to note that till 1980 not a single women from Odisha was elected to the Lok Sabha. It was only 1980

Smt. Jayanti Patnaik, wife of former Chief Minister; J.B. Patnaik was elected to the Lok Sabha. Since 1980 only ten women so far have been elected to the Lok Sabha and since 1952 ten women have been elected to the Rajya Sabha (Tables 5.1 and 5.2). Most women representatives who have entered into politics are highly educated with a good social and economic background. The Congress nominee for Cuttack Lok Sabha seat, Jayanti Patnaik, has been elected to Parliament four times—thrice to Lok Sabha and once to Rajya Sabha. She also headed the All India Mahila Congress once. The BJP candidate from Bolangir, Sangeeta Singhdeo fought for her third consecutive terms in Lok Sabha, but she lost the election in 2009. Of course, Mrs. Patnaik and Mrs. Singhdeo had the backing of their husbands in their political journeys. While Mrs. Patnaik is the wife of former chief minister and current PCC chief J.B. Patnaik, Mrs. Singhdeo is the better half of senior BJP leader, K.B. Singhdeo, who was the state industries minister.

(xiii) **Frequency is very low: known faces are elected more times:** The elitist nature of women politics in Odisha is further evident from Table 5.12, which indicates that some women leaders have been elected more than once to the Legislative Assembly. It is because of the factors like their own personality, socio-economic factors; education; family background etc. counts more. The total number of women MLAs elected to the Legislative Assembly between 1936 and 2014 was 64. Among them 44 women MLAs were elected for one time, 11women MLAs were elected twice, 5 women MLAs were elected thrice, 3 women MLAs were elected four times, 1 women MLAs was elected for seven times and 1 women MLAs was elected for 10 times. Among them V. Sugyan Kumari Devi had been elected for 10 times and this is the highest number of frequency in Odisha Legislative Assembly in terms of winning the election and representing the state legislature by a woman. As Mrs. V. Sugyan Kumari Devi has no family burdens and she is the only existing members of the royal family of erstwhile Royal family of Khallikote and the traditional loyalty of the people towards their ex-ruler is more responsible for electing her to the State Legislature for several times. Next to her Nandini Satpathy had won 7 times. Satpathy had shot into national prominence in the seventies when she served as a close aide of former Prime

Minister Indira Gandhi. Known as "The Iron Lady of Orissa", she was Orissa CM for about three years in two spells—from 1972 to 1973 and 1974 to 1976. Satpathy was born to an illustrious family in 1931 at Christian street, Cuttack. Her father Padmabhusan Kalindi Charan Panigrahi was a renowned Oriya litterateur. Her uncle Bhagabati Charan Panigrahi was a leading Left leader, poet and founder-member of CPI in Orissa. Satpathy demonstrated her leadership abilities quite early and made a mark in student politics. She took the plunge into mainstream politics and became a Rajya Sabha member from 1962 to 1972. She served as a Union Minister from 1966 to 1972 and was an All India Congress Committee member in 1972. She was elected to Orissa House as a Congress candidate from Cuttack city in 1972 and took over as CM.

Conclusion

Women empowerment in a general sense, it refers to empowering women to be self-dependent by providing them access to all the freedoms and opportunities, which they were denied in the past only because of their being women. In a specific sense, women empowerment refers to enhancing their position in the power structure of the society. The word women empowerment essentially means that the women have the power or capacity to regulate their day-to-day lives in the social, political and economic terms—a power which enables them to move from the periphery to the centre stage (Bhuiyan, 2006).

The Constitution of India not only grants equality to women but also empowers the state to adopt measures, a position; indiscrimination in favour of women. Within the framework of democratic polity, our laws, developmental policies, plans and programmes are aimed at women's advancement in different spheres. India has also ratified various international conventions to secure rights of women. Women of India are now uplifted and emancipated and granted equal status with men in all walks of life—political, social, domestic and educational. Their voice is now as forceful and important as that of men. They are becoming equal partners in making or dismissing of a government (Bhuiyan, 2006).

But Women Empowerment is still an illusion of reality. Notwithstanding the remarkable changes in the position of women in free India, there is still a great divergence between the constitutional position and stark reality of deprivation and degradation. There still exists a wide gulf between the goals enunciated in the Constitution, legislations, policies, plans, programmes and related mechanisms on the one hand and the situational reality on the status of women in India, on the other.

There is a strong relationship between access to economic resources and participation in the political sphere. As such, they did not have their own resources to enter or participate in the political process. One major finding was that education and household income of women leaders have significant positive relationship with their political status, modernisation and role performance. The lack of access to economic resources results in low representation of women as elected members at all levels of governance. Similarly, lack of access to information, results in women members not being taken seriously. The most effective way to provide women with information is through training and capacity building.

Restricting women's participation in trade unions and cooperative movements has resulted in denying women the opportunity to gain similar experience like men, which enables them to participate in mainstream political activities. The cultural norms operate both as a restriction on a woman's mobility as well as an impediment for her participation in the public sphere. These cultural norms are perpetuated and sustained by powerful institutions of family, caste and religion.

Women in the family are viewed as liabilities because of which gender-based discrimination in all dimensions of their lives prevails. This is reflected in the alarming proportions of violence against women within the family—female foeticide, infanticide, malnourishment, school dropouts, neglect and deprivation through limited access to resources, dowry violence and torture, etc. Women having a new born baby in the family do not have the support system that can free them to participate in the political activities outside the home. Younger women and unmarried women have more restrictions placed on their participation because of the control exercised on their sexuality.

Women receive minimal support from their families. The nature of this support tends to be in the form of encouragement to run for elections but rarely does it extend to helping them fulfil their responsibilities as elected representatives by taking the burden of domestic work off them. Usually women elected officials get help from their husbands in the form of their initial contacts and encouragement to join politics. But in some cases resistance from in-laws proves to be another major detriment for women participating in political activities. Sometimes, support from in-laws is purely for the women getting elected but not to carry out her duties. Even if there is family support if the community does not accept the women they are faced with difficulties. Support of the community is as important as that of thc family and the two needs to go together, and this support ideally should be there from the beginning. Patriarchal values relegate women to the home. By the very nature of this value system, any woman bold enough to come out in the open and into politics is viewed with suspicion. It is natural that she is particularly targeted for slander and character assassination.

Women typically are forced to play a triple role when they enter politics, namely they have to work at home, in their jobs and in the political institutions. Since, it is hard for a woman to sustain this triple burden, it can pose as a barrier to her political work or her political work can interfere with her work at home or in her vocation. There are no mechanisms to reduce the burden of women in fulfilling their domestic responsibilities.

Caste has played an instrumental role in raising issues related to the more marginalised among women. In a highly hierarchical society, women belonging to the lower castes have lesser access to public fora, which is compounded by their gender. This exclusion makes it difficult for these women to represent and articulate the voices of their constituencies and their demands are often overlooked or subsumed by the dominant sections of the society. Though higher castes are associated with higher positions with more access to economic resources, women in this category are subjected to more social controls in accessing these resources. Lower castes on the other hand, are economically weak, have to struggle for their livelihood, and therefore, cannot afford to give up their daily wage to attend meetings. Neither are they able to easily meet the demands of the community.

Literacy on the one hand is linked to women's socio-economic status and on the other, her status as a woman has an independent and equally strong implication for her access to this realm. The world's largest numbers of illiterate women are in India. Money and muscle power are used to threaten opponents and the voters; and impose their decisions on the electorate and to raise the kinds of funds required to get into and stay in power. Violating women's dignity is an integral part of politics instilling fear in women, thereby restraining their entry into politics. In addition corruption is also institutionalized systematically. Women who have entered the political process are faced with a lot of resistance. There are many instances where they have been subjected to physical violence, threats and intimidation. This has especially occurred when elected women representatives aspired to be articulate, assertive and effective in discharging their responsibilities.

Women's decision-making is prevented due to party interference. Political parties do not want to transfer control to women and are reluctant to invest in women as candidates fearing that they do not have the capacity to draw votes, and finally, they do not see women as having financial credibility to compete with male contestants. In such circumstances, women who do occupy positions in politics, either through support from political parties or through reservation, do not find the space to participate fully without interference.

It is probably most useful to look at challenges by sphere, notably socio-cultural, economic and political. Compulsory gender quotas to be applied in the elections should be legalized. Women's branches of political parties should be granted an autonomous status in order to protect them from being kept under tutelage by the party administration. The political parties should undertake necessary alterations in their administrative system in order to facilitate women's participation and representation in the decision-making bodies and executive boards of the party. Women's branches should be organized in the way that endows their members with necessary political skills and experience. The nomination process of candidates in the political parties should be carried out in a non-arbitrary and transparent manner. The establishment of equality committees, which would monitor the observation of the principle of gender equality in political parties, should be encouraged.

For true equality to become a reality for women, the sharing of power on equal terms with men is essential. The government has acknowledged the need to increase the number of women in decision-making processes at all levels, as early as in 1976. As a first step to facilitate women's participation in politics, in 1993, it introduced 33 per cent reservation for women in institutions of local governance through the 73rd and 74th Constitutional Amendments. While the government has succeeded in facilitating women's participation by providing for reservation at the lower levels of governance, it has failed to do so in passing the reservation Bill for women in the higher echelons of political institutions, i.e. in the State Assemblies and the Parliament.

The government has attempted to introduce reservation for women at the legislature and parliament levels on three occasions in the years 1996, 1999 and 2000, which have lapsed. Further, women, being in insignificant numbers, are often pressurised to align with men along their caste, class, religion and ethnic identities rather than on the basis of gender. This has resulted in dividing women on the one hand from centre-staging gender issues and concerns and on the other their solidarity.

List 1: Women M.Ps. (Lok Sabha) from Odisha (Women representation from 1st Lok Sabha to 6th Lok Sabha was Nil)

7th Lok Sabha 1980 Election

Name	*Name of Constituency*	*Party Affiliation*
1. Smt. Jayanti Patnaik	Cuttack	Congress

8th Lok Sabha 1984 Election

	Name	*Name of Constituency*	*Party Affiliation*
1.	Smt. Jayanti Patnaik	Cuttack	Congress

10th Lok Sabha 1991 Election

	Name	*Name of Constituency*	*Party Affiliation*
1.	Frida Topno	Sundargarh	Congress

11th Lok Sabha 1996 Election

	Name	*Name of Constituency*	*Party Affiliation*
1.	Susila Tiriya	Mayurbhanj	Congress
2.	Frida Topno	Sundargarh	Congress

12th Lok Sabha 1998 Election

Name	*Name of Constituency*	*Party Affiliation*
1. Smt. Jayanti Patnaik	Brahmapur	Congress
2. Sangita Kumari Singhdeo	Balangir	BJP

13th Lok Sabha 1999 Elections

Name	*Name of Constituency*	*Party Affiliation*
1. Kumudini Patnaik	Aska	Biju Janata Dal
2. Sangita Kumari Singh Deo	Balangir	BJP

14th Lok Sabha 2004 Elections

Name	*Name of Constituency*	*Party Affiliation*
1. Sangita Kumari Singh Deo	Balangir	BJP

- *No women candidate was elected to Lok Sabha in 2009 election*

15th Lok Sabha 2014

1. Sakuntala Laguri, Keonjhar—BJD
2. Rita Tarai, Jajpur—BJD

List 2: Women Members of Rajya Sabha from Odisha 1952-2014

Name	*Term*	*Date of Election*
1. Sailabala Das	1952-54	31-3-1952
2. Nandini Satpathy	1962-68	19-3-1962
3. Nandini Satpathy	1968-71	28-3-1968
4. Saraswti Pradhan	1972-78	31-3-1972
5. Susila Tiriya	1996-92	21-6-1986
6. Mira Das	1990-96	21-3-1990
7. Illa Panda	1992-98	25-6-1992
8. Pramila Bahidar	2002-08	27-3-2002
9. Susree Devi	2002-08	27-3-2002
10. Renubala Pradhan	2008-2014	14-4-2008
11. Sarojini Hembram	2-4-2014 to 2-4-2020	

Notes

1. A. Lakshmi Bai was sister of former President of India Dr. V.V. Giri; Deputy Speaker of Orissa Legislative Assembly 29.5.1946–20.2.1952.

She represented the Berhampur Town (W) assembly constituency as a Congress candidate from 1937-1946 in 1st Pre-Independent Assembly and in the 2nd Pre-Independent from 1946 to 1952. She expired on 27-1-1986.

2. Odisha became a separate state in 1936 and elections were held on the basis of limited franchise till independence. The provincial head was known as Prime Minister of Odisha. It was only in 1952 that the members of Odisha Legislative Assembly were elected on the basis of Universal Franchise under the new Constitution of India and the same Prime Minister came to known as the Chief Minister.
3. Swatantra-Jana Congress coalition ministry was formed in 1967. That ministry did not include any woman in ministry though 4 women members were elected to Odisha Assembly from both the parties.
4. Late Nandini Satpathy, daughter of famous writer Padmabhusan Kalindi Charan Panigrahi. She was the Member, Rajya Sabha as Congress Candidate, 1962-1968, Member, Rajya Sabha as Congress candidate, 1968-1972, Member, Working Committee of A.I.C.C., Chairperson, State Planning Board Odisha, 1989-1990, Chairperson, State Planning Board, Orissa in March, 1995. She was the Chief Minister of Odisha from 1971 to 1976.
5. Smt. V. Sugnana Kumari Deo wife of Late Purna Chandra Mardaraj Deo of Khalikote royal family in Ganjam district represented the Odisha Assembly in 3rd (1961-1967), 6th (1974-1977), 7th (1977-1980), 9th (1985-1990), 10th (1990-1995), 11th (1995-2000), 12th (2000-2004), 13th (2004-2009), 14th (2009-2014). She has the highest record of representation in the Odisha Assembly.
6. Janaki Ballav Patnaik resigned on the ground of moral responsibilities for the spate of violent incidents, especially gruesome attacks on Christians by the communal forces in the State on 7th February, 1999. J.B. Patnaik was replaced by Giridhara Gomango to save the party's image. during October 1999 the coastal areas of the State were flattened by a killer Super cyclone. Giridhar Gomango's government proved total inefficiency in providing relief. He was replaced by Hemananda Biswal. Both Gomango and Biswal accommodated all the women ministers of J. B. Patnaik.
7. Naveen Patnaik reshuffled his ministry on August 7, 2002 and suspended three MPs of the party for anti-party activities. The suspensions of Jagannath Mallick, Prabhat Kumar Samantray and Kumudini Patnaik, who were representing Jajpur, Kendrapada and Aska constituencies respectively, was aimed at pre-empting any move by the dissident MPs to split the 10 member BJD group in Lok Sabha. The three MPs tried to win one more MP to its fold so that the suspended MPs can avoid disqualification under the Anti-defection Act in case of split. In order to prevent a formal split in the parliamentary party, Bishnu Priya Behera, wife of party MP Padmanabha Behera were accommodated in the Ministry.

References

Ashalata Parija, S.B. (1988). Women Politcs in Odisha. In B.B. Jena and J.K. Baral, *Government and Politcs in Odisha* (pp. 402-4013). Lucknow: Print House.

B.B. Jena, J.B. (1988). Government and Politcs in Orissa,. In J.B. B.B. Jena, *Government and Politcs in Orissa*, (p. 405). Lucknow: Print House.

Bhuyan, D. (2006). Empowerment of Indian Women: A challange of 21st Century. *Odisha Review*, 61.

Ghosh, S. (1979). *Odisha in Turmoil*. Bhubaneswar: Bookland International.

Harihara Das, B.C. (1990). Role Perception of Women Participants in the Electoral Politcs of Orissa. In B.C. Harihara Das, *Federal and State Politics in India* (pp. 223-248). New Delhli: Discovery Publishing House.

Irwin, G. (New York). The Matrimonial Connections: The Nomination of Congressmen Widows for the House of Representatives. *Journal of Politics*, Vol. 42, Issue 3, pp. 820-833.

Nuwer, D.S. (September 2000). Southern Women Legislators and Partriarchy in the South. *South Eastern Political Review*, Vol. 28, Issue 3, New York.

Orissa Reference Annual (2004). Bhubaneswar, Odisha: Department of Information and Public Relations.

Rout, B. (2006). Orissa Legislative Assembly: An Analytical Study. In B. Rout, *The State Government and Administration* (p. 23). Bhubaneswar: Panchashila.

6

Transnational Terrorism in the Discourse of Globalisation

A Perspective

Midatala Rani

> *The world is a dangerous place to live, not because of the people who are evil, but because of the people who don't do anything about it.*
> —Albert Einstein

All social movements started with positivism. When movements fail to achieve the goals and when state and non-state actors fail to achieve their objectives through conventional, legal, constitutional means, violence is practised and imposed on the people. Such violence is branded as terrorism. There is no universally accepted definition on terrorism either at academic or policy levels. United Nations has made number of attempts after 9/11 attack on USA to define terrorism satisfactorily. But it has remained as a futile exercise. The major difficulty is one person's terrorist is another person's freedom fighter. Until recently liberation movements and their leaders were branded as terrorist organisations and their leaders spearheading the movement as terrorists. It may be recalled here that the African National Congress was to the United States a terrorist organisation till early 1990s and Nelson Mandela was in a 'special list' of those associated with terrorist organisations till four years ago. Although, the historical roots of terrorism can be traced to the beginning of man, contemporary terrorism poses many challenges to mankind which have never been experienced before and has become a permanent phenomenon of the present world society.

As a form of political action terrorism is totally unacceptable. By passing history it cannot be treated as a 'generic' phenomenon. Terrorism as a strategy is rooted in political discontent and is used in the service of many different beliefs and doctrines that seek to legitimize and sustain violence. Ideologies associated with nationalism, revolution, religion and defence of *status quo* have all inspired terrorism. There exists numerous typologies of violent terrorist movements such as ethnic, religions, minority, ideological, autonomy, liberation, separatist. In 1960s the character of political terrorism changed when it acquired a transnational character and emerged as a self-sufficient strategy, owing to revolutions in communications and modern urban civilization. Seen as a new trend in terrorism it remained as a serious problem in 1990s and will continue to confront the nations of the world well into the next century. It is important to note that terrorism is not an ideology by itself. It is a tool employed at specific times by specific actors and for specific political goals. The label terrorist is never a fixed or essential identity and terrorists may choose to abandon its use as a tactic for achieving political aims. Once a terrorist is not always a terrorist. The inability of the UK and US Governments to agree on a common list of prescribed terrorist organisations despite holding similar definitions of terrorism speaks to the inherent subjectivity of applying this label in the real world.

Traditionally terrorism was confined within national borders with specific state centric objectives. But today the new "transnational terrorism" has become a critical component. Transnational terrorism transcends the nation state boundaries both in terms of objectives and operations. Transnational terrorist groups are usually characterised by a universalist ideology enhanced mobility and communication networks, multinational sources of recruitment and funding as well as cross-border operations. Al-Qaeda network is the best example of transnational terrorist group. Other organisations such as Hamas, Hizbollah, LTTE have also displayed transnational features. Almost a decade before the terrorist attack against the United States on 11th September, 2001 and followed by the terrorist attacks in Mumbai on 26th November, 2008, two eminent political scientists Samuel Huntington and Benjamin Barber had predicted about the nature of post-cold war conflict. These predictions have strengthened the present notion that transnational terrorism is a reaction against the forces of globalisation emerging from the inequality between secular, capitalist globalisation and cultural, religious conservatism. Globalisation which is a process rather than an outcome emerged in 1990s following the fall of communism, consolidation of the capitalism and coinciding with internet revolution and global communication network. Modern globalisation has taken place in three forms including economic, cultural and political. All of them have their own features and effects. It is believed that globalisation and brutalization of violence with emphasis on four 'A's (assassination, abduction, assault and arson) have ushered a new "Age of terrorism" with all its frightening ramifications.

In the year 2006, the US State Department has identified three main trends in terrorism. They include, firstly, the emergence of 'micro actors' (US and allied success in isolating Al-Qaeda leadership resulting in its subdued operational role and assuming more of propaganda role). Secondly, sophistication whereby terrorists use advanced technology to their benefit. Lastly, increasing overlapping between terrorist activity and international crime which expose terrorists to law enforcement activities. The modern global terrorists groups even though claim to be explicitly anti-modern and backward looking have four main features—to seek political power and control the state, to see themselves as opposed to modernity, emphasis is placed on the need to regenerate and unify the corrupt society. They believe that they are part of a great war against another.

New global terrorism differs from old terrorism in organisation, use of media and funding methods. The transnational character of terrorist movements has led to a shift from vertical forms of organisation to horizontal networking structures. In the horizontal network there is anonymity, absence of publicly identifiable command structures. Many terrorist groups are a part of family of organisations. All these groups use the new median including television, internet, video cassettes as their transnational network. Some of the groups have their own radio and TV channels. It is true that substantial technological advances have influenced transnational terrorism. Funding to extremist groups are channeled through religious NGOs. Apart from this funding for terrorists are from supporters, wealthy individuals and even through smuggling and kidnapping.

Transnational Terrorism as a Reaction Against Globalisation

One of the paradoxes of globalisation is it engenders terrorism. Globalisation is a critical factor for the growth of transnational terrorism. Even though the current transnational terrorism is believed to have religious inspiration, it needs to be pointed out that transnational terrorism emerges from the inequalities within nations and between nations. Globalisation in different forms including westernization, secularization, democratization, consumerism and the growth of market capitalism signifies destructive attack in traditional conservative societies. Globalisation is viewed in terms of threatening traditional way of life, religion and leading to unfair distribution of income and power. Therefore, the development of dissatisfied communities has proved to be the important means of recruitment and support for transnational terrorists globally.

In the economic field, it was hoped that globalisation would bring in economic prosperity. On the contrary in 1999 United Nations Development Programme (UNDP) Report pointed out that globalisation was partially responsible for an accelerating gap between rich and poor states and between people in global economy. Added to this the wealthiest oil producing countries of the Middle East are confronting internal economic inequalities. Further the neo liberal economic reforms thrust on developing countries through World Bank and International Monetary Fund (IMF) included the dismantling of welfare programmes and removal of safety nets for poor. The *International Herald Tribune* (December, 2001) viewed the terrorist attacks as symbol of bitter polarization between 'haves' and 'have-nots'. As Marvan Bishara (Israeli Arab Commentator) points out that when people feel so inferior militarily and economically they adopt asymmetric means to achieve what they want. Likewise in April 2001 a British economist Robert Wade hinted of a probable threat posed by those whom economic globalisation has left out. He further adds that while the West has been trumpeting the virtues of globalisation the gap between rich and poor has widened.

Cultural globalisation has made images of western life and transmission of western values across the world through the media and internet. Benjamin Barber argues that globalisation is leading to a homogenized 'McWorld' where American popular culture and consumerism is overtaking the globe. Rejecting perceived cultural domination, conservative elements of society revile this as an attack on religious teachings and cultural traditions and are generating movements of resistance and are supporting transnational terrorism.

Terrorism can also be traced to the struggle for power. Political globalisation has extended US supremacy and interests worldwide forming strong alliances with national governments. The need to protect its strategic interests obliges US to extend its military might internationally establishing bases in Middle East to protect the strategic Persian Gulf. This is unacceptable to the extremists who see this land as sacred and hence feel the need to resist by any means. Thus the economic, cultural and political dimensions of globalisation are seen to impinge on Muslim ways of life and evoke violent responses, framed in the idiom of '*jihad*'.

Globalisation and Transnational Terrorism

The relationship between globalisation and transnational terrorism is a paradoxical one. Transnational terrorism is an authentic product of the globalised world and yet in fundamental conflict with it. While it aims to repel US-led globalisation transnational terrorism has harnessed globalisation features in three ways, viz. exploitation of new technologies, global financial networks and reduced barriers to cross-border interactions. Globally connected networks facilitate the recourse to asymmetric attacks and are thus key enablers of transnational terrorism. Modern transnational terrorism is very dangerous as it derives its power from globalisation.

Firstly, globalisation has enabled transnational terrorism through the exploitation of new technologies. The information revolution has speeded up computing, telecommunications and data transference capabilities. The use of internet, mobile phones and satellite telecommunications has increased terrorist related activities and extended the global reach of terrorist groups. The global information age enhanced terrorist planning and coordination of operations, recruitment of members, communication among adherents, attraction of supporters across national borders. Terrorist activities are no longer confined to defined regions but enjoy expanded range and impact of operations. The internet is also used clandestinely for passing encrypted messages in graphic codes. The reliance on advanced telecommunication networks has defined the organisational structures of transnational terrorist groups. Networks have enabled terrorist groups across regions to rely on one another for technology, expertise and resources. Thus the level of inter-connectivity between terrorist groups has increased even between those of different aims or ideologies.

Secondly, integrated global financial networks are a key supporting mechanism for funding the operations of transnational terrorist groups. Integrated financial markets are exploited and adapted by terrorist organisations and "digitization of money" facilitates instantaneous transfer of funds across the borders. Also financial globalisation limits the level of control that governments have over financial matters as huge volume of transactions occurs on daily basis. This makes tracing terrorist funds extremely difficult. The integrated global economy provides transnational terrorist groups the chance to accumulate wealth and ability to redistribute it quickly under garb of anonymity.

Finally, with globalisation physical and commercial barriers have become more permeable to facilitate trade and immigrate movements. Open borders and visa free travel policies have become common place. This allows terrorist organisations to establish their cells easily and operate across borders virtually undetected.

Globalisation as a Weapon Against Terrorism

Even though globalisation has enabled the growth of transnational terrorism the mechanisms of globalisation must be used to counter the globalisation of terror. Transnational terrorism is a global problem. Certain policy initiatives can be made to combat transnational terrorism.

Firstly, counter-terrorism tools between states must be integrated to utilize inter-governmental networks to achieve maximum cooperation.

Secondly, countries cannot tackle the menace of terrorism alone. So a truly integrated and multifaceted approach combining cooperation and coordination in diplomacy, law, finance, economics and law enforcement, intelligence is essential. This inturn will encourage intergovernmental linkages which are themselves products of globalisation.

Thirdly, nation states must brush aside narrow defined national interests and go in for multilateral response against transnational terrorism. This will serve national and international interests.

Fourthly, international laws and institutions must be integrated. Apart from strengthening domestic legal codes in international institutions or terrorist fighting agency should be established to coordinate investigation, intelligence and jurisdiction of transnational terrorist activities. Globalisation must be used as an advantage rather than an obstacle in counter-terrorism.

Lastly, globalisation must promote equitable global economic development. There is a need for sustainable development in poor countries because poor economic conditions create terrorist breeding grounds. Economic development has an important role to play in the fight against terrorism.

Summing Up

Terrorism emerging along with globalisation process is a major challenge to the nation states in contemporary period. One of the paradoxes of globalisation is it engenders terrorism with the wish to protect traditional cultures. Clearly globalisation changed the nature of terrorism and is a key motivator and enabler of transnational terrorism. The 9/11 terror attack has forced the nation states to adopt a new kind of conception and idea of security. It has also brought into focus as to whether safety and risk should be first taken care of instead of security and what kind of discourses and practices are to be found related to the notion of security in the world of the current threat of terrorism.

The discourse on the war on terrorism is slowly beginning to consolidate. It is very important to develop a strategy for countering the growth of terrorist groups based on law and morality rather than war. Perhaps it may never be possible to eliminate terrorist groups but it is possible to reduce their recruiting power and minimise the damage they are able to inflict. Apart from a global agenda for progressive governance, more specific policies are needed to tackle transnational terrorism. First, the strategy to protect civilians against all forms of illegal violence. Second, is to counter the ideology of terrorist groups through grassroots political mobilisation by involving civil society groups. Third is the strategy to counter the sophisticated organisational infrastructure of the terrorist groups. Four factors including education, media, welfare and jobs are part of this strategy to reduce global insecurity.

Just as globalisation facilitates transnational terrorism it can also be used as a weapon against terrorism. Transnational terrorism is inherently global and a clearly unified global response is required. The multifaceted transnational terrorism must be comprehended through other perspectives like history, politics, psychology and religion. A comprehensive approach is to be applied to defeat transnational terrorism. Transnational terrorism and globalisation are although paradoxical are connected with the present international security system. As such they cannot be viewed separately. A wholistic approach instead of nationally autonomous approach is the only preferable solution to rid off global terrorism for a peaceful secure world.

References

Aleksander, Kwasnic Wski (2002), *Stop Terrorism*, Warsaw, Perspekty Press.

Alvin Toeffler (1980), *The Third Wave*, New York, William Marrow and Company.

Andrew Johnston (2001), 'Disparities in Wealth are Seen as Fuel for Terrorism', In *Herald Tribute*, December 19, 2001.

Christopher Coker (2002), 'Globalisatist Terrorism,' Paper presented at a Seminar on "The Prospects for the Canadian Summit" at Tokyo on 10 January, 2002.

David E. Long (1990), *The Anatomy of Terrorism*, New York, Maxwell MacMillan International.

Deepa M. Ollappally (2009), *The Politics of Extremism in South Asia*, ND, Cambridge University Press.

LTA Wee Wci Sheng, *Edward, Globalisation and Transnational Terrorism—Ironies, Interactions and Implications*, www.mindef.gov.sg/imindef/publications/pointer/cdjessay/past/html.

Mary Kaldor, *Terrorism as regressive globalisation*, www.opendemocracy.net/democracy-american-power.

Michael J. Sandel (1996), *Democracy's Discontent*, Cambridge, Harvard Univ. Press.

Ninan Koshy (2010), Current Trends in Terrorism, *SAJOSPS*, Vol. 10, No. 2, January-June.

Paul R. Pillar (1996), *Terrorism and US FP*, Cambridge, Harvard Univ. Press.

Rajit K. Pachnanda (2002), *Terrorism and Response to Terrorist Threat*, ND, UBSPD.

Samuel P. Huntington (1996), *The Clash of Civilization and the Remarking of World Order*, New York, Simon and Schuster.

Trends in Terrorism, US State Dept. Report, April 18, 2006.

7

Gender, Poverty and Globalization in India

Padmalaya Mahapatra and *Niranjan Pani*

Introduction

Globalization has been described as the gradual elimination of economic borders and concomitant increase in international exchange and transnational interaction. It has been identified with economic reform, Structural Adjustment Programmes (SAP), New World Trade order and the opening up of the commercial markets and the global communicatior village. Anthony Giddens in his book *The Edge: Living with Global Capitalism* identifies multiple meaning of Globalization. To it he refers the world-wide communication revolution, for instance (this is not only air travel, but the opening up of worldwide, e-mail, internet). Secondly, he refers to what he terms the 'weightless economy'. By this he means the new 'Knowledge Economy' with financial markets at its leading edge. Financial markets today are stunning in their scope, their instantaneous nature and their enormous turnover.

In the contemporary scenario development issues are intertwined with globalization and structural adjustment in India. With the economic climate altering drastically, a contradictory situation is developing. On the one hand, there is a developed India that has got the benefits of globalization. On the other, there is an undeveloped India which is very backward and remains poor. After 67 years of independence, large scale poverty remains a reality in India. The poor can be defined as those who are deprived of basic human needs. But there are differences on what exactly constitutes these basic needs. Most national governments associate poverty with deprivation of basic needs required for physical survival such as food, nutrition, clothing, shelter, water and education.

India still has the world's largest number of poor people. Out of it about one billion inhabitants an estimated 350-400 million are below the poverty line. Particularly, 75 per cent of them live in rural areas. The main causes of poverty are illiteracy and population growth. To be specific population growth rate is far exceeding economic growth rate of the past 67 years. This is so because protectionist policies were pursued since 1947 to 1991. To add to it, failure of industrialization coupled with infrastructural inadequacy are other causes of poverty in India.

Development

Today, on the one hand, it is seen that the paradoxical co-existence of unprecedented accomplishments in technological and economic spheres. On the other hand, persisting discrimination, deprivation and marginalization of vast populace, particularly women deter development. In the opinion of Nobel laureate Amartya Sen overcoming this is the central part of the exercise of development.

It is clear that development, hitherto conceived primarily as a West-Centric project to modernize the post-colonial societies. It has fallen short of realizing the promised utopia of improved quality of life for all and greater equity. Instead, the dominant model of development has resulted in jobless, poverty, greater economic and gender inequalities and degradation of environment. Globalization driven growth model has multiplied the socio-economic costs of development further. In this context women have been worst sufferers in this process.

Globalization: Challenges and Opportunities

Globalization provides many challenges as well as opportunities. While opportunities have come in some sectors like IT mostly in urban areas, there are challenges in rural areas where agriculture still predominates. India had adopted the New Economic Policy (NEP) in 1991 in the wake of the debt crisis, as an essential part of the structural adjustment policy urged by the IMF and the World Bank. The new economic programmes have not changed the basic structure in Indian society. It has often reinforced preexisting inequalities. Human development in India prior to this was characterized by low levels of attainment and sharp regional and gender disparities. By 1993, it was recognized that India lagged behind many of the Asian Countries in human development indicators such as life expectancy, literacy, school enrolment and medical care (Government of India, 1992). The dominance of rich nations, multi-national corporations and international capital over markets, resources and labour in the developing countries through trade, aid and technology transfer has greatly weakened the capacity of nation states and governments to promote human development and offer protection to the poor people. The process of globalization, particularly the post-cold war economic restructuring in the area of trade and financial liberalization has adversely affected vulnerable social groups such as women. If global opportunities continue to be unevenly distributed, the consequences of the most pressing problem, poverty, would increasingly overflow national frontiers (UNDP, 1995b). The worst hit in this transformation is the informal sector, marked with income disparity and dominated by the poor and underprivileged women. To this women's attitude to Globalization is presented here for a greater positive reception.

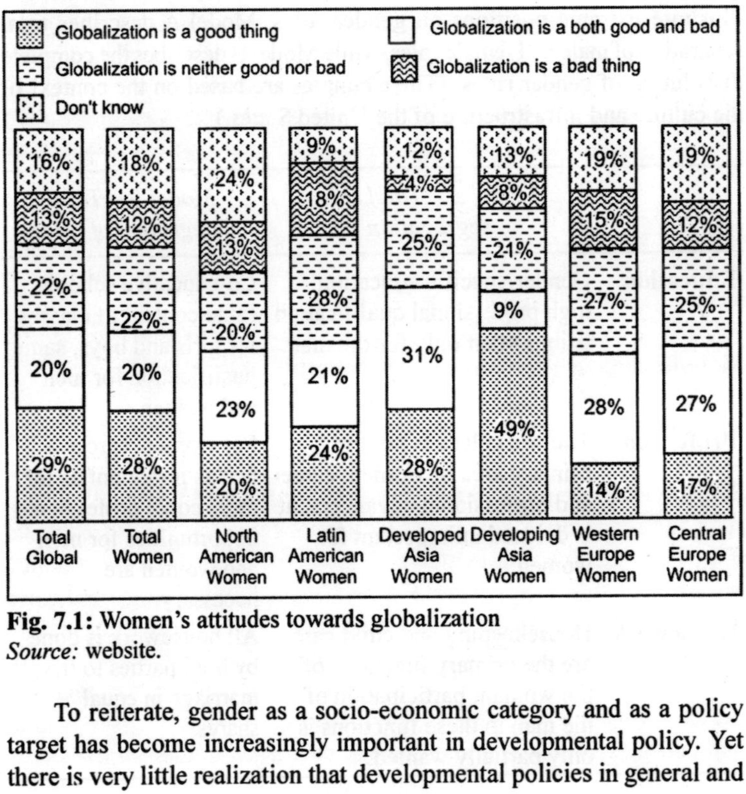

Fig. 7.1: Women's attitudes towards globalization
Source: website.

To reiterate, gender as a socio-economic category and as a policy target has become increasingly important in developmental policy. Yet there is very little realization that developmental policies in general and structural adjustment in particular is not gender neutral. These policies affect various classes as well as men and women differently. It is women who carry the double burden of poverty and discrimination. They are almost invariably paid less than men for the same work. They have less access than men to credit and limited access to productive resources such as irrigation, water, fertilizers and technologies. These women were already exploited now suffer tremendous disadvantages due to globalization. Women disproportionately bear the burden of structural adjustment in the sense that they are more represented in the growing informal sector and they constitute a large chunk of the reserve army of labour that is called in and thrown out when necessary. Structural adjustment is followed by the withdrawal of the state from more and more welfare oriented activities, which leads to more poverty.

To this Parson's Gender Role model is put here for appreciation in the context of US scenario. The Parsons Model was used to contrast and illustrate extreme positions on gender roles. Model A describes total separation of male and female roles, while Model B describes the complete dissolution of gender roles. (The examples are based on the context of the culture and infrastructure of the United States.)

	Model A – Total role segregation	*Model B – Total integration of roles*
Education	Gender-specific education; high professional qualification is important only for the man.	Co-educative schools, same content of classes for girls and boys, same qualification for men and women.
Profession	The workplace is not the primary area of women; career and professional advancement is deemed unimportant for women.	For women, career is just as important as for men; equal professional opportunities for men and women are necessary.
Housework	Housekeeping and child care are the primary functions of the woman; participation of the man in these functions is only partially wanted.	All housework is done by both parties to the marriage in equal shares.

(*Contd.*)

	Model A – Total role segregation	*Model B – Total integration of roles*
Decision-making	In case of conflict, man has the last say, for example in choosing the place to live, choice of school for children, buying decisions.	Neither partner dominates; solutions do not always follow the principle of finding a concerted decision; *status quo* is maintained if disagreement occurs.
Child care and education	Woman takes care of the largest part of these functions; she educates children and cares for them in every way.	Man and woman share these functions equally.

Source: Wikipedia.

Women in Informal Sectors

International Women's Day is March 8. And this year's (2014) theme is "Equality for women is progress for all." Despite there is gender discrimination in many sectors. India has a labour force of over 400 million. Certainly, a large portion of which is women workers. Nearly 90 per cent of this labour force belongs to the unorganized or informal sectors. A large number of women work at home and have to carry a double burden. Noticeably, they are vulnerable to exploitation. These activities are characterized by reliance on indigenous sources, family ownership of enterprises, small-scale operations, labour intensive and adopted technology, skills acquired outside the formal school system, and the unregulated and competitive market (Kalpagam, 1994). True, women is not a homogenous group by way of caste, class or economic activity, deprivation and discrimination. But they are common to all the workers in the informal sectors. They suffer from lack of opportunity to work, low and discriminatory wages and exploitative conditions. These women working in the informal sector have long and inconsistent working hours, fragmentation and atomization of workforce and the absence of any form of workers organization. They lack social security, face occupational health hazards, and do not have access to new technologies, skills and knowledge (*Shramshakti*, 1988). Most of their work is under-valued and classified as subsidiary activities. This is so because women tend to do this work alongside their unpaid domestic task. The employers enjoy tremendous advantages because there are no overhead costs or need to invest in tools or machinery, no trade unions to contend with and partially no legislation defining workers rights or requiring welfare measures, minimum wages or social security benefits. The wages here are much low that every family member is called upon to assist in some aspect of production, resulting in large-scale child labour. Children in general and girls in particular are easy prey as 'complaint workers'. Although there is a high rate of women's participation in the informal sectors, neither the strategy for development nor the specific programmes aiming at betterment of the situation have taken this into consideration. By and large women continue to be invisible.

Indian Women as Farmer

In rural India, the percentage of women who depend on agriculture for their livelihood is as high as 84 per cent. Further, women constitute about 33 per cent of cultivators and about 47 per cent per cent of agricultural labourers (Rao, E. Krishna, 2006). Within the informal sector, agriculture is an area that has seen a lot of changes due to globalization. A large number of adult women in India are in fact agricultural labourers. However, agricultural policy is still dominated by the false view that farm labourers are men and women are only housewives. In fact, agriculture employs 85 per cent of all economically active women. Female participation rates are noticeably higher among scheduled castes, scheduled tribes population of BPL category. There is considerable inter-state variation in the distribution of female agricultural labourers. As a whole about 17 per cent of female agricultural labourers in India are from scheduled tribes. In contrast this figure ranges roughly between 30 and 40 per cent in Odisha, West Bengal, Gujarat and Madhya Pradesh. The increase in the number of agricultural labourers from 12.6 million in 1951 to 15.7 million in 1971, a shift from less than one-third to more than half of the total women workforce, is the greatest indicator of increasing poverty and reduction in the level of employment (Shiva, 1991). More recently, the increased commercialization of agriculture and magnetization of economy have resulted in the transformation of agriculture labour into wage employment. In order to survive, these farmers have no choice but to encroach on forestlands and other fragile environmental areas where the climate and soil do not permit sustainable agriculture. Throughout the country, women's loss of control over production processes has been associated with an increase in the burden of work and increased dependence on wage labour (Mies, 1987). Globalization has increased the number of displaced farmers, as more land is now being used for large-scale commercial export-led production of cash crops.

In this connection it is to be mentioned that according to United Nations Human Development Report only 32.8 per cent of Indian women formally participate in the labour force. This rate of participation has remained same since 2009 statistics. Besides according to another estimate 52-75 per cent of women engaged in agriculture are illiterate. As a matter of fact an education barrier prevents women from participating in more skilled labour sectors. They are not ICT savvy yet. Fact is, to restate, in all activities there is an average gender wage disparity. To put succinctly, women earning is only 70 per cent of men's wage. As well, many women participate in agricultural work as unpaid subsistence labour. 'The lack of employment mobility and education render the majority of women in India vulnerable, as dependents on the growth and stability of the agricultural market' (Satyavathi, C. Tara; Bharadwaj, Ch.; Brahmanand, P.S., 2010). A picture is presented below showing sole women are working in agriculture sector.

Fig. 7.2: Women working in agriculture sector

Cultivators hiring agricultural labourers by the day have for the most part replaced long-term agreements between persons with rights on the land and landless labourers. Instead of whole families working for a landlord, individuals are hired. Agricultural labour is seasonal work with long period of unemployment and underemployment during the year. The landless were certainly oppressed by the earlier ties of dependence on landlords. There was some chance of aid when times were hard. Today operating in the cash nexus, labourers eat only when they can find work. It has been shown that a shift from cultivator to labourer status can only be explained by loss of land for subsistence cultivation and inadequate growth of productive employment opportunities of family structure (Brandtzaeg, 1979). As a majority of these women are in the subsistence sector with no marketable surplus available, there are no gains accruing to them. Since globalization and the reform package place greater emphasis on market forces, the relationship between women and the market assumes greater importance.

In the increasing cash-based economy, the conversion of cash into grains and dry fodder has become an expensive proposition for poor households. In the absence of alternative avenues of employment and other important sources of subsistence, the poor landless are being increasingly marginalized and pauperized (Tanwar, 1999).

It has been pointed out that women as consumers stand to lose under protectionism if the price of domestic goods is higher than those in the world markets, while women as producers stand to gain through the liberalization of trade in agricultural production and exports only if they belong to the category of surplus farmers, but not that of subsistence production (Mehta, 1999). Since most women are in subsistence economy, globalization is deterrent to the poor women and contributes to the feminization of poverty. Today the shifting market considerations have created unforeseen economic hardships for the weaker nations and more so for the poor women who suffer from a double disadvantage of belonging to both the underprivileged class and the underprivileged gender. Modernization and mechanization has brought many paradoxical situations for poor household women.

For an Indian woman farmer, rice is not only a food but also a source of fodder for cattle and straw for thatch. High yielding varieties have increased women's work. The destruction of biological diversity undermines women's diverse contribution to agriculture by eroding biological sources of food, fodder, fertilizer, fuel and fibre (Shiva, 1991). The shift from local varieties and local indigenous crop improvement can also take away women's control over seeds and genetic resources

(Government of India, 1974). Similarly, women's access to credit is also severely restricted. They do not have the collateral (land title and cattle) required for agricultural loans and hence cannot access credit.

With the process of commercialization women's traditional land rights were eroded. Land reform programmes as well as the tendency towards the breakup of communal land holding especially ideas of tribal and customary tenures have led to the transfer of exclusive land rights to males as head of households. The head of the family concept that issued as the basis for land redistribution has historically ignored both the existence of the female headed households and the rights of married women to a joint share in land.

For Indian agriculture multiplication, distribution and availability of good quality seed is crucial to accelerated food production. With the entry of multinational companies in seed production and distribution and the consequent effects of patenting under the WTO regime, providing good quality seeds at affordable prices is becoming a challenge. Women are repositories of knowledge on seed production and the misuse of bio-technology also indicates a decline in the role of women in agriculture (Shiva, 1996).

Government's growth oriented policies have taken away whatever control women had over traditional occupations. With a decline in State's interventionist role, the marketization of the economy has led to an increased burden for women and growing inequalities between regions, men and women and an increased feminization of poverty (Pande, 2000).

It is pertinent to note that there is strong evidence to show that the contemporary process of globalization put emphasis on technical change in agriculture. Further, it is associated with higher capital intensity, greater mechanization of production and post-harvest operations. The development of crop and livestock with varied characteristics geared to the requirement of commercial commodity production. These have been accompanied by changes that women experience in unique ways. These include the loss of knowledge, skills and production contributions.

Women and Households

Today, major economic and social transformations are very common. Besides, the cultural position of men and women in society, are changing household formations. It also changes patterns of obligations rapidly and substantially. The household gains particular significance as the locus of production of human capital in the wake of globalization. The effects of macro policies percolate down to the level of the household. It is within this locus that women's lives are deeply entrenched. As a matter of fact women head 35 per cent of the households below the poverty line. It is a fact which challenges the image of the model poor rural household headed by male. Even where there is a male earner, women's earnings form a major part of poor household's income. Moreover, women contribute a larger share of what they earn to basic family maintenance than men. An increase in women's income translates more directly into better child health and nutrition. It also increases women's personal security and hence the security of children in poverty-stricken households.

Women's role in food production is linked to family welfare. Besides farming, women have also been experts in breeding and feeding of farm animals. In forestry too, women's knowledge is crucial to the use of biomass for feed and fertilizer. Knowledge of the feed value of different fodder species is essential to agriculture related forestry in which women are predominantly active. In low input agriculture fertility is transferred from the forest and farm trees to the field by women's work, either directly or *via* animals.

Migration and Women

It is very well documented that in today's globalized world many women working in urban factories and service industries are migrants from the countryside. Young women are preferred by employers because they are more likely to work with low pay, short-term employment, and repetitive, labour-intensive work. Female migration is described, as economic exploitation and rural-urban income disparities. One can see a similar trend in India. In a study of Odde caste women agricultural labourers from Salem district in Tamil Nadu, it has been shown that agricultural mechanization and inflation has contributed towards the pauperization of female agricultural labourers (Padmavathi and Ramamohan, 1999). Because of modernization and technological transfer, this particular caste group was forced to migrate to the cities in search of employment. Before migrating they sold their lands to the big farmers with whom they were unable to compete because of changes in the economy. Globalization has only compounded the situation by pushing women further down the occupational hierarchy. Women as consumers stand to lose under protectionism if the prices of domestic goods exceed those of the world market, while women as producers gain through liberalization of trade if they belong to the category of surplus farmers (Mehta, 1999). Most women farmers are in subsistence production. Due to these changes, lack of work all year round and slack and drought seasons, they have little choice but to migrate to other areas. Due to migration women are now being trafficked. Eventually, this has emerged as a serious issue.

The guidelines for the New Economic Policy of 1991 for small-scale industrial sectors have legitimized sub-contracting operations of big businesses and foreign firms by permitting them to have ownership stakes. This has affected small-scale industries like weaving, garment making and others in the informal sector. In the wake of these forces women are hardly able to withstand the onslaught of big companies with sophisticated tools and machinery (Sundaram and Tendulkar, 1988). The conditions of the marginalized and dependent wavers are becoming more pathetic. The worst hits are the women. For them weaving has always been a traditional source of livelihood. Multinationals in their efforts to maintain and increase profits have tried to relocate the industry to areas where labour costs are cheap. They have also utilized the most vulnerable sections of the workforce such as immigrants and women. The nature of relocation of the clothing industry in India has not taken the form of factories set up by multinationals. Instead local clothing manufacturing companies have formed links with international buying houses or manufacturing companies. This maintains the dependence of Indian companies on foreign buyers while foreign capital is not utilized (Mitra, 1987). In this process of global reorganization the most important link are these home-based workers, who are sliding down into poverty more and more.

Winding Up

The rhetoric of globalization promises to remove backwardness through a worldwide exchange of information and skills in order to establish a truly cosmopolitan culture. There is an underlying belief that mutual cooperation and concern for social justice is automatically cared for under this system. In actual practice since the global order is based on unequal power relations these concerns are put on hold. Globalization seems to increase choices but only for those with money and access to the market. Women in the informal sector continue to bear the brunt of gender and class inequalities, experience increasing marginalization and pauperization. These growth-oriented policies have taken away whatever control women had over traditional occupations and denied those better avenues of employment. In the shift from welfare development to economic development women have been the worst affected, because a large number of them are in the informal sector.

Yet it cannot be denied that there is an irreversibility of the reform process that has already been initiated. There is a need to make a collective and concentrated effort to accommodate the strategic gender needs. Moreover, in this period of transition social safety nets are created for the women—the vulnerable sections of society. Also there is a need of policy, action and research to protect the interests of especially women, the marginalized sections, in the informal sector, so that they have better access and control of resources.

References

Giddens, Anthony and Will Hutton (eds.) (2000), *On the Edge: Living with Global Capitalism*, London, Jonathan Cape.

Gorringe, Timothy (1999), *Fair Shares: Ethics and Global Economy*, London, Thames and Hudson.

Kalpagam, U. (2011), *Gender and Development in India: Current Issues*, Jaipur, Rawat Publications, p. 64.

Kaushik, Asha (2013), *Development, Globalization and Women*, Jaipur, Rawat Publications.

Mehta, Asha Kapur (1999), "Globalization and the Third World", in Rajmohan Sethi (ed.), *Globalization, Culture and Women's Development*, New Delhi.

Shiva, V. (1988), *Staying Alive: Women, Ecology and Development*, London, Zed Books.

UNDP (1995), *Human Development Report*, New York, Oxford University Press.

World Bank (1991), *Gender and Poverty in India*, a World Bank Country Study, Washington.

Yadav, Ravi Prasad, Kumar Chandradeep, Barsa (Ed.) (2012), *Women Workers in India*, New Delhi, New Century Publications.

8

Agrarian Crises Faced by the Farmers of Vidarbha with Special Reference to Its Cotton Growers

Neelima Deshmukh

Agriculture is a largest economic sector and plays a very significant role in the socio-economic development of our country, which is now in crises. The farmers of various states particularly in Maharashtra are in distress due to multiple factors ending in suicide in large scale. Agriculture farmer's suicides in growing numbers throughout the states of Maharashtra, Karnataka, Andhra Pradesh and Punjab is the most crucial problem and calls for the topmost priority in the agenda of rulers and policy-makers. The suicidal trend set in 1991 by the farmers of Andhra Pradesh has spread to Maharashtra in 2000-01 and has been continued even today. Vidarbha is more suicide prone danger zone of the State. In Vidarbha region alone till the date about 2932 farmers have committed suicide to overcome the miseries due to non-production of crops, bad debts, drought, lack of markets, marketing and irrigation facilities exploitation by private money-lenders and other social and family causes arising out of the combination of various factors, and no one particular reason could be attributed to this saddest event of the mankind in the Indian history.

The Eastern part of Vidarbha comprising Nagpur, Bhandara, Chandarpur, Gondia, Gadchiroli, known as rice belt is less affected area in comparison to the western part including Wardha, Amaravati, Akola, Yeotmal, Washim, Buldhana districts which are referred to as cotton belt where maximum number of cotton growers have committed suicides. Once upon a time cotton was one of the rich natural resource contributing to the state economy to a very great extent. Now the scenario is extremely grim since the 'Cotton' as a backbone of Vidarbha is breaking, imagine the pangs! The challenges of LPG are making this white gold undergo the acid test. The same gold which gave the extreme wealthy status to all of us is now becoming a means to farmers for buying the poison for committing suicides. The farmers are caught in the vicious cycle of tremendous losses of the crop leading to hunger deaths followed by their inabilities to carry on family obligation ultimately leading to suicide. The same insecticide which once upon a time was a tonic for the healthy crop has now turned to be deadly poison releasing the poor farmer from this devastating situation. Till now about 8410 cotton growers of Vidarbha has committed suicide within the period of last 3 years. Hence, this attempt to study the various aspects of crises, on the cotton growers of this region. Though disheartening the figures shows the trend of suicide comparatively more prevalent in the cotton belt of Vidarbha which constrains us to probe into the issue from this particular aspect. All the top political leaders including President, Prime Minister, Chief Ministers, administrators, social workers, researchers, academicians, media have shown their concern for the tragedy through their visits, relief packages, focusing this problem before the world but it did not prove beyond lip sympathy as there are no visible results as yet and the suicides are continued even to this date when I started writing this paper for it's presentation. There has been suicides in a day, every three and half hour one farmer is ending his life.

II. Divisionwise Number of farmers Committing Suicide in Vidarbha Region 2011

(Six out of 35 Districts of Maharashtra account for 76 per cent Suicides)

Amraoti Division	*2034*	*72%*
Yeotmal		28%
Amraoti		16%
Buldhana		10%
Akola		8%
Washim		7%
Aurangabad Division	321	11%
Nagpur Division	251	9%
Nashik Division	174	6%
Pune Division	62	2%

During the period of 2001-2011 Amravati division comprising six districts has suffered from highest number of suicides. Till June 3, 2012 total number 8410 farmers committed suicides out of which only 2843 were considered eligible for the relief from PM package. In 2006 the

Table 8.1: Farmer's Suicides: Big 5 States *vis-à-vis* all-India

Year	*Maharashtra*	*Andhra Pradesh*	*Karnataka*	*Madhya Pradesh & Chhatisgarh**	*Farm suicides In Big 5 states yearly total*	*Farm suicides All-India yearly total*	*All suicides in India yearly total*	*Big 5 as % of all farm suicides*	*Big 5 as % of all suicides*
1997	1917	1097	1832	2390	7236	13622	95829	53.1	7.6
1998	2409	1813	1883	2278	8383	16015	104713	52.3	8.0
1999	2423	1974	2379	2654	9430	16082	110587	58.6	8.5
2000	3022	1525	2630	2660	9837	16603	108593	59.2	9.1
2001	3536	1509	2505	2824	10374	16415	108506	63.2	9.6
2002	3695	1896	2340	2578	10509	17971	110417	58.5	9.5
Totals 1997-2002	**17002**	**9814**	**13569**	**15384**	**55769**	**96708**	**638645**	**57.5**	**8.7**
2003	3836	1800	2678	2511	10825	17164	110851	63.1	**9.8**
2004	4147	2666	1963	3033	11809	18241	113697	64.7	**10.4**
2005	3926	2490	1883	2660	10959	17131	113914	64.0	**9.6**
2006	4453	2607	1720	2858	11638	17060	118112	68.2	**9.9**
2007	4238	1797	2135	2856	11026	16632	122637	66.3	**9.0**
2008	3802	2105	1737	3152	10797	16196	125017	66.7	**8.6**
Totals 2003-2008	**24402**	**13465**	**12116**	**17070**	**67054**	**102424**	**704228**	**65.5**	**9.6**
Totals 1997-2008	**41404**	**23279**	**25685**	**32454**	**122823**	**199132**	**1342873**	**61.5**	**9.1**

Source: www, India together.org. 3rd November, 2011.

Farmer's Suicides in Maharashtra 1997-2008			
1997-1999	*1999-2002*	*2003-2005*	*2006-2008*
1917	3022	3836	4453
2409	3536	4147	4238
2423	3695	3926	3802
6749	10253	11909	12493

Farmers Suicide in Vidarbha (2001 to Sep. 2011)		
Sr. No.	*Year*	*No. of farmers committing suicide in Vidarbha region*
1.	2001	52
2.	2002	104
3.	2003	148
4.	2004	447
5.	2005	445
6.	2006	1448
7.	2007	1246
8.	2008	1252
9.	2009	1054
10.	2010	706
11.	Sep. 2011	903

Source: *Lokmat Marathi, The Hitavada, Times of India, Indian Express, Sakal Marathi* (2002 to 2012).

Government has started a survey of farmers which shows 17.64 lakh farmers including 3.00 lakh young females in very crucial phase (*Source*: *Daily, Lokmat Samachar,* Nagpur dated 3/6/2012 p. 6). In 2010 all over state 15,916 suicide cases were recorded out of which 3141 are farmers (*Source:* National Crime Bureau). On account of relief from CM, PM Package Agriculture coordination project in the division the number of suicide cases in the district have been reduced, but did not stop fully.

III. Causes of Suicide by Farmers

In Vidarbha Yeotmal, Washim, Wardha, Buldhana, Akola, Amaravati districts show high incidences of farmer's suicide during last five years. Print media brought it to the public notice repeated incidences whereas the government is blamed for giving incorrect figures misguiding the public at large on the basis of data gathered from various sources. The main causes identified by various surveys media reports are as follows:

1. Indebtedness: 93 per cent

Table 8.2: Districtwise Suicides in Vidarbha (2001 to September 2011)

Districts	*2001*	*2002*	*2003*	*2004*	*2005*	*2006*	*2007*	*2008*	*2009*	*2010*	*2011*
Amaravati	11	20	40	101	102	269	264	263	122	185	12
Akola	6	7	21	46	43	174	125	165	136	114	102
Yeotmal	17	38	52	142	167	360	359	311	325	175	12
Buldhana	8	9	14	85	81	306	193	195	54	66	7
Washim	7	6	6	44	26	185	177	125	66	76	11
Wardha	3	24	14	29	26	154	128	88	35	39	6
Bhandara	–	–	3	7	12	50	50	62	30	31	27
Nagpur	5	8	9	15	19	41	39	68	36	29	9
	57	112	159	469	476	1539	1335	1277	804	715	186

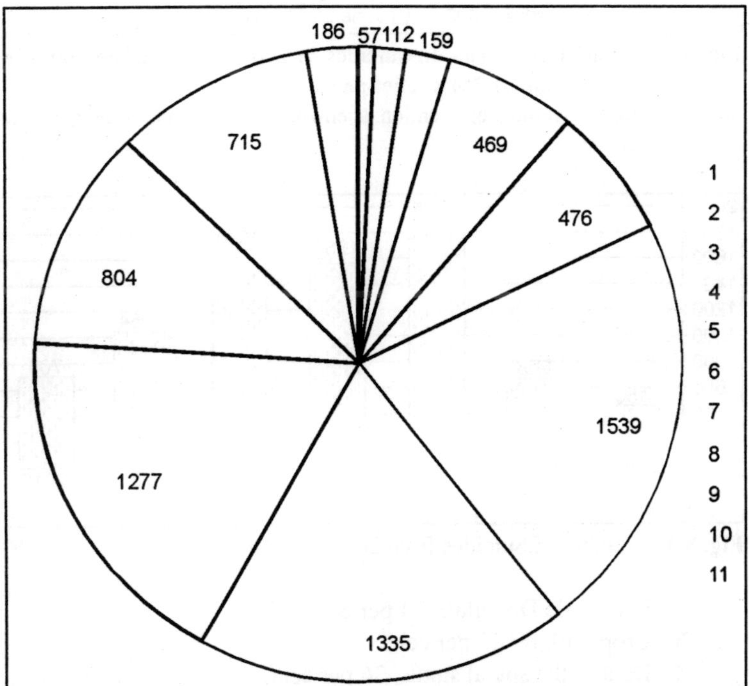

Fig. 8.1: Year-wise Suicides, 2001 to September 2011

Source: *Lokmat Marathi, The Hitavada, Times of India, Indian Express, Sakal Marathi* (2001 to 2012).

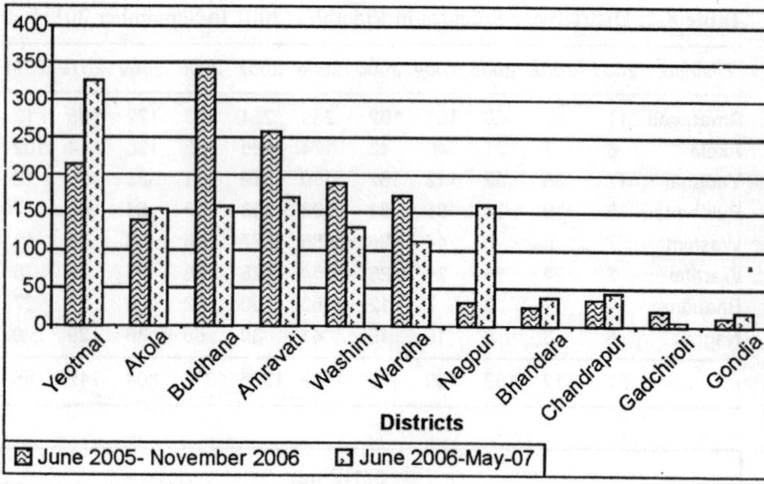

Fig. 8.2: District-wise data on suicides in 2005-2007 (Before and after declaration of PM's relief package)

Source: http:://covering deprivention.acjenwline.org./vidarbha sayantami news suicide

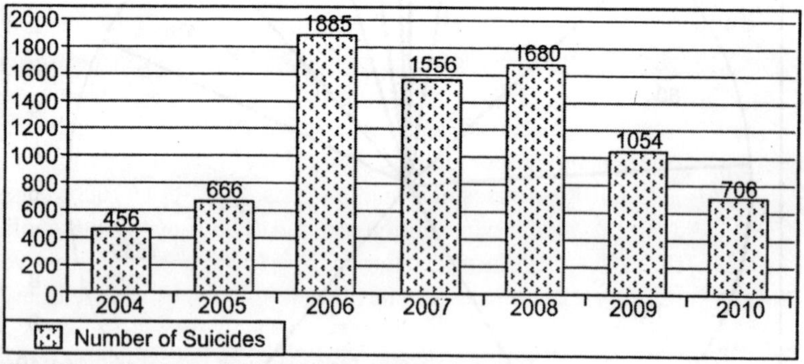

Fig. 8.3: Number of Suicides from 2004 to 2010

2. Economic Downfall: 74 per cent.
3. Crop Failure: 41 per cent.
4. Dent in the social status: 36 per cent.
5. Health Problems: 21 per cent.
6. Conflict in the family: 55 per cent.
7. Daughter/Sister's marriage: 34 per cent.
8. Addiction: 28 per cent.
9. Mismatch between expected and actual yield of cotton.

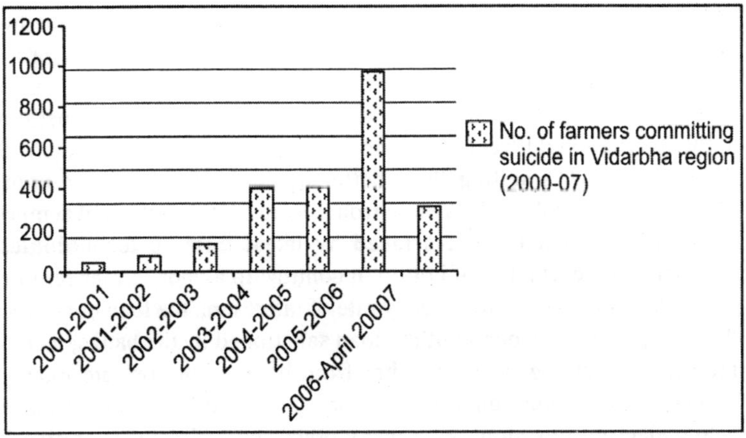

Fig. 8.4: No. of farmers committing suicide in Vidarbha region (2000-07)
Source: http//covering deprivention.acjenwline.org./vidarbha sayantami news suicide.

10. Natural calamities adulterated and spurious inputs.
11. Poor extension services.
12. Lopsided flow of institutional credits.
13. Warning out of joint family system and declining concern for others misery. Psychological aspects like stress which an individual in an unusual situation is confronted which has emerged as another factor.
14. Ecological Factors: soil formation takes about 500 to 1000 years. About 80 crores to one billion soil is washed away. On the whole the soil has been degraded turning it infertile due to the excessive use of the chemicals and fertilizers which does not yield any crop.
15. Lack of irrigation, electricity, bullocks and carts, water supply facilities.
16. Inappropriate government policies.
17. Apathy of the government and lack of good governance and policies.
18. Administrative maladies in agriculture ministry, cotton federation.
19. Impact of LPG on the cotton growers and inability to compete in the international market.

Aforesaid problems of the farmers of Vidarbha are further exaggerated with the impact of process of libéralization, privatization and globalization (LPG). In the present globalised scenario dominated by WTO and GATT where the market operates at cut-throat competition at the international level these poor farmers are unable to compete with their counterparts selling their better quality cotton to the ginning factories of the Maharashtra State from Sudan, Egypt and Israel at much cheaper rates. Rich farmers laced by latest farming technologies, producing better quality of cotton in contrast to a poor farmer farming manually with little money, heavy rate of interest on the loan borrowed, delayed payment disbursal of the loan sanctioned by the banks, lack of facilities, surviving on loan either from bank or the private money-lenders, lack of good quality seeds, irrigation facilities, no subsidies, heavy electric bills along with many other constraints of operating in domestic market are making it extremely difficult to attain the sustainability from the any angle, resultantly the poor farmer has no access neither to domestic nor international market making his life most miserable, unable to seek even two meals a day for himself and the family. Finding themselves unable to meet the family obligations most of them are committing suicide.

IV. Cotton Crop and its Problems

The socio-economic and political set up of the country are highly influenced by cotton. Millions of people earn their bread due to direct and indirect employment in cotton fields and cotton-based industries. Hence, investment in Cotton R&D has been playing back richly to our country as today; we enjoy security for clothing and earn valuable foreign exchange. At independence due to partition, major cotton growing area went to Pakistan while textile industries remained here. However, due to very systematic planning, today our country is third in the world in cotton production after China and USA. The country's policies are shaped by Agriculture and Textile Ministries. Eco-friendly attitude of the consumer would have given rise to the need for researching on highly productive varieties of natural colour cotton. Natural colours are ranges of brown in addition to green. Efforts to develop high yielding colour cotton cultivation with good fibre properties have commenced in order to meet the anticipated demand for this type of cotton on the next decade.

V. Nature Strikes Cotton Crop Hard

The cotton growing region of Vidarbha received a big setback as unseasonably rains, coupled with hail storms and pests, destroyed almost the entire cultivation during last decade in particular. It has left behind a trail of destruction, with the whole lot of cotton cultivators finding themselves trapped between zero income and mounting debts. But, if nature played villain to perfection, man was equally to blame for the havoc wreaked. It was one of those fatal combinations, which apart from affecting the cotton cultivation and growers also hit the region where it hurts—the economy. In terms of quantity, the loss is estimated at 8 lakhs quintals of cotton. At an average procurement price of Rs. 1,850 per quintal (2006), the total loss amounted to Rs. 150 crore. It would be difficult to calculate monetary losses due to the inferior quality cotton yield in the region. Yet, even if the same is procured at the lowest rate possible, the losses would be as trinomials.

VI. Marketing of Crop through Cotton Monopoly Scheme and the Role of Maharashtra State Cotton Federation

The low procurement at the Maharashtra State Cotton Co-operative Marketing Federation centres is an indicator of the grim scenario. The procurement at 33 centres in Nagpur zone was 7,79,920 quintals in 2006. The same dropped to a record low of 2,92,398 quintals in 2007. In Wani zone, procurement figures for 16 centres last year were 3,17,905 quintals; the same at 14 centres this year is 2,46,998 quintals. Yeotmal zone accounted for 6,31,463 quintals cotton procurement in 2006. The corresponding figures in the year 2007 were 4,76,264. The figures for Amravati zone for 2006 and 2007 year are 4,69,336 and 2,14,831 quintals respectively. The situation was not different in Khamgaon zone where the figures for the 2 years stood at 3,69,951 and 2,01,110 quintals. In contrast to these figures only 13 private businessmen from three centres from Yeotmal purchased 56,000 quintals of cotton in November 2010 whereas in November 2011 they have purchased about 82,000 quintal cotton as a private party because there were no purchases by Cotton Federation during this period. These purchases were made initially at the rate of Rs. 4,200 per quintal which was then reduced to Rs. 3,600–3,800. Cost of production of cotton per acre is 15,000–20,000 rupees where as maximum purchase price in open market is not more than Rs. 4,000 per quintal. A post-mortem of the events, which plunged the region into one of its worst crises ever, reveals that though nature initiated the downward swing, man-made errors accentuated the slide.

VII. Problems of Sale of Cotton in the Domestic Market

1. Cotton is not sold at right time.
2. Due to partial grading the farmers do not get appropriate money, i.e. selling cost.
3. Graders sweet will prevails in the pricing matter which sellers have to accept, without any questions asked for.
4. Due to the incapability to use the proper transportation for carrying the crop to the market they have to sale it lower prices.
5. Cotton seeds are very expensive farming is very difficult wages of minimum 250 Rs. per day are required which the farmers are unable to pay in cash daily.
6. Ecological problems like rains, attack of insects, fire are beyond humanly controls to save them.
7. Weighing system does not properly operate if at all it operates weighing is not done properly and the differences of the weights could be located.
8. The farmers are unwilling to sale their crops to cotton federation because of the various problems associated with payment in installment system known as "*chukara*" many a times left over payments remains unpaid.
9. Role of cotton broker is unfair and ditching the farmers. Most of the times they are constrained to sale their products through brokers on lower rates selling further in his own name to the federation and as against that part payment is made to the original producer.
10. Cotton Federation starts their business quite late, therefore, most of the time the farmers go to different places for selling their crops. And their functioning is very unsystematic irresponsible and most unsatisfactory with many prevailing corrupt practices.
11. The loaded bullock carts remain lying in the federation premises for minimum 8-10 days where by the owner lives on road without food, water and other facilities along with their bulls.
12. The cost of production of cotton is much higher than the selling cost as most of the buyers take the undue advantage of farmers helplessness to seek the price for his hard work added to his simplicity, ignorance and illiteracy.

VIII. Performance and Working of Cotton Federation

Maharashtra Cotton Federation started its business of purchasing in 1972 under the leadership of the then Chief Minister late Shri Vasantraoji Naik with the intention to stop the interference of cotton brokers in this business and sale on no profit or no loss basis through its Centres located districts wise but every year the federation is recurring losses in various sectors (15 crores turnover) is known for its malfunctioning. Sometimes ago the farmers were getting good prices for their produce under cotton monopoly purchase scheme which has been discontinued since 5 years. CAG has recommended merging of various district cotton federations in State federation and as such there is no one to look after proper administration and facing the closure. Presently in April 2011 the government declared the rate of Rs. 3,200–4,000 per quintal as a purchase rate in comparison to Rs. 3,800 in October, 2010. Quantity of cotton purchased in 2001-02 amounting to 1 crore 53 lakh quintals has been regularly reduced to 13,000 quintals in 2009-10 finally leading to no purchase in 2010-11. (*Source*: *Daily Lokshahi Varta*, Nagpur dated 25th May, 2011 page no.7). Still the Chief Minister is repeatedly assuring the farmers that the government is committed to buy even the last bail of cotton procuring entire crop of the region, which is part of his political tricks. Initially the private businessmen were giving the rate of Rs. 1900 per quintal but by the end of the season the rate closedown at Rs. 3000 per quintal the farmers preferred to sell their crop in the neighbouring place "PANDHURNA" in Madhya Pradesh because for more price and the cash payments in hand. They preferred to sell the product to private businessman at the rate of Rs. 2000–2200 per quintal because of the cash dealing in contrast to the rate of Rs. 2300 per quintal but payment by cheques in 3 installments by the federation making their choice absolutely clear that they are not happy with the Federation and don't mind to sell to the private parties for the clear on the spot dealing though at losses. People opine that the government is more concerned about the cloth producer rather than cotton producer and the economical picture would be different. Hence, there is an acute need of the changes in policies. People are disgusted with the cheque system requiring 2 to 3 years for the realization of the due payment. They are unable to pay interest charges on the loan borrowed from the private money-lender. Marriages and other family responsibilities make his life absolutely miserable. Two decades ago they were below poverty line but now are above it but still very poor not able to seek two meals a day for himself and the family thereby committing suicides, sometimes *en mass*.

Purchase of Cotton by Cotton Federation 2000-2001: 74 lakh quintals

2001-02	1 crore 53 lakh quintals
2002-03	23 lakh quintals
2003-04	32 lakh quintals
2004-05	2 crore 11 lakh quintals
2005-06	18 lakh quintals
2006-07	32 lakh quintals
2007-08	1 lakh quintals
2008-09	1 crore 67 lakh quintals
2009-10	13 lakh quintals
2010-11	No Purchases

Purchase Rates of Cotton Federation 2010-11

October 2010	Rs. 3800/quintal
November 2010	Rs. 4600/quintal
December 2010	Rs. 4400/quintal
January 2011	Rs. 4800/quintal
February-March 2011	Rs. 6800/quintal
April 2011	Rs. 3200-4000/quintal

Source: *Daily Lokshahi Varta*, Nagpur dt. 25th May 2011, page no. 7.

IX. Problem Areas of the Cotton Federation

(i) *Not adhering to the declared rates; Fluctuating rates*: The buying price of the Federation is very low than what is declared as a policy matter. This year the government has declared the rate of Rs. 3700-4000 per quintal but they are not buying beyond 3800 per quintal.

(ii) *Varying rates for purchase of cotton*: The rates differ from person to person in the name of grading, obliging the favourite ones. More influential you are better the deal you get.

(iii) *Mode of payment*: Payment is by cheque and too much delayed ranging from 6 months to 3 years. Many times the farmers do not even have the Bank account. Further the payment cheque of the rich businessman or the brokers from cotton Federations are cleared very rapidly in comparison to that of the poor farmer. Here also he is helpless.

(iv) *Rampant corruption*: Visible at every step from Class IV employees to the higher ups depending upon the nature of work.

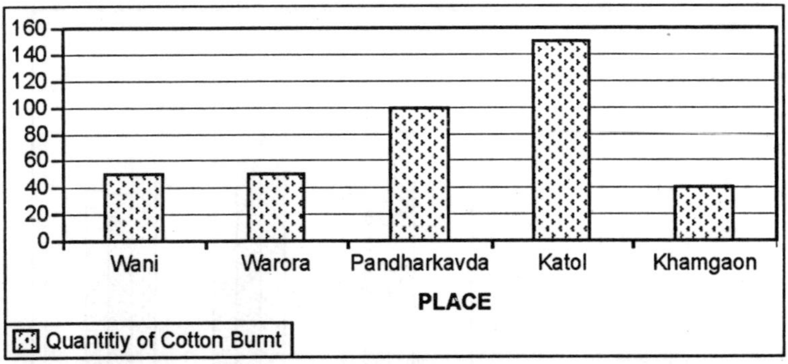

Fig. 8.5: Quantity of Cotton Burnt Deliberately

(v) *Deliberate pre-planned destruction of the cotton stock*: Owing to the corrupt practices of the federation the huge quantities of cotton are burnt to obtain heavy claims from the insurance companies. The proportion of fire is more only in case federation owned cotton in comparison to the privately owned by business men.

Value of the Quantity of the Cotton Destroyed (2005)

Sl. No.	*Place*	*Quantity of Cotton Burnt*
1.	Wani	50.00 lakhs
2.	Warora	50.00 lakhs
3.	Pandharkavda	1 crore
4.	Katol	1.50 crores
5.	Khamgaon	40 lakhs

The available data of 2005 shows events of deliberately burning of cotton and reimbursing the costs from insurance claim. Though the data is old it is more or less same even to this date, illustrating the malpractices.

X. Comparative Purchase Rates of Cotton in the Region

Here's the comparison of purchase rate of cotton for the period of 5 years by federation, private businessmen and (Madhya Pradesh) Pandurna's rate are compared for the farmers of Linga village.

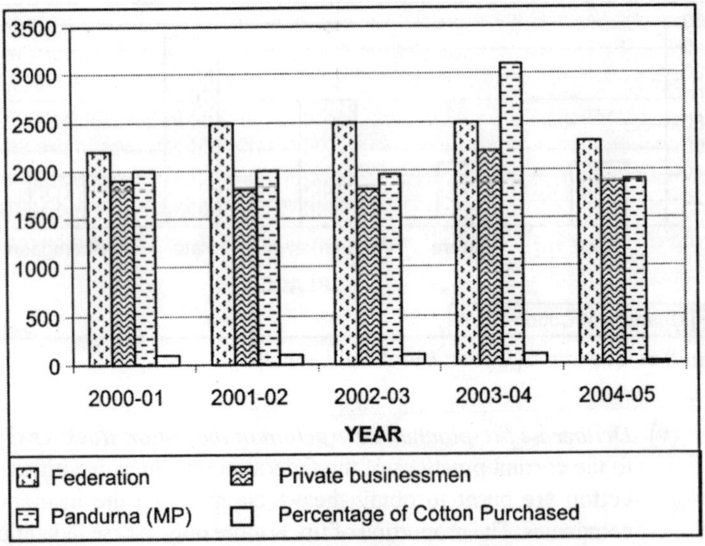

Fig. 8.6: Comparative Purchase Rates of Cotton in the Region

Year	*Federation*	*Private Businessmen*	*Pandurna (MP)*	*Percentage of Cotton Purchased*
2000-01	2200-60%	1900-10%	2000-30%	100%
2001-02	2500-60%	1800-5%	2000-25%	100%
2002-03	2500-60%	1800-5%	1950-35%	100%
2003-04	2500-40%	2200-5%	2000 to 3100-55%	100%
2004-05	2300-20%	1875-5%	1900-10%	35%

The above mentioned comparative chart clearly indicates the declining percentage of cotton purchased by the federation solely because of its late payments and the defective operational modalities. Year 2004-05 is not cleared yet because state government had declared the rate of Rs. 2700 per quintal but paying only Rs. 2300 in reality. The farmers prefers to sale their crop to the private party at comparatively lesser price and get cash payment rather than waiting for cheque which may be sometimes dishonoured also.

XI. Cotton: The Deciding Factor of Politics in Maharashtra

Needless to emphasize that the cotton is a decisive factor in the state politics challenging the government on the point of tariff. Many large rallies, agitations, warning for the suicides are given from the public platform by the leaders cashing on the sympathy of those farmers with the eye on the vote bank. Many a times the opposition and the pressure groups pressurizes the CM to such an extent that he has to announce his decision on the spot to save his skin. Always there is a furore in the State Assembly about this burning issues but the outcome for farmers is big zero. Nobody in government seems to be bothered for their suicides but using it just as a weapon to clean swipe the individual vested interest of the political leaders.

XII. Prime Minister's Relief Package and its Implementation

In response to the ever swelling number of suicides by the farmers of Vidarbha, Prime Minister Dr. Manmohan Singh visited the affected area along with his paraphernalia on 1st July, 2006 and declared the relief package of Rs. 3750 crore to bail out the Vidarbha's farmers including the waiver of Rs. 712 crore overdue interest for six districts of Vidarbha which witnessed spate of suicides by debt-ridden farmers till 30th June, 2006 so that it could provide immediate relief to the farmers, who would be getting the fresh loans. Identifying rural indebtedness as a major cause of agrarian distress he also declared one year moratorium on Rs. 1300 crore overdue loan as on the same date to restart the process of credit flow so that the farmers can resume normal agriculture activities and obtain regular livelihood. The other major components of the package include Rs. 2177 crore special grant for expediting major and medium irrigation projects aimed at irrigating 1.59 lakh hectares land of these six districts over the period of next three years, Rs. 180 crore for seed replacement and purchase of cotton seeds, Rs. 242 crore for watershed development and the construction of check dams Rs. 225 crore for subsidy under National Horticulture Mission, Rs. 78 crore for micro irrigation and Rs. 135 crore for improving the cattle and fishery activities in those districts.

The implementation of this special package was to be personally monitored by Prime Minister's Office and a special monitoring cell headed by Principle Secretary to the Prime Minister would oversee its effective implementation by state and local level agencies. This was a welcome step into this direction to handle the devastating crises. Unfortunately even after the declaration of this package as many as 1377 farmers again committed suicide. The said package could not be implemented properly and the relief did not reach the concerned ones, resultantly the same situation prevailed despite the tall claims of the top leaders and policy makers. In order to save his skin the Chief Minister of the state stated that the government has not received the grants from the Centre. Which later on was corrected by him by filing an affidavit. In a way the State Government has not attached the deserving priority to this crucial issue. The Parliamentary Standing Committee on Agriculture has expressed its displeasure about implementation of the PM's package in a report tabled in Lok Sabha indicting the State Government and Agriculture Ministry. It says, aid is not reaching to the farmers and called for the restructuring of the debts. Further rapped Agriculture Department and Planning Commission for the lack of coordination. Increasingly out of Rs.1075 crore whopping of Rs. 735 crores was returned to the farmers from their own 3 per cent under Monopoly Cotton Procurement Scheme which means the Government has spent only Rs. 150 crore from its kitty to wipe out the tears of the farmers during last 16 months. Further only those farmers who took the loan of Rs. 25000 could get the benefit of interest waiving but the farmer with more than Rs. 25000 loan, principle amount along with long outstanding interest was disqualified as a beneficiary for the said package. This reflects the differentiating attitude of the Govenment. Also this package is only for the worst affected six districts of the cotton belt, what about the others? Needless to say it calls for uniform policy for all the affected farmers and their future generations.

XIII. Non-conducive Economic Reforms

The New Economic Policy (NEP) and Economic Reforms were formally adopted and made operational in 1991. These invited various changes in the institutional set up suiting to the need of hour. Ever since the period of last 2 decades lot of debates had been invoked about the gap between the results expected and delivered. These reforms have not been proved effective rather they have created many obstacles in the way of industrialization undercutting the industrial development particularly in the agro-based industries located in rural areas, units which were contributing to the rural economy to a great extent. Vidarbha region of the Maharashtra State comprising 11 districts is known for fine cotton which is a raw material for cotton yarn required by the textile mills which are in quite large numbers scattered all over the state. Further, the cloth from textile mills is in great demand for the readymade cotton garments being exported in huge quantity earning the profits made by textile mills. Those rich businessmen in exports business are becoming more and more rich but the poor farmer—the cotton grower, producer of the raw material is becoming poor to the extent to commit suicide. Obviously, the reform had devastating impact and there is an acute need for coming out of it. Cotton was not included in the list till very recent past.

The Ministry has short listed 10 agriculture products for export boost.

The Preference List

- Floriculture products
- Wheat products
- Coarse grains
- Processed foods
- Spices
- Horticulture
- Cashew
- Oil meals
- Rice
- Sugar

Cotton imports in India 1996-97 onwards

Year	*Quantity (In lakh bales of 170 kgs.)*	*Value (Rs. crores)*
1996-1997	0.30	56.42
1997-1998	4.13	497.93
1998-1999	7.87	772.64
1999-2000	22.01	1967.92
2000-2001	22.13	2029.18
2001-2002	25.26	2150.01
2002-2003	17.67	1789.92
2003-2004	7.21	880.10
2004-2005	12.17	1338.04
2005-2006	5.00	695.77
2006-2007	5.53	752.29
2007-2008	6.38	986.33
2008-2009	10.00	1377.80
2009-2010	7.00	1195.64
2010-2011	5.00	N.A

Note: Value figures are estimated.
Source: Cotton Advisory Board for Quantity figures.

The Union Commerce Ministry has identified 10 agricultural products to be promoted in the next couple of years to capitalize on the over $ 600 billion agri-products market which does not include cotton. Further, the import duties on cotton are nominal, therefore, cotton from abroad finds no problem in seeking and capturing Indian market. Success has been achieved where growers and processors have been integrated, as in the case of sugar. For the success of other agro-based industries also, close links must be forged between the growers and processor units. Industrial policy would, therefore, especially promote projects which are organized in close co-operation on the basis of joint ownership. Growers will be encouraged to set up processing units within the framework. This will also ensure the transmission of better technology for enhanced agricultural production. Agro-processing industry would receive high priority in credit allocation from financial institutions.

The growth of agriculture has been fluctuating in the nineties; the double-digit industrial growth of 1993-96 has receded subsequently and in the recent years, the growth of services-income has been the mainstay of the State's economy. The share of the agriculture, industry and services sectors was 17.59, 27.9 and 54.6 per cent, respectively in 2005-06. This suggests that from 1980-81 to 1997-98, 2005-06 the share of services has been steadily increasing, at the cost of the share of agriculture, with the share of industry remaining stagnant throughout the two-decade period.

Conclusion

1. The cotton farmers in India are paying more prices for the inputs like seeds, pesticides, fertilizers, electricity, water, labour and whereas the price of cotton has gone down, along with the diseased productivity. In contrast to this picture in India, US government is giving USD 4.0 billion to cotton farmers and asking for further Liberalisation of cotton trade in USA.

The provided Prime Ministers relief packages are the amalgamation of existing schemes. Apart from the helpline and direct financial assistance there was hardly anything new being offered. Pumping extra funds into additional schemes shows that no new idea was applied to overcome the grave situation, where existing measures have obviously failed. Farmers helpline did not give them any substantial help to them. Also the basis of selection of beneficiaries under the assistance scheme was not well defined. Further the type of assistance to be given to deal with problems, like a farmer needing pair of bullock cart, pump set etc. is very low. Awareness regarding this package is also pretty low.

2. We are strong in economic reforms as a result of which GDP has been raised. India's ranking as 127 in the year 2000 has gone up to 103 in 2004 is indicative of improved aspect of development. Challenges ahead with regard to management of economic situation are for market places. Imperial evidences suggest that liberalisation has to be in terms of economic policies and governance. As the lower societies have gone much beyond their capacities to bear with the globalisation. We should have gone in for internal reforms first rather than external directly. The reforms *vis-à-vis* changes in the policy have not been conducive to the changing economic scenario in the global perspective and has failed to bring out the desired result at local level. As a result of this rich have become more richer and poor have become more poorer widening the gap between the rich and poor.

3. In order to meet the challenges of WTO, GATT, various facilities, finances, subsidies and incentives have been provided by the Maharashtra Government to encourage direct foreign investment, and industrialisation all over the state but again due to regional disparities Vidarbha region remains neglected. Further these facilities are given to ginning factories, textile mills, garment manufacturers, and exporters but the poor cotton producer remains deprived of all the basic inputs, including the credit facilities from the banks and other financial institutions.

4. Due to encouraged privatisation policy more and more private parties have entered the market and captured most of the business. Due to the various lapses and inefficiency of State Cotton Federation the farmers prefer to sell their crops to private parties at a lower rate than that of the federation as they have lost their faith in it's working. Inefficient, corrupt, opaque administrative practices of the federation have been supporting factors to the rich and powerful persons to manipulate the business in their own vested interest which everyone cannot do.

5. As a impact of globalisation countries, like Sudan, Israel, Egypt, have also entered into domestic market, selling their quality crops at much cheaper rates to local factories leaving no scope for the son of the soil neither in domestic nor international markets.

6. Further looking at the intricacies of rural life and the agro-based business the farmers have started converting the agricultural land into non-agriculture for the urban usage, selling the same lands and migrating to cities, living much substandard life than what they were leading in the

village. Decreased farming, and increased migration resulting in burden on urban local bodies.

7. Maharashtra's cotton monopoly scheme has failed to render the expected desired results in cotton procurement particularly in Vidarbha region which is being implemented through Maharashtra State Cotton Federation and calls for further administrative reforms.

Suggestions

(a) Cotton procurement scheme of the Maharashtra Government should be revamped thoroughly suiting to the new market needs and fast changing grim scenario.

(b) According to Ted Gebler's model market oriented, consumer and mission driven result oriented, profit centred, curbing wastages, efficient, competitive, quality conscious administrative reforms may be introduced by the State Ministry of Agriculture and Cotton Federation, APMC, etc. leading to innovations and effective implementation. There is an acute need for reinventing the Government as per paradigm of NPM.

(c) Fool proof grading system for judging the quality of the cotton for deciding the price rates be developed which should be fully computerized leaving no scope for manipulation.

(d) The Import duty on cotton from abroad be raised to 300 per cent from the present rate of 130 per cent and further the various controls on agro-products be relaxed to boost up the export of cotton which has been very recently included in the export promotion list.

(e) Various subsidies, ensured loan disbursement from the nationalized banks at comparatively lower rates be availed to those cotton growers.

(f) In accordance with the Schedule XI of the 73rd Constitutional Amendment Act, out of the 29 items covered by the Panchayati Raj Institutions the local bodies should take over the supply of quality seeds and required inputs for the quality production. Further the Gram Panchayat should purchase tractors and advanced equipments of farming and those be availed to the farmers on rental basis so as to provide access to the infrastructural facilities.

(g) Pattern of cooperative farming should be encouraged.

(h) Undertaking the effective programme of water conservation, stopping degradation of soil, increased irrigation facilities and the electricity supply at subsidized rates.

(i) The present generation of the farmer's children is reasonably educated they should be given a practical training of crop management pattern by the research institutions like Vasantrao Naik Krishi Pratishthan working for the development of agricultural sector of the region.

(j) Majority of the efforts should be taken to improve the quality of the soil which has turned into a barren land due to its degradation and poor fertility.

(k) Since 85 per cent of the total land under the crop production is dry and barren due to lack of irrigation facilities more dams, canals, wells, tube-wells be constructed to irrigate the land for the proper crops.

(l) As suggested always, that the farming be connected to allied business of dairy, poultry, goatery, piggery, etc. are not feasible and unable to cope with the challenges of all-round development of the farming communities in the years to come.

(m) The cooperative activity, programme similar to that of "Kutumbshree" of Kerla state, based on the building and developing the self-help groups movement should be strengthened involving the women members of the families of the farming community. Same pattern developed by Dr. Mohammed Yunus could bring revolution in the lives of poor people in Bangladesh could be implemented which will lead to the desired results also proved very successful in the state of Maharashtra.

(n) More and more number of small and large industries be developed in the region, encouraging the industrialization through subsidies and incentives which will provide employment more specifically to the distressed families of the region. With the take off of the Multimodal International Hub Airport at Nagpur (MIHAN) future of the region seems brighter which will take minimum one more decade for its practical shape.

(o) Provision of e-choupals (Electronic Market) and electronic auction halls which are connected to national, international market places in each district for the sale of farm produce which is the key of ensuring free, competitive marketing system. The use of such market places would improve prices for the produce, they would also improve traceability, tagging systems which are very important for supply chain management.

(p) Prime Ministers relief fund package should be redesigned considering the practical problems and loopholes.

(q) Backward and Forward linkages be developed to process Cotton as yarn and readymade cotton garments for the export. Further to provide storage, grading, and product handling facilities which means more investment in warehousing. With the coming up of MIHAN this objective could be easily met with the strong political will and bureaucratic support.

(r) Free education with more stress on skill-oriented vocational training programmes be imparted to their children.

(s) Elimination of middlemen and touts from the market chain involved in the sales of the produce.

(t) Last and the most important factor is remunerative prices for the agricultural produces be availed to the farmers by Government.

Notes and References

1. Editorial Sakal, *Daily Monday*, 4th January 2005.
2. District information (Yeotmal) presented by Nitin Raut: Sakal, *Daily Monday*, 3rd January2005.
3. Sai Y.V.S.T. (2 araph of 001) Monograph on support by liberal procurement policy as socio-economic stability factor in the lives of small farmers: Shyamprasad Institute of Social Service. October 2001.
4. Surjit Mishra: Note prepared for discussion during the inception workshop for the study on 'suicide of farmers in Maharashtra, at IGIDR on 11th January, 2005.
5. Suman Sahai (2002) 'What's worng with BT cotton?' *Economic Times*, 2nd April, 2002.
6. *The Hindu*, Friday, July 23, 2004. June 2004.
7. Vyas, V.S. (2004), 'Agrarian Distress: Strategies to protect Vulnerable sections', *Economic and Political Weekly,* December 25-31, 2004.
8. Gary Grander, *State of the World 1998*, Earth Scan Publications Ltd.
9. Surendra Bahuguna: Development redefined, *The Journal of Public Administration*, July-September 1993.
10. Editor, *Independent daily Newspaper*, London, September 30, 1992.
11. Kawaljeet Singh, Congress (I) blamed for Farmers Suicides, *The Hindu*, 27 June, 1998.
12. G. Parthasarathy Shameem: 'Suicides of Cotton farmers in Andhra Pradesh', *Economic and Political Weekly*, March 28, 1998.
13. Deshpande, R.S., 2002, "Suicides by farmers in Karnataka Agrarian

Distress and possible Alleviatory Steps", *Economic and Political Weekly*, Vol. 1.

14. Government of Maharashtra, 2001: "Report on monopoly cotton inequality: Case study of Satara District", *Economic and Political Weekly*, Vol. 34, No. 13.
15. Vyas, V.S. (2002), 'Agriculture: Second round of Economic Reforms', *Economic and Political Weekly*, Vol. 36, No. 10.
16. Surendram, K. and S.D. Tendulkar (2003), "Poverty in India in the 1990s, Revised Results, *Economic and Political Weekly*, Vol. 38, No. 46.
17. Data is collected from websites, Local dailies, *The Hitavada, Sakal, Nav Bharat*, Government officers off the records, and personal interviews of the affected family members of the farmers.

9

Public Private Partnerships

Successful Strategies Adopted by Indian States

Vijayaraj Kumar Charles

1. Introduction

1.1 Public Private Partnerships (PPP) in General

Despite becoming the second fastest growing and the fourth largest economy of the world, India continues to face large gaps in the demand and supply of essential social and economic infrastructure and services. Rapidly growing economy, increased industrial activity, burgeoning population pressure, and all-round economic and social development have led to greater demand for better quality and coverage of water and sanitation services, sewerage and drainage systems, solid-waste management, roads and seaports, and power supply. Increased demand has put the existing infrastructure under tremendous pressure and far outstripped its supply.[1]

Many analysts argue that the best way to improve service provision is to change the way in which governments administer them in India. For those who believe in neo-liberal ideology, privatization is the only way to solve this problem. According to the World Bank, the key task is to 'manage infrastructure like a business, and not like a bureaucracy' (World Bank, 1994, p. 2). The neo-liberals call for 'reinventing government' by inspiring a new entrepreneurial spirit (Osbome and Gaebler, 1992; Hammer and Champy, 1993). They propose a lean state and lean government and advocate a greater role for private sector in service provision and they argue that 'market type management approaches could be effectively applied to the public sector' (Hood, 1991; Osbome &

Gaebler, 1992). The proponents of New Public Management emphasize the need for 'speed and flexibility and touted the advantages of markets for both greater private sector engagement and consumer voice for citizens' (Savas, 1987). The New Public Management reform is focused on competition and entrepreneurialism (Warner, 2008). The belief is that the market would make government service provision self-correcting in three ways: efficiency, cost minimization and quality delivery.[2]

The recent trend of infrastructure provision in India shows that many of the persuasive arguments and ideologists have influenced the way a number of state governments administer basic services. This includes acknowledging the vital role that private enterprises can play in service delivery and subsequently decentralizing responsibilities to them in the form of Public-Private Partnerships (PPPs). 'Most scholars and public decision-makers advocate thus for a more pragmatic approach which consists of promoting efficient (or at least as efficient as possible) partnership between the public and the private sectors for the provision of major services and public goods' (Martimort, 2008: 393).

PPPs have acquired different meanings in different parts of the world. In the United States, PPPs have traditionally been associated with urban renewal and downtown economic development, In the United Kingdom, the Private Finance Initiative (PFI) has become a cornerstone of New Labour's stakeholder society notion. Osborne (2001) notes that PPPs have become a tool for providing public services through Public Community partnerships, and developing a civil society in post-communist regimes such as Hungary, and a mechanism for combating social exclusion and enhancing community development under European union policy. Therefore, it is clear that the PPPs are a family of different possible approaches to providing public sector infrastructure and services (Hodge, 2004:156)

If we judge by the way many governments are currently committing themselves to PPP approach, it is evident that Public Private Partnerships (PPPs) have become a popular way of providing public sector infrastructure and services. However, the approach to PPPs should be based on the principles, which ensure that PPPs are formulated and executed in public interest with a view to achieving additional capacity and delivery of public services at reasonable cost. These partnerships must supplement the scarce public resources for improving the investment in infrastructure sectors, and at the same time improving efficiencies and reducing costs. 'Public private partnerships must aim at bringing private resources into public projects, not public resources into private' (GOI, 2007: 256) see also (Datta, 2009: 73).

Although the Government of India has been encouraging private sector investment and participation in all sectors of infrastructure, and there has been considerable innovation in the design of PPPs, it is clear that the progress has been uneven. 'There are islands of progress, with some states having undertaken far more PPPs than others, and a much heavier use PPPs in some sectors than others' (World Bank, 2006:21). There is considerable diversity in both the legal and institutional frameworks in place, and the level of transaction capacities and experiences.

In this regard, there are several related questions that need to be addressed, which include; Are there some developmental conditions (Legal and Institutional frameworks) which are essential for any state to get investments in PPPs ? Why some states are able to attract more number of PPP projects, compared to other states? Are there any commonalities in the policy environment which make these states more conducive for PPP projects?

In order to answer the above and other related questions, this research propose to examine the effectiveness of policy and legal frameworks in place, in both high and low performing states in India (based on per capita investment in PPPs) and will try to identify, critical factors which determine investment inflows in PPPs, which are most essential for investments in PPP projects.

1.2 Relevance of PPPs for India

Investment Required in Infrastructure

'The economic strength of a country is primarily built upon a good infrastructure' (Sarangi, 2002: 267). 'Since the early 1990s India has come a long way in improving its infrastructure, but is still unable to meet the demand that has arisen in the areas of roads, railways, ports and power. It is in this context that PPPs are fast emerging way for India to grow'[Global Business Coalition (GBC), 2008:1]. It is generally recognized that lack of infrastructure is one of the major constraints on India's ability to achieve 9 to 10 per cent growth in GDP, which is the rate required to make a significant difference to living conditions in the country and achieve inclusiveness over the next ten years.

The Eleventh Five Year Plan has set an ambitious target of increasing total investment in infrastructure from around 5 per cent of GDP in the base year of the Plan 2006-07 to 9 per cent by the terminal year 2011-12. This projection results in a total investment requirement of Rs. 2,056,150 crore ($ 514 billion) for ten infrastructure sectors over the five year period.

Growing Emphasis on Private Sector Participation

The pronounced demand for investment cannot be met by government alone and private capital from both home and abroad has to be mobilized. 'Many scholars believe that the public sector organizations that failed to provide these (infrastructure) services in a cost-effective manner have instead blocked enormous capital resources of the state without yielding adequate returns'(Kundu, 2001:1). The Government realizes this and 'the consequences have been an increase in public-private partnerships and greater scope for foreign investment in comprehensive projects' (Heymann, 2007: 6).

The combined deficit of the Union and State Governments is around 10 per cent of GDP. Governments can not also borrow arbitrarily to meet out their requirements for investment in infrastructure. The Approach Paper to the Eleventh Plan states that 'One has to reach out to the private sector, and private savings, and to the other mechanisms available in the market today to raise funds' (Planning Commission, 2006, "An Approach Paper to the Eleventh Plan"). The National Development Council (NDC) has passed resolution which mentions that 'increased private participation has now become a necessity' to mobilize the resources needed for infrastructure expansion and upgradation.

Given the large resource requirements and the budgetary and borrowing constraints, Government of India has been encouraging private sector investment and participation in all sectors of infrastructure. The expected investment by the private sector, which includes Public-Private Partnership (PPP) Projects, is approximately to the tune of Rs. 6,19,591 crore, which is 30 per cent of the required total investment during the Eleventh Plan, a much higher share than 20 per cent anticipated to be realized during the Tenth Plan. 'The idea behind such project is most often expressed in general language as harnessing the efficiencies and innovativeness associated with a competitive private sector to help government achieve its public service goals at lower cost' (Bettignies, 2009: 358).

However, there are policy gaps in many states, because most state governments in India are at an early stage in the development of their PPP programmes. 'Considerable experience has rendered the conclusion that little can be accomplished to encourage economic growth and improved social welfare unless policies create a climate to promote these goals and institutions are organized to support them' (Grindle and Thomas, 1990: 1163). Therefore, it is important that the right framework and capacities are further developed in the states and agencies where PPP programmes are under way already and especially where these are going to be pursued.

As part of infrastructure policy, various investment models such as voluntary cooperation, establishing coalitions and the partnership model discussed here, have been adopted by India based on the area and level of investment. 'The partnership model is a joint venture between the government and the private sector, where the responsibilities as well as the benefits would be shared equally or even enjoyed more by the private partner depending upon the level of involvement' (Sarangi, 2002: 268). Apart from that, maximum leverage of private investment is possible in partnership model. 'In other worlds, the partnership model lends itself to investments in infrastructure which are large and have a long gestation period' (Sarangi, 2002: 268).

According to Sarangi (2002) the project viability, scale of benefit to the community and community acceptance for such joint ventures are the important criteria for proceeding with PPP projects. Though there were many studies made on individual PPP projects in India analyzing the factors contributing to their success or failure, there were no attempts to comprehensively study the effectiveness of the polices and transaction capabilities for PPPs at state level in India in relation to the incidence of PPPs. This research propose to examine the effectiveness of policy and legal frameworks in place, and the level of transaction capacities and experiences in both high and poorly performing states (based on per capita investment in PPPs) in India and identify the most suitable/needed frameworks and capacities to be developed in states for PPP Programmes.

1.3 Scope and Methodology

Research Objectives

Firstly the study is going to look at the patterns of PPP Project formulations in 12 states (both good and bad performing, based on per capita investment in PPPs).

Secondly, to explore the effectiveness of the strategies policy frameworks as well as legal frameworks and procedures adapted by these states, to attract more investments in PPP Projects.

Thirdly, to identify other critical factors which determine investment inflows in PPPs.

Finally, this study also seeks to examine the first Water Supply PPP project in India (New Tirupur Area Development Company Ltd. in Tamil Nadu) in depth and make a critical analysis to understand the positive and negative outcomes of this project.

Research Questions

Main Research Question: What are the critical factors that determine investment inflows in PPPs in Indian States?

Sub-Questions

1. Are there some commonalities in policy environment which makes certain Indian states as more attractive destinations for PPP projects?
2. How do the cost of corruption and cost of regulation, influence the investment inflows in to PPP projects in Indian states?
3. How does the availability of infrastructure, power supply and transportation facilities influence the investment inflows into PPP projects in Indian states?
4. How does the access to land and availability of external finance influence the investment inflows in to PPP projects in Indian states?
5. What are the positive and negative outcomes of the Tirupur Water Supply Project which is the first water supply PPP project in India?

1.4 Analytical Framework

The first empirical attempt to analyze the determinants of PPPs in infrastructure projects was the World Bank's Private Participation in Infrastructure (PPI) database on projects for developing countries during 1990-2003. According to the study the determinants of PPPs have been classified into seven channels, taking into account different incentives and constraints in both public and private sectors. 'These channels are Government constraints, political environment, market conditions, macroeconomic stability, institutional quality, the legal system, and past experience with PPPs' (Hamami *et al.*, 2006: 4).

Sachs (Sachs, 2002: 1) in his study identifies Currency inconvertibility and Transfer Restriction, Expropriation, Breach of Contract, Political Violence as risks that are insurable and legal, regulatory and bureaucratic risks, and Non-Governmental action risks as key non-insurable risks that influence the investment inflows in PPP projects. 'With increasing political risks, PPP (investment) opportunities become less and the costs of PPPs increase as well' (*Ibid.*, 1).

Existence of policies need not necessarily motivate the investors to choose a particular state for investment in PPP projects. More than the existence of policies, hassle free implementation of policies matters, when it comes to investment, because bureaucratic inefficiencies and delay add to transaction costs and red-tape/bureaucratic delays often cause holdups in obtaining various clearances and permits, essential for starting a project. 'Nonetheless, poor economic governance due to bureaucratic inefficiencies and cumbersome regulations create additional fixed costs for investments and particularly hamper firms in the small-scale and medium-scale sectors which typically do not possess the political contacts required to circumvent bureaucratic hassles' (Chakravarthi, 2009: 13).

Since most of the states spend a huge portion of their earnings for payment of salaries rather than on investing in infrastructure a 'contraction in the size of the bureaucracy also has the potential to reduce corruption through reduction of red-tape and removal of inefficient officers'. Ahluwalia (2002), for example, mentions that the prevalence of large bureaucracies often forces entrepreneurs to fall prey to the "triple vicissitudes of harassment, delay and corruption."

Infrastructure and availability of power supply are other important factors that influence any investment decision in infrastructure projects. Since, any shortage in infrastructure like power supply, transportation facilities add up to the project cost and affect timely completion of projects, 'a state which can offer reliable power supply at a low cost to industrial and commercial consumers will provide investors with a lower cost of production and be preferred as an investment destination' (Chakravarthi, 2009: 13).

According to Veeramani and Goldar (2004) a constant supply of power is one of the factors viewed favourably by investors while evaluating a state's investment climate. They also report that irregular power supply leading to stoppage of work adds to the project cost. 'A high level of physical infrastructure coupled with reliable power supply betters investment prospects in the state by facilitating connectivity with markets and lowering input costs' (Chakravarthi, 2009: 13-19). Therefore, a positive relationship is expected between the power generation capacity in a state and the per capital investment proposals received by the state.

'Prudent fiscal management can have positive impacts on the state's investment climate through enhanced infrastructure development and labour productivity along with a reduction in corruption and bureaucratic delays' (Chakravarthi, 2009: 13). Therefore, it leads us to expect a negative correlation between the level of bureaucratic corruption and investment proposals in a state.

Deutsche Bank (2007) has undertaken a more comprehensive study in ranking states according to their investment climates with a more empirically grounded methodology. According to this survey 'the investment climate is expressed as a function of the growth rate of state domestic product, population growth rates, share of manufacturing and construction in SDP, and level of infrastructure, measured through the length of roads constructed under the Golden Quadrilateral programme in the State' (Chakravarthi, 2009: 22).

However, for our purpose of our study, the explanatory variables for answering the research questions can be identified as follows:

1. Legal and Institutional frameworks,
2. Cost of Corruption,
3. Transaction costs,
4. Availability of infrastructure, and
5. Accessibility to land and external finance in the states.

In this research, it is proposed to analyze the data collected on the above variables and establish the patterns of relationship between these variables and the performance of top ranking states in utilizing the PPP model for infrastructural service delivery, so that lessons can be drawn for capacity building in public sector for robust PPP programme.

The analytical framework followed in this research is summarized and given below:

1. Investment Climate for PPPs in States is a function of various critical governance and infrastructure dimensions such as Legal and Institutional framework, Cost of Corruption, Transaction Costs, Availability of Infrastructure and Accessibility to land and external finance etc.

2. Proper legal and Institutional framework in place instills investor's confidence and creates a positive environment for investments in projects, therefore, it should have a positive correlation with the performance of states in PPP investments.
3. Cost of Corruption and Cost of Regulation increases the Project Cost, therefore, it has a negative correlation with performance of states in PPP investments. States with low cost of corruption and low cost of regulation may be assumed to attract more investment in PPP projects compared to other states.
4. Availability of Reliable Power supply reduces the cost and time over runs of any infrastructure projects, similarly availability of good road infrastructure reduces the transportation cost of raw material for the infrastructure projects, therefore, they have a positive correlation with the performance of states in PPP investments. States with good infrastructure, and reliable power supply and good transportation facilities attract more investment in PPP projects compared to other states.
5. Accessibility to land is not a major problem foreseen in PPP projects, because in PPPs States take the responsibility of providing required land to the concession contractor for the execution of the projects. However, any delay in acquisition of land for the infrastructure projects will increase the overheads and cost of plant and machinery. Similarly, access to external finance for the project is also going to affect the project finance. Therefore, these factors have a positive correlation with the performance of states in PPP investments. States with better access to land and external finance can be assumed to attract more investment in PPP projects compared to other states.

1.5 Research Methodology and Boundaries of the Study

This research will be based on both secondary data and primary data collected from different sources. All the data relevant to PPP projects in India and different states are available in the Government of India official website, namely *http://www.pppinindia.com* and this is the main data source, which is secondary in nature. Apart from that there is useful information on infrastructure, investments PPP's etc. on the official website of the committee on infrastructure, Planning Commission at *http://www.infrasturcture.gov.in* and the official website of Investment Commission of India *http://www.investmentcommission.in.* The data available on these websites are regularly updated and the website is directly under the control of Ministry of Finance, Government of India.

Primary data collection was done through semi-structured interviews and focus group discussions. A few interviews with senior level Indian Administrative Service Officers who are in charge of implementing PPP projects in India and responsible persons like State level nodal officers for PPP projects were conducted in order to fully understand the emerging patterns in PPP's in India. Interviews have been conducted with the Managing Director and other Senior level officials of New Tirupur Area Development Corporation Ltd., and focus group discussions with other stake holders in the project like public representatives at Panchayat level were also conducted to understand the positive and negative outcomes of the Tirupur Water Supply Project.

The data collected have been analyzed to understand the patterns of project formations in infrastructure across states in PPP mode. The states are ranked according to the per capita investment in PPP projects in infrastructure and the relationships between the legal and institutional frameworks and the performance of states in getting PPP investments were studied and analyzed. To understand the other critical factors which influence the investment flow in infrastructure under PPP mode, a large number of proxies and variables have been analyzed and for this purpose, the findings of Investment Climate Survey jointly conducted by World Bank and CII has been extensively used.

Limitations of the Study

Though every attempt has been made to study all the important factors that influence inflow of investment into states under PPP mode, it might have missed out some factors due to non-availability of data and time constraint. Regarding the case selected for the study, some of the information required might not be available to the public, or may be restricted or confidential, due to political interests, and there may be so many factors that make a state more conducive for PPP projects, for example, political environment in terms of stable and accountable governments, track record of the governments in honouring the commitments, previous PPP experience with the governments, etc. Considering these limitations, this study is going to mainly focus on, (1) Legal and Institutional frameworks, (2) Cost of Corruption, (3) Transaction costs, (4) Availability of infrastructure, and (5) Accessibility to land and external finance at state level, that make a state more conducive for PPPs, so that lessons can be drawn for building capacities in public sector for better use of PPPs.

2. Theoretical and Conceptual Framework

This research paper will focus on Policy measures undertaken by State governments to create enabling environments for PPPs. New Public Management (NPM) and the Theory of policy credibility, suggest some basic fundamentals that need to be right if the expected results of PPPs are not to be elusive.

2.1 Public-Private Partnership

The public sector includes all 'organizations and institutions that are financed by state revenue and functions under government budgets. They include government departments, semi-autonomous bodies, civic bodies, agencies, etc.' (Venkatraman and Bjorkman, 2006:2). National governments, district administration, municipal authorities, local government bodies, parastatal corporations, state universities and research organizations can be considered as a Public sector partners. The private sector consists of both private for profit and not for profit organizations.

Paoletto (2000) defines partnership as 'collaborative activities among interested groups, based on mutual recognition of respective strengths and weaknesses, working towards common agreed objectives developed through effective and timely communication' (Paoletto, 2000). For Brinkerhoff, partnership is a 'dynamic relationship among diverse actors, based on mutually agreed objectives, pursued through a shared understanding of the most rational division of labour based on the respective comparative advantages of each partner' (Brinkerhoff, 2002: 21). According to Venkatraman and Bjorkman, the common elements that determine partnership are 'beneficence, non-malfeasance, autonomy (of each partner), jointness (shared decision making) and equity (benefits to be distributed to those in need)' (Venkatraman and Bjorkman, 2006: 4).

'The term Public Private Partnership (PPP) describes a spectrum of possible relationships between public and private actors for the cooperative provision of infrastructure services. The only essential ingredient is some degree of private participation in the delivery of traditionally public-domain services' (Kumar & Prasad, 2004: 36). This definition covers almost all possible investment models like voluntary, coalition, and partnership models. However, Government of India's (GOI) definition on Public Private Partnership (PPP) will be more relevant here, since this study is going to focus on the PPPs in infrastructure in Indian states. According to GOI, 'Public Private Partnership (PPP) Project means a project based on contract or concession agreement, between a Government or statutory entity on the one side and private sector company on the other side, for delivering an infrastructure service on payment of user charges. Private Sector Company means a company in which 51 per cent or more of the subscribed and paid up equity is owned and controlled by a private entity.'[3]

Though private procurement is not new in government, the 'PPP is the new face of development where the state and private actors, who have had a long history of conflict now work in collaboration' (Datta, 2009: 73). Although many commentators consider PPPs to be a new version of privatisation (Minow, 2003), PPPs are not privatisation because, in PPP the government retains ultimate responsibility where else in privatisation the government does not exercise any direct role in ongoing operation. When it comes to infrastructure development PPPs are considered as a 'refinement of the private financing initiatives for infrastructure that started in the early 1990s and describe the provision of public assets and services through the participation of the government, the private sector and the consumers' (Grimsey, 2005: 346). The difference with the traditional form of procurement is that in PPPs the government takes a more minimalist stance it chooses a private consortium which is asked to design, build and ultimately maintain it as efficiently as possible. 'The PPP alternative is thus characterized by two important features. First, the two tasks of building and managing assets are now bundled. Second, the ownership pattern is also quite different' (Martimort, 2008: 394).

According to Martimort (2008), the key advantage of bundling both the building and management of infrastructure is getting good design and technology and its impact on operating costs. A 'better design of the infrastructure may help to save on operating costs, the case of a positive externality', 'A better design may also require learning new procedures for managing assets and thus increase operating costs, the case of a negative externality' (Martimort, 2008: 394). The idea is that if both the tasks are performed by the same firm the firm will built a quality infrastructure because if building and managing are bundled the firm can internalize the impact that a better infrastructure design has on operating costs. 'The builder and the operator should thus be merged into a single entity. The optimal organization form exhibits thus an important feature found in public-private partnerships' (Martimort, 2008: 394). Also the delay normally found in a publicly procured contracts adds to the costs of the project. Therefore, 'transferring these risks to the private sector under a PPP structure and having it bear the cost of design and construction overruns is one way in which a PPP can potentially add value for money in a public project' (Grimsey, 2005: 346).

2.2 Are PPPs Value for Money?

The Private Finance Initiative of UK offers valuable information on this question. According to Hodge, 'The early analysis of Hall (1998) (also) noted that value for money in PFI Schemes depended on any gains in efficiency through private sector involvement more than compensating for higher finance costs and that it was difficult to obtain clear evidence on this in the absence of an accurate and uncontroversial public sector comparator' (Hodge, 2004: 157).

After careful analysis, Arthur Andersen (2000), suggests that there are 'six main determinants of value for money, namely risk transfer; the long-term nature of contracts (including whole-of-life cycle costing); the use of an output specification; competition; performance measurement and incentives; private sector management skills. Of these, competition and risk are seen to be the most important' (Grimsey, 2005: 347). If we apply these norms to study PPPs, they have an appeal to be value for money (especially to those in charge of allocating public sector resources) 'because they offer one way of resolving the large cost overruns and delays in traditional public procurement methods for infrastructure phenomena known as 'optimism bias' (Grimsey, 2005: 373).

Grimsey, after quoting two studies of optimum bias in 2002, which confirmed the results of earlier research by Pickrell, argues that the government is in a disadvantageous position, particularly the government cannot create incentives to the managers as it is done in the commercial organizations, 'By contrast, market competition can be seen as a form of coordination with intrinsic advantages over bureaucratic organizational forms and the discipline and incentives embodied in market contracting arrangements are valuable in injecting greater efficiency into infrastructure delivery' (Grimsey, 2005: 373). Therefore, on number of scores PPPs have proved to be value for money compared to the traditional form of government procurements.

2.3 New Public Management

There has been a shift in understanding the role of the states in public service delivery over the last few decades. The old public administration emphasized direct government delivery, hierarchical control, and a separation of politics and management to ensure due process for citizens and limit outside influence among public employees. This system was criticized as too slow and inflexible by proponents of the New Public Management who argued market type management approaches could be effectively applied to the public sector (Hood, 1991: Osborne & Gaebler, 1992). The New public management emphasized the speed and flexibility and touted the advantages of markets for both greater private sector engagement and consumer voice for citizens (Savas, 1987). The new public management reform focused on enhancing values and practices relating to competition and entrepreneurialism inside the public sector (Warner, 2008).

The argument in favour of New Public Management is 'that policy-making and service delivery are distinct tasks and that each benefits from the additional attention it receives if it is not competing for management time with the other. In addition, of course, once purchasing has been detached from policy-making, there are opportunities for creating contract-like arrangements to provide performance incentives' (Manning, 2001: 299).

2.4 Policy Credibility

Reforms agenda will fail to achieve its intended results, if the overall 'policy environment' in which the reforms and programmes are undertaken. Investors make their investment decisions based on their perception about the viability and effectiveness of announced policies by the governments, which is again judged by the likelihood of policy reversal or collapse (Grabel, 1999: 3-4). The policy credibility then 'depends on a kind of circular logic: economic policies are deemed effective only if they are credible to private agents; but policies are deemed credible only if they are seen to be effective' (Blackburn and Chiristensen, 1989: 1).

If success of policy depends on the perception of investors on its viability, then what should be done by the states on the policy? Should they implement a 'correct policy' or should they shade the policy towards the existing sentiments? Kydland and Prescott (1977) offer their valuable suggestion that 'Policy-makers should follow rules rather than have discretion' because 'discretion implies selecting the decision which is best, given the current situation. Such behaviour either results in consistent but suboptimal planning or in economic instability' (Kydland & Prescott, 1977: 487).

Incorrect policy cannot retain its credibility in case of disruptions that it would encounter in future. 'If in each period, the policy decision selected is the one which maximizes the sum of the value of current outcomes and the discounted valuation of the end-of-period state, the policy selected will be consistent but not optimal' (Kydland & Prescott 1977: 486).

Decision-makers and implementers inevitably face opposition when they attempt to pursue reform initiatives, therefore, it is important to analyze the feasibility of policy or reform proposals by analyzing the support and opposition for change. It is also important to understand, what interest the reformers and the government which is undertaking reforms are going to serve, and the political and bureaucratic resources need to sustain such initiatives (Grindle & Thomas, 1991). A business environment in which the rules are incredible such as unclear property rights, constant policy surprises and reversals, uncertain contract enforcement, and high corruption most likely translates into lower investment and growth (Brunetti, 1998). The need for political continuity and stability are vital for investments in infrastructure, since they have a long-time horizon. 'Investment in infrastructure is highly political in nature and it is often the lack of political stability that holds back necessary investment. Investors are hesitant to make long-term commitments for fear of government intervention and breaches of contractual obligations' (Heymann, 2007: 6).

3. PPPs in India

3.1 Status of PPPs in India

Public Private Partnerships (PPPs) are not new to India. India had a few notable PPPs like, the Great Indian Peninsular Railway Company operating between Bombay (now Mumbai) and Thana (now Thane) (1853), the Bombay Tramway Company running tramway services in Bombay (1874) even in the nineteenth century. The Great Indian Peninsular Railway Company, and the Power Generation and Distribution companies in Bombay and Calcutta (now Kolkata) in the early 20th century are some of the earliest examples of PPP in India.

Since the opening of the economy in 1991 there have been several cautious and tentative attempts to bring investments through PPPs in India. However, most PPPs have been restricted to the roads sector. Large-scale private financing in water supply has so far been limited to a few cities like Visakhapatnam and Tirupur. Most PPPs in water supply projects have been through municipal bonds in cities such as Ahmedabad, Ludhiana, and Nagpur. West Bengal has recorded significant success in using PPPs in housing and health sectors. Gujarat and Maharashtra have had success especially in ports, roads, and urban infrastructure.

However, successfully working PPP models are a more recent phenomenon. The NOIDA toll bridge, Tirupur water supply project, national highways, port development, and telecom industry are some notable examples of successful PPPs. It took a long time for many of these projects to take shape from concept and financial closure and commissioning. Nevertheless, they have offered valuable lessons on how not to handle PPPs and they have been internalized well. However, the commercial viability of water supply and sanitation projects are yet to demonstrated to the public. Absence of regulatory authorities and the desired legal framework are some of the hurdles in the water supply and sanitation sectors (DEA & ADB-Workshop Report, 2006).

In the last 10 years, Indian states have made considerable innovation with different structures to attract private participation in delivering infrastructure services. But at the same time progress has been uneven; there are islands of progress, with some states having under taken far more PPPs than others, and a much heavier use of PPPs in some sectors than others. In terms of frameworks for PPPs, some states have made maximum effort to develop this, including cross-cutting legislation and the development of cross-sectoral units that play a role in the identification and preparation of PPPs. Others, however, have worked within the bounds of their existing organizational structure (World Bank, 2006: 21).

The Role of PPPs so far in India

The data related to PPP projects as on 31st July, 2009, from the Government of India's database is compiled and given in Table 9.1.

As per the database, both the Central and State agencies put together, there are 402 PPP Projects in various stages from bidding to completion. The total value of the PPP Projects is Rs. 1,77,972 crores (Rs.17,797 bn). Karnataka has the maximum number of projects, i.e. 92 (23%), followed by NHAI 82 (20%), Andhra Pradesh 39 (10%), Rajasthan 32

Table 9.1: PPP Projects in India (Implemented through both the Central and State Agencies)

Contacting Agencies and States	*Total Number of PPP Projects*	*% of PPP Project*	*Value of Contract in Crores*	*% of Value of Contracts*	*Value of Contracts in billion (Indian Rs.)*
Karnataka	92	22.89	34795	19.55	3479.5
NHAI	82	20.40	31335	17.61	3133.5
Andhra Pradesh	39	9.70	7774	4.37	777.4
Rajasthan	32	7.96	450	0.25	45.0
Madhya Pradesh	29	7.21	5748	3.23	574.8
Sikkim	23	5.72	16961	9.53	1696.1
Gujarat	17	4.23	13613	7.65	1361.3
Punjab	15	3.73	767	0.43	76.7
Maharashtra	14	3.48	20329	11.42	2032.9
Ministry of Shipping	14	3.48	7592	4.27	789.2
Tamil Nadu	9	2.24	2114	1.19	211.4
Kerala	8	1.99	9547	5.36	954.7
Delhi	6	1.49	503	0.28	50.3
Jharkhand	3	0.75	681	0.38	68.1
Ministry of Civil Aviation	3	0.75	19111	10.74	1911.1
Odisha	3	0.75	3225	1.81	322.5
Ministry of Railways	3	0.75	1007	0.57	100.7
Puducherry	2	0.50	2286	1.28	228.6
Andaman and Nicobar Islands	1	0.25	85	0.05	8.5
Bihar	1	0.25	4	0.00	0.4
Chandigarh	1	0.25	15	0.01	1.5
Goa	1	0.25	30	0.02	3.0
Total	402		177972		17797.2

Source: Author's own compilation, Data source *www.pppinindia.com.*

(8%), Madhya Pradesh 29 (7%), Sikkim 23 (6%). All other central agencies and state have less than 5 per cent of share in total number of projects.

According to the value of projects, the State of Karnataka tops the list with 92 projects at an estimated value of Rs. 34,795 crore (Rs. 3,479 bn.) which is 20 per cent of total value of all projects put together for the entire country, followed by NHAI Rs. 3133 bn (18%), Maharashtra Rs. 2031 bn (11%), Ministry of Civil Aviation Rs. 1911 bn (11%), Sikkim Rs. 1696 bn (10%), Gujarat Rs. 1361 bn (8%). All other central agencies and States have less than 5 per cent of share in total value of projects so far in the entire country.

Sector-wise analysis indicates that, Road sector dominates the list with maximum number of PPP Projects 264 (67%), followed by urban development with 52 Nos. (13%), Ports with 41 Nos. (10%), energy sector 30 (7%), Air port projects 6, and tourism projects 6, and 3 projects in Railways. Annexure-I gives details about the sectorwise PPP variants. BOT-Toll model is the most popular PPP model (187 are BOT-Toll type out of 402 projects) adopted by central sector agencies in 227 Road sector projects and 21 Port projects, followed by BOOT model in 51 projects. Again from the figures it is clear that BOOT model has been adopted for almost all the projects in the Energy sector.

When looking at the total estimated project cost of PPPs in terms of projects, we see that Road Sector account for 46 per cent of the total (Rs. 8171 bn), because of the small average size of project. Ports, with a much larger average size of project, account for 26 per cent of the total (Rs. 4515 bn). The value of the 6 Airports project is 11 per cent of the total value (Rs. 2004 bn). It is noteworthy that if ports and central road projects and airport projects are excluded from the total, there is in fact a relatively small value of flow, at only Rs. 3000 bn in basic infrastructure PPPs to-date suggesting a significant potential upside for PPP projects across sectors, where states, municipalities have primary responsibilities.

3.2 PPPs in Central Government Agencies

Across central agencies, the leading users of PPPs by number of projects have been the Road sector, and the National High Ways Authority of India (NHAI), with 82 projects (Table 9.2). The other central agencies that have been important users of PPPs are Ministry of Shipping, Road Transport and Highways (MOSRTH) (14 projects), Ministry of Civil Aviation (5 projects) and the Ministry of Railways with 3 PPP projects. However, looking at the break up by the estimated project size, we see that Road Projects accounts for 53 per cent of total project cost (Rs. 3133 bn)

Table 9.2: Central Agency-wise PPP Projects

Central Government Agencies	*No. of Projects*	*Value in crores*
NHAI	82	31335
Ministry of Shipping	14	7592
Ministry of Civil Aviation	5	19111
Ministry of Railways	3	1007
Total	104	59045

due to its four large projects. Ministry of Civil Aviation with Rs.1911 bn (32%) and MOSRTH with Rs. 759 bn (13%) are other significant players.

Table 9.3 gives the details of State-wise investment in PPP Projects implemented through Central Agencies. Delhi tops the list with maximum per capita investment in PPPs though there were only two PPP projects from central agencies followed by Goa with only one PPP project. This is because of the high value of the projects and low population in these states. Among the comparable states like Tamil Nadu, Andhra Pradesh, Karnataka, Maharashtra and Gujarat, Tamil Nadu is able to get maximum number of projects and maximum per capita investment, from central agencies.

Table 9.3: State-wise investment in PPP Projects (Implemented through Central Agencies)

Sl. No.	*States*	*Total No. of PPP Projects*	*Value of contracts in crores*	*Per capita investment in Rs.*
1.	Tamil Nadu	21	8489	1360.3
2.	Andhra Pradesh	15	7409	972.2
3.	Maharashtra	11	10813	1116.1
4.	Gujarat	10	4087	806.6
5.	Karnataka	7	4314	816.3
6.	Madhya Pradesh	7	2515	416.7
7.	Rajasthan	5	1590	281.4
8.	Uttar Pradesh	5	2108	126.8
9.	West Bengal	5	2055	256.3
10.	Chhattisgarh	4	838	402.2
11.	Haryana	3	863	408.1
12.	Kerala	3	2733	858.3
13.	Punjab	3	778	319.4
14.	Delhi	2	9310	6721.8
15.	Bihar	1	418	50.4
16.	Goa	1	220	1632.4
17.	Odisha	1	505	137.2
	Total	104	59045	631.2

Source: Author's own compilation. Data source *www.pppinindia.com.*

An analysis of State-wise and Sector-wise details on PPP projects implemented through central agencies (Table 9.4) shows that, the top performers like Tamil Nadu, Maharashtra, Andhra Pradesh have maximum projects in Road sectors and Tamil Nadu, Maharashtra and Gujarat have got the maximum number of Port Projects as well. In terms of main types of PPP contracts, (Table 9.5) out of 104 PPP Projects in central sector 73

Table 9.4: State-wise and Sector-wise details on PPP Projects implemented through Central Agencies

Sl. No.	States	Roads	Ports	Air Ports	Railways	Total number of PPP Projects
1.	Andhra Pradesh	14		1		15
2.	Bihar	1				1
3.	Chhattisgarh	4				4
4.	Delhi	1		1		2
5.	Gujarat	4	3		3	10
6.	Goa		1			1
7.	Haryana	3				3
8.	Karnataka	6		1		7
9.	Kerala	1	1	1		3
10.	Madhya Pradesh	7				7
11.	Maharashtra	7	3	1		11
12.	Odisha		1			1
13.	Punjab	3				3
14.	Rajasthan	5				5
15.	Tamil Nadu	17	4			21
16.	Uttar Pradesh	5				5
17.	West Bengal	4	1			5
	Total	82	14	5	3	104

Source: Author's own compilation. Data source *www.pppinindia.com.*

Table 9.5: Sector-wise details on various PPP Project Models adopted by Central Agencies

Sector	BOOT		BOT-TOLL		BOT Annuity		BOO		LDOT		Total	
	No. of Projects	Value	No.of Projects	Value	No. of Projects	Value	No. of Projects	Value	No. of Projects	Value	No. of Projects	Value
Roads			56	21254	26	10081					82	31335
Ports			14	7592							14	7592
Airports	2	4408					1	303	2	14400	5	19111
Railways			3	1007							3	1007
Total	2	4408	73	29853	26	10081	1	303	2	14400	104	59045

are BOT-Toll, followed by 26 under BOT Annuity, 2 each under BOOT and LDOT and one BOO type.

3.3 PPPs in States

Across states, the leading user of PPPs by number of projects is Karnataka with 92 projects, followed by Andhra Pradesh (39 Projects), Rajasthan

(32 Projects), Madhya Pradesh (29 Projects), Sikkim (23 Projects) and Gujarat (17 Projects). However, looking at the break up, by estimated project size, we see that Karnataka dominates with Rs.349 bn (29%), followed by Maharashtra Rs.2032 bn (17%), Sikkim Rs.1696 bn (14%), Gujarat Rs.1361 bn (11%), and Kerala Rs.954 bn (8%). Andhra Pradesh accounts for 7 per cent of total project costs with Rs.777 bn and Madhya Pradesh 5 per cent with Rs.574 bn.

Table 9.6: State-wise Investment in PPP Projects implemented by State Governments

Sl. No.	*States*	*Total No. of PPP Projects*	*Value of Contracts in crores*	*Population*	*Per capita investment in Rs.*
1.	Andaman & Nicobar	1	85	356152	2386.6
2.	Andhra Pradesh	39	7774	76210007	1020.1
3.	Bihar	1	4	82998509	0.5
4.	Chandigarh	1	15	900655	166.5
5.	Delhi	6	503	13850507	363.2
6.	Gujarat	17	13613	50671017	2686.5
7.	Goa	1	30	1347668	222.6
8.	Jharkhand	5	681	26945829	252.7
9.	Karnataka	92	34795	52850562	6583.7
10.	Kerala	8	9547	31841374	2998.3
11.	Madhya Pradesh	29	5748	60348023	952.5
12.	Maharashtra	14	20329	96878627	2098.4
13.	Odisha	3	3225	36804660	876.2
14.	Puducherry	2	2286	974345	23461.9
15.	Punjab	15	767	24358999	314.9
16.	Rajasthan	32	450	56507188	79.6
17.	Sikkim	23	16961	540851	313598.4
18.	Tamil Nadu	9	2114	62405679	338.8
	Total	298	118927	676790652	1757.2

Source: Author's own compilation. Data source: *www.pppinindia.com.*

Sector-wise analysis of PPP projects implemented by the state governments shows that, there are some similarities in project formations compared to central agencies. Here again, Road sector dominates with 185 projects out of 298 projects formed by state governments, followed by Urban development (52 projects), Energy (30 projects) and Ports (24 projects). A very clear indication that both the Central Government and State Governments are developing Roads on priority. In Urban development again, a close analysis indicates that more number of projects are being undertaken by States for developing urban transportations like

Table 9.7: Sector-wise PPP Projects implemented by the State Governments

Sl. No.	*States*	*Roads*	*Ports*	*Air ports*	*Urban Dovelopment*	*Energy*	*Tourism*	*Total No. of PPP Projects*
1.	Andaman & Nicobar					1		1
2.	Andhra Pradesh	36	2		1			39
3.	Bihar				1			1
4.	Chandigarh				1			1
5.	Delhi	1			5			6
6.	Gujarat	10	7					17
7.	Goa		1					1
8.	Jharkhand	1			4			5
9.	Karnataka	55	3		23	6	5	92
10.	Kerala	1	2	1	3		1	8
11.	Madhya Pradesh	23			6			29
12.	Maharashtra	7	7					14
13.	Odisha	1	2					3
14.	Puducherry	2						2
15.	Punjab	12						15
16.	Rajasthan	32						32
17.	Sikkim					23		23
18.	Tamil Nadu	4			5			9
	Total	185	24	1	52	30	6	298

Source: Author's own compilation. Data source: *www.pppinindia.com.*

flyovers etc. Some states such as Sikkim and Kerala which have natural advantages have developed projects in Energy sector and most of them are Hydro Electric projects. Similarly some states with natural advantages could develop projects for Minor Ports.

In terms of main types of PPP contracts among the states (Annexure-II), almost all contracts have been of the BOT/BOOT type or close variants. Out of 298 total number of PPP Projects 187 are BOT-Toll, followed by 51 under BOOT type, 29 under BOT Annuity, 16 under DBFOT and 10 under BOOST Type. World Bank (2006:34-36) report suggests that a considerable number of unbankable and unrealistic PPP projects are brought to the market by State Governments. Data from the Government of India database show that there were 14 projects that have been moved from PPP mode to Public domain and 4 projects have been cancelled[4]. Of these, several had no good offers forthcoming from private sector firms in response to successive requests for expressions of interest. Although this number is not obviously high compared to the number of projects underway, it nonetheless suggests that there may be significant benefits from capacity building in identification and preparation of PPPs to ensure that more bankable projects are brought to market by the states and private firms.

4. Legal and Institutional Frameworks for PPPs Presentation of Data

4.1 Legal and Institutional Framework for PPPs at State Level

In India, State Governments have understood that achieving high volumes of private investment in infrastructure is not easy, therefore, they found it necessary to develop an environment which is both attractive to investors and also seen to be fair to consumers. 'The concept and implementation of PPPs is still very nascent in India. Diverse models are being operationalised by multiple stake holders in a wide variety of sectors. Government policy regarding regulatory, legal and institutional framework is still evolving' (Datta, 2009: 74). Following are the three main approaches followed by Indian states in structuring the legal and institutional frameworks for PPPs:

- combining dedicated institutions with cross-cutting legislation;
- establishing and using cross-sectoral PPP advisory units to help line departments in the absence of overarching legislation; and
- relying on line departments and sectoral agencies to build capacities.

If we apply this framework to analyze the legal and institutional set up, Indian states can be grouped in to three categories.

Category-I

The States of Andhra Pradesh, Gujarat, Karnataka, Odisha and Punjab have developed enabling legislation and established dedicated cross-sectoral institutions. These states have constituted specialized agencies and passed legislations to promote PPPs in infrastructure. (Example: Gujarat Infrastructure Development Board, The Andhra Pradesh Infrastructure Authority and the Punjab Infrastructure Development Board).

Andhra Pradesh

The State of Andhra Pradesh has enacted the Infrastructure Authority Act, to facilitate private investors in securing the required administrative approvals and lays down provisions for arbitrations and fiscal regulation. The legislation covers the infrastructure sectors of highways/bridges, airports, seaports, power, water supply and sanitation, telecommunication networks, gas distribution and waste management. It also covers urban infrastructure, including housing, urban development, medical facilities, and leisure facilities (DEA & ADB, 2006: 44).

Gujarat

The State of Gujarat has enacted the Gujarat Infrastructure Development Act, 1999 (GID Act), which provides for a regulatory framework for private sector participation in financing, construction, maintenance and operation of infrastructure projects. This Act provides transparent procedures for selection of private developers and levying user charges for the facilities provided by the developer. The government had set up the Gujarat Infrastructure Development Board (GIDB) as a specialized agency under an ADB-assisted TA Project to promote PPPs in infrastructure. GIDB is responsible for overall planning, removal of policy impediments, coordination between various departments and monitoring the progress. During 1995-99, various sectoral policies have been framed by Gujarat government, covering ports (1995), power (1995), roads (1996) and BOOT policy for ports (1997).

Karnataka

Karnataka has enacted an Infrastructure policy, which provides an option for Public Private Partnerships and collection of user charges for the services provided by the Private investors. This policy applies to township development, commercial development with common-user facilities, water supply and sewerage, waste water recycling, underground drainage, waste management (solid waste/biomedical/hazardous waste), tourism, energy, industrial infrastructure, agricultural infrastructure, education and health care (DEA & ADB 2006: 46).

Infrastructure Development Corporation Karnataka Limited (IDCK) is a cross-sectoral entity established by Government of Karnataka for project development activities. It is a joint venture of the state government, IDFC and HDFC modelled on 'Partnerships' in UK. It undertakes policy work, development studies, documentation, bid process management and provides advisory services to other departmental government agencies. It also provides advisory services such as enabling frameworks, project development and structuring and management of a Project Investment Fund.

Odisha

The Industrial Policy Resolution (IPR), 2001, of the state has accorded high priority for development of physical and social infrastructure through PPPs. A committee on Infrastructure has been set up to formulate strategies, identify projects, develop model documents and establish processes and procedures related to PPPs. A PPP Cell has also been created and a Secretary-level officer has been posted exclusively for it. A PPP Technical Secretariat is being created with subject experts from outside government. Institutional arrangement with ILFS has been put in place with focus on development and implementation of projects in PPP mode and provide direction.

Punjab

The Government has established the Punjab Infrastructure Development Board (PIDB) and passed the Punjab Infrastructure (Development & Regulation) Act, 2002. The PIDB acts as an apex empowered body responsible for overall planning of infrastructure sector and infrastructure projects in the state. It undertakes the policy formulation and regulation, single-window approvals and award of concession. It also acts as a body to find alternative funding.

The Government has also established the Punjab Infrastructure Initiative Fund, with a corpus of Rs. 20 crore to finance project developmental costs, is intended to identify, develop and structure projects to prepare a shelf of financially viable projects, and create a superior model for PPPs in the state through modern project management, monitoring and execution practices (DEA and ADB, 2006: 55).

Category-II

A second category of States, such as Rajasthan, Uttarakhand, Kerala and West Bengal have developed cross-sectoral facilitation entities, but have not passed comprehensive legislation.

Rajasthan

Rajasthan has established Rajasthan Project Development Corporation (PDCOR) as a cross-sectoral agency to facilitate private investment in infrastructure, including policy advisory services to the state government and institutional support to structure and implement PPPs. Apart from PDCOR, Rajasthan has the following other institutional arrangements as well for facilitating investment in infrastructure and PPPs.

- Economic Policy and Reforms Council (EPRC): It is a state-level think-tank comprising corporate leaders, eminent educationalists, specialists and economists with the chief Minister as Chairperson.
- Board of Infrastructure Development and Investment (BIDI): It is an empowered committee which accords approvals, including concessions to major projects.
- Bureau of Investment Promotion (BIP): It is a single-window agency to facilitate approvals from various departments.
- Empowered Committee on Infrastructure Development (ECID): It is the nodal body for conceptualizing and approving projects, including PPPs.

Rajasthan has enacted Rajasthan Road Development Act, in 2002 to encourage PPPs in the construction of financially viable bridges, bypasses, rail over-bridges, tunnels, etc.

Uttarakhand

The Government of Uttarakhand has identified tourism, energy, IT and horticulture sectors as future drivers of the state's GDP, and aims to achieve this by improving communication and transport infrastructure. It has developed an Infrastructure Vision with professional support. It has established a Infrastructure Board chaired by the Chief Minister, and two joint venture companies with IDFC and ILFS for developing PPP projects.

West Bengal

West Bengal has established a cross-sectoral entity IWIN (ICICI-West Bengal Infrastructure Developmental Corporation Limited) which is a joint venture between ICICI Bank Group and Government of West Bengal. It is formed with the objective of accelerating the development of infrastructure in the state. West Bengal Government has also notified its policy on Infrastructure Development through Public Private Partnership in August 2003. The major elements of the policy are to ensure reasonable returns on private investment by way of extending 'concessions' tax incentives, VGF (Capital grant/revenue grant), government guarantee, shorter period for deferred annuity, and providing possible safeguard against political and social uncertainty.

Kerala

Kerala Industrial Infrastructure Corporation (KINFRA) is the key organization to develop infrastructural projects and investments in Kerala. The Government of Kerala, through KINFRA has formed a public private joint venture company called Infrastructure Kerala Limited (INKEL) as a Special purpose vehicle to develop PPP Projects for infrastructure development. Kerala's port policy facilitates Private Partnerships in Port development, it allows the investors to decide tariffs and employee policies.

Category-III

Finally, a third category of states, including Madhya Pradesh, Maharashtra and Tamil Nadu, have relied on sectoral and line agencies to develop and implement PPPs.

Madhya Pradesh

In Madhya Pradesh (MP), initially the MP Public Works Department (MPPWD) and then the specially created MP Road Development Corporation (MPRDC) have acted as the agency for development of road projects on BOT basis in the state. In the process of developing projects, MPRDC has developed policy, guidance, materials and skills for facilitating PPPs in Road sector.

Maharashtra

In Maharashtra, the State Road Development Corporation (MSRDC) and Mumbai Metropolitan Region Development Authority (MMRDA) have developed policies for infrastructure development through private sector participation, including a "Policy on implementation of Road and Bridge Projects" through private sector participation.

Tamil Nadu

There is no state PPP Policy in Tamil Nadu. However, the Government of Tamil Nadu has enacted an Act in 1998 the "Tamil Nadu Transparency in Tender Act, 1998" and relevant rules under "Tamil Nadu Transparency in Tender Rules, 2000". This act and rules give clear procedure for the departments for the procurement of goods and services, construction, etc.

Government has given thrust to Public Private Partnerships in its following Policy Documents:

1. The New Industrial Policy 2007.
2. Housing Policy.
3. IT Department G.O. Ms. No. 18 dated 11.6.2007.
4. Health and Family Welfare Department G.O. Ms. No. 33 Dated 31.1.2008, Facilitating Public Private Partnership in the improvements and upkeep of health facilities in the State.
5. Highways Department (Roads, Bridges, Minor Ports and Shipping) Policy note 2008-2009.
6. Municipal Administration and Water Supply Department Policy Note on administration of ULBs 2008-2009.
7. Tourism and Culture Department Policy Note 2008-2009.
8. Agriculture Department Policy Note 2005-2006.

The State government has also established several PPP agencies like, Tamil Nadu Water Investment Company (TWIC); New Tirupur Area Development Corporation Limited (NTADCL) as SPVs for supply of industrial and drinking water under Tirupur Water and Sanitation Project; Tamil Nadu Road Development Company (TNRDC) to develop road projects.

Annexures III and IV gives a compiled version of Legal and Institutional framework for PPPs in selected Indian states.

5. Case Study

5.1 Tirupur Water Supply Project

The entire chapter 5.1 on Tirupur Water Supply Project is prepared based on the factual information from the Power Point presentation on "Tirupur Area Development Programme—Financing and Structuring PPP projects—The Tirupur experience"—prepared on 24th October 2007, by the NTADCL, which is authentic and collected by the author of this Research Paper, from the Managing Director of the NTADCL, Chennai. The data collected from the fieldwork is discussed separately in Chapter 5.2.

Background

Tirupur is located in Tamil Nadu state 60 km from Coimbatore, in the Coimbatore-Erode textile belt, and it was part of the Coimbatore district till 2008, when the government created Tirupur district with Tirupur as its head quarters. Tirupur Municipality covers an area of 27 sq. km and the Tirupur Local Planning Area (TLPA) covers an area of 220 sq. km, Tirupur Municipality had a population of 235,000 (as per Census 1991) and its population as on date is around 4,50,000, most of them employed in the textile industry.

Knitting as an industry in Tirupur dates back to early 1900s. The number of units has increased from 100 in 1930s to over 8000 now. The town has evolved from a domestic supplier, to supporting exporters from Mumbai and Delhi, to a "direct" exporter (US & EU). Taking into account the indirect exports the town today caters to 50 per cent of India's knitwear exports (direct), valued at over 1.5 billion USD (both direct and indirect).

Water is the key resource used in the processing (bleaching and dying) of knitwear industry. Due to lack of adequate water supply, the industries have turned to groundwater and private tankers for getting assured supply of water. Prior to the NTADCL project 700 tankers operated daily on the average making 10-15 trips, with demand exceeding 100 MLD. The municipal area was not having an organized drainage system and a sewage collection and treatment system.

The unregulated drawal of groundwater not only damaged the underground aquifers, it also had the effect of crowding out water required for agriculture. Water availability is not consistent throughout the year and acute shortage being felt in the summer months. In addition to that the traditional sources of water was inconsistent in quality and has high Total Dissolved Solids (TDS) and hardness, which needs treatment before use. The opportunity cost of water for Industry is in the range of Rs.70-80 per kilo litre. Therefore, in response to the call by the Tirupur Exporters Association (TEA), and the people of Tirupur, Government of Tamil Nadu has announced the launch of the Tirupur Area Development Project in 1991, as a comprehensive solution for meeting the infrastructure requirements of the town.

Features of the Tirupur Area Development Project

The Tirupur Area Development Project (TADP) was set-up as a PPP by three partners—the Tamil Nadu Corporation for Industrial Development (TACID), the Tirupur Exporters Association (TEA), and the Infrastructure Leasing and Financial Services (IL&FS). They have signed an agreement in August 1994 to develop the TADP on a commercial format.

Tamil Nadu Water Investment Company Limited (TWICL)has been formed as a SPV by Government of Tamil Nadu and IL&FS. TWICL has a paid up capital of Rs. 65 crore, of which IL&FS holds Rs. 35 crore and Government of Tamil Nadu holds Rs. 30 crore of equity. TWICL has also raised subordinate debt of Rs. 40 crore from its promoters. TWICL has promoted New Tirupur Area Development Corporation Limited (NTADCL) for implementing various infrastructure projects in Tirupur, including water supply and sewerage and has invested a sum of Rs. 105 crores in NTADCL as equity.

Scope of the Project

The scope of work under the water and waste water project includes:

1. Integrated Water Supply Services

- ➢ Bulk Water supply to Tirupur Municipality (TM).
- ➢ Bulk Water Supply to Industries located in the TLPA
- ➢ Bulk water Supply of Wayside villages (Agreements executed with Government/agencies for supply).

2. Improvement of distribution network within Tirupur Municipality.
3. Sewerage collection treatment and disposal for Tirupur Municipality.
4. Low cost sanitation facility within Tirupur Municipality.

The NTADCL would be responsible for the operation and maintenance of the project outside the municipal area and Tirupur Municipality would be responsible for operation maintenance within the municipal area. Water for the project would be drawn from the river Cauvery. The Off-take point is downstream of the confluence of the river Cauvery with Bhavani. The spruce is located at a distance of 55 kms from Tirupur town. The NTADCL has received permission from Government of Tamil Nadu for drawal of 185 MLD of water from the river (can be increased to 250 MLD later).

The water is allocated in the following manner (net supply):

- Industries 105 MLD
- Tirupur Municipality (domestic) 26 MLD
- Way side Villages 31 MLD

The Project has three separate contracts, two awarded on an Engineer, Procure and Construct (EPC) basis, and one contract on Operate and Maintain (O&M) basis. The EPC1 contractor (Hindustan Construction Company Ltd.) is responsible for building a river intake, well and pumping station, a water treatment plant and booster pumping station; a transmission main, and a master balancing reservoir. The EPC2 contractor (Mahindra & Mahindra, L&T Ltd.) is responsible for three feeder mains, water distribution stations, distribution networks, a sewerage system and a low cost sanitation. The O&M contractor (Mahindra United Utilities) is responsible for operation and maintenance of the finished water and sewerage facilities.

Financing Structure

The project cost of Rs. 1023 crore is proposed to be financed through a mixture of debt and equity taken on by government, various commercial financial institutions, and international financing agencies, with debt-equity ratio of 1.5:1.

Item	*Rs in crores*	*US $ (in millions)*
Equity	322.7	69
Senior Debt	613.8	132
Subordinate Debt	86.5	18
Total	1023.0	219

Details on the Equity Structure of the Project is given in the Annexure-V.

Security Structure

A comprehensive security package has been put in place for the assignment of project agreements and step in rights, Charge on assets, Charge on receivables (post O&M expenses), Charge on residual insurance proceeds and for securing Cash Flows.

A lean period fund ("Water shortage fund") has been established by GoTN with initial corpus equivalent to six months revenue. This special fund, will be parked in a public deposit account to be drawn by NTADCL. It will be large enough to pay the interest and operative expenses of the project in the event of water shortage in the Bhavani river. For ensuring the receivables from the Tirupur Municipality an irrevocable letter of credit equivalent to one month receivables are escrowed into a special account (3 months reserves) and charged to NTADCL. For ensuring the receivables from industries Bank guarantees from local banks equal to 3 months receivables have been obtained.

Following is the Off-take and Revenue distribution among the intended beneficiaries.

Water Users	*Supply*	*Revenue*	*Unit Price*
Industry	67%	94%	4.5 paise/litre
Tirupur Municipality	16%	3%	0.5 paise/litre
Way side Panchayats	17%	3%	0.35 paise/litre

The pricing of water supply to industry has been determined on the basis of its opportunity cost, considered to be the rates paid to private tankers. Therefore, the price for industry will be five to six times the amount charged to domestic users. The tariff is linked to the basket of expenditure like power, consumables, O&M costs, etc. The weighted average increase in expenditure is automatically applied to the tariff in July every year and re-priced for industrial consumers, whereas for domestic consumers the revision is done once in three years. The subsidy structure will be maintained throughout the concession period.

This innovative financing structure has facilitated the repayment of funds raised in international and domestic markets, while balancing the interest of share holders. Infrastructure Leasing and Financial Services (IL & FS) and USAID provided loan guarantees over 30 years for US$ 25 million. The World Bank provided a line of credit to IL&FS. In addition, the Asian Development Bank through its private arm has a 27 per cent stake in the project. Although ownership of the project assets lay exclusively with NTADCL in its capacity as concessionaire, the consortium has an equity share in NTADCL. The return on equity amounts to 20 per cent per annum, and the average cost of debt is 17 per cent. Most importantly for the government implementation of the project leveraged its investment by about 100 times.

Intended Benefits of the Project

On completion, the Tirupur water supply and sewerage project is expected to deliver the following benefits.

Benefits to the Industry

Availability	: 24 hr availability
Delivery	: Water at the door step
Quality	: Superior and consistent quality
Cost	: Overall savings including in process costs
Realization	: Improvements in quality (RFT) leading to higher realization
Environment	: Helps the industry meet TDS norms

Improvement in quality and availability of water would lead to improvement in export competitiveness and it would act as a catalyst for attracting higher investment in core areas.

5.2 Analysis of the Data with Respect to Tirupur Water Supply Project

As this project is intended to supply water to 13 wayside villages, to assess impact of the scheme the researcher has collected data from all panchayats on the quantity of water they used to have before the project and the quantity of water available after the implementation of the project.

Since the project intends to supply treated water to way side panchayats, it has to reduce the drawal of groundwater by the panchayats and intern is expected to reduce the electricity bill. Therefore, to assess the financial implication of the project on panchayats the data relevant to payment of electricity bill before and after the project is collected and it is given in the (Annexure-VI).

The researcher had also discussed about the impact of the project with all 13 panchayat presidents, and with the Assistant Director of Panchayats who looks after the panchayat administration at district level and Engineers of the Water Board and also with the District Collector of Tirupur District. The researcher also had discussions with the Managing Director of NTADCL at Chennai and with the General manager and Manager (Technical) of Tirupur Water Supply Project at Tirupur.

From Table 9.6 it can be understood that the population has increased many fold from 2001 to 2009. It makes our job difficult to assess the satisfaction level as far as the quantity of water made available to the panchayats through this scheme is concerned. Though the scheme has fetched more water to panchayats, still there is an acute shortage of water in all the 13 panchayats selected for study. Correspondingly the electricity charges have not reduced, because the NTADCL makes the water available to one of the tanks available in all these panchayats, and pumping of water to the house hold connections and public fountains still remains the responsibility of panchayats. Because more water is made available to panchayats by NTADCL, now the panchayats have to spent more money on electricity for the internal pumping of water. Apart from that the panchayats have not done away with their old water resources because of this new projects. Still they continue to use the old resources, and it gets reflected in the electricity charges that the panchayats have to spent.

Regarding the quality of water supplied by the NTADCL, the feed back from the panchayat presidents and fieldwork gives a different picture than what is expected from a world class project. Mr. Rangasamy, the Thottipalayam Panchayat president said, “if the water is kept unused for 5 days, it gets spoiled and cannot be used for drinking, the odour is bad and people have a dislike for L&T water”, the Chettipalayam Panchayat president Mr. Marappan said, "This water is not fit for drinking, still I buy water from L&T, as it can be supplied and people will use it for other than drinking", and a more apt comment is made by the Pudupalayam Panchayat president Mr. Ramasamy: "third water scheme offers only a 3rd quality water". Apart from the above presidents almost all people, I have interacted with have expressed the same concern about the quality and odour of the water supplied through this scheme. Interaction with general public and other officials, engineers of this project confirmed these statements. One thing is that the people were comparing the quality of water which was available through other water supply schemes (all these panchayats were getting water from two other different government water supply schemes before the implementation of this project and people generally refer this project as 3rd scheme or as L&T scheme), and the engineers also confirm that there is difference in taste of water from this source. The other reason is that the water supplied to panchayats in this scheme is not fully treated, in the sense that the NTADCL is supplying water without proper chlorination. When enquired, the engineers said that, in the beginning they were supplying water after chlorination, and as it was causing damage to the fabrics in the textile industries and textile exporters were objecting to the chlorination, they stopped the chlorination and started to supply water without chlorination to panchayats as well. The panchayats are expected to supply the water to public for consumption, only after proper chlorination, which is not done properly and that's why there is a complaint on the quality and odour. This argument is not valid as the NTADCL is expected to supply potable water ready for consumption to way side panchayats as stipulated in the concession agreement.

As there is acute shortage of water every panchayat president have said that they require more water from NTADCL, however, the rate should be the same as it is supplied now. Though it is not part of the concession agreement, they expect that the NTADCL should help the panchayats to construct additional tanks in their panchayats for NTADCL water, and to supply water after full treatment including chlorination. The other interesting phenomena noticed in this project was, that it has improved the compliance of panchayats in their payments to the corporation. All these panchayats have paid the cost of water to NTADCL without any due till date.

The panchayat presidents have also informed that the compliance of people paying water charges has improved drastically, now 90 per cent of the people pay water charges due to panchayats on time. The panchayats adjacent to Tirupur municipality went in to say even they are ready to pay more provided if their full demand for water is met by the NTADCL.

From the discussions the researcher had with the Officials the following interesting points came to light. The Tirupur Water Supply Project was originally conceived by the Government agency TWAD (Tamil Nadu Water Supply and Drainage Board), to be executed through government funding. Since, the government funding was not coming through as expected, the Tirupur Exporters Association had put up more pressure on the Government for speedy execution of the project for their benefit, the Government had to resort to alternate form of financing the project and ultimately it evolved as a PPP project.

Regarding the PPP mode of procurement the Public sector engineers have a different say, at least for this project they are of the opinion, that the project cost is high compared to the government mode of execution. It is evident from the figures that the project cost went up because in Tirupur Water Supply Project, the Concessions were based on three contracts, two on Engineer, Procure and Construct (EPC) basis and one is an Operate and Maintain (O&M) contract. In EPC contract, the EPC agency or engineering firm is allowed to undertake design, engineering and execution of the project, and the procuring agency (NTADCL), is particular about the quantity and quality of the water supplied (that is the final product) and not the cost involved in design, engineering and execution of the projects. Because of this the engineers feel that the project cost went up. For example in BECTEL design they used MS Pipes where we can use PVC pipes, though MS pipes ensure long life and reduction of leakage, the cost involved is very high. The other interesting example is that the BECTEL has designed the pumping station with a 11 KVA motor, where only a 33 KVA supply is available from Tamil Nadu Electricity Board (TNEB), and as per the concession contract the Government has to make the required power supply available to the project execution agency. Here, the government had no other option to go for a separate 11 KVA substation which would have been avoided if the contract agency was ready to change the 11 KVA motor to a 33 KVA motor of the same capacity, it involved an extra expenditure of Rs. 9 crore to the government, which could have been avoided if the care was taken while preparing the concession contract.

In general the engineers feel that in such a sensitive project like water supply project the government should always have an upper hand. Even when we have to adopt the PPP mode for its technical superiority the government agency should have a say in design and execution, as it will give option for the government agency to adopt the design to local conditions and requirements and thereby reduce the unnecessary costs involved in procurement of customized spare parts from single agency.

From the discussions the researcher had with the field level officers working in Tirupur Water Supply Project, it was evident that all is not well with the project, as the private textile units have not come forwarded to take water from the NTADCL. Though the NTADCL can deliver water at their door steps, they don't want to buy the water from NTADCL, because, if industries buy water from NTADCL it is properly accounted for and they become responsible for letting out the untreated water into the river source. Because of the stringent norms enforced by Tamil Nadu Pollution Control Board (TNPCB) following a Supreme Court order the industries have become cautious and they make a nominal purchase of water from NTADCL and, still they buy water from other sources, since it is not accounted for. Since the entire project is based on the differential pricing mechanism adopted for supply of water to industries and Panchayats, as such it is very difficult to meet out the O&M costs and if the present trend continues and if there is no binding on the textile units to buy water from NTADCL, it will be very difficult for the corporation to ensure continuous supply of water to Panchayats at concessional rates.

Though the NTADCL is running in to rough weather now, still it can become a successful project if the illicit tapping of ground water in the surrounding areas of Tirupur for the industrial purpose is totally curbed and the textile units opt to buy water from NTADCL only. The free power supply made available for the agricultural purpose should not be misused for commercial exploitation of water for the industrial purposes.

6. Data Analysis

6.1 Analysis of Legal and Institutional Framework and Performance in PPPs

In the past, Central Government was dominant in infrastructure planning. 'At the moment the state governments are playing an increasingly important role, as regional parties have grown in strength' (Heymann, 2007:6). This is also related to decentralization trends in states particularly in infrastructure sectors. It has resulted in a complex bureaucratic system that foreign players find difficult to understand and it has slowed the process of infrastructure development in India. Since the investment flow in infrastructure is governed by the market principles and the incentive schemes offered by the particular regulatory regimes, the 'entry decisions of new infrastructure firms have been associated with sunk cost (i.e. assets-specific investment in infrastructures) and entry assistance such as incentive to invest' (Devapriya, 2006: 558).

As discussed in detail in the analytical framework the existence of proper legal and institutional framework can be assumed to instill the investor's confidence and creates a positive environment for investments in projects, therefore, it should have a positive correlation with the performance of states in PPP investments. To test this proposition we make the following leading hypothesis which is again later assessed for separate dimensions.

- There are commonalities in policy environment which makes certain states more attractive destination for PPP projects.

This overall hypothesis leads to:

Hypothesis-1

- Legal and Institutional framework for PPPs in States make the States more attractive destination for investment in PPP projects.

Table 9.8: Legal and Institutional Framework and Performance of in PPP Investments

States	*Legal and Institutional framework*	*Total Number of PPP Projects (Ranking shown in brackets)*		*Value of contracts in crores (Ranking shown in brackets)*		*Per capita investment in crores (Ranking shown in brackets)*	
Karnataka	Category - I	92	(1)	34795	(1)	6583.7	(1)
Kerala	Category - II	8	(8)	9547	(4)	2998.3	(2)
Gujarat	Category - I	17	(5)	13613	(3)	2686.5	(3)
Maharashtra	Category - III	14	(7)	20329	(2)	2098.4	(4)
Andhra Pradesh	Category - I	39	(2)	7774	(5)	1020.1	(5)
Madhya Pradesh	Category - III	29	(4)	5748	(6)	952.5	(6)
Odisha	Category - I	3	(10)	3225	(7)	876.2	(7)
Tamil Nadu	Category - III	9	(9)	2114	(8)	338.8	(8)
Punjab	Category - I	15	(6)	767	(9)	314.9	(9)
Rajasthan	Category - II	32	(3)	450	(10)	79.6	(10)
West Bengal	Category - II	NA		NA		NA	

Source: Author's own compilation. Data source: WB-IFC Investment Climate Survey, 2004 and www.pppinindia.com.

A detailed analysis has been made on different legal and institutional arrangements in different states in Chapter 4 (Tables 4.1.1 and 4.1.2). Based on the analysis the states have been grouped into three categories. Now to test the hypothesis a comparison has been made between the performance of these states in getting investment under PPP mode and the legal and institutional framework that were established in these states.

Category-I

Among the category-1 States (Andhra Pradesh, Gujarat, Karnataka, Odisha and Punjab) which have developed enabling legislation and established dedicated cross-sectoral institutions and constituted specialized agencies and passed legislations to promote PPPs in infrastructure, there is no consistency in performance with respect to the total investment under PPP mode and the per capita investment these states were able to generate under PPP mode.

Among the 11 states compared, the state of Karnataka distinctly occupies the number one position both in respect of total PPP investments and in per capita investment in PPP, followed by the Gujarat, and Andhra Pradesh occupying 3rd and 5th position respectively in respect of total PPP investments and in per capita investment in PPPs. Where else the performance of the States of Orissa and Punjab is not up to the mark, even though they have established legislation, dedicated cross-sectoral institutions and specialized agencies, they occupy only the 7th and 9th position respectively in respect of total investment in PPP projects and in the per capita investment in PPP projects.

Category-II

Among the second category of States (Kerala, Rajasthan, Uttarakhand and West Bengal), who have developed cross-sectoral facilitation entities, but have not passed comprehensive legislation to facilitate PPPs. The performance of Kerala is impressive, it occupies the 2nd position with Rs. 2998 crore as per capita investment in PPPs and 4th position with Rs. 9547 crore, as far as total investment in PPP is concerned. The performance of other States like Rajasthan, Uttarakhand and West Bengal who are in the same category is not comparable with Kerala. Rajasthan occupies only the 10th position in the comparison list of 11 states. West Bengal and Uttarakhand don't have even a single project under PPP mode in state sectors.

Category-III

Among the third category of states including Madhya Pradesh, Maharashtra and Tamil Nadu which have relied on sectoral and line agencies to develop and implement PPPs, the performance of Maharashtra is very impressive. It occupies 2nd position with Rs. 20329 crores as for as total investment in PPPs are concerned and 4th position with Rs. 2098 crore, with respect to per capita investment in PPP projects. Elsewhere the performance of Madhya Pradesh and Tamil Nadu are not so impressive occupying only the 6th and 9th position respectively both in total investment and per capita investment in PPPs.

The above analysis shows that, there is no clear link between institutional structures and success in developing PPPs in Indian states. It would seem clear from the experience of Karnataka, Andhra Pradesh, Rajasthan, Madhya Pradesh, Punjab and Gujarat in the development of PPPs for roads that, it is possible to develop a PPP programme in a single sector by building up capacities in line departments. The States of Gujarat and Maharashtra have developed capacities for port projects under PPP mode.

The reasons for the inconsistency in performance and the legal and institutional framework could be the following:

1. India has a well-developed rule of law, but its current legal and regulatory framework is not robust enough to give investors full confidence and therefore, it is a serious obstacle blocking the necessary injections of (foreign) private capital into India's infrastructure. The tariff and performance standards for Infrastructure projects are often governed by Concession agreements and they are typically matters of independent regulation (Heymann, 2007: 9).
2. In India, many (local) authorities are taking an adhoc approach and applying inconsistent and overly complex rules related to Investments. The reasons are: (a) the regulatory framework for infrastructure has developed autonomously within each sector. (b) Political constraints and vested interests. 'This has resulted in delays, corruption, incompetence and uneven regulatory framework' (Heymann, 2007: 9).
3. For Investors, the enforceability of obligations and concessions arrangements are very important. Since, India's Constitution distributes legislative and executive powers vertically between

the Union, states and local government, enforceability is a major problem in India. 'In reality, each of the sectors is regulated differently' (Heymann, 2007: 9).

To quote from the words of Mr. Paneendra Reddy, Managing Director of Tamil Nadu Urban Infrastructural Finance Services Limited, who handled the Tirupur Water Supply Project earlier, "Legal and Institutional arrangements may help or may not help in getting investments, but that itself may bind you sometimes." According to him it is better to keep the option opened, as it gives more flexibility, and we need not necessarily rely on legislative framework and it is not a prerequisite. According to him the key elements in deciding about PPP mode of investment are "cost of fund" and "risk sharing". There should not be any blind following for PPP model, we have to pick and choose depending upon the cost of funds and identification and sharing of risks.

According to Mr. Dawidar, Secretary to Government of Tamil Nadu, Energy and Information Technology Department, "Policy framework is not so important in choosing PPP mode of infrastructure financing, if PPP model can offer a better solution to a problem, we can go for it or we may choose PPP model if it brings better technology for a problem solving." According to him more than the legal and institutional framework, the criteria that should be adopted while choosing PPP model are efficiency, accountability and managerial skills. In his view fundamentals such as investment climate in the states, political commitment towards the use of PPPs, sufficient trained staff, and strong links between built-up capacity and implementation responsibility in the respective line departments are probably the most important ingredients of success.

6.2 Analysis of Investment Climate in States and Performance of States in PPPs

Infrastructure development through PPP mode means increased private sector participation in terms of investment in infrastructure projects. According to the World Bank, the key task is to 'manage infrastructure like a business and not like bureaucracy' (World Bank, 1994: 2). Any private sector investment in a country whether it is in infrastructure projects or industrial projects, it has 'much to do with the quality of India's investment climate with other investment destinations in Asia' (WB-IFC, 2004: 4). Since Investments in infrastructure have a long-term horizon, investors look at political continuity and stability in a state before making investment decisions. They also fear about government intervention and breaches of contractual obligations. 'This implies that investment in infrastructure is highly political in nature and it is often the lack of political stability that holds back necessary investment' (Heymann, 2007: 6).

A study using a disaggregated analysis, predicts that 'states successful in maintaining political and fiscal stability stand to gain most from public investments in human capital formation in terms of increased investment inflows,' and the 'investors select states as investment destinations predominantly on the basis of their contemporary social-economic performance as opposed to their past images as investment destinations' (Chakravarthi, 2009: 9).

Differences in Investment Climate within India

Ahluwalia (2002) indentifies private investments as the primary determinant of economic growth across states. Dollar, Iarossi and Mengistae (2002) also expect a good investment climate to facilitate a higher volume of investment inflows, particularly in the high productivity manufacturing and services sectors, leading to job creating, income growth and ultimately, poverty reduction. There are certain critical factors which determine investment inflows across Indian states and these factors are state specific. 'Though the federal frameworks of India cause all states to face certain common macroeconomic policies such as monetary policy and trade policy, states too retain extensive control over local administrative regulations, provision of infrastructure' (Chakravarthi, 2009: 11).

The determinants' of investment inflow into a state makes up the Investment Climate of that state. The Investment Climate Survey 2003, conducted jointly by World Bank and Confederation of Indian Industries (CII) shows that "significant investment climate variations exits among India's many states." The ICS of India 2003 asked respondents, to rate the general investment climate in all states other than their own. The resulting pattern was analyzed and found that Maharashtra, Delhi, Gujarat, Andhra Pradesh, Karnataka, Punjab, Tamil Nadu and Haryana were rated as better investment climate states and these states have attracted almost all the FDI in the past (WB-IFC, 2004: 5-6). The survey also asked the respondents 'to name which states had the best investment climate and which had the worst. Each of the other eleven states is ranked between these extremes by the difference between the percentage of those identifying it as a better-climate state and the percentage of those identifying it as worse-climate state' (WB-IFC, 2004: 44).

Since the investors have the liberty to choose their preferred investment destination amongst the various states in the Indian Union, there is an intense competition across states to get a maximum share in the upcoming investment projects. It has 'resulted in most state governments striving to better the investment climate prevailing in their respective states to make them conducive to inflows of domestic and foreign investment' (Chakravarthi, 2009: 10). If we look at the total investment over an extended post-reform period, investment trends between 1992 and 1998, we can find that, most "new" private sector investments have a strong coastal bias and were made in previously established locations. There is also evidence to show the 'path dependence' in the process of investment location. Investors, in seeking efficient locations, tend to favour existing industrial clusters with access to the coast (Chakravorty, 2003). 'At the same time, they show that investors avoid regions with inhospitable investment climates and friendly local governments' (WB-IFC, 2004: 42).

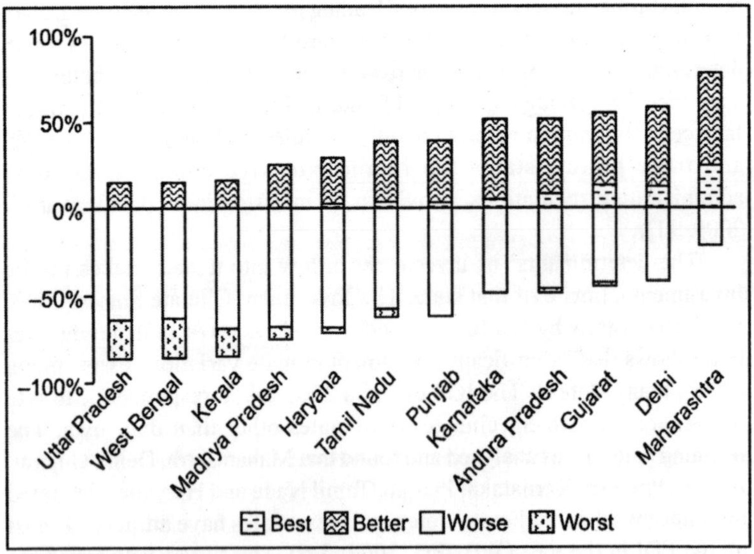

(Adopted from WB-IFC, Investment Climate Survey Report, 2004, p. 44).

Fig. 9.1: Outside Respondents Ranking a State's Investment Climate Relative to that of their Own

Yet another alternative index to rank investment climate is "state's average cost advantage" according to those who thought it had the best climate less its average cost disadvantage according to those who thought it had the worst climate. This is plotted against the percentage of outside respondents rating the investment climate of a state better than their own, and given in Figure 9.2. It brings out the following list of "better climate" States; Andhra Pradesh, Delhi, Gujarat, Haryana, Karnataka, Punjab and Tamil Nadu (WB-IFC, 2004: 44-46).

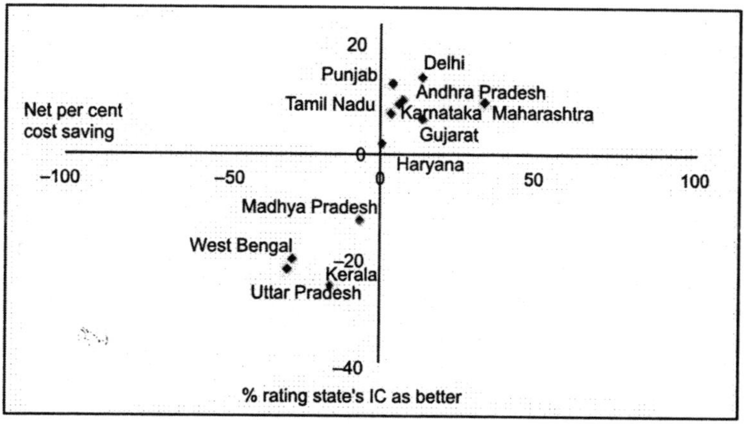

(Adopted from WB-IFC, Investment Climate Survey Report, 2004, pp. 44 & 46)
Fig. 9.2: Better Climate States

Location Modelling Approach

Location Modelling is an economic model used to understand the profit-maximizing location decision. It shows that agglomeration economies tend to push new investment to established locations and there is an element of path dependency. Analysis of firm-level data also shows that key investment climate indicators are closely correlated with productivity and business growth rates. Investment climate indicators such as unreliable and costly power supply, burdensome tax and customs administration, excessive labour regulation, inadequate land access, lack of access to formal external finance and finally corruption all are negatively correlated with productivity and business growth rates (WB-IFC, 2004: 8).

From the above analysis it is clear that there are two main factors that affect the individual firm's location decision. They are: (1) "Business environment" which includes access to inputs (quality and cost of labour and capital); access to markets; provision of basic infrastructure; institutional environment; and industry-specific subsides or tax breaks. (2) "Agglomeration economies" which are external economies from localization and urbanization that increase returns on scale and can lead to cumulative causation (WB-IFC, 2004: 42). It is also clear that the "better climate" States—Karnataka, Gujarat, Maharashtra, Andhra Pradesh, Tamil Nadu and Punjab—have fared well in attracting PPP investment in infrastructure projects. The states of Kerala, Madhya Pradesh and Odisha have also done well compared to other states in spite of being rated as not having better investment climate in the IC survey. Therefore, to explore the reasons for some states attracting more PPP investments compared to other states, and the factors that influence the investment location decisions, we propose to test the following hypotheses 2, 3 and 4.

Hypothesis-2

- States with low cost of corruption and low cost of regulation, tend to attract more investment in PPP projects compared to other states.

Analysis

The data related to perception criteria on level of corruption, cost of labour regulation and Tax and customs administration has been compiled from the IC survey and presented in Table 9.9.

Among the issues that influence investment in a state 'regulatory and corruption issues are top priorities for the business community in the "better climate" states, just as they are in other states; infrastructure, customs administration and the rest have more or less the same order of priority across states' (WB-IFC, 2004: 6). Karnataka has attracted the maximum per capita investment in PPPs, however, the percentage of respondents identifying corruption as a major bottleneck for investment is very high (66.4%) compare to other states. The objective proxies of burden of regulation are also high for Karnataka compared to other states. Same is the case with other better investment climate States such as Gujarat, Maharashtra, Andhra Pradesh, Tamil Nadu and Punjab. One-to two-thirds of respondents have responded that corruption is a bottleneck in these better climate states, a result reflected in all our objective proxies

Table 9.9: Cost of Corruption, Cost of Regulation in States and their Performance in PPP investment

States	*Per Capita investment in Rs. (Ranking shown in brackets)*	*Investment Climate*	*Corruption as major obstacle*	*Tax and Customs as major obstacle*	*Labour Regulation as major obstacle*	*Number of Inspections by Govt., officials*	*Senior Mgt. time spent in dealing with Regulations*	*Days to clear customs*
Karnataka	6583.7 (1)	Better IC	66.4%	54.7%	51.8%	5.6	11.2%	7.1
Kerala	2998.3 (2)	Not Better	42.6%	23.0%	5.9%	13.6	21.0%	5.7
Gujarat	2686.5 (3)	Better IC	62.0%	39.3%	7.0%	7.6	24.3%	8.8
Maharashtra	2098.4 (4)	Better IC	46.2%	31.3%	18.9%	5.4	15.7%	8.1
Andhra Pradesh	1020.1 (5)	Better IC	37.5%	16.8%	2.4%	9.3	10.7%	7.1
Madhya Pradesh	952.5 (5)	Not Better	33.6%	17.9%	2.1%	1.9	7.0%	2.6
Odisha	876.2 (7)	Not Better	NA	NA	NA	NA	NA	NA
Tamil Nadu	338.8 (8)	Better IC	65.3%	43.2%	30.3%	10.8	13.4%	7.6
Punjab	314.9 (9)	Better IC	54.2%	15.8%	2.8%	6.8	12.7%	2.6
Rajasthan	79.6 (10)	Not Better	NA	NA	NA	NA	NA	NA
West Bengal	—	Not Better	51.6%	43.5%	9.1%	13.0	17.8%	10.1

Source: Author's own compilation. Data source: WB-IFC Investment Climate Survey, 2004 and www.pppinindia.com.

of the burden of regulation, which are all higher for these better climate states, including the frequency of inspection visits, management time, cost of regulation and the duration of customs clearance. The better investment climate states have attracted more investment in PPP in spite of rated as having high cost of corruption and high cost of regulation. This suggests that the better climate states are not, after all, rated because the burden of regulation and corruption is less onerous. A state could be an attractive investment destination because of so many other factors such as availability of input materials, availability of electricity, transportation facilities, and natural advantages such as close to ports etc. It disproves the assumptions made in the hypothesis.

Hypothesis-3

- States with good infrastructure and reliable power supply and good transportation facilities attract more investment in PPP projects compared to other states.

Analysis

Table 9.10: Availability of Infrastructure, Power Supply and Transportation facilities and the Performance of States in getting investment in PPPs

States	*Per Capita investment in Rs. (Ranking shown in brackets)*	*Investment Climate*	*Infrastructure as major obstacle*	*Power supply as major obstacle*	*Transport as major obstacle*
Karnataka	6583.7 (1)	Better IC	61.2%	59.3%	50.3%
Kerala	2998.3 (2)	Not Better	19.8%	5.9%	29.0%
Gujarat	2686.5 (3)	Better IC	24.3%	5.7%	3.1%
Maharashtra	2098.4 (4)	Better IC	31.6%	22.3%	3.5%
Andhra Pradesh	1020.1 (5)	Better IC	17.2%	41.1%	1.4%
Madhya Pradesh	952.5 (6)	Not Better	49.2%	54.0%	2.4%
Odisha	876.2 (7)	Not Better	NA	NA	NA
Tamil Nadu	338.8 (8)	Better IC	40.9%	46.3%	43.5%
Punjab	314.9 (9)	Better IC	11.6%	3.9%	60.0%
Rajasthan	79.6 (10)	Not Better	NA	NA	NA
West Bengal	—	Not Better	31.6%	5.2%	7.8%

Source: Author's own compilation. Data source: WB-IFC Investment Climate Survey, 2004 and www.pppinindia.com.

The data related to perception indicators for infrastructure, power supply and transportation has been compiled from the IC survey and presented in Table 9.10. Contrary to the assumption, in the states having better investment climate which have attracted more investment in PPP projects, the percentage of respondents identifying Infrastructure, Power supply and Transportation as major obstacles for investment is quite high. For example, in the state of Karnataka where the per capita investment in PPP is maximum compared to other states, 61.2 per cent of the respondents identify Infrastructure as major obstacle, 59.3 per cent respondents identify Power Supply as major obstacle and 50.3 per cent of respondents identify Transportation as a major obstacle. Same is the case with Tamil Nadu, the other better investment climate state where 40.2 per cent of respondents identify Infrastructure as a major obstacle, 46.3 per cent of the respondents identify Power supply as a major bottleneck and 43.5 per cent respondents identify Transportation as an obstacle. The hypothesis holds good with the other better investment climate states such as Gujarat, Maharashtra and Andhra Pradesh.

Hypothesis-4

- States with greater access to land and external finance attract more investment in PPP projects compared to other states.

Analysis

Table 9.11: Access to Land and Availability of External Finance for Projects in States and their performance in getting investments in PPPs

States	*Per Capita investment in Rs. (Ranking shown in brackets)*	*Investment Climate*	*Access to and as major obstacle*	*External finance as major obstacle*
Karnataka	6583.7 (1)	Better IC	14.5%	37.6%
Kerala	2998.3 (2)	Not Better	11.9%	31.7%
Gujarat	2686.5 (3)	Better IC	6.0%	30.0%
Maharashtra	2098.4 (4)	Better IC	11.2%	24.6%
Andhra Pradesh	1020.1 (5)	Better IC	8.3%	25.9%
Madhya Pradesh	952.5 (6)	Not Better	3.6%	7.9%
Odisha	876.2 (7)	Not Better	NA	NA
Tamil Nadu	338.8 (8)	Better IC	12.6%	43.4%
Punjab	314.9 (9)	Better IC	1.7%	22.5%
Rajasthan	314.9 (10)	Not Better	NA	NA
West Bengal	—	Not Better	26.3%	30.3%

Source: Author's own compilation. Data source: WB-IFC Investment Climate Survey, 2004 and www.pppinindia.com.

The data related to perception indicators for the Access to land and Access to external finance, has been compiled from the Investment Climate Survey results and presented in Table 9.11. Compared to other indicators that determine investment climate in a state, the percentage of respondents identifying Access to land as a major obstacle is very less. However, among the better investment climate states in Karnataka where the investment in PPP is very high, the percentage of respondents identifying access to land as major obstacle is 14.5 per cent and it is 6 per cent, 11.2 per cent, 8.3 per cent and 12.6 per cent respectively for Gujarat, Maharashtra, Andhra Pradesh and Tamil Nadu. It only shows that there is no consistency between investment in PPP and access to land as a constraint. It only indicates that, accessability to land is not a critical factor for PPP investments, since government is a party in PPPs and normally the government undertakes to provide the required land for the PPP projects.

Contrary to the assumption, more respondents have identified external finance as a major obstacle in states which have higher investment in PPP projects. Here again, it indicates that the perception indicator may be applicable to industrial investment generally and not for the investment in PPPs.

7. Findings and Conclusions

Policy Environment and Performance in Getting Investment in PPP Projects

As mentioned earlier in data analysis there is no clear link between policy environment and institutional structures in a state and its success in getting PPP investments. There are no clear and obvious commonalities in policy environment among Indian states which were successful in getting more PPP projects compared to other states. However, proactive states like Karnataka, Andhra Pradesh and Gujarat who have exhibited their political commitment by enacting cross-sectoral legislation and establishing dedicated institutions, stand out in their performance in getting PPP investments compared to other states in spite of actually being seen as states which have many adverse investment characteristics. It is also clear from the experience of Karnataka, Andhra Pradesh, Rajasthan, Madhya Pradesh, Punjab and Gujarat in the development of PPPs for roads that, it is possible for states to get more investments in PPP mode if they develop a PPP programme in a single sector by building up capacities in line departments. For example, the state of Gujarat and Maharashtra have developed capacities for Port projects under PPP mode and they have attracted more PPP projects in these sectors. Also it is clear that, because of the vertical distribution of legislative and executive powers between Central Government and States, Indian states have adopted different legal and institutional frameworks and there is no uniformity even within the sectors among the states for PPP investments. More than the legal and institutional framework, the investment in PPP projects in infrastructure are governed by Concession Agreements, which determines the tariff and performance standards. Therefore, the actual enforceability of tariff and performance standards are more important, for which the investors look for Independent Regulatory Authorities, which are free from political constraints and vested interests. Therefore, from the data available on legal and Institutional framework, we can conclude that the Indian states have adopted only an *ad hoc* approach instead of developing a robust legal and institutional framework required for attracting more investment in infrastructure sector.

Influence of Cost of Corruption and Cost of Regulation, in the Investment Inflows into PPP Projects

One very striking and important outcome from the analysis of data related to perceived corruption levels and cost of regulation in states that the states which have been rated as better investment climate states need not necessarily to have low level of corruption and regulation. The top five states which have attracted more per capita investment in PPP projects are Karnataka, Kerala, Gujarat, Maharashtra and Andhra Pradesh. All these states except Kerala have been rated as states having better investment climate, which shows a positive correlation between perceived investment climate and investment in PPPs. However, when we compare the perceived corruption levels in these states, to our surprise these states have been perceived by investors as having high level of corruption. Same way if we compare the proxies for cost of regulation, again these states give a different picture than normally expected, that they have attracted more PPP investment in spite of having high cost of regulation. Therefore, we can conclude that, when it comes to investment in infrastructure particularly in PPP mode, if the overall cost benefit of the project in the entire concession period is higher, and if the cost benefit can absorb the cost of corruption and cost of regulation, than the states still tend to attract more investment in PPP in spite of high costs of corruption and high cost of regulation. There is no doubt that, to make these states even more attractive for investment, the states have to minimize the cost of corruption and regulation.

Availability of Infrastructure, Power Supply and Transportation Facilities and the Investment Inflows into PPP Projects

From the data analysis it can be seen that in spite of having maximum per capita investment in PPP, the state of Karnataka has been perceived to have more bottlenecks in Infrastructure, Power Supply and Transportation facilities. It only indicates that there is growing demand for these services in Karnataka and Karnataka couldn't match its requirements with the supply. It is clear from the fact that in spite of having good power supply and transportation network, the states of Gujarat and Maharashtra have been perceived to have infrastructure bottlenecks due to the mismatch in the demand and supply of these services in these states. The objective proxies for infrastructure like availability of power supply and transport facilities show a positive correlation with the high performance in attracting more investment in PPP projects. The other way to look at the performance in investment in infrastructure projects is that the states which have high demand for such infrastructural services like power supply, and transportation facilities have attracted more such projects in PPP mode.

Access to Land and Availability of External Finance and the Investment Inflows into PPP Projects

From the data analysis it can be seen that the states which have more PPP investment in infrastructure, except Gujarat and Andhra Pradesh have been perceived to have problems in getting access to land. It may be true to some extent for the projects in the industries sector, as the investment climate survey is conducted by the World Bank and CII, taking opinion from the investors and top management professionals from industries sector. It may not hold good for the PPP projects, since in the infrastructure projects, the government takes responsibility for making the land available for the projects. Coming to the availability of external finance, there is again a contradiction between the assumptions postulated in chapter one and the data presented. The analysis shows that the perception indicator may be applicable to the industrial investment and not to the PPP infrastructure projects. Since Investments in infrastructure have a long-term horizon, and decided based on the factors like value for money, competition and policy credibility which again depends on political stability and other factors.

Critical Factors that Determine Investment Inflows in PPPs in Indian States

Availability and Enforcement of Legal and Institutional frameworks that are conducive for PPP investment are is no doubt important factors, for the investors while deciding about investment in PPP projects, but it is not a pre-requisite for any PPP investment flow into any states. To some extent they exhibit the government's commitment and willingness for collaborating with private partners in infrastructure projects, but that alone is not sufficient. In fact the investors look for Independent regulatory authorities to enforce the tariff and performance standards agreed upon in a concession contract. If Indian states want to attract more investment in infrastructure projects through PPP mode they should give up the *ad hoc* approaches they were following so far and develop a robust legal and institutional framework required for attracting more investment in infrastructure sector.

Though the analysis shows that the investment flow in PPP projects in infrastructure into a state is based on the overall estimated actual net-cost benefits by private sector investors, than the cost of corruption and cost of regulation, it indicates that if the cost of corruption and the cost of regulation are less, then the state's investment climate make it more attractive for PPP projects in infrastructure, as it will reduce the project cost and make it more viable.

The availability of infrastructure like power supply and transport facilities in a state shows a positive correlation with the high performance in attracting more investment in PPP projects as it will reduce the project cost and make it more viable in long term. Similarly, the states which have high demand for such infrastructural services like power supply, and transportation facilities have the capacity to attract more such projects in PPP.

In infrastructure projects, the government takes responsibility for making the land available for the projects, therefore, availability of land is not a major factor that determine investment decision for infrastructure projects under PPP mode. Since investments in infrastructure have a long-term horizon, and are decided based on the factors like value for money, competition and policy credibility which again depends on political stability and other factors availability of external finance locally in a state is not a major deciding factor when it comes to investment in infrastructure projects in PPP mode.

As far as the Tirupur Water Supply Project is concerned, the NTADCL was able to complete the project on time, because of its innovative financing structure, which has facilitated the repayment of funds raised in international and domestic markets, while balancing the interest of shareholders. No doubt the project design is technically superior, however, the project cost could have been further reduced, if it was designed to suit the local conditions. This project has improved the water availability in the wayside panchayats, though the quality is not up to the expected level. This project has made Panchayats accountable for the water usage. It has also brought discipline among the water users as, as it has improved the payment of water charges by the users up to 90 per cent. The differential pricing mechanism can work, only when the textile units consume the NTADCL water only as promised before the starting of the project. It can happen only when the illicit tapping of groundwater for commercial use is stopped completely. This project gives a positive hope that with the support of stakeholders, including industry, the donar community, local government and residents, more such PPPs are possible in future in Water Supply sector in India.

Notes

1. www.adb.org/Documents/Reports/Consultant/39659-IND/39659-IND-TACR.pdf
2. http://siteresources.worldbank.org/INTAMSTERDAM/Resources/Awortwi.pdf
3. *www.adb.org/Documents/Reports/Consultant/39659-IND/39659-IND-TACR.pdf*
4. http://www.pppinindia.com/database.asp

References

Ahluwalia, Montek S. (2002), "State level Performance under Economic Reforms", *Economic Policy Reforms and the Indian Economy*. ED. Anne O. Krueger, 91-129. Chicago and London:University of Chicago Press, 2002.

Asian Development Bank (2006), 'Facilitating Public Private Partnership for Accelerated Infrastructure Development in India'—available at *www.adb.org/Documents/Reports/Consultant/39659-IND/39659-IND-TACR.pdf*

Awortwi, Nicholas, (2005), '*Getting the Fundamentals Wrong. Lessons for policy makers, practitioners, and researchers. from the delivery of basic services in Ghanaian cities*'—available at *http://siteresources.worldbank.org/INTAMSTERDAM/Resources/Awortwi.pdf*

Batley, Richard (2004), 'The Politics of Service Delivery', *Development and Change* 35(1): 35-56, Oxford, Blackwell Publishing.

Bettingnies, Jean-Etienne de, Thomas W. Ross. (2009), 'Public Private Partnerships and the Privatization of financing: An incomplete contracts approach', *International Journal of Industrial Organization*, 27 (2009) 358-368.

Brinkerhoff, J.M. (2002), "Government-Nonprofit Partnership: A defining Framework." *Public Administration and Development Journal*, 22:19-30

Brunetti, A., Kisunko, G. and Weder, B. 'Credibility of Rules and Economic Growth: Evidence from a Worldwide survey of the Private Sector', *The World Bank Economic Review*, Vol. 12, No. 3:353-84.

Burnett, Michael (2007), '*Public-Private Partnerships (PPP)—A Decision Maker's Guide*, Maastricht; European Institute of Public Administration.

Chakravarti, Ritadhi (2008), 'An Empirical Analysis of Investment Determinants in Indian States: 1998-2006', *The Michigan Journal of Business.*

Chakravorty, S. (2000), 'How Does Structural Reform Affect Regional Development? Resolving Contradictory Theory with Evidence from India.' *Economic Geography*, 76:367-394.

Committee on Infrastructure, Planning Commission, Government of India (2008). 'Projections of Investment in Infrastructure during the Eleventh Plan'—available at *www.infrastructure.gov.in/pdf/Inv_Projection2.pdf*

Datta, Amrita (2009), 'Public Private Partnerships in India: A Case for Reforms', *Economic and Political Weekly*, August 15, 2009, Vol. XLIV, No. 33.

Department of Economic Affairs (DEA), Ministry of Finance, Government of India and Asian Development Bank (ADB) (2006). 'Facilitating Public-Private Partnership for Accelerated Infrastructure Development in India', Regional Workshops of Chief Secretaries on Public-Private Partnership Workshop Report.

Devapriya, K.A.K. (2006), 'Governance issues in financing of public-private partnership organizations in network infrastructure industries', *International Journal of Project Management*, 24 (2006), 557-565.

Dollar, David, Iarossi, Giuseppe and Mengistae, Taye (2002), 'Investment Climate and Economic Performance: Some Firm Level Evidence from India' (Working Paper No.143). Centre for Research on Economic Development and Policy Reform, Stanford University. 2002.

Fafchamps, M. (1996), 'The enforcement of commercial contracts in Ghana'. *World Development*, 24(3): 427-448.

Ghobadian Abby, David Gallear, Nicholas O'Regan, Howard Viney (2004), '*Public-Private Parnerships—Policy and Experience*'.

GBC, Global Business Coalition (2008), 'Legislative and institutional framework for Public-private partnership in India'.

GOI, Government of India (2006), 'India. Building Capacities for Public Private Partnerships'.—available at *www.pppinindia.com/pdf/india_building_capacities_for_PPPs_june2006.pdf*

Grimsey Darrin, Mervyn K. Lewis (2005), 'Are Public Private Partnerships value for money? Evaluating alternative approaches and comparing academic and practitioners views', *Accounting Forum*, 29 (2005), 345-378.

Grindle, M.S. and Thomas, J.W. (1991), 'Implementing Reform: Arenas, Stakes and Resources.' Public choices and policy change: The Political Economy of Reform in Developing Countries'. Baltimore: Johns Hopkins University Press.

Grindle, M.S. and Thomas, J.W. (1990), '*After the Decision: Implementing policy reforms in developing countries*'. Cambridge: Harvard Institute for International Development.

Guasch J. Luis, 'Granting and Renegotiating. Infrastructure Concessions. Doing it Right', The World Bank—available at *http://crgp.stanford.edu/events/presentations/gcr2/Guasch3.pdf*

Hammami, Mona; Ruhashyankiko, Jean-François; Yehoue, Etienne B. (2006), "Determinants of Public-Private Partnerships in Infrastructure".—available at *www.imf.org/External/Pubs/FT/irb/2006/eng/04/index.pdf*

Heymann Eric, Tobias Just, Lonneke Löwik, Maren Väth. (2007), 'Deutsche Bank Research—450 bn reasons to invest in India's infrastructure'.

Hodge, A. Graeme (2004), 'Risks in Public-Private Partnerships: Shifting, Sharing or Shirking?' *The Asia Pacific Journal of Public Administration*, Vol. 26, No. 2, December 2004, 155-179.

Kumar, Sasi, and C. Jayasankar Prasad. (2004), 'Public-Private Partnerships in Urban Infrastructure.' *Kerala Calling*. February 2004. Available at: *www.kerala.gov.in/keralacallfeb04/p36-37.pdf*

Kundu, Amitabh (2001), 'Institutional innovations for urban infrastructural development: the Indian Scenario', *Development in Practice*, Volume 11, Numbers 2 & 3, May 2001.

Lane, J.E. (2000), '*The Public Sector: Concepts, Models and Approaches*.' 3rd edition, London, Newbury Park, CA and New Delhi: Sage Publications.

Leibenstein, Harlay, (1966), "Allocative Efficiency vs. 'X-Efficiency'," *American Economic Review*, Vol. 56, No. 3 (June), pp. 392-415.

Martimort David, Jerome Pouyet (2008), 'To build or not to build: Normative and Positive theories of public-private partnerships', *International Journal of Industrial Organization*, 26, 393-411.

National Council for Applied Economic Research (NCER), Quarterly News Letter on NCAER—CEPR—IEDI—ECARESECCP Project—May 2006- 'Public-Private Partnership for Infrastructure Development: Lessons for India'—available at *http://www.cepr.org/eeaii/connexions_May_2006.pdf*

OECD, 'OECD Principles for Private. Sector Participation in Infrastructure'—available at *http://www.oecd.org/dataoecd/41/33/38309896.pdf*

Osborne, D., Gaebler, T. (1992), *Reinventing Government: How the Entrepreneurial Spirit Is Transforming the Public Sector.* Addison-Wesley.

Paoletto, G. (2000), 'Public-Private Sector Partnerships: An Overview of Cause and Effect', In Wang, Yiden (Ed.) *Public-Private Partnerships in the Social Sector. Tokyo,* Asian Development Bank Institute: 30-47.

Plummer, Janelle, (2002), 'Focusing Partnerships—A Sourcebook for Municipal Capacity Building in Public-Private Partnerships'.

Sarangi, Debendranath (2002), 'Infrastructure development: a public-private partnership in india', *International Social Science Journal*, 172/2002, UNESCO 2002, Published by Blackwell Publishers, Oxford, UK.

Sachs, Jeffery, Bajpai, Nirupam and Ramiah Ananthi (2002), 'Understanding Regional Economic Growth in India' (Working Paper No. 88). Center for International Development, Harvard University, March 2002.

Savas, E.S. (1987), '*Privatization: The key to better government'*. Chatham, NJ: Chatham House Publishers.

Stiglitz, J. (1987), 'Principal and Agent,' in J. Eatwell, M. Milgate and P. Nennan (eds.), *The New Palgrave Dictionary of Economics*, pp. 241-53. Basingstoke and London: Palgrave.

Venkatraman, A. and J.W. Bjorkman (2006), 'Public-Private Partnership in the Provision of Health Care Services to the Poor.' Unpublished draft report of Project supported by Indo-Dutch Programme on Alternatives to Development: 1-20.

Vinod, B. Annigeri, Lizann Prosser Jack Reynolds, Raghu Roy (2004), 'An Assessment of Public-Private Partnership Opportunities in India'—available at-*http://pdf.dec.org/pdf docs/PNADC694.pdf*

Veeramani, C. and Goldar, Bishwanath (2004), 'Investment Climate and Total Factor Productivity in Manufacturing: Analysis of Indian States' (Working Paper No.127), Indian Council for Research on International Economic Relations. April 2004.

Walsh, K. (1995), *'Public Services and Market Mechanisms: Competition, Contracting and the New Public Management'*. Basingstoke and London; Macmillan.

Warner, M.E. (2008), 'Reversing privatization, rebalancing government reform: Markets. Deliberation and Planning'. *Journal of Policy and Society*, 27(2008), 163-174.

World Bank. (1994), 'World Development Report: Infrastructure for Development'. Oxford University Press: Oxford and New York.

World Bank, (2006), 'India-Building Capacities for Public Private Partnerships' Energy and Infrastructure Unit and Finance and Private Sector Development Unit, South Asia Region, June 2006.

World Bank (WB) and International Finance Corporation (IFC). (2004), "India: Investment Climate and Manufacturing Industry".

Annexure-I

Sector-wise PPP Types (Both Central and State Agencies put Together)

Sectors	BOOT		BOT-Toll		BOT-Annuity		BOO		LDOT		Mgt Contract		Lease		BOOST		DBFOT		Total	
	No., of Projects	Value	No., of Projects	Value	No., of Projects	Value	No., of Projects	Value	No., of Projects	Value	No., of Projects	Value	No., of Projects	Value	No., of Projects	Value	No., of Projects	Value	No., of Projects	Value
Roads	1	408	227	63553	35	10605							1	2150					264	81715
Ports	8	10546	21	16820	2	5378									10	13415			41	46159
Air Ports	2	4403			1	930	1	303	2	14400									6	20041
Urban Development	12	1202	9	2714	16	4838					3	224	1	250			11	1985	52	11213
Energy	30	17640																	30	17640
Tourism					1	17											5	179	6	196
Railways			3	1007															3	1007
Total	51	29796	187	59241	29	11687	1	303	2	14400	3	224	2	2400	10	13415	16	2164	402	177972

Source: Author's own compilation. Data source *www.pppinindia.com.*

Annexure-II

Sector-wise PPP Project Types (Implemented by State Governments)

Sectors	BOOT		BOT-Toll		BOT-Annuity		BOO		LDOT		Mgt Contract		Lease		BOOST		DBFOT		Total	
	No. of Projects	Value	No. of Projects	Value	No. of Projects	Value	No.of Projects	Value	No. of Projects	Value	No. of Projects	Value	No. of Projects	Value	No. of Projects	Value	No. of Projects	Value	No.of Projects	Value
Roads	1	408	227	68553	35	10605							1	2150					182	81716
Ports	8	10546	21	16820	2	5378									10	13415			27	46159
Air Ports	2	4408			1	930	1	303	2	14400									1	930
Urban Development	12	1202	9	2714	16	4838					3	224	1	250			11	1985	52	11213
Energy	30	17640																	30	17640
Tourism					1	17											5	179	6	196
Railways			3	1007															3	1007
Total	51	29796	187	59241	29	11687	1	303	2	14400	3	224	2	2400	10	13415	16	2164	298	118927

Source: Author's own compilation. Data source *www.pppinindia.com.*

Annexure-III

Institutional Frameworks for PPPs in India

State	*Framework Law*	*Nature of PPP unit*	*Approval Power over PPPs*	*Project advice*	*Resource centre*	*Guidance material*	*Funding for PPP preparation*
Andhra Pradesh	Enacted	Autonomous/Quasi	Dedicatee PPP unit	Dedicated PPP unit	Dedicated PPP unit	Dedicated PPP unit	Dedicated PPP unit
Gujarat	Enacted	Autonomous/Quasi	Dedicated PPP unit	Dedicated PPP unit	Dedicated PPP unit	Dedicated PPP unit	Dedicated PPP unit
Karnataka	Enacted	State level PPP Cell (Statutory), and iDeCK- Pub/Pvt Joint Venture	Dedicated PPP unit	Dedicated PPP unit	Dedicated PPP unit	Dedicated PPP unit	Limited to some sector/projects
Kerala	X	State level PPP Cell (Statutory), and INKEL-Pub/Pvt Joint Venture	X	Dedicated PPP unit	Dedicated PPP unit	Sector Specific	Limited to some sector/projects
Madhya Pradesh	X	PPP-Cell under Finance Department	X	X	X	Sector Specific	Limited to some sector/projects
Maharashtra	X	PPP-Cell and MUINFRA (Statutory Board)	X	Dedicated PPP unit	Dedicated PPP unit	Sector Specific	Limited to some sector/projects
Odisha	Enacted	PPP-Cell under Planning and Coordination Department	Dedicated PPP unit	Dedicated PPP unit	Dedicated PPP unit	Sector Specific	Limited to some sector/projects
Punjab	Enacted	Autonomous/Quasi	Dedicated PPP unit	Dedicated PPP unit	X	Dedicated PPP unit	Limited to some sector/projects
Rajasthan	X	State level PPP Cell (Statutory), and PDCOR-Pub/Pvt Joint	Dedicated PPP unit	Dedicated PPP unit	Dedicated PPP unit	Sector Specific	Dedicated PPP unit
Tamil Nadu	X	PPP-Cell under Finance Department	X	X	X	Sector Specific	Limited to some sector/projects
West Bengal	X	Pub/Pvt Joint Venture	X	X	X	Sector Specific	Limited to some sector/projects

Source: Author's own compilation. Data source: World Bank 2006, p. 24 and www.pppinindia.com.

Annexure-IV

Legal and Institutional Framework – States

State/ Agency	Legal Framework		Decision-Making Responsibility	Project development Responsibility	State support Funding	Conflict Resolution within Govt.	Guidelines Materials			Established Regulatory Agency	Dispute Resolution
	Cross-sectoral policy	Sectoral Policies					Standard Document	Model Contracts	Project Preparation Guidelines		
Andhra Pradesh	Infrastructure Policy-2000, AP-Infrastructure Development Enabling Act, 2001	AP-Electricity Reforms Act-1998, Information Technology and Communication Policy-2005, AP Tourism Policy-2006,Industrial Promotion Policy-2005, AP Road Toll Policy	Infrastructure Authority	APIIC (as a nodal agency)	Departments: case to case basis; APIIC/ IA involved	Infrastructure Authority	✓	✓	✓	0	Conciliation Board
Gujarat	Gujarat Infrastructure Development Act,1999	Power Policy-1995, Port Policy-1995, Road Policy-1996, IT Policy-1999, Gas Distribution Policy-2002	Infrastructure Authority	GIDB	Departments; case to case basis	GIDB	✓	✓	✓	×	GIDB: Case to case basis EX: Power sector -GERC
Kerala	×	Kerala Road Fund Act-2001, Kerala Infrastructure Development Bill, Industrial Policy-2001, Bio Technology Policy-2003, Policy guidelines for development of Wind Power-2007	Departments and Government agencies	Departments and government agencies such as Kerala Industrial Infrastructure Corporation (KINFRA), KSIDC, Infrastructure Kerala Ltd (INKEL)- a Public Private joint	Departments; case to case basis	×	×	×	×	×	Contractual
Madhya Pradesh	×	M.P. Highway Bill 2001, Tourism Policy 1995, Eco and Adventure Tourism Policy 2001, Captive Power Policy 2001, Industrial Policy and Action Plan 1994	State Level Committee on PPPs, and Departments	Departments and agencies such as MPRDC and MPPWD	Departments: case to case basis;	×	×	×	×	×	Contractual
Maharashtra	×	Sector Specific Guidelines in, State Road Policy-1996, Port Policy-2002, Tourism Policy-2006	Departments	Departments and agencies such as MSRDC	Departments; case to case basis	×	×	×	×	×	Contractual

Source: Author's own compilation. Data source: World Bank 2006, pp. 62, 63 and www.pppinindia.com

Annexure-IV (Continued.)

Institutional Framework–States

State/ Agency	Legal Frame Work		Decision Making Responsibility	Project development Responsibility	State support Funding	Conflict Resolution within Govt.	Guidance Materials			Established Regulatory Agency	Dispute Resolution
	Cross-sectoral policy	Sectoral policy					Standard Document	Mode Contracts	Project Preparation Guidelines		
Odisha	Orissa Public Private Partnership (PPP; Policy-2007	Infrastructure Policy 2001, Port Policy-2003, Revised I Policy Guidelines for Electricity Projects-2003, Orissa Industrial Policy -2007	Up to 500 Crores-Empowered Committee on Infrastructure (EOI), more than 500 Crores—High Level Clearance Authority (HLCA)	Departments and government agencies such as Orissa Industrial Infrastructure Development Corporation (IDCO)	Orissa Infrastructure Development Fund (OIDF) In addition to VGF of Govt, of India, Departments; case to case basis	×	×	×	×	×	Contractual
Rajasthan	×	State Road Policy-1994, Rajasthan Road Projects Act-2002, State Road Projects Fund Act-2004, Power Generation Policy (Amendment)-2005, Industrial Policy-1998, Tourism Policy, Tourism Unit Policy-2007, Rajasthan Investment Promotion	Empowered Committee On Infrastructure Development (ECID), Board of Infrastructure Development and Investment BIDI)	Departments and other agencies such as Project Development Company of Rajasthan (PDCOR)—a joint between Govt, and IL&FS	Rajasthan Project Development Fund (RPDF), Rajasthan Social Sector Viability Gap Funding Scheme	×	×	×	×	×	Contractual

Annexure-IV (Continued.)

Institutional Framework–States

State/ Agency	Legal Framework		Decision Making Responsibility	Project development Responsibility	State support Funding	Conflict Resolution within Govt.	Guidance Materials			Esta-blished Regu-latory Agency	Dispute Resolution
	Cross-sectoral policy	Sectoral policy					Standard Document	Mode Con-tracts	Project Pre-paration Guidelines		
Punjab	Punjab Infrastructure Development Act, 1998, Punjab Infrastructure (Development & Regulation) Act, 2002		Punjab Infrastructure Development Board (also other agencies such as Punjab Urban Development Authority-PUDA)	Punjab Infrastructure Development Board	Punjab Infrastructure Incentive Fund (PIIF)	Executive Committee of PIDB	×	×	×	×	Contractual
Tamil Nadu	×	The New Industrial Policy 2007, Housing Policy, Information Technology-GO 18/2007, Health & Family Welfare-GO-33/2008, Highways Policy Note-2008,Tourism Policy Note-2008, Agriculture Policy Note-2005-6	Departments	Departments and agencies such as TIDCO, TNRDC, TWIC	Departments; case to case basis	×	×	×	×	×	Contractual
West Bengal	×		Departments	ICICI-WINFRA—A joint venture company, WBIDC, KMDA and Departments	Departments; case to case basis	×	×	×	×	×	Contractual

Annexure-V

Equity Structure of Tirupur Water Supply Project

Equity and Subordinate Debt Plan

Equity	*Rs. in crores*	
Sponsor holding Company (TWICL)	105.00	Committed
Asian Infrastructure Development Co. Ltd.	90.00	Committed
Contractor Consortium	45.00	Committed
Tirupur Exporters Association	10.00	Committed
Life Insurance Corporation of India	20.00	Committed
General /insurance Corporation of India	15.00	Committed
IL & FS	37.70	
Total	322.70	
Subordinate Debt Plan		
IL & FS	66.50	Committed
TWICL	20.00	
Total	86.50	

List of Rupee Term Lenders

	Rs. in crores
Industrial Development Bank of India	75.00
Small Industrial Development Bank of India	60.00
Life Insurance Corporation of India	40.00
General Insurance Corporation of India	15.00
IL & FS	180.00
State Bank of India and Associate Banks	70.00
Indian Overseas Bank	25.00
Central Bank of India	30.00
Punjab National Bank	15.00
Bank of India	10.00
Canara Bank	48.80
Bank of Baroda	20.00
Oriental Bank of Commerce	25.00
Total Debt	613.80

Annexure-VI

Quantity of Water supplied to Panchayats and EB charges paid by Panchayats before and after the Implementation of Tirupur Water Supply Scheme

Sl. No.	Name of Panchayat	2001 Census	2009 Census	Quantity of drinking water supply in litres		Electricity Charges paid	
				Before NTADC implementation scheme (Before 2005) Litres	After NTADC implementation scheme (After 2005) Litres	Before NTADC implementation scheme (Before 2005) Rs.	After NTADC implementation scheme (After 2005) Rs.
1.	Kaniyampoondi	1540	4580	200000	217000	15000	20000
2.	Pudhupalayam	6084	7500	60000	200000	20000	60000
3.	A. Periyapalayam	2026	6400	70000	207000	184560	34315
4.	S. Periyapalayam	4007	15850	100000	364500	236353	151462
5.	Andipalayam	11350	68100	297000	1407000	1020000	1860000
6.	Chettipalayam	20184	77754	381000	2020000	600000	2709000
7.	Iduvai	4413	12563	506000	240000	325000	345000
8.	Mangalam	10016	35280	380000	1280000	1022400	1345400
9.	Muthanampalayam	9548	45645	293000	1276000	1365000	1869000
10.	Mudalipalayam	6267	35960	222000	811000	85000	52000
11.	Neruperichal	16372	45866	1011000	1716000	230000	460000
12.	Thottipalayam	26818	108118	330000	216000	585600	2550400
13.	T. Mannarai	8496	36790	140000	840000	2186540	4075000

Source: Author's own compilation. Data source: Assistant Director of Panchayats, Tirupur District.

Annexure-VII

List of Persons Interviewed

Sl. No.	*Name*
1.	Mr. PWC Dawidar,.IAS, Secretary to the Government, Energy, Information Technology Department, Government of Tamil Nadu, Chennai
2.	Mr. Paneendra Reddy, IAS, Managing Director, Tamil Nadu Urban Infrastructural Finance Services Limited and Formerly Managing Director of New Tirupur Area Development Corporation Ltd., Chennai.
3.	Mr. R.Thiagarajan, IAS, Special Secretary to Government, Finance Department, in charge of Special Cell for PPPs in Finance Department, Government of Tamil Nadu, Chennai.
4.	Mr. C. Samayamoorthy, IAS, District Collector, Tirupur District.
5.	Mr. S.S. Palanisamy, General Manager (Operations), New Tirupur Area Development Corporation Ltd., Tirupur.
6.	Mr. C. Elangovan, Manager (Technical), New Tirupur Area Development Corporation Ltd., Tirupur.
7.	Mrs. S.I. Padmavathy, Assistant Director of Rural Development (Panchayats), Tirupur.
8.	Mr. Chetti Kaliyappan, President, Kaniyampoondi Panchayat, Tirupur District.
9.	Mr. Ramasamy, President, Pudhupalayam Panchayat, Tirupur District.
10.	Mr. C. Rengasamy, President, A. Periyapalayam Panchayat, Tirupur District.
11.	Mr. D. Ganesan, President, S. Periyapalayam Panchayat, Tirupur District.
12.	Mr. Murugasamy, President, Andipalayam Panchayat, Tirupur District.
13.	Mr. K. Marappan, President, Chettipalayam Panchayat, Tirupur District.
14.	Mrs. Poongodi, President, Iduvai Panchayat, Tirupur District.
15.	Mrs. Balamani, President, Mangalam Panchayat, Tirupur District.

Sl. No.	*Name*
16.	Mrs. D. Baby, President, Muthanampalayam Panchayat, Tirupur District.
17.	Mr. Viswalingasamy, President, Mudalipalayam Panchayat, Tirupur District.
18.	Mr. P. Balan, President, Neruperichal Panchayat, Tirupur District.
19.	Mr. G. Rengasamy, President, Thottipalayam Panchayat, Tirupur District.
20.	Mr. M. Rengasamy, President, T. Mannarai Panchayat, Tirupur District.

10

Income Inequality among Small-Scale Fishery Households

A Case Study in a Coastal Village of Kerala

R. Mahesh and *D. Rajasenan*

In Kerala, the open access marine fishery is unregulated and is characterized by dualism in the form of co-existence of a small-scale sector side by side with a large-scale sector; but their activities are largely concentrated in the inshore areas. In the last two decades there has been enormous increase in fishing pressure as a result of increase in the number of fishing crafts, particularly in the number of motorised crafts in the small-scale sector. In spite of this increase in the number of fishing crafts the annual fish production remains stagnant around 5.9 lakh tonnes, against the optimal sustainable yield of 5.7 lakh tonnes, thus leading to resource depletion crisis (GOK, 2002). Under the open access regime, larger and faster vessels meant larger share of the common wealth of marine fishery. The official statistics of fish landing show a declining share to the small-scale sector, especially to the non-motorised sector. Within the traditional sector itself, the introduction of motorisation and ring seine brought new appropriation and technological dilemmas for the non-motorised and non-ring seine using segment (Paul, 2003). With about 50 per cent of the fish output cornered by the large-scale sector and another 40 per cent by operators of large seines in the motorised sector, the traditional fishermen especially those in the non-motorised sector find themselves to be marginalized (Yohannan *et al.*, 1999).

The process of modernisation of the fishery industry through the induction of technology has also changed the labour process by converting the immediate producers into wage-earners and also depriving and marginalizing the real fishermen (Rajasenan, 2001).

The costs of resource degradation are disproportionately paid by the poor who are the primary users of the commons and environmental resources. For many fisherfolk in the small-scale sector daily earnings from fisheries are low, fluctuating and often uncertain affecting their livelihood security. For them outward movement to non-fishing activities is difficult because of lack of knowledge of opportunities and lack of skills.

The real benefits of fisheries development policies followed by the Government and the general economic growth do not seem to have reached the people in the lower strata of the fishing community[1]. According to the socio-economic survey of fisherfolk conducted by the Department of Fisheries in 2004, 64.1 per cent of the families in the marine fishery sector are below the poverty line on the basis of ration card issued by the revenue authorities (GOK, 2005).

It is believed that with modernization of fishing technology, economic and social stratification and inequality in the fishing communities have increased. The conventional view is that a society's welfare is contributed by two factors, the level of income and the extent of inequality in the distribution of income. The notions of poverty and inequality are closely related—for a given mean income the more unequal the income distribution the larger would be the population living in poverty. In this article, an attempt is made to examine the pattern and the inequality of income distribution in detail in order to get a clear picture of the well-being of the small-scale fishing community.

Materials and Methods

In order to examine the income structure, data on consumer expenditure from a sample survey of 282 fishery households carried out in a typical coastal village Pulluvilla in Thiruvananthapuram district are used. The data were collected through personal interviews using a structured interview schedule. In order to overcome the effect of seasonality the interviews were spread over a period of eight months with a break of one month during the monsoon period June-July.

For households dependent on fishery resources, access to the resources is one of the main factors contributing to household income. Since access to the resources depends mainly on the possession and utilisation of fishing assets, it can be assumed that households possessing fishing assets are better-off than the other households. To verify this, in this study households have been classified as those 'with fishing assets', and those 'without fishing assets' and the extent of income inequality between the two groups of fishery households and within the groups is examined.

In order to examine the pattern of income distribution it will be useful to fit a suitable mathematical model to the data collected.

Scme of the desirable properties of such a mathematical formulation are:

(i) the form of the function can be derived from realistic elementary assumptions,
(ii) the mathematical form is amenable to statistical analysis,
(iii) the parameters have economic significance, and
(iv) the fitted function approximates the data.

However, in many practical situations the overriding requirement may be that the function should adequately graduate the data, sometimes over a given portion of the range only. In economic analysis the choice has been narrowed down to the 'lognormal' and 'Pareto' models. Empirical studies show that lognormal distribution is a better approximation at lower ranges of income, while Pareto distribution is better in the higher ranges[2]. Since, the interest in the present study is in the lower range lognormal distribution seems to be a better choice to represent the data on household income. An examination of the histogram of the household Monthly Per Capita Consumption Expenditure (MPCE) also indicates that lognormal distribution is a better choice. A commonly used measure of inequality, namely the Gini coefficient and Theil index have been used when the Lorenz Curve intersects.

Distribution of Household Income

Fishing income is derived from the ownership of fishing crafts, engine, and fishing gear, from employment of household members in their own fishing crafts and/or other crafts for a share of the earnings, from ownership of other fishing assets yielding rent, and from employment of household members in fish related activities like fish processing and vending. The activities of fish processing and vending are usually attended to by the female members of the household. There are a few instances in which male members are also engaged in fish vending. A fishery household may receive income from non-fishing activities also. The non-fishery activities mainly relate to self-employment in small trade or business, employment as hired labour in construction and repair activities and in a few cases as salaried or regular wage paid employment in institutions.

The standard of living is one of the most commonly used indicators of well-being and is represented by household income, from all sources and in all forms (i.e. cash as well as kind). Adjustments are to be made in the gross income for tax payments, receipts of subsidies, etc. to arrive at the disposable income. For comparison across households, age structure, household size, etc. are also to be taken into account. In the analysis of inequality the concept of income is defined as the increase in a person's command over resources during a given time period and is considered to represent the person's well-being. Since it is difficult to get reliable data on household income, household consumption expenditure is often used as a proxy variable. According to Coudouel *et al.* (2002), consumption is considered to be a better outcome indicator, better measure than income, and it better reflects a household's actual standard of living and ability to meet basic needs. Consumer expenditure is considered a proxy for income and for the sake of convenience in the discussions that follow; the term 'income' is used even though the data used relate to consumer expenditure[3].

The distribution of households and persons according to MPCE by asset categories is given in Table 10.1. Even though the average MPCE of the households is Rs. 1363, there are about 10 per cent households in the lowest class of Rs. 350 and below, and about 7 per cent in the upper class or above Rs. 3000, indicating large disparity in expenditure among

Table 10.1: Percentage Distribution of Households and Persons by Category for each MPCE class

MPCE (in Rs.)	*With fishing assets*		*Without fishing assets*		*All*	
	Households	*Persons*	*Households*	*Persons*	*Households*	*Persons*
< = 350	—	—	11.7	10.6	9.2	8.0
351-500	3.3	2.5	6.3	6.6	5.7	5.6
501-1000	10.2	10.9	31.8	35.3	27.3	29.2
1001-1500	27.1	30.6	22.4	24.5	23.4	26.0
1501-2000	17.0	17.3	10.8	9.8	12.1	11.7
2001-3000	35.6	34.0	10.3	8.6	15.6	14.9
3001 = >	6.8	4.7	6.7	4.6	6.7	4.6
Total	100.0 (1790)	100.0 (1733)	100.0 (1250)	100.0 (1155)	100.0 (1363)	100.0 (1298)

Source: Survey data.

Note: Figures in parentheses are mean expenditure.

households. Further, the median expenditure was found to be Rs. 1139 and is less than the mean. This shows that the distribution is positively skewed indicating large disparity in household expenditure with a comparatively large number of households in the lower income groups.

Fitting the Lognormal Distribution

A random variable X $[0< x<\infty]$ is said to be lognormally distributed if Y = log X is normally distributed with mean — and variance σ^2. The distribution of X is completely specified by the two parameters μ and σ^2. The distribution is positively skewed, and the greater the value of σ^2 the higher the skewness. The relative positions of the mean, median and mode are at $X = e^{\mu + \sigma^2/2}$, e^{μ}, and $e^{\mu-\sigma^2}$ respectively. A simple relation exists between the quintiles of the lognormal distribution and the corresponding quintiles of the standard normal distribution. From this relation we get the lower and upper quintiles of the lognormal distribution as $e^{\mu-0.67\sigma}$ and $e^{\mu + 0.67\sigma}$ respectively.

It is worthwhile to submit the data to some kind of graphical scrutiny as a preliminary to detailed analysis. To visually test the lognormality of the distribution a probability-probability (p-p) plot of households by MPCE was taken. A p-p plot is a graph of the empirical cumulative distribution function values plotted against the theoretical cumulative distribution function values and is widely used for assessing the goodness of fit of a hypothesized distribution[4]. The plot will be approximately linear if the specified model matches the given distribution. The plotted graph is given in Figure 10.1, and it indicates a good fit of the lognormal distribution for the household data; the fitted parameters are given in Table 10.2, where $\mu = 6.981$ and $\sigma = 0.7389$. To test the goodness of fit of the fitted distribution the 'Chi-square' test was carried out. The computed statistics are given in Table 10.3. The given *p* value for the Chi-square statistics indicates that the difference is not significant which means that lognormal can be considered as a good fit. The fitted plot of the probability density curve over the histogram of the MPCE is given in Figure 10.2.

Since the arithmetic mean of the fitted lognormal distribution $\alpha = e^{\mu + \sigma^2/2}$ involves both the location and dispersion parameters, it is not a pure measure of the level of income under the lognormal hypothesis. For this the median is to be preferred. In the present case the median income is estimated at Rs. 1076.5.

The dispersion parameter σ^2 is of greater interest by virtue of its

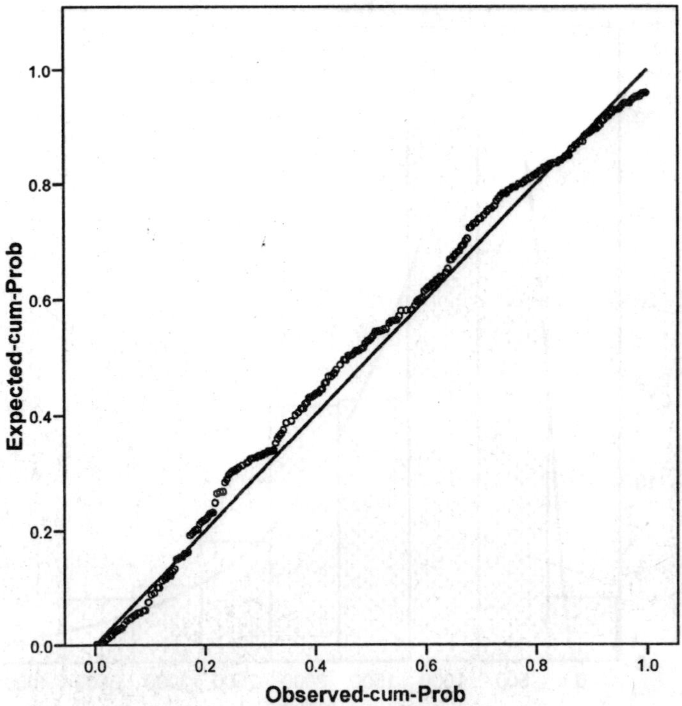

Fig. 10.1: Lognormal p-p plot for household MPCE

Table 10.2: Parameters of the fitted lognormal distribution

Parameter	*Symbol*	*Estimate*
Scale	Mu	6.981468
Shape	Sigma	0.738881
Mean		1414.371
Median		1076.498
Std. Dev.		1205.322

Table 10.3: Goodness-of-fit test for lognormal distribution

Null hypothesis			*Distribution fits the data*	
Alternative hypothesis			*Distribution does not fit the data*	
	Statistic	*DF*	*p Value*	
Chi-square	12.7992825	7	Pr > Ch-Sq	0.077

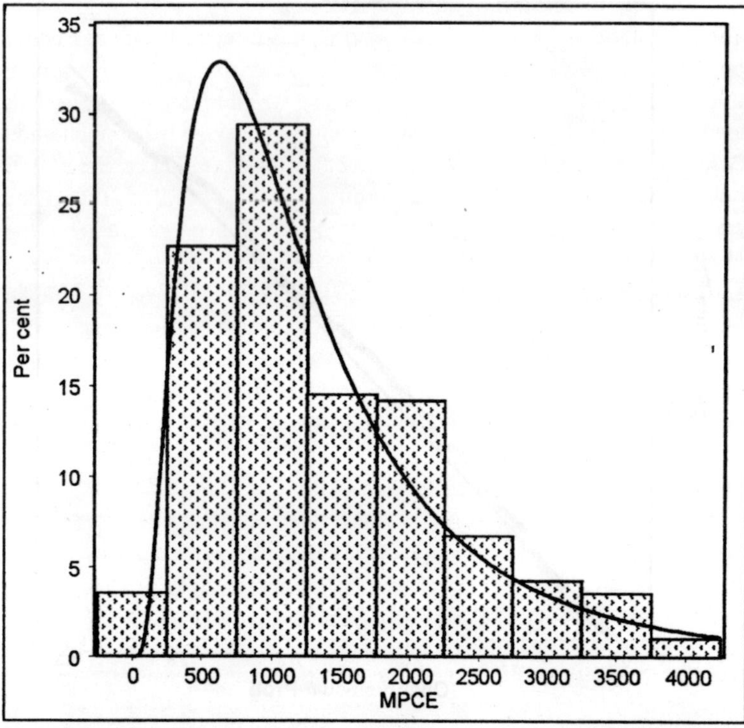

Fig. 10.2: Histogram and fitted lognormal curve for household MPCE

relation to the concept of 'concentration of income' (L) suggested by the Lorenz ratio. The measure is monotonically related to the value of σ^2 and is independent of the value of μ. The measure varies from zero, when all persons have the same income, to unity, when all available income accrues to one person. The measure of concentration of income corresponding to 0.74 the value of σ in the fitted distribution is 0.40 indicating significant concentration of income especially since consumer expenditure is used as a proxy for income.

In order to measure inequality of income and the extent of poverty among the fishing community, the pattern of income distribution by persons has to be examined. The next step, therefore, is to fit the lognormal model to the sample distribution of MPCE by persons. The attempt however, did not succeed as the model was not found to be a good fit in this case. So, inequality measures have to be computed directly from the survey data.

Further examination of the tabulated survey results given in Table 10.1 shows the fisher population with fishing assets are in a better position than their counterparts without fishing assets. The average MPCE of the fisher population 'with fishing assets' was found to be Rs. 1733 as against Rs. 1155 for those in the latter group. Among the fisher population 'without fishing assets' 10.6 per cent are in the MPCE class Rs. 350 or below and 6.6 per cent in the expenditure class Rs. 351 to 500. At the same time among the group 'with fishing assets' there were none in the lowest expenditure class Rs. 350 or less and only 2.5 per cent in the expenditure class Rs. 351 to 500. In the upper class Rs. 3001 and above the percentage of persons in both the sub-groups are almost same. These estimates indicate that the group 'with fishing asset' is economically in a better position as compared to their counterpart, and that there is wide disparity of income within both categories.

Inequality Measurement

It is worthwhile to quantify the extent of inequality since it can be used to compare the inequalities between and within the two sub-groups. Income differentials in the population can be shown by Lorenz curve. However, because of interpretation difficulty when the Lorenz curves intersect, we use the more commonly used measures of inequality, namely the Gini coefficient and the Theil index[5]. Both have certain desirable properties. The Theil index has an additional advantage; that is, for a given point of time it can be decomposed as the sum of inequalities between the chosen groups and the remaining inequality within groups. Gini coefficient (or Gini ratio) G, is a summary statistic of the Lorenz curve and a measure of inequality in a population. Graphically, the area between the Lorenz curve and the 'line of equality' can represent the index. The Gini coefficient can be calculated from unordered size data as the 'relative mean difference', i.e. the mean of the difference between every possible pair of individuals, divided by the mean size μ. Thus

$$G = \frac{\sum_{i=1}^{n}\sum_{j=1}^{n}|Xi - Xj|}{2n^2\mu} I \qquad ...(1)$$

If the data are ordered by non-descending size of individuals, G can be [Dixon *et al.* (1987) and Damgaard and Weiner (2000)], expressed as,

$$G = \frac{\sum_{i=1}^{n}(2i-n-1)x_i}{n^2\mu} \qquad ...(2)$$

where i is the individual's rank order number, n is the total number of individuals, x_i is the individual's variable value, and μ is the population average.

The Gini coefficient ranges from a minimum value of zero, when all individuals are of equal size, to a theoretical maximum of one in an infinite population in which every individual except one has a size of zero. It has been shown that the sample Gini coefficients defined above need to be multiplied by $n/(n-1)$ in order to become unbiased estimators for the population coefficients.

The extent of overall inequality in the population in our study area as measured by Gini coefficient works out to be 0.33. Considering that we are dealing with consumer expenditure rather than income, and given the low levels of consumer expenditure that are obtained, a Gini coefficient of 0.30 and above must be judged to signal substantial inequality[6]. In the present case since the Gini coefficient of income inequality is more than 0.30 the inequality could be considered as substantial. The Gini coefficients computed separately for each of the two sub-groups were found to be 0.24 for the sub-group 'with fishing assets' and 0.35 for the sub-group 'without fishing asset', indicating that the inequality is higher in the latter sub-group (See Table 10.5). When the level of income is also taken into account we see that the 'without fishing asset' sub-group has a lower level of mean income but a higher level of inequality, suggesting that this sub-group has a larger percentage of population living in income poverty. The indication is that possession of fishing assets significantly contributes to the well-being of the population. It is also seen that asset concentration is another pronounced feature of the sector. Only one-fifth of the households had any fishing asset of substantial value and even here some of them had only low valued assets (See Table 10.4).

Decomposition of Inequality

Even though the above analysis is indicative of the difference in the income and inequality levels between the two subgroups 'with fishing assets' and 'without fishing assets', it does not provide insight into the contribution of asset holding to the overall inequality. This is because the Gini coefficient is not additively decomposable across groups; that is, the total

Table 10.4: Distribution of households by value of fishing assets

Value of fishing assets (Rs.)	*% of households*
No fishing assets	78.7
Less than 10000	2.1
1000 – 25000	3.2
25001 – 75000	1.1
75001 – 150000	1.4
150001 –250000	11.3
Above 250000	2.1
All	100.0

Source: Survey data.

Gini of a population is not equal to the sum of the Ginis for its subgroups. Hence, the inequality analysis is continued using the Theil index of inequality, which has the advantage of being additive across subgroups. Theil's (1967) elegant first presentation of this measure of inequality was based on statistical information theory. The Theil index, however, lacks the appealing interpretation of the Gini coefficient.

The Theil index is a particular form of the Generalised Entropy (GE) class measures given by:

$$GE(\alpha) = \frac{1}{\alpha^2 - \alpha}\left[\frac{1}{n}\sum\left(\frac{y_i}{\bar{y}}\right)^{\alpha} - 1\right] \qquad \ldots(3)$$

Where y_i—income of the *i*th individual, n—number of individuals in the sample, $\bar{y}$—arithmetic mean of incomes in the sample, α—a number representing the weight given to the distance between incomes at different parts of the income distribution. For lower values of 'α', the measure is sensitive to lower tail values of the distribution. The value of GE ranges from zero to infinity with zero representing an equal distribution (all incomes identical) and higher values represent higher levels of inequality.

In particular, when $\alpha \leq 2$, we have

$$GE(0) = \frac{1}{n}\sum \log\frac{\bar{y}}{y_i} \qquad \ldots(4)$$

$$GE(1) = \frac{1}{n}\sum\frac{y_i}{\bar{y}} \cdot \log\left(\frac{y_i}{\bar{y}}\right) \qquad \ldots(5)$$

$$GE(2) = \frac{1}{\bar{y}}\left[\frac{1}{n}\sum(y_i - \bar{y})^2\right]^{1/2} \qquad \ldots(6)$$

GE (1) is the Theil index.
GE (2) is half the square of the coefficient of variation (CV).

The Theil index *GE* (1) varies from 0 to log *n* and is mean independent; population size independent satisfies Pigou-Dalton condition and is decomposable[7]. Decomposition of inequality can give insights into the structure of inequality. It can be used to examine the contribution of particular characteristics (e.g. ownership of productive assets) to inequality. The method is to separate the overall inequality (I) into a component of inequality between the chosen groups (I_b) and the remaining inequality within groups (I_w). When inequality is decomposed at one point of time, it is referred to as static decomposition and when over a period of time, it is dynamic decomposition.

The Theil index can be decomposed as the sum of inequalities explained by within group disparity (I_w) and between group disparity (I_b). Thus,

$$I = Iw + Ib \qquad ...(7)$$

Here,

$$I_w = \sum_{j=1}^{k} \left[\frac{Y_j}{Y}\right] GE(1)_j \text{—inequality explained by within group disparity.} \qquad ...(8)$$

$$I_b = \sum_{j=1}^{k} \left[\frac{Y_j}{Y}\right] \log \left[\frac{Y_j/Y}{n_j/n}\right] \text{—inequality explained by between group disparity.} \qquad ...(9)$$

where

Y — total income
Y_j — income of the *j*th group
n_j — number of individuals in the *j*th group
$GE(1)_j$ — inequality measure for group *j*
k — number of groups
n — total number of individuals

Thus to calculate I_w, the first step is to calculate *GE* (1) for each sub-group and then to compute the weighted sum of the sub-group indices with income shares as weights. The overall inequality *I* can be expressed as $I = I_w + I_b$; and this can be used to compute I_b, the between group inequality.

Intuitively, $R = I_b/I$ can be considered as a measure of the amount of inequality explained by difference between groups with a particular characteristic. Thus, if $R = 0.8$, it can be concluded that 80 per cent of the inequality is explained by the characteristic used for sub-group formation.

The measure is calculated directly from the data using the formula (5). In the present case, since the number of persons is 1446 the Theil index can range from 0 to 7.3; zero indicating perfect equality and 7.3 maximum inequality. From the survey data, the Theil index for the overall inequality works out to 0.18 (See Table 10.5).

As pointed out earlier, the main purpose of decomposing overall inequality is to understand the contribution of the sub-groups of the population to overall inequality, in this case between the sub-groups 'with' fissing assets and 'without' fishing assets. The distribution of MPCE for persons within each subgroup is given in Table 10.1. In order to compute the within sub-group share of inequality the fist step is to calculate inequality measure for each sub-group and then to take the weighted sum of these measures, the weights being the share of income of each sub-group (See Table 10.5).

Table 10.5: Indicators of inequality

Subgroups	*Theil index*	*% Income share*	*Gini ratio*
With fishing assets	0.0915	33.2	0.24
Without fishing assets	0.2040	66.8	0.35
All	0.1842	100.0	0.33

Source: Computed from survey data.

Since Gini coefficient ranges from 0 to 1, the inequality measured using the Gini coefficient can be better appreciated compared to Theil index. Both measures indicate that the extent of inequality is less in the subgroup 'with fishing assets' as compared to the other. To get an idea of the contribution to the overall inequality by sub-groups 'with fishing assets' and 'without fishing assets', the overall inequality has been decomposed as shown in Table 10.6.

From these figures we get an idea to the extent of inequality explained by the difference between the two groups namely, 'with fishing assets' and 'without fishing assets'. This measure (R) I_b/I is 9.5 per cent, which means that only about one-tenth of the inequality is explained by

Table 10.6: Decomposition of Theil index

Inequality level	*Theil index*
(i) Overall inequality (I)	0.1842
(ii) Inequality within groups (I_w)	0.1667
(iii) Inequality between groups ($I_b = I - I_w$)	0.0175
(iv) Inequality explained by difference between groups with and without fishing assets ($R = I_b / I$)	0.0950

Source: Computed from survey data.

'possession of fishing assets', the characteristic used for sub-group formation. The inference is that ownership of fishing assets is not the main factor for the observed difference in the level of inequality of income. That is to say, the means of access to fishery resources is not the deciding factor in the variation of income.

The results show that while possession of fishing assets influences the level of household income, the inequality in income is mainly due to other factors. The reason for this finding seems to be the method of income-sharing in the fishing activity. From ownership of fishing assets, the owner gets a fixed share of the net sale value of the catch and the remaining catch is shared among the crew. Households with fishing assets and labour thus get a larger share of the income and the variation depends to a large extent on the number of workers contributed by the household.

A disadvantage of both the Gini coefficient and the Theil index is that they vary when the distribution varies, no matter if the change occurs at the top, the bottom, or the middle. If one is more concerned about the share of income of the people at the bottom, a better indicator may be a direct measure, such as the share of income that goes to the poorest, say 10 to 20 per cent. This leads to the concept of poverty.

From the distribution of per capita income shown in Table 10.1, it is seen that about 43 per cent of the population has very low monthly income of less than Rs. 1000 per capita. Further, nearly 14 per cent have less than Rs. 500. These point to the prevalence of poverty in the coastal community.

Conclusion

The socio-economic condition of the fishing community in the small-scale sector has to be seen in the context of modernization of fishing technology, over fishing and consequent degradation of marine fishery resources. While households possessing fishing assets are financially in a better position, households depending solely on fishing labour and other fish related activities face insecurity due to fluctuating and often uncertain daily income. This situation is reflected in the low average income, wide income inequality and severe poverty of households in the small-scale fishery sector. The inequality of income in the small-scale fishery sector as measured by the Gini coefficient worked out to 0.33; and considering the low levels of consumer expenditure that has been obtained from the survey data it must be judged to signal substantial inequality. Within the community, the inequality of income was found to be higher for the subgroup of the fisher population 'without fishing assets' (0.24 for the subgroups 'with fishing assets' and 0.35 for the subgroups 'without fishing assets'). At the same time the income level of this subgroup is lower than the subgroup 'with fishing assets'. That is to say, 'without fishing assets' group has a lower mean income and a higher level of inequality. In economic terms the households depending only on fishing labour occupy the lower stratum compared to those with fishing crafts.

The lower income inequality of the 'with fishing asset' group suggests that income inequality of the population may have some relation with asset possession. In order to verify this, using the Theil index, the overall income inequality was decomposed as the sum of inequalities between and within the subgroups. However, this exercise showed that only less than 10 per cent of the overall inequality could be explained by the inequality between the two subgroups, suggesting that possession of fishing assets does not have a major contribution in explaining income inequality. The cause of income inequality has, therefore, to be sought elsewhere.

The comparatively better economic condition of the households owning fishing assets can be traced to the pattern of sharing sale value of catch prevailing in the coastal area. If the owner along with the fishing vessel goes for fishing, he gets a share as wage for the labour in addition to the share as rent. Usually, the owner and often other members of the household go for fishing. This has the effect of enhancing household income and also of smoothing inequality of income. As a result the group of households 'with fishing assets' is seen to have a higher average income and lower income inequality as compared to 'without fishing assets' who are really the fishery labour households.

In spite of this difference in income pattern, it cannot be said that households 'with fishing assets' and 'without fishing assets' are two isolated independent groups; on the contrary the two are closely related to each other by an exploitation linkage rooted in technology and the socio-cultural system prevailing in the community which perceives the fishery resources as common property.

Notes

1. The Government started its attempt to modernise the fishery sector as early as 1953 by introducing the Indo-Norwegian Project (INP) which was mainly intended to increase the productivity of the traditional fishery sector. According to various studies which evaluated the project these attempts from the Government was a failure. See Kurien (1985); Galtung (1969).
2. For details see Aitchison and Brown (1969).
3. For poverty calculations expenditure data are more reliable than income data due to several reasons such as biased reporting of the respondents, recall bias, instability of the income, seasonal fluctuations of income, etc. (Lipton and Ravallion, 1995).
4. For more about p-p plots, see Vogel (1986), Johnson and Wichern (1982), and Mage (1982).
5. See Theil (1967).
6. See Subramanian (1997) for a detailed discussion on Gini inequality index.
7. The Theil index can also be computed directly from the distribution of income in certain particular cases. For example, if the distribution is lognormal $L(Y; \mu, \sigma^2)$ then the Theil index is $\frac{1}{2}\sigma^2$ and if the distribution is Pareto form $\Pi(Y; \chi, \alpha)$ then the Theil index is $\frac{1}{\alpha-1} - \log\frac{\alpha}{\alpha-1}$. For details see Cowell, (1995).

References

Aitchison, J. and J.A.C. Brown (1969), *The Lognormal Distribution—with Special Reference to its Uses in Economics*; Cambridge University Press.

Coudouel, A., Jesko, S. Hentschel and Quentin T. Wodon (2002), *Poverty Measurement and Analysis*, in the PRSP Sourcebook, World Bank, Washington D.C.

Cowell, F.A., (1995), *Measuring Inequality*, Phillip Allan, Oxford, 2nd edition.

Damgaard, C. and Weiner, J. (2000), "Describing Inequality in Plant Size or Fecundity," *Ecology*, 81, 1139-1142.

Dixon, P.M.; Weiner, J.; Mitchell-Olds, T.; and Woodley, R. (1987),

"Bootstrapping the Gini Coefficient of Inequality," *Ecology,* Vol. 68, pp. 1548-1551.

Galtung, J. (1969), *Development from Above and the Blue Revolution: The Indo-Norwegian Project in Kerala*, International Peace Research Institute, Paper No. 2-12, Olso.

GOK (Government of Kerala) (2002), *Facts and Figures,* Department of Fisheries, Kerala.

GOK (Government of Kerala) (2005), *Socio-Techno Economic Survey of Fisherfolk in Kerala 2004*, Department of Fisheries, Thiruvananthapuram.

Johnson, R.A. and D.W. Wichern (1982), *Applied Multivariate Statistical Analysis,* Prentice-Hall, Englewood Cliffs, N.J.

Kurien, J. (1985), "Technical Assistance Projects and Socio-Economic Change—Norwegian Intervention in Kerala Fisheries Development," *Economic and Political Weekly*, 20 (25&26), pp. A70-A88.

Lipton, M. and M. Ravallion (1995), "Poverty and Policy", in J. Breman and T.N., Srinivasan (eds), *Handbook of Development Economics,* Vol. III B, Amsterdam; Elsevier, pp. 2551-2657.

Mage, D.T. (1982), "An Objective Graphical Method for Testing Normal Distributional Assumptions using Probability Plots", *Am. Statistician,* Vol. 36(2).

Paul, Antonyto (2003): "Evolution and Performance of Institutions in Common-Pool Resource Management: A Study of Kerala's Marine *Fishery",* Unpublished Ph.D. Thesis, JNU, Centre for Development Studies, Thiruvananthapuram.

Rajasenan, D. (2001). "Technology and Labour Process in Marine Fishery: The Kerala Experience", *The Indian Journal of Labour Economics*, Vol. 44, No. 2.

Subramanian, S. (1997). "Introduction: The Measurement of Inequality and Poverty", in S. Subramanian (ed.), *The Measurement of Inequality and Poverty*, Delhi, Oxford University Press.

Theil, H. (1967). *Economics and Information Theory*, Amsterdam: North Holland.

Vogel, M. Richard (1986). "The Probability Plot Correlation Coefficient Test for the Normal, Lognormal, and Gumbel Distributional Hypothesis", *Water Resources Research*, April, Vol. 22(4), pp. 587-590.

Yohannan, T.M.; P.N. Radhakrishnan, Nair; N.G.K. Pillai and P.L. Ammini (1999). "Marine Fisheries in Kerala," *Marine Fisheries Information Service*, No. 160, ICAR, April-June.

11
Municipal Solid Waste (MSW) Management and Its Future Impact on Sustainable Energy Generation in India

Swami Prakash Srivastava

Introduction

Solid waste is the unwanted or useless solid materials generated from combined residential, industrial and commercial activities in a given area. Municipal solid waste (MSW) originates in homes, businesses, and other urban areas. It may be categorized according to its origin (domestic, industrial, commercial, construction or institutional); according to its contents (organic material, glass, metal, plastic paper etc.); or according to hazard potential (toxic, non-toxin, flammable, radio-active, infectious etc.). Management of solid waste reduces or eliminates adverse impacts on the environment and human health and supports economic development and improved quality of life. A number of processes are involved in effectively managing waste for a municipality. These include monitoring, collection, transport, processing, recycling and disposal.

Solid-waste management has become an important issue in the Asia-Pacific region, and it needs to be resolved through an integrated community, private sector, and policy-based approach. Solid-waste management is a major challenge in urban areas throughout the world. Without an effective and efficient solid-waste management programme, the waste generated from various human activities, both industrial and domestic, can result in health hazards and have a negative impact on the environment. Understanding the waste generated, the availability of resources, and the environmental conditions of a particular society are important to developing an appropriate waste-management system.

REVIEW OF LITERATURE

Gore (1992): Even the landfills still operating are reaching grand proportions of refuse; a Staten Island landfill receives twenty-two thousand tons of trash from New York City on a daily basis. It will soon be the highest point on the Eastern Seaboard south of Maine. Landfills are clearly the largest refuse heaps in the world.

Anonymous (1992): In Canada, many cities have several options besides landfilling (which is, unfortunately, the most popular method). Recycling, composting, and incineration systems are working now in various provinces, and the country has established a target of reducing the national amount of municipal solid waste by fifty per cent by the turn of the millennium.

Earth Works (1990): In today's world, active citizens take offense when our waste, which we thought was being taken care of, needs immediate attention. This is happening while sanitary landfills spill over the land we call home, industrial machines pollute the air we breathe, and other cities and states try to dump their garbage problems on our own land.

Anonymous (1992): By 2009, four of five landfills operating today will be full, and a new landfill can cost near $90 million.

TERI (2010): The Energy and Resources Institute (TERI) has estimated that by 2047, waste generation in Indian cities will increase five-fold to touch 260 million tonnes per year, implying that the current solid waste generation is over 50 million tonne per year.

World Bank (2006): A study by the World Bank puts India's annual generation of municipal solid waste to be somewhat lower, i.e. in the range of 35 to 45 million tonnes, amounting to about 100,000 to 120,000 metric tonnes everyday.

Asnani (2006): Estimates the annual increase in the quantity of solid waste in India's cities to be at the rate of 5 per cent per annum.

SOLID WASTE MANAGEMENT

Solid-waste management may be defined as the discipline associated with controlling the generation, storage, collection, transfer and transport, processing, and disposal of solid waste in a manner that is in accordance with the best principles of health, economics, engineering, conservation, aesthetics, and other environmental considerations, and that is also responsive to public attitudes. In its scope, solid-waste management includes all administrative, financial, legal, planning, and engineering functions involved in the solutions to all problems of solid waste. The solutions may involve complex interdisciplinary fields such as political science, city and regional planning, geography, economics, public health, sociology, demography, communications, and conservation, as well engineering and materials science. For instance, if waste is wet or has a low heating value, it would not be possible to incinerate it without adding supplemental fuel. If a portion of the waste stream consists of organics and can be easily separated from other waste materials, bioconversion of the waste may become a viable strategy. On the other hand, the waste generated by industrialized countries may be different from those generated by non-industrialized countries. Non-industrialized societies may have more organic waste than those generated by industrialized countries. If this is the case, composting or anaerobic digestion may be more suitable for organic waste management.

The activities associated with managing solid waste from the generation point to final disposal normally include generation, reduction, reuse, recycling, handling, collection, transfer and transport, transformation (e.g., recovery and treatment), and disposal. Depending on site specific conditions, a sound waste-management programme can be established by combining some of the necessary activities into integrated solid-waste management. On the other hand, legislative efforts and effective implementation are vital for the safe management and disposal of solid waste. Incentives may be provided for the development and practice of safe treatments, harmless manufacturing processes, and methods for converting solid waste into valuable resources by recycling and reuse. On the part of industry, industrial waste-management is also indispensable from the viewpoint of both the social responsibility of business corporations and ISO: 14000, which will influence their survival in global markets.

Historical Background

In times long past, when the population of the earth and the amount of garbage created were both much smaller (and when highly toxic wastes were highly uncommon), we trusted that the earth's absorption of our waste meant that we never had to give it a second thought. That has changed completely. In today's world, active citizens take offense when our waste, which we thought was being taken care of, needs immediate attention. This is happening while sanitary landfills spill over the land we call home, industrial machines pollute the air we breathe, and other cities and states try to dump their garbage problems on our own land (Earth Works, 1990). About 5000 years ago, the world's first recorded landfill was built in Knossos, Greece. Huge questions of waste were buried in large pits, with soil layered throughout. Landfills have since remained a popular idea, not because of their usefulness but because of the dearth of disposal options—what exactly can one do with garbage?

Significance of Solid Waste Management

All over the world, Solid Waste Management (SWM) has occupied huge significance. SWM is an organized process of storage, collection, transportation, processing and disposal of solid refuse residuals in an engineered sanitary landfill. It is an integrated process comprising several collection methods, varied transportation equipments, storage, recovery mechanisms for recyclable material, reduction of waste volume and quantity by methods such as composting, waste-to-power and disposal in a designated engineered sanitary landfill.

Management of Solid Wastes is a growing concern to the general public at large, local authorities and business communities in cities across the country. The problem is aggravating in urban areas due to swift strides in population growth coupled by an economic boom that has marked a huge surge in consumption of goods leading to generation of wastes by leaps and bounds. Hence, it becomes the need of the States'/Union Territory to take plunge into managing the solid waste since its accumulation in open areas lead to multifarious problems such as:

1. Negative impact on the living conditions of human beings as well as the overall environment.
2. Spread of communicable and non-communicable diseases among human beings and animals, thus affecting the welfare, livelihood and economic productivity.
3. Contamination of soil, surface water, ground water and generation of toxic and green-house gases.
4. A breeding ground for insects and other vectors as well as human beings.
5. Diminishing real estate and property value.
6. Causes odour nuisance, reflects the unorganized nature of the community.

Solid Waste Management in India and its Challenges

Solid waste is a major source of environmental pollution in Indian cities and towns. The Energy and Resources Institute (TERI) has estimated that by 2047, waste generation in Indian cities will increase five-fold to touch 260 million tonnes per year, implying that the current solid waste generation is over 50 million tonnes per year (Asnani, 2006). A study by the World Bank (2006) puts india's annual generation of municipal solid waste to be somewhat lower, i.e. in the range of 35 to 45 million tonnes, amounting to about 100,000 to 120,000 metric tonnes every day. Asnani (2006) estimates the annual increase in the quantity of solid waste in India's cities to be at the rate of 5 per cent per annum. Further, disposal practices at the solid waste open dumping sites are highly unsatisfactory. The poor management of solid waste has led to contamination of ground water and surface water through leachate and pollution of air through unregulated burning of waste. Unscientific practices in processing and disposal compound the environmental hazards posed by solid waste. It is estimated that anywhere between 30-35 per cent of the total waste remains uncollected from the city roads; similarly, the waste disposal services in most cities and towns are archaic and inadequate, and carry high environmental risks. The combined effect of the inefficiencies in collection and inadequate and unsafe disposal is evident in widespread insanitation, contaminated water and high incidence of chronic respiratory and communicable diseases found in India's cities.

Future Projections for Solid Waste Generation

As the world hurtles towards its urban future, the amount of Municipal Solid Waste (MSW), one of the most important by-products of an urban lifestyle, is growing even faster than the rate of urbanization. Ten years ago there were 2.9 billion urban residents who generated about 0.64 kg of MSW per person per day (0.68 billion tonnes per year). According to one estimates (report) that today these amounts have increased to about 3 billion residents generating 1.2 kg per person per day (1.3 billion tonnes per year). By 2025 this will likely increase to 4.3 billion urban residents generating about 1.42 kg/capita/day of municipal solid waste (2.2 billion tonnes per year). This estimates (report) provides consolidated data on MSW generation, collection, composition, and disposal by country and by region. Despite its importance, reliable global MSW information is not typically available. The report also makes projections on MSW generation and composition for 2025 in order for decision makers to prepare plans and budgets for solid waste management in the coming years.

CONDITION OF SEWAGE SYSTEM IN INDIA

In developed countries, the standard practice for sanitary disposal of human waste and waste water is the sewerage system. However, the system appears to unviable due to high capital and O&M (Operations and Maintenance) costs as well as huge water requirement for effective flushing. Sewerage was first introduced in London in the 1850s followed by New York in the 1860s. Calcutta was the next city in the world to have the privilege during the 1870s. Yet today, out of over 5,000 odd cities and towns in the country, only a few over 200 have sewerage systems. In developing countries like India, neither the government nor the urban local bodies could sustain the capital and O&M expenditure associated with the sewerage system. It requires skilled persons and technical management for O&M, which is critically lacking in the municipal authorities. It requires over 10 to 15 litres of water to flush human excreta and carry the same through the sewers. Most of the waste water treatment plants are ill-functioning and most of the rivers are heavily polluted due to untreated domestic sewage loads from urban habitats. This is borne out by the fact that majority of the rivers in India have a faecal coliform count.

LEADING URBAN ENVIRONMENTAL CHALLENGES INDIA FACES

Major environmental challenges in India are as follows:

1. **Change in Land Use/Land Cover:** As urban population increases, the demand of land for various urban activities increases. Forests need to be cleared, grasslands ploughed or grazed, wetlands drained and croplands are encroached upon due to expanding cities. This is a challenge because it reduces the green covers and increases the consumption of fossil fuels and GHGs emissions, and leads to increase in surface temperature.
2. **Solid Waste Generation, Collection and its Management**: This is the major challenge because a large amount of solid waste is left by the side of streets, to decay, which is a major source of

health concerns. Further, there are no appropriate mechanisms to collect and dispose of the waste thus generated.

3. **Poor Sanitation:** This is a challenge because there is still a large proportion of population which practices open defection; hence this plays a role in the pollution of surface and ground water sources.

SUSTAINABLE USE OF SOLID WASTE IN INDIA AND USA

Sustainable Solid Waste Management in India

As far as a desired level of service is concerned with respect to solid waste, various committees have recommended 100 per cent collection of the generated waste, with its proper disposal. For instance, see the Report of the Third Working Group on Norms and Standards for Provision of Basic Infrstructure and Services, prepared for State Finance Commission, 1995. To implement this 100 per cent norm, India's urban local bodies are guided by the directives in the Municipal Solid Waste (Management and Handling Rules 2000, issued by the Ministry of Environment and Forest, Government of India. According to a study by Da Zhu *et al.* (2008) of the World Bank, the composition of Indian waste is such that close to 55 per cent is organic and can be converted into compost and another 15 per cent is recyclable.

Waste-to-Energy

Waste-to-Energy or Energy-from-Waste is the process of generating energy in the form of electricity and/or heat from the incineration of waste. WtE is a form of energy recovery.

Popular Process of Solid Waste to Energy

Most Waste to Energy processes produce electricity and/or heat directly through combustion, or produce a combustible fuel commodity, such as methane, methanol, ethanol or synthetic fuels.

Waste Plastic to Energy

Plastic Pyrolysis can convert petroleum based waste streams such as plastics into char, tar and pyrolysis gas. Given below is the list of suitable plastic raw materials for pyrolysis:

- Mixed plastic (HDPE, LDPE, PE, PP, Nylon, Teflon, PS, ABS, FRP etc.)
- Mixed waste plastic from waste

Sustainable Solid Waste Management in USA

Modern waste-to-energy plants in other countries have been providing sustainable means of waste management, with minimum side effects on the environment. One example is of SEMASS, a waste to energy facility in Massachusetts, in the US, which uses 1 million tonnes of municipals solid waste to generate 600 million kilowatt-hours of electricity every year and recycles 40,000 tonnes of metals. The annual toxic emission is less than half a gram annually. This seems like a win-win situation for everyone, which Indian cities should more proactively adopt.

IMPORTANCE OF SOLID WASTE IN ENERGY GENERATION IN INDIA

Most wastes that are generated, find their way into land and water bodies without proper treatment, causing severe water pollution. They also emit greenhouse gases like methane and carbon dioxide, and add to air pollution. Any organic waste from urban and rural areas and industries is a resource due to its ability to get degraded, resulting in energy generation. The problems caused by solid and liquid wastes can be significantly mitigated through the adoption of environment-friendly waste-to-energy technologies that will allow treatment and processing of wastes before their disposal. These measures would reduce the quantity of wastes, generate a substantial quantity of energy from them, and greatly reduce environmental pollution. India's growing energy deficit is making the government—Central and State Governments become keen on alternative and renewable energy sources. Waste to energy is one of these, and it is garnering increasing attention from both the Central and State Governments. While the Indian Government's own figures would suggest that the cost of waste to energy is somewhat higher than other renewable sources, it is still an attractive option, as it serves a dual role of waste disposal and energy production.

Solid Waste to Energy Potential in India

According to the Ministry of New and Renewable Energy (MNRE), there exists a potential of about 1700 MW from urban waste (1500 from MSW and 225 MW from sewage) and about 1300 MW from industrial waste. The ministry is also actively promoting the generation of energy from waste, by providing subsidies and incentives for the projects. Indian Renewable Energy Development Agency (IREDA) estimates indicate that India has so far realized only about 2 per cent of its waste-to-energy potential. A market analysis from Frost and Sullivan predicts that the Indian municipal solid waste to energy market could be growing at a compound annual growth rate of 9.7 per cent by 2013.

Indian Government Initiatives for Waste to Energy

The Government of India has recognized waste to energy as a renewable technology and supports it through various subsidies and incentives. The Ministry of New and Renewable Energy (MNRE) is actively promoting all the technology options available for energy recovery from urban and industrial wastes. MNRE is also promoting the research on waste to energy by providing financial support for R&D projects on cost sharing basis in accordance with the R&D Policy of the MNRE. In addition to that, MNRE also provides financial support for projects involving applied R&D and studies on resource assessment, technology upgradation and performance evaluation.

The launching of New Energy Policy by Government of India, "Energy for all by 2012", and the policy on liberalization of energy production have opened a number of opportunities in power sector. Independent Power Producers (IPP) are exploring many renewable energy sources like fuel cells, solar, wind, etc. for production of energy at affordable rates. The Municipal Solid Waste (MSW), which is available abundantly, is now gaining importance as a source of energy in many places in India.

Global Solid Waste to Energy Developments in Other Countries (China, Japan, Canada and USA)

During the 2001-2007 period, the WTE capacity increased by about four million tonnes per annum. Japan and China built several plants that were based on direct smelting or on fluidized bed combustion of solid waste. In China there are about 50 Waste to Energy plants.

Japan is the largest user in thermal treatment of MSW in the world with 40 million tonnes. Some of the newest plants use stoker technology and others use the advanced oxygen enrichment technology. There are also over one hundred thermal treatment plants using relatively novel processes such as direct smelting, the Ebara fluidization process and the Thermo-select-JFE gasification and melting technology process.

In Patras, Greece, a Greek company just finished testing a system that shows potential. It generates 25 kWs of electricity and 25 kWs of heat from waste water. In India its first energy bio-science centre was developed to reduce the country's green house gases and its dependency on fossil fuel.

In USA, Biofuel Energy Corporation of Denver, CO, opened two new biofuel plants in Wood River, NE, and Fairmont, MN, in July 2008. These plants use distillation to make ethanol for use in motor vehicles and other engines. Both plants are currently reported to be working at over 90 per cent capacity. Fulcrum BioEnergy incorporated located in Pleasanton, CA, is currently building a WTE plant near Reno, NV. The plant is scheduled to open in early 2010 under the name of Sierra BioFuels plant. BioEnergy incorporated predicts that the plant will produce approximately 10.5 million gallons per year of ethanol from nearly 90,000 tons per year of MSW.

TECHNOLOGIES FOR THE GENERATION OF ENERGY FROM WASTE

Energy can be recovered from the organic fraction of waste (biodegradable as well as non-biodegradable) through thermal, thermo-chemical, biochemical and electrochemical methods.

Thermal Conversion

The process involves thermal degradation of waste under high temperature. In this complete oxidation of the waste occurs under high temperature. *The major technological option under this category is incineration*. But incineration has been losing attention these days because of its emission characteristics.

Incineration

The new age ideas for garbage disposal began with trials and errors between 1885 and 1908, the US sought to tackle the problem *via* incineration, aptly known as 'destructors' at that time, by building close to 200 incinerators. In 1905, NewYork city even used the incinerators to generate electricity to light the Williamsburg Bridge. But by 1909, as many as 102 of 180 incinerators were defunct or dismantled because they had either been inadequately built or had outlived their purpose; apparently the vast tracts of free land in the country meant that its government did not place the same premium on land that we do today. Thus, dumping garbage was the cheaper option. Reclaiming (a fancy word for filling) wetlands near cities with garbage also becomes a preferred disposal method. Incineration, the combustion of organic material such as waste with energy recovery, is the most common Waste to Energy implementation. All new WtE plants in OECD countries incinerating waste (residual MSW, commercial, industrial or RDF) must meet strict emission standards, including those on nitrogen oxides (NO_x), sulphur dioxide (SO_2), heavy metals and dioxins. Hence, modern incineration plants are vastly different from old types, some of which neither recovered energy nor materials. Modern incinerators reduce the volume of the original waste by 95-96 per cent, depending upon composition and degree of recovery of materials such as metals from the ash for recycling. Incinerators have electric efficiencies of 14-28 per cent.

The method of using incineration to convert Municipal Solid Waste (MSW) to energy is a relatively old method of waste-to-energy production. Incineration generally entails burning waste (residual MSW, commercial, industrial and RDF) to boil water which powers steam generators that make electric energy and heat to be used in homes, businesses, institutions and industries. One problem associated with incinerating MSW to make electrical energy, is the potential for pollutants to enter the atmosphere with the flue gases from the boiler. These pollutants can be acidic and in the 1980s were reported to cause environmental damage by turning rain into acid rain. Since then, the industry has removed this problem by the use of lime scrubbers and electro-static precipitators on smokestacks. By passing the smoke through the basic lime scrubbers, any acids that may be in the smoke are neutralized which prevents the acid from reaching the atmosphere and hurting the environment.

New and Emerging Technologies Other than Incineration for Electric Power

There are a number of other new and emerging technologies that are able to produce energy from waste and other fuels without direct combustion.

Many of these technologies have the potential to produce more electric power from the same amount of fuel than would be possible by direct combustion. This is mainly due to the separation of corrosive components (ash) from the converted fuel, thereby allowing higher combustion temperatures in e.g. boilers, gas turbines, internal combustion engines, fuel cells. Some are able to efficiently convert the energy into liquid or gaseous fuels.

(i) Thermo-chemical Conversion: This process entails high temperature driven decomposition of organic matter to produce either heat energy or fuel oil or gas. They are useful for wastes containing high percentage of organic non-biodegradable matter and low moisture content. *The main technological options under this category include Pyrolysis and Gasification.* The products of these processes (producer gas, exhaust gases etc.) can be used purely as heat energy or further processed chemically, to produce a range of end products.

(ii) Bio-chemical Conversion: This process is based on enzymatic decomposition of organic matter by microbial action to produce methane gas, and alcohol etc. This process, on the other hand, is preferred for wastes having high percentage of organic, bio-degradable (putrescible) matter and high level of moisture/water content, which aids microbial activity. *The major technological options under this category are anaerobic digestion (bio-methanation) and fermentation.* Of the two, anaerobic digestion is the most frequently used method for waste to energy, and fermentation is emerging.

(iii) Electrochemical Conversion: Electrochemical conversion in the context of waste to energy refers typically to Microbial Fuel Cells (MFC). These systems are developed to trap the energy from wastes, where the reduction-oxidation machinery of immobilized microbial cells is catalytically exploited, for the accelerated transfer of electrons from organic wastes, to generate electricity and bio-hydrogen gas. However, this methodology needs extensive evaluation studies on bulk scale liquid waste treatments and stands at a nascent level in India as well as worldwide.

SUSTAINABLE MANAGEMENT OF SOLID WASTE-WAYS

There are two ways to manage Municipal Solid Waste (MSW). The high-waste approach involves leaving it somewhere, burning it, or burying it. Landfills, the symbol of *the high-waste approach*, have the proven reputation of *preventing* MSW from degrading, not to mention attracting a lot of traffic, noise, and dust to the surrounding areas. On a side note, burning MSW in incinerators disinfects it and reduces the volume and weight, but incinerators emit small but noticeable amounts of lead, cadmium, mercury, and other toxic substances into the air we breathe. The most frightening item piped into the atmosphere due to this method are dioxins. *The low-waste approach* is twofold: attempting to produce as little solid waste as possible, and diverting as much solid waste away from landfills and incinerators. The recycling bin is the symbol of the low-waste approach, but it hasn't caught on in this country to make a noticeable difference. In today's times of scientific progress and technology, a plethora of alternatives to landfills do exist, and all of them have much better degradability results.

Over the past few years, the former has been viewed as cheap and irresponsible, and the latter has been viewed as initially expensive but morally gratifying. People are sick of looking at and living with the landfills. And the landfills are filling up fast—too fast. We all grew up believing that once we threw something away, it all went to some hole in the ground that would always have more space for next week's trash pickup. But the volume of garbage is reaching sizes so immense that we are running out of places to put it. In this country prior to 1988, over 5,500 landfills took 80 per cent of MSW. By 2009, four of five landfills operating today will be full, and a new landfill can cost near $90 million (Anonymous, 1992).

E-WASTE IN INDIA

With income rising steadily over the last decade, more and more people have been purchasing and discarding mobile devices, computers, television, air-conditioners and refrigerators etc. This has created a mountain of e-waste in the country. According to Central Pollution Control Board data, India will generate 800,000 metric tonnes in 2013 compared to 1,47,000 metric tonnes in 2005.

Nearly 90 per cent of India's e-waste is processed by the unorganized sector, mostly comprising small sweet shops in urban slums. These outfits use hazardous methods—pouring acid over circuit-boards, for instance—to extract valuable element such as iron, gold, silver and copper. These un-scientific methods pose a health risk. Moreover, the unusable junk is discarded, causing environmental damage. But there is hope in the form of the growing organized sector, which is using technology to process e-waste in a safe and environmental friendly manner.

Nearly 95 per cent of the electronic waste is converted into re-usable material like plastic, copper, aluminum, iron etc. Noida based Attero Recycling claims to extract 12 elements from the Junk, which it sells to companies and vendors. The remaining 5 per cent hazardous waste goes to government approved treatment, storage and disposal facilities. Today, there are 64 authorised recyclers, including Atters, e-Parisaraa and Ramsky Enviro Engineers. Most have tie ups with large businesses to process their e-waste.

According to Manufacturers' Association of Technology, India generates 400,000 tonnes of e-waste every year. Industry experts have been citing this figure for the past three years. However, only 19,000 tonnes of this e-waste is recycled. An additional 50,000 tonnes of e-waste is illegally imported into the country. Some 95 per cent of this e-waste is dismantled manually by scrap dealers. The dismantling methods they use are extremely harmful to the environment and human health, state studies by several environmental agencies, including the Central Pollution Control Board (CPCB). The either immerse printed circuit boards and electronic parts into chemical solutions or burn them to obtain metal extracts. These processes release toxic gases. Certain electronic components contain potential carcinogenic substances such as lead and cadmium. To get the upper hand over e-waste management, CPCB plans to begin a nation-wide survey along with state pollution control boards. The exercise would help identify the challenges faced by the government as well as private companies in managing e-waste. The survey would also determine the type of waste, its source, destination and aspects related to its treatment and recycling.

Legal (Act) concerning e-waste in India: In May (2013), the e-waste (Management and Handling) Rules, 2011, came into force. The Rules have made manufacturers responsible for regulating and reducing e-waste and requires them to open collection centres or introduce take back systems. In the long term, the policy will have a major impact or recyclers in the formal sectors.

SOLID WASTE MANAGEMENT POLICY AND LEGISLATION IN DEVELOPING COUNTRIES

The legislation for water- and air-pollution control are comprehensive and well established, but not for solid-waste management. Solid-waste management is still very much a municipal government responsibility. A long-term strategy on solid-waste management is still lacking in the developing countries. Like many other developing countries in the world, concerns in the region are growing in both the governmental and public sectors for an effective and economic management of solid waste. The lack of awareness, technical knowledge, legislation, policies, and long-term strategy are major issues for solid-waste management in developing countries.

SOLID-WASTE MANAGEMENT IN ASIAN COUNTRIES

Solid-Waste Management in Asian Countries has given alarming signals because of their improper waste management. The urbanization, industrialization, and an increase in economic status and activities have increased the quantity of municipal solid waste and altered its contents. A lack of motivation on the part of the municipalities has created a grave situation. Although the developing countries generate less solid waste per capita in comparison to developed countries, the collection, storage, transportation, processing, and disposal of solid waste is highly ineffective, and consequently damaging to the environment. A poor understanding of solid-waste management leads to different kinds of environmental problems within urban metropolises. The emission of greenhouse gases and air pollutants, the pollution of groundwater, occupational hazards, etc. are other areas of concern.

The new millennium has introduced the global focus on sustainable development, especially in the area of solid waste. Solid-waste management is the responsibility of the municipalities under the provision of their respective acts. Solid-waste management practices in developing countries like India are far from satisfactory, and the associated problems are due to a lack of technical expertise, financial constraints, and legal provisions. Generally, state and municipal governments consider solid waste a low priority, and consequently give less budgetary support to this field. Slow decision-making processes in the municipalities create an additional hindrance. In a broader sense, municipal solid-waste management is a very complex task, as the social, economic, and cultural cooperation among households, communities, enterprises, and municipal authorities is minimal and a lack of awareness of the rules and regulations, as well as environmental concerns with poor resources, have created a chaotic situation. Although India has formulated legislation relating to municipal solid waste, hazardous waste, and biomedical waste, the compliance and awareness of rules among communities and municipalities are lagging behind. Waste collectors and rag pickers take out the recyclable portion of solid waste and sell it to retailers, which is recycled in the informal sector to the extent of 10 per cent of the waste generated, but no efforts have been made by the government to encourage a recycling industry.

The municipal corporations and municipalities generally collect solid waste through various modes of transportation like handcarts, animal-driven carts, rickshaws, etc. and street sweeping is carried out manually. Generally, municipal solid waste is dumped in low-lying areas by the smaller town municipalities without caring about the environment, whereas a regulatory framework is being partially followed by metro-cities. Cities with a million-plus population are complying with some of the regulations and Green Productivity practices in various activities of solid-waste management, namely the segregation of solid waste, composting at the community level, the transportation of solid waste in closed vehicles, and its disposal in controlled landfill sites having weighbridge facilities with a leachate-management facility. Solid-waste management, especially in India, can be practiced efficiently and in an ecofriendly manner through Green Productivity measures, and by considering and incorporating various policy, legislative, financial, technology, and management issues.

GROWTH OF SOLID WASTE AND ITS IMPACT ON ENVIRONMENT, HUMAN HEALTH AND COLLECTION WORKERS

The growth in the amount of solid-waste generation in India poses many threats to the environment and to occupational health. The improper and manual handling of solid waste and the transfer of waste in open vehicles create unhygienic conditions. Disposal of waste in low-lying areas without proper liners, leachate collection, and treatment systems creates groundwater pollution, and the disposal of solid waste into streams and rivers creates water pollution. Air pollution is created by odour nuisances and the generation of greenhouse gases from most of the landfill sites. In brief, open dumping of waste adversely affects the environment and human health. All the vectors of disease like flies, mosquitoes, rats, and stray animals like cows, dogs, and pigs breed at receptacles due to a very conducive atmosphere. They then multiply and become the causes of diseases like plague, malaria, typhoid, and cholera.

Environmental Impact of MSW

The environmental problems caused by MSW can be summarized as follows:

1. Uncollected waste often ends up in drains, causing blockages that result in flooding and unhealthy conditions.
2. Flies breed in some constituents of solid wastes and are very effective vectors that spread diseases. They have spread cholera in Delhi for many years.
3. Rats find shelter and food in waste dumps. Rats consume and spoil food, spread diseases, damage electrical cables and other materials, and inflict unpleasant bites. In fact plague was caused in the city of Surat in 1999 by an increase in the rat population.
4. Waste plastic bags are a particular aesthetic nuisance. They also cause the death of the grazing animals that eat them.

Impact on Collection Workers

Solid-waste collection workers face particular occupational hazards including strains from lifting, injuries from sharp objects, and traffic accidents. Dangerous items (such as broken glass, razor blades, hypodermic needles and other healthcare wastes, aerosol cans, and potentially explosive industrial containers and chemicals) pose risks of injury or poisoning, particularly to the rag pickers who sort recyclables from waste.

EXISTING PRACTICES IN SOLID WASTE MANAGEMENT IN INDIA

The existing practices in solid-waste management can be classified at three levels, depending upon the quantity of solid waste and the physical area covered.

1. *Rural Level*: Rural people generally do not use plastic or metal containers to keep waste segregated as to biodegradable and non-biodegradable. Instead, they throw it in the open fields. Sometimes it is naturally composted at the local level.
2. *Town Level*: In most towns in India, the practices for the

collection and transportation of waste are not defined. No specific mode of collection, transportation, and disposal exists. The garbage is generally dumped in low-lying areas and burned openly.

3. *Big-City Level*: A more defined system of collection, transportation, and disposal/composting exists. People send their waste through locally hired waste collectors and organizations to the community bin. From the community bin, it is transported by various methods to sanitary landfill sites. Rag pickers can be seen at waste collection and disposal points.

LEGISLATION, REGULATION, AND POLICIES FOR SOLID-WASTE MANAGEMENT IN INDIA

The Government of India has taken various steps to improve solid-waste management. The following are some of the steps taken.

1. *National Waste Management Committee*: It was constituted in 1990 with the objective of identifying the contents of recyclables in solid waste picked up by rag pickers through Kabariwal.
2. *Strategy Paper*: The Ministry of Urban Development in collaboration with the National Environmental Engineering Research Institute (NEERI) formulated strategy papers and was asked to prepare a manual on solid-waste management.
3. *Policy Paper*: The Ministry of Urban Development in association with the Central Public Health and Environmental Engineering Institute prepared a policy for the disposal of wastewater, sanitation, solid-waste management, and drainage utilities.
4. *Master Plan of Municipal Solid Waste*: The Ministry of Environment and Forest, the Central Pollution Control Board, and municipal authorities devised a strategy and a master plan for managing solid waste including biomedical waste.
5. *High Powered Committee*: A High Powered Committee was constituted in 1995 and headed by Dr. Bajaj. The objective of the committee was to suggest a long-term strategy for the collection, loading, transportation, composting, treatment, and disposal of solid waste using appropriate technology.

LEGISLATION AND REGULATION (ACTS) ON SOLID WASTE MANAGEMENT

Many acts and regulations relating to protecting the environment have come up from time to time. The rules pertaining to solid-waste management are as follows:

1. *Hazardous Waste (Management and Handling) Rules (1989, amended in January 2003)*: These rules deal with controlling the generation, collection, treatment, disposal, import, storage, transport, and handling of hazardous waste.
2. *Biomedical Waste (Management and Handling) Rules (1998)*: These rules are legally binding on healthcare institutions to streamline the process of proper handling (segregation, collection, treatment, and disposal) of hospital waste.
3. *Municipal Solid Waste (Management and Handling) Rules, 2000*: These rules deal with the scientific management of municipal solid waste by ensuring proper collection, segregation, storage, transportation, processing, and disposal of municipal solid waste.
4. *The Batteries (Management and Handling) Rules (2001)*: These rules apply to every manufacturer, importer, re-conditioner, assembler, dealer, recycler, auctioneer, consumer, and bulk consumer involved in the manufacture, processing, sale, purchase, and use of batteries or components thereof.

REDUCE, REUSE, RECYCLE

Methods of waste reduction, waste reuse and recycling are the preferred options when managing waste. There are many environmental benefits that can be derived from the use of these methods. They reduce or prevent greenhouse gas emissions, reduce the release of pollutants, conserve resources, save energy and reduce the demand for waste treatment technology and landfill space. Therefore, it is advisable that these methods be adopted and incorporated as part of the waste management plan.

Waste Reduction and Reuse

Waste reduction and reuse of products are both methods of waste prevention. They eliminate the production of waste at the source of usual generation and reduce the demands for large scale treatment and disposal facilities. Methods of waste reduction include manufacturing products with less packaging, encouraging customers to bring their own reusable bags for packaging, encouraging the public to choose reusable products such as cloth napkins and reusable plastic and glass containers, backyard composting and sharing and donating any unwanted items rather than discarding them.

Recycling

Recycling refers to the removal of items from the waste stream to be used as raw materials in the manufacture of new products. Thus from this definition recycling occurs in three phases: first the waste is sorted and recyclables collected, the recyclables are used to create raw materials. These raw materials are then used in the production of new products.

The sorting of recyclables may be done at the source (i.e. within the household or office) for selective collection by the municipality or to be dropped off by the waste producer at a recycling centres. The pre-sorting at the source requires public participation which may not be forthcoming if there are no benefits to be derived. Also a system of selective collection by the government can be costly. It would require more frequent circulation of trucks within a neighbourhood or the importation of more vehicles to facilitate the collection.

INTEGRATED SOLID WASTE MANAGEMENT (ISWM)

Integrated Solid Waste Management (ISWM) takes an overall approach to creating sustainable systems that are economically affordable, socially acceptable and environmentally effective. An integrated solid waste management system involves the use of a range of different treatment methods, and key to the functioning of such a system is the collection and sorting of the waste.

It is important to note that no one single treatment method can manage all the waste materials in an environmentally effective way. Thus all of the available treatment and disposal options must be evaluated equally and the best combination of the available options suited to the particular community chosen. Effective management schemes, therefore, need to operate in ways which best meet current social, economic, and environmental conditions of the municipality.

IMPLEMENTATION OF SOLID WASTE MANAGEMENT PROJECTS IN UTTAR PRADESH

Considering the importance of management of solid waste in various parts of the U.P., the Government is implementing SWM projects under Public-Private Partnership (PPP) model in 26 cities. Under this model, a concessionaire shall operate the projects in these cities, the responsibilities of whom would include door-to-door collection of waste, primary storage, secondary collection, transfer, transportation, development of processing plant and landfill etc. The private agency has to manage and maintain the project for a period of 30 years and also would have to shoulder the responsibilities of replacement and capacity enhancement etc. and has to make all related investments during the concession period. The tipping fees shall be paid to them by the concerned Nagar Nigam. All the projects shall be implemented under JNNRUM scheme of Government of India, which is a reforms-driven, fast-track, planned development of identified towns with focus on efficiency in urban infrastructure.

Cities where Solid Waste Management Projects are being implemented in Uttar Pradesh

Kanpur, Lucknow, Agra, Varanasi, Allahabad, Meerut, Mathura, Moradabad, Gorakhpur, Aligarh, Jhansi, Muzaffarnagar, Mirzapur, Jaunpur, Sambhal, Etawah, Rai Bareilly, Badaun, Fatehpur, Ballia, Mainpuri, Barabanki, Kannauj, Ferozabad, Loni, Basti.

The purpose of adopting PPP in SWM projects in these cities is to impart more efficiency and cost effective services which may not be effectively provided by the existing infrastructure/manpower of the municipality. The projects are under various stages of implementation. In 10 cities, door-to-door collection has been commenced, in 10 cities processing plant work is in progress whereas land has been acquired in 3 cities. The concentrated endeavour of the Government of U.P. bore fruitful results and in a near future, citizens of Uttar Pradesh can enjoy a cleaner, contamination-free environment. It will also boost confidence amongst prospective investors across the globe to step in here and set up their dream projects in states.

Role of US based Company, Renewable Energy Alternatives (REA) in Energy Generation in UP with the help of Solid Waste

UP may lose a Rs. 4000 crore 'waste-to-energy project as the US based

Renewable Energy Alternatives (REA), which sent the proposal in June 2013, has hinted at approaching Tamil Nadu or Kernataka following no response from urban development department. The US Renewable Energy Alternatives (REA) had approached the UP Government in June 2013 to set up a 500 MW 'waste-to-energy' project in the state but the proposal gathers dust despite many reminders. According to REA, it was initially decided that the project would be set up on a Public Private Partnership (PPP) model with the 20 per cent funding from the state government. Later, the Company had offered 100 per cent investment. The Company employs the latest techniques for producing electricity from garbage and tapping of solar energy. The REA adopts a technique by which garbage is used to produce synthetic gas, also, referred to as, 'Sin Gas' which further leads to produce of power. The quality of the ash left behind is well suited for use in laying roads and construction purposes.

CONCLUSIONS AND SUGGESTIONS

All this does not mean recycling is bad or land filling (not indiscriminate dumping; the two are different) is the last resort. Overall, summarizing, we find that India's major urban environmental concerns pertain to changes in land use cover, solid waste management and better management of sanitation to make cities open defecation free. Based on the estimates of the high powered expert committee on urban infrastructure, finances still are the biggest constraint to management of India's urban environmental concerns. However, there is hope. There are a large number of win-win situations such as roping in private sector partners for better solid waste management and sanitation. Government's need to think up novel ways to help (mostly coerce) citizens to manage their waste responsibly. This needs a strong will backed with sound knowledge and vision.

A number of key statistics, such as the value of recyclables, the amount of environmental pollution from waste sources, and the quantity of industrial waste generated, need to be computed to gain a better understanding of this sector. In terms of research related to waste to energy, detailed analysis of costs and available funding is needed.

References

A. Sz. Váradi, L. Strand, and J. Takács, "Clean Electrical Power Generation from Municipal Solid Waste", *IEEE trans. Energy Conversion*, pp. 293-300.

A. Sz. Váradi and J. Takács, "Electricity Generation from Solid Waste by Pilot Projects", International Symposium on Power Electronics.

Aarne Vesilind, William Worrel, Reinhax, (2002), "Solid Waste Engineering", Thomson Asia Pte. Ltd.

Anonymous, (1992). *The 1992 Information Please Environmental Almanac*. World Resources Institute, New York, NY.

Belmont, Lawrence P. (1995), *Louisiana's Chemical Causeway: What Pollutes the Mississippi River?* Tulane University, New Orleans, LA.

Business Today (2013), January 6, 2013, pp. 35.

C. Palanichamy, (2002), "MSW fuelled Power Generation for India", *IEEE trans on Energy Conversion*, Vol. 17, December 2002, pp. 556-563.

Dastur, Mahazareen (2013), *Down to Earth*, July 16-31, p. 53.

Electrical Drives, (2008), *Automation and Motion*, pp. 826-831.

Eric. Solano, (2002), "Life Cycle based Solid Waste Management", Vols. 1 and 2, *Journal of Environmental Engg.*, 128, pp. 993-1005.

Gore, Albert. (1992), *Earth in The Balance*. Plume Publishing, New York.

George Tchobanoglous, Hillary Theisen, Samuel A. Vigil, (1993), *Integrated Solid Waste Management*, McGraw Hill International Editions.

Miller, G. Tyler Jr. (1990), *Living in the Environment: An Introduction to Environmental Science*. Wadsworth Publishing Company, Belmont, CA.

The Earth Works Group. (1990), *The Recycler's Handbook*. The Earthworks Group, New York.

The Times of India, September 25, 2013, p. 5.

Young and Sachs. (1995), Creating a sustainable materials economy. In: *State of the World*. W.W. Norton and Company, New York.

12

Naxalbari to Today's Naxalite Movement

Its Genesis, Goals and Leaders

Kartick Das

Introduction

Naxalite or Naxalism is an informal name given to Communist groups that were born out of the Sino-Soviet split in the Communist movement in India. Ideologically they belong to various trends of Maoism[1]. Initially the movement had its centre in West Bengal. In recent years, they have spread into less developed areas of rural central and eastern India, such as Chhattisgarh and Andhra Pradesh *http://en.wikipedia.org/wiki/Andhra_Pradesh*, through the activities of underground groups like the Communist Party of India (Maoist) [CPI(M)]. They are conducting an insurgency, typically called the Naxalite-Maoist insurgency. Naxals hold sway in about 180 districts across ten states of India, accounting for about 40 per cent of India's geographical area. They are especially concentrated in an area known as the 'Red Corridor[2], where they control 92,000 square kilometres. According to India's intelligence agency, the Research and Analysis Wing, 20,000 Naxalites were in April 2006 in operation[3] and their growing influence prompted Indian Prime Minister Monmohan Singh to declare them as the most serious threat to India's national security.

Genesis

The term Naxalites comes from Naxalbari[4], where a section of Communist Party of India (Marxist), led by Charu Majumdar[5] and Kanu Sanyal[6] led a violent uprising in 1967, trying to develop a 'revolutionary opposition' in opposition to the Communist Party of India (Marxist), leadership. The insurrection started on May 25, 1967 in Naxalbari village when a peasant was attacked by hired hands over a land dispute. Local peasants retaliated by attacking the local landlords and the violence escalated. Majumdar greatly admired Mao Zedong of China and advocated that Indian peasants and lower classes must follow in his footsteps and overthrow the government and upper classes whom he held responsible for their plight. He engendered the Naxalite movement through his writings, the most famous being the 'Historic Eight Documents' which formed the basis of Naxalite ideology. In 1967 'Naxalites' organized the All India Coordination Committee of Communist Revolutionaries (AICCCR), and later broke away from CPI (Marxist). Uprisings were organized in several parts of the country. In 1969 AICCCR gave birth to Communist Party of India (Marxist-Leninist). Ironically enough, although the uprising in Naxalbari in May 1967 was crushed by the police within two months, the Naxalite ideology gained rapid currency in other parts of West Bengal and India within a few years. By the early 1970s, the Naxalite movement had spread from far-flung areas like Andhra Pradesh and Kerala in the south, to Bihar in the east, and Uttar Pradesh and Punjab in the north. Incidentally, in Andhra Pradesh and in West Bengal, the Naxalites found their main support among the aboriginal tribal communities, who had been the most oppressed and marginalized in Indian society—the Girijans in Andhra Pradesh and the Santhals in West Bengal. The Naxalite movement, which began as a violent peasant response to oppression by landlords, has undergone severe conflicts and innumerable splits over ideological and political positions before the regrouping attempt[7].

The Maoist Communist Centre of India (MCCI) and the Communist Party of India (Marxist-Leninist) People's War (also known as the People's War Group or PWG) merged to form a new entity, the Communist Party of India-Maoist (CPI-Maoist) on September 21, 2004, somewhere in the projected 'liberated zone'. Officially, the merger was announced on October 14, 2004, by the PWG Andhra Pradesh 'state secretary', Ramakrishna, at a news conference in Hyderabad, on the eve of peace talks between the PWG and the State Government[8]. The military wings of the respective organizations, People's Liberation Guerrilla Army (military wing of MCCI) and People's Guerrilla Army (military wing of PWG), were also merged. The name of the unified military organization is People's Liberation Guerrilla Army. P.V. Ramana, of the Observer Research Foundation in Delhi estimates the Naxilities' current strength at 9,000-10,000 armed fighters, with access to about 6,500 firearms[9].

Other estimates by Indian intelligence officials and Maoist leaders suggest that the rebel ranks in India have swelled to 20,000, though the number is impossible to verify[10].

Birth of CPI (Maoist)

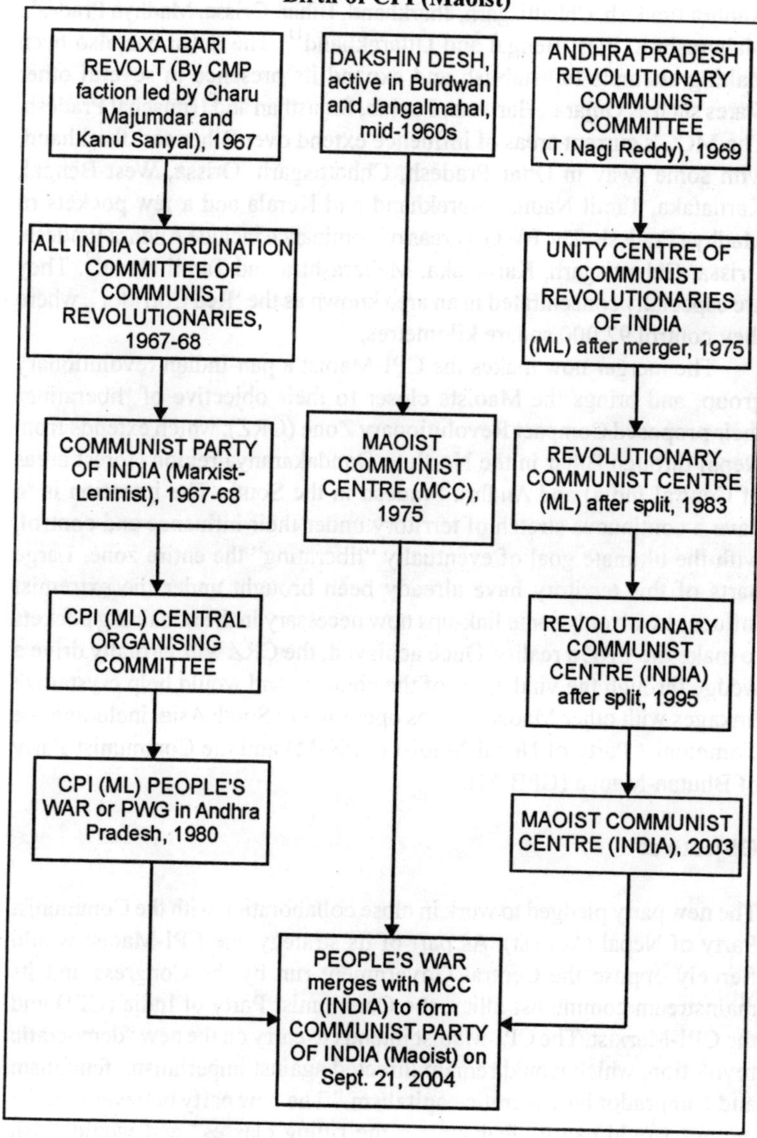

Jurisdiction

Naxals hold sway in about 180 districts across ten states of India, accounting for about 40 per cent of India's geographical area that include Andhra Pradesh, Chhattisgarh, Jharkhand, Bihar, Orissa, Madhya Pradesh, Maharashtra, West Bengal and Uttarakhand[11]. The outfit has also been making attempts to establish and expand its presence in several other States such as Gujarat, Haryana, Punjab, Rajasthan and Himachal Pradesh. The MCC's current areas of influence extend over Bihar and Jharkhand, with some sway in Uttar Pradesh, Chhattisgarh, Orissa, West Bengal, Karnataka, Tamil Nadu, Uttarakhand and Kerala and a few pockets of Madhya Pradesh. The PWG's areas of dominance include Andhra Pradesh, Orissa, Chhattisgarh, Karnataka, Maharashtra and Tamil Nadu[12]. They are especially concentrated in an area known as the 'Red Corridor', where they control 92,000 square kilometres.

The merger now makes the CPI-Maoist a pan-Indian revolutionary group, and brings the Maoists closer to their objective of 'liberating' their proposed Compact Revolutionary Zone (CRZ), which extends from Nepal through Bihar in the North to Dandakaranya region (forest areas of Central India) and Andhra Pradesh in the South. The intention is to have a continuous stretch of territory under their influence and control, with the ultimate goal of eventually "liberating" the entire zone. Large parts of this territory have already been brought under the extremist influence with only some link-ups now necessary in the remaining pockets to make the CRZ a reality. Once achieved, the CRZ will virtually drive a wedge through the vital areas of the country, and would help crystallize linkages with other Maoist groups operating in South Asia, including the Communist Party of Nepal-Maoist (CPN-M) and the Communist Party of Bhutan-Maoist (CPB-M).

Objectives

The new party pledged to work in close collaboration with the Communist Party of Nepal (Maoist). As part of its strategy, the CPI-Maoist would fiercely oppose the Central Government run by the Congress and its mainstream communist allies, the Communist Party of India (CPI) and the CPI-Marxist. The CPI-Maoist intends to carry on the new "democratic revolution, which would remain directed against imperialism, feudalism and comprador bureaucratic capitalism." The new party believes that the merger would cause "fear among the ruling classes" and would fulfil "the aspirations of the masses" for a strong revolutionary party that would usher in a "new democratic society" by advancing towards socialism and communism.

According to a CPI-Maoist press release issued by Muppala Lakshman Rao *alias* Ganapathi, the 'General Secretary' of the CPI (Maoist), the unity was aimed at furthering the cause of "revolution" in India. The new party also pledged to work in close collaboration with the Communist Party of Nepal (Maoist). As part of its strategy, the CPI-Maoist would fiercely oppose the Central Government run by the Congress and its mainstream communist allies, the Communist Party of India (CPI) and the CPI-Marxist. Ganapathi also announced the formation of a 'People's Liberation Guerrilla Army' and extended support to "revolutionary struggles" in Nepal, Peru, the Philippines, Turkey and "other places". The CPI-Maoist intends to carry on the new "democratic revolution, which would remain directed against imperialism, feudalism and comprador bureaucratic capitalism." The new party believes that the merger would cause "fear among the ruling classes" and would fulfil "the aspirations of the masses" for a strong revolutionary party that would usher in a "new democratic society" by advancing towards socialism and communism.

Both organizations shared their belief in the 'annihilation of class enemies' and in extreme violence as a means to secure organizational goals. However, significant ideological divisions did exist in the past, with the PWG adhering to a Marxist-Leninist 'line', while the MCCI embraced Maoism. These differences have now been ironed over, with Maoism prevailing, in the words of PWG Andhra Pradesh State 'Secretary', as "the higher stage of the M-L (Marxist-Leninist) philosophy. Marxism-Leninism-Maoism will be the ideological basis guiding its (CPI-Maoist's) thinking in all spheres of its activities". The new entity has reaffirmed its commitment to the classical Maoist strategy of 'protracted armed struggle' which defines its objectives not in terms of the seizure of lands, crops, or other immediate goals, but the seizure of power. Within this perspective, participation in elections is rejected, and all efforts and attention is firmly focused on 'revolutionary activities' to undermine the state and seize power. In a press statement dated October 14, 2004, General Secretaries of the Central Committee of the two outfits, Kishenji of the MCCI and Ganapathi of the PWG, declared that

> "The immediate aim and programme of the Maoist party is to carry on and complete the already ongoing and advancing New

> Democratic Revolution in India as a part of the world proletarian revolution by overthrowing the semi-colonial, semi-feudal system under the neo-colonial form of indirect rule, exploitation and control... This revolution will be carried out and completed through armed agrarian revolutionary war, i.e. protracted people's war with the armed seizure of power remaining as its central and principal task, encircling the cities from the countryside and thereby finally capturing them. Hence the countryside as well as the Protracted People's War will remain as the "centre of gravity" of the party's work, while urban work will be complimentary to it."[13]

The new organization continues to employ violence to achieve its goals—peasant revolution, abolition of class hierarchies, and expansion of Maoist-controlled "liberated zones," eventually leading to the creation of an independent "Maoist" state. The CPI (Maoist) reportedly has a significant cadre of women. Important leaders include Ganapati (the PW leader from Andhra Pradesh), Pramod Mishra, Uma Shankar, and P.N.G. (*alias* Nathuni Mistry, arrested by Jharkhand police in 2002). Prior to its consolidation with the PW, the MCCI ran a virtual parallel government in remote areas, where it collected a "tax" from the villagers and, in turn, provided infrastructure improvements such as building hospitals, schools, and irrigation projects. It ran a parallel court system wherein allegedly corrupt block development officials and landlords—frequent MCCI targets—had been punished by amputation and even death. People's War conducted a low-intensity insurgency that included attempted political assassination, theft of weapons from police stations, kidnapping police officers, assaulting civilians, extorting money from construction firms, and vandalizing the property of multinational corporations.

Ideologies—Muzumdar's Eight Theses

Charu Mazumdar engendered the Naxalite movement through his writings, the most famous being the 'Historic Eight Documents'[14], which formed the basis of Naxalite ideology. Mazumdars[15] eight documents laid in the foundation of what would constitute the severest internal security the severest internal security challenge to Indian almost half-century down the line. Had the North Block man drains cared to trace the genesis of the ultra-Left insurgency, they would have found that much of the Maoist mayhem be it in Dantewada or else where closely followed Mazumdar's script. With a hind sight, the rare documents seem to have provided the guidelines to the Maoists for their massive strikes in recent months.

- His first thesis, completed on January 28, 1965, instructed the communist cadres to set up secret and armed 'activist groups' in rural areas. Every such unit, Mazumder said, should have a minimum of five members who would hold regular meetings, prepare hiding calls and propagate the doctrine of a peasant revolution.
- The second thesis called for creating 'liberated zones' where 'class enemies' had been eliminated. The next paper gave a direct call for taking to arms to liberate more and more areas.
- The arms, Mazumdar said, would have to be snatched away from the people and big landlords. "He termed as tit-for-tat the strategy of revolutionary violence", his biographer and close associate Souren Basu said in his book.
- The fourth paper put the emphasis on building a clan destine but effective organization to wage the armed struggle. The police forces, Mazumdar explained, would be confused in tackling a large number of armed, well trained, unknown radicals.
- In the fifth document, he asked the Maoist cadres at that time a breakaway faction from the CPM to be armed, to set up secret units and politicize the followers. Even before he could complete the fifth thesis. Mazumdar was arrested in September 1965.
- In the sixth thesis, he rejected the system of parliamentary democracy and criticized the conventional Left's practice of organizing strikes industry in his last two documents; he recognized the importance of drafting the students and youths from middle class homes for 'revolutionary' activity, called for concentrating on rural areas and attacked revisionism in the established communist movement.

Status

The party was banned on 22 June, 2009 by the Central Home Ministry keeping in mind the growing unlawful activities by the group. The party is regarded by some as a "left-wing extremist entity" and a terrorist outfit and several of their members have been arrested by the Indian Government under the Prevention of Terrorism Act (POTA). The group is officially banned by the State Governments of Orissa, Chhattisgarh and Andhra

Pradesh, among others[16]. The party has protested these bans. They are regarded as a serious security threat and the Indian government is taking countermeasures, pulling the affected states together to coordinate their response. It says it will combine improved policing with socio-economic measures to defuse grievances that fuel the Maoist cause. *(http://www.alertnet.org/printable.htm?URL=/db/crisisprofiles/IN MAO.htm).* In many states, private armies and vigilante groups, often government-sponsored, have sprung up to counter the Maoists. It is alleged that these private armies have also forcibly recruited villagers against the Maoists. Special insurance provisions have been made by the Indian government for paramilitary forces stationed in regions affected by the militant Maoists.

Military Might

Naxalites are not a few men and women gone astray. After the regrouping of the country's Maoists under the banner of the CPI (Maoist), it has dedicated cadre that operates military lines. According to the government's own estimates, Maoists have around 10,000 combat cadres operating in nine states. According to Rural Development Minister Jairam Ramesh, 9,000 sq. km in southern Chhattisgarh is a "free zone" where the Indian flag doesn't fly. Armed with sophisticated weapons and tools the top leadership is believed to be safely ensconced in the "liberated" expanse of Dandkaranya forests straddling Chhattisgarh, Odisha and Andhra Pradesh, while the cadres move freely across state jurisdictions. The Maoists use local support and have cultivated a section of the intelligentsia in the cities that helps project them as victims of state oppression rather than as reckless killers.

India's war against Naxalism is turning out be a one sided bloody affair as Maoist dominate a battlefield of dispirited security forces with no credible intelligence flow. The level of sophistication shown by the Maoists, in inflicting large scale casualties on civilians and security personnel with minimum damage to themselves, is turning out to be far superior to that of any other guerrilla group in India, including Kashmiri terrorists with suicide bombers.

Statistics (Table 12.1) show that the fight between an insurgent group and Indian security agencies has never been so one-sided. Just one Naxalite gets killed against four deaths among civilians and security personnel in Left-wing extremism affected areas. Even at the peak of Kashmir insurgency, the casualty rate was almost equal on both sides—a terrorist

Table 12.1: Deaths in Naxal Violence

Years	*Civilians*	*Security Forces*	*Naxals*	*Total*
2005	281	150	286	717
2006	266	128	348	742
2007	240	218	192	650
2008	210	214	214	638
2009	392	312	294	998
2010	258	167	107	532
All total	1,647	1,189	1,441	4,277

Source: South Asia Terrorism Portal.

was killed by security agencies for every death among civilian and security force personnel. It was always an equal fight in that sense. 1996 may have been the bloodiest year in Jammu and Kashmir, when a total of 2,822 lives were lost—1,424 civilians, 189 security personnel and 1,209 terrorists. Even then, the ratio between the number of civilians and security personnel killed against slain terrorists was 1:33. The ratio gradually declined over the years, and over a period of time, the security forces were able to reverse the trend.

Table 12.2: State-wise deaths in Naxal violence

States	*2009*		*2010 (Till May)*	
	Civilian	*Security Forces*	*Civilian*	*Security Forces*
Andhra Pradesh	18	0	4	0
Bihar	47	25	29	6
Chhattisgarh	163	127	43	103
Jharkhand	140	68	28	9
Maharashtra	41	52	4	0
Odisha	36	31	22	17
West Bengal	144	14	128	32
Total	589	317	258	167
Jammu & Kashmir	55	78	16	34

Source: South Asia Terrorism Portal.

The Maoists have far less sophisticated weaponry and explosives than the Kashmiri terrorists, and they do not carry out suicide attacks like the Kashmiri groups. Suicides attacked are believed to be the most powerful means of inflicting large scale casualties in modern day terrorism. But still, thanks to the lack of credible intelligence, coordination and ill-prepared security forces, the Maoists are able to dominate the cat—and mouse game. By the end of April 2010, over four civilians and security personnel were losing their lives against one Maoist casualty (Table 12.2). This ratio may actually go up, or remain alarmingly high, as long as Maoists are able to carry out train sabotages, remote controlled explosives targeted at crowded buses etc.

Political Implications

In the Chief Ministers' meet of the nine Maoist-affected states on 5th June, 2013 in the wake of the May 25, 2013 Naxal attack in Chhattisgarh, two adverse opinions comes out on the issue of tackling of Left-wing extremist movement. The Chief Ministers of the two badly affected states—Chhattisgarh and Bihar have advocated diverse strategies to tackle the militant, exemplifying the challenges for the centre to organize a coordinated offensive. Chhattisgarh Chief Minister Raman Singh called for some hard decisions and a unified national policy to treat Maoists as terrorists and fight a decisive battle. While Bihar Chief Minister Nitish Kumar maintained that a multi-dimensional strategy based on the theme of governance with justice was required. Kumar said "we must work together to launch serious developmental schemes so that misdirected people can be brought back into the socio-economic mainstream." While Singh said it was a battle of democratic forces against the perpetrators of violence. He further said "to call naxals as defenders of rights of anyone in society would only be a cruel joke. The battles being fought in Sukma, Dantewada, Baster and Narayanpur are not Chhattisgarh's alone. We are fighting those whose ultimate aim is to capture Delhi and the Red Fort through power of the gun." Maharashtra, Chhattisgarh, Andhra Pradesh and Odisha agreed to be on board for a coordination offensive with the central forces in the tri-junction of the Baster jungles from where the senior Maoist leadership operates. The Central Government decided to progressively enhance the development level of central forces in the worst-affected states and stressed on surgical operations to take out the top leadership of the CPI (Maoist).

Prime Minister Dr. Monmohan Singh in his opening remarks at the all-party meet on 10th June, 2013 said "the strength and robustness of the democratic forces in our country would suffer if the space for political activity gets restricted because of fear or terror." The political party in the meeting resolved that "it was an attack on democracy, freedom, and free speech and expression. Nothing can be more dangerous to our Republic than the insurgency of the CPI (Maoist) in pursuit of its misguided goal of overthrowing Parliamentary democracy and the Constitution of India through violent means. The Indian State cannot, and will not, accept the pernicious Maoist doctrine".

Remedies

The Maoist movement has evolved into an insurgency, at least in its strongholds in central and eastern India. The government must devise countermeasures accordingly. Half measures like local militias will not help. A well-trained and well equipped police and paramilitary force with the ability to source information about local Maoist activity is necessary to fight the battle. There's no need to deploy the army but its expertise could be sought to train and provide logistical back up for police personnel. There ought to be, as well, proper coordination among the various agencies involved in anti-Maoist operations. The Maoist challenge is not merely about the rights of adivasi people; it's essentially about what ought to be the nature of the Indian state. A democratic state as envisaged in the Indian Constitution is unacceptable to Maoists. The adivasis, a victim of the inefficiency and callousness of elected representatives and public officials, are only used as a front to promote an ideology that is inherently undemocratic. The plight of the adivasi community can, and must, be addressed through democratic means.

The government's strategy, of course, should not be limited to military action in-areas dominated by Maoists. A purely security-based approach, an all-out assault that does not distinguish between Maoists and the local people, the tribal, will be counter-productive, yielding exactly what the Maoists want. Portraying the operation against them as the state's war against the dispossessed, impoverished people in order to grab their natural resources is central to Maoist ideology and strategy.

A fight against insurgency is also a fight to win the hearts and minds of people. Issues that have bothered the adivasi community must be engaged with sympathetically and developmental initiatives designed accordingly. Maoist cadres willing to shun violence and work with the government and the civil society could be encouraged to join the social mainstream. A part from effective police action, another reason for the failure of the Maoist rebellion in Andhra Pradesh was that a number of party members, fed up with the endless violence, took up rehabilitation packages offered by the government and left the movement.

Conclusion

The rule of law, one of the pillars of a democratic polity and society, is based on an element of trust and reciprocity. It is not farfetched to assume that those who expect protection under the rule of law are also upholders of it and respect it in their politics and in their daily lives. Terrorists and Maoists do not fall into this category since they believe that political and socio-economic grievances entitle them to kill innocent people and those they consider to be their enemies. They have no respect for the rule of law and therefore, logically, they cannot expect any protection from it. All such rebels always have a specific and clear agenda, but here the Maoists' agenda is not clear. What Maoists are doing is just anarchism against Parliamentary democracy and the Constitution of India.

The Centre, in consultation with the state governments, must formulate a multidimensional strategy to end the Maoist terror. There is a false opposition between security and development in our public discourse. These paradigms can, and ought to, coexist in the government's vision of the battle against Maoists. That, by no means, is an impossible task.

Notes

1. Established the Chinese Peoples' Republic. Maoism, formally known as Mao Zedong Thought, is a political theory derived from his teachings. Maoism sees the agrarian peasantry, rather than the working classes, as the key revolutionary force which can fundamentally transform capitalist society towards socialism.
2. Naxal-affected area covering in Andhra Pradesh, Bihar, Chhattisgarh, Jharkhand, Madhya Pradesh, Odisha, Uttar Pradesh and West Bengal.
3. Guerilla zone, *Frontline Magazine*, October 8, 2006.
4. Naxalbari is the name of a village and a region in northern part of the state of West Bengal. It is famous for being the site of a revolutionary peasant uprising in 1967, which began with the 'land to tiller' slogan and inspired similar revolts in other parts of the India, popularly known as Naxalite movement. For details see Sohail Jawa, (1979). The Naxalite Movement in India: Origin and Failure of the Maoist Revolutionary Strategy in West Bengal, 1967-1971, Associated Publication House, New Delhi, p.53.

5. The founder of the Naxalbari peasant uprising in 1967, who is up there in the ultra-left pantheon along with Lenin, Stalin and Mao.
6. A section of the CPM led by Kanu Sanyal and Jangal Santhal initiated a violent uprising in 1967 in West Bengal.
7. Venkitesh Ramakrishna, The road from Naxalbari, *Frontline Magazine*, Volume 22, Issue 21, October 8-21, 2005.
8. The MCCI was originally formed in the early 1970s, while People's War was founded in 1975. Both groups are referred to as Naxalites, after the West Bengal village where a revolutionary radical Left movement originated in 1967. For details see "Centre declares Maoists a terrorist organization", *Times of India*, June 22, 2009.
9. A specter haunting India, *The Economist*, Volume 380 Number 8491, August 19th-25th, 2006.
10. Naxalites lay siege to Jehanabad 25 killed in Maoist attack, *The Hindu*, November 14, 2005.
11. Singh, Prakash, (1999). *The Naxalite Movement in India*, New Delhi, Rupa & Co., p. 101.
12. South Asia Intelligence Review, *Weekly Assessments and Briefings*, Volume 6, No. 8, September 3, 2007.
13. Left-wing extremist group—Communist Party of India-Maoist (CPI-Maoist), South Asia Terrorism Portal.
14. Recovering from the heart ailment in January 1965, Charu Majumdar, a little known communist activist in a small town at the foothills of the Himalayas propounded the first of his eight theses for an armed struggle. Written in the backdrop of the 1964 split in the communist movement, worsening food crisis and a radical mood in Europe, Latin America and much of Asia, Mazumdar's eight documents laid in the foundation of what would constitute the severest internal security the severest internal security challenge to Indian almost half-century down the line. For details see Jawaid, Sohail (1979). *The Naxalite Movement in India: Origin and Failure of the Maoist Revolutionary Strategy in West Bengal-1967-1971*, Associated Publication House, New Delhi, p. 53.
15. A section of Communist Party of India (Marxist) led by Charu Majumdar and Kanu Sanyal led a violent uprising in 1967, trying to develop a 'revolutionary opposition' in opposition to the CPI(Marxist) leadership. Majumdar greatly admired Mao Zedong of China and advocated that Indian peasants and lower classes must follow in his footsteps and overthrow the government and upper classes whom he held responsible for their plight. For details see Prakash Singh, (1999), *The Naxalite Movement in India*, New Delhi, Rupa & Co. p. 101.
16. "Naxal (Maoist) movement is little more than in the past." Shivraj Patil, Union Home Minister, August 14, 2007. Another official 'assessment' of the Maoist challenge was placed on record in the Lok Sabha (Lower House of the Indian Parliament) on August 14, 2007.

13

Naxal Problem in India

An Economic Analysis

Raj Kishor Pradhan

Introduction

India, having one of the fastest growing economies in the world, and being the most populous democratic country, has great potential to become a future superpower. However, in this increasingly globalised environment, India faces several threats to its security. The Naxalites has been identified as the biggest internal security threat to India by none other than the Prime Minister Manmohan Singh. The complex and structural causes of the problem support this proposition. The Naxal movement also presents the greatest overall threat to India in the future, as it highlights various underlying weaknesses of India's governance, political institutions and socio-economic structure.

Naxal, naxalite are generic terms used to refer various militant communist groups operating in different parts of India under different organization structures. Naxalism is the biggest threat because it affects several areas including the economy, security and foreign affairs, its citizens and rule of law. Because of the multi-dimensional aspect of the Naxal problem, a three-pronged approach should be taken in dealing with the threat. It calls for a balance between military forces, social and economic development, as well as dialogue between all parties. Therefore, it is realised by the different strata's of the society to understand the root cause of the Naxal problem and its solution.

The objective of the chapter is to present different methods of solution and particularly give emphasis on economic solution. The plan of the paper is divided into three parts. In first part we will analyse the brief history of naxal problem. In second part we will discuss the various factors responsible for Naxalism. Thirdly, we discuss the possible solution of the problem.

The Maoist movement may have started off on purely altruistic terms but has metamorphosed over the years into an ugly monster indecipherable from its original avatar as encapsulated in this incisive description (R.S.N. Singh, Associate Editor IDR. Maoist Threat and Politics. *India Defence Review,* Vol. 25.1. Jan.-March 2010): Naxal, Naxalite and Naksalvadi are generic terms used to refer to various militant communist groups operating in different parts of india. In the eastern states of the mainland India (Chhattisgarh, Jharkhand, West Bengal and Odisha), they are usually known as, or refer to themselves as Maoists while in southern states like Andhra Pradesh they are known under other titles. The term Naxalites comes from Naxalbari, a small village in West Bengal in 1967. The Naxals are considered far-left radical communists, supportive of Maoist political sentiment and ideology. Their origin can be traced to the split in 1967 of the Communist Party of India (Marxist), leading to the formation of the Communist Party of India (Marxist-Leninist). Initially, the movement had its centre in West Bengal. In later years, it spread into less developed areas of rural southern and eastern India, such as Chhattisgarh, Odisha and Andhra Pradesh through the activities of underground groups like the CPI(M). For the past 10 years, it has grown mostly displaced tribal and natives who are fighting against exploitation from major Indian corporations and local officials whom they believe to be corrupt. Now they resort to mean of violence to achieve their goal. Therefore, Naxalites or red violence is one of the growing menaces in India. Now, for last forty years Naxalism has been spread from an obscure village of Naxalbari in West Bengal to rest of the country. Now, even our Prime Minister has also admitted that Naxal or Maoist is great internal threat to our country. The so called "Red Corridor" of India has hugely attracted domestic and international attention. In last few years their bloody game has not only put common people on spot but also the government. The 'Red terror' spots have begun to pop up in India's capital and northern States' forest and hilly areas too. It seems that the Maoists are interested in enlarging their area of influence outside the jungles of the 'Red Corridor' that runs from the Nepal border down to Andhra Pradesh. Lately, they have begun targeting India's seat of power—New Delhi—and many other cities by setting up urban bases with the aim to penetrate and influence policy makers, judiciary, media, civil liberty, human rights, cultural, Dalit, women and youth organisations. So far, the urban units are not indulging in violence. But who knows when they may start firing guns. Their fearless and bold attack on our paramilitary forces, police forces, common citizens, political leaders and also on government properties took a huge toll in term of property and human lives. Human lives are precious. The preceding five years was a watershed period in the fight against Naxalism for it was marked by an exponential and dangorous growth in this scourge. In 2004, Naxalites were confined to 156 of India's 602 districts. By 2008, Naxalites had expanded their reach into 180 districts or roughly one-third of the nation's territory.

The same period saw Naxalites-related incidents assume alarming proportions, both in terms of frequency and intensity. In 2003 there were 1,597 incidents. By 2009, this number had shot up to 2,239—an increase of nearly 40 per cent. Additionally the number of casualties suffered by security forces reached an all time high of 317 in 2009 compared to 217 Naxal casualties. And for three years running the annual death toll of security personnel has consistently exceeded the corresponding figures for Naxalites deaths—not a reassuring statistics.

There are various factors responsible for Naxalism. These are the political, social, historical and economical factor. It should bear in the mind that naxal problems are not merely a media propaganda. Definitely it is a serious problem, which going to hurt our ambition of next economic superpower.

The main factor is India's long neglect to develop the tribal areas which has created large pockets of alienation against the government and these pockets have become the spawning ground of Maoist terrorism. The governments concerned have to take note of the genuine grievances of the tribal's and deal with them in a sympathetic manner. There has to be a system for a prompt enquiry into all allegations of excess. Naxal problem has its origin in deeply rooted negligence of tribal and landless people by the Government. After sixty-four years of independence the government is unable to provide the basic necessity to the bottom half of the population. Naxalism never flourish in northern part of India but obscure central and eastern part of India. In this part of country basically the States of West Bengal, Bihar, Odisha, Jharkhand, Chhattisgarh and Andhra Pradesh etc. are basically hugely tribal dominated area. Historically, these tribal people are more freedom minded, they deeply attached to their land, forest. They neither interfere others life, nor they prefer the interference of others. But the development of the economy definitely affects the interest of the common man. Here, the lack of basic governance is main problem. In these areas there is lack of communication, basic health care facility and education, banking facility etc. Therefore, the government machinery are virtually failed. Government officials are scared to be posted here. Therefore, the decentralisation of the local government has not been fulfilled here. Therefore, these people are alienated from the mainstream of the nation. This vacuum has been fulfilled by the Maoists in these areas. Therefore, the Maoist terrorism cannot be effectively countered without modernising and strengthening our rural policing and the rural presence of the intelligence agencies. The tribal areas, which have not yet been affected by the Maoist virus, have to be developed on a crash basis in order to prevent the spread of the virus to them.

There are various factors responsible for rise of Naxalism. Important among them are political and economical factors. But here we focused on economic perspectives of Naxalism. Besides, the political factors, economic factors have also acted as a catalyst in giving momentum to the movement. Economically, the problem of poverty and economic inequality can be identified as vital in accelerating the pace of movement. The absolute numbers of the poor have fallen over the decades. According to the Planning Commission report now the people below poverty line is 22 per cent of the population (in the year 2009-10, NSSO Report); the statistical averages do not capture the intensity of distress in certain pockets despite the high growth in recent years. To be poor is one thing and to seem condemned to one's fate quite another. Rising incomes in the post-reform India have created a rapidly growing aspirational class but these have also contributed to an army of socio-economic orphans who have been rejected by all mainstream political parties. These downtrodden people comprises tribal, *dalits*, landless poor are the majority of the population. They are depriving of the basic necessities of the human life. The fruit of economic growth has not reached to them. In addition, a contractor-politician nexus controls the wealth of the forests and pushes tribal's to the margin. A repressive state apparatus, represented by the police and the black laws, they use their advantage, helps keep this exploitative system going.

The situation has further worsened by the opening up of the Indian economy to trade and investment; the entry of the multinational companies in Odisha and Chhattisgarh poses a threat to the livelihoods of tribal and their way of life. These MNCs are eyeing on the vast natural resources like minerals, forest products etc. The SEZ and demand of raw materials for the industrial development has put pressure on forest and mining areas. But the then government law regarding mining etc. has underestimated the interests of the tribal. Large-scale displacement has been taken place due to establishment of large-scale mineral based industries and hydel dams. Thus economic exploitation of the tribal, a problem that is unattended by the political system, creates a fertile soul for the Naxals to play an important role.

The study of various factors thus indicates that Naxalism is the outcome of not just one factor but a number of various factors. One can really have a proper grip of the problem by focusing on the psychology of the individuals who are a part of the movement. The psychological factors synthesise well the above mentioned factors—political and economic—and facilitate a clear understanding of the roots of the movement.

The impact of Naxalism on economic growth and development is very severe. For sound development of the economy it requires a peaceful environment. But Naxalism is now creating a war like situation in certain states. They are operating a parallel rules in that states. Unfortunately, these areas are increasing day by day. For example, the Bastar region of Chhattisgarh, undivided Koraput district of Odisha is the hotbed of Maoist activities. In these areas the rule of law is absent. Therefore, economic activities remain standstill.

Therefore, Government has understood the gravity of the situation. It has formed various committees to deal with the naxal problem. In May 2006, the Planning Commission appointed an expert committee headed by D. Bandopadhyay, a retired IAS officer instrumental in dealing with the Naxalites in West Bengal in the 1970s. The expert committee has underscored the social, political, economic and cultural discrimination faced by the SCs/STs across the country as a key factor in drawing large number of discontented people towards the Naxalites. The committee established the lack of empowerment of local communities as the main reason for the spread of the Naxal movement. Choosing its words carefully, the report states that "We have two worlds of education, two worlds of health, two worlds of transport and two worlds of housing."

The expert committee delved deep into the new conflict zones of India, i.e. the mines and mineral rich areas, steel zones, as well as the SEZs. The report holds the faulty system of land acquisition and a non-existent R&R Policy largely responsible for the support enjoyed by the Naxalites. On the other hand, the committee makes a forceful plea for a policy and legal framework to enable small and marginal farmers to lease-in land with secure rights while landless poor occupying government land should not be treated as encroachers.

For the first time in the history of the Naxal movement, a government appointed committee has put the blame on the State for the growth of the movement. Providing statistics of 125 districts from the Naxal-affected States, the committee finds out that the state bureaucracy has pitiably failed in delivering good governance in these areas. The report recommends rigorous training for the police force, not only on humane tactics of controlling rural violence but also on the constitutional obligation of the State for the protection of fundamental rights.

Making a departure from the usual government position, the expert committee concludes that development paradigm pursued since independence has aggravated the prevailing discontent among the marginalized sections of society. Citing democratic principles, the report also argues for the right to protest and discovers that unrest is often the only thing that actually puts pressure on the government to make things work and for the government to live up to its own promises. Dealing with Naxalism needs a holistic approach with development initiatives as an integral part of the security approach.

Solutions

The complexity of the causes of the Naxalite problem as well as its implications both for internal and external security reflect a solution that is multi-dimensional and calls for a synergy between the Central Government and the States. In order to comprehensively dissolve the Naxalite threat, the government has to address its root causes. Socio-economic alienation and the dissatisfaction with the widening economic and political inequality will not be solved by military force alone, which seems to be the main instrument employed by the government. The problem calls for a three-pronged solution: social and economic development, multi-lateral dialogue and military force.

Socio-economic Development

As the Naxalites are fuelled by discontent from the marginalised and the poor, a larger percentage of the national budget must be allocated to addressing the needs of these regions. More of the national expenditure needs to be focused on developing these poorer regions through initiatives regarding health, education, social welfare and rural and urban development. Government service delivery should be improved in these tribal areas. Both state and government must ensure that things such as statutory minimum wages, access to land and water sources initiatives are implemented. In coming up with strategies for national economic growth, the government must always bear in mind the possible effects of fast growth for all socio-economic groups in a country as large and diverse as India. If the social needs of these marginalised people are addressed, there will be no discontent to fuel the Naxalite movements.

Governance

The growing Naxalite insurgency also reflects a flaw in the federal structure. Because law and order is seen as a state responsibility, the Central Government is unable to be implementing a coherent national strategy to address the threat. Ganguly notes that "in the absence of a near complete breakdown of public order or without the express request of the afflicted state, the Central Government cannot… [Intervene]." The government has the overall responsibility of mobilising development, but it cannot do so without the support of the states. The Central Government and the States need to cooperate together to solve the internal security threats and coordinate the implementation of this multi-dimensional approach. Both organisations must complement and support each other's initiatives and strategies. But the present economic growth models are advocating of that type of economic growth which is not sustainable. For example, this part of our country is mineral rich. Therefore, multinational companies are interested to exploit these areas at any cost. But at the cost of lower strata of the people, these people are tribal people and landless farmers. These are the persons who have to be displaced but not gained anything in return. Therefore, large scale dissatisfaction is arising. Governance is totally absent there. Recent lethal attack of Naxalites on Congress leaders in Chhattisgarh are pointer of lack of Government coordination there. Although government policy is good, if implementation is nil then serious problems arise. This is the main reason for rising of Maoist insurgency in these areas. Counter-terrorism activity like 'Operation green hunt' is never a solution for this problem. Then what is the solution? Actually there is no quick fix solution of this problem. The need of the hour is good governance. The public also do their bit to solve this problem. We cannot criticise the establishment for each and every problem. Here, the role of public or civil society is very important. Government is making every possible effort by making all possible policies and instruments. But to implement all the policies and to create awareness among the public, the role of civil society is also very important.

References

Aletha Cherian, 'Naxalism—The Biggest Security Threat to India', 2010.

Naxalites—Wikipedia.

Sarabjit Kaur, 'Towards Understanding Naxalism', *Mainstream*, Vol. XLVIII, No. 12, March 13, 2010.

'The Naxalite Problem of India', *Competition Master*, 2009.

Vivek Gumaste, 'The Naxal Problem: 'Failure of Political leadership', Rediff.com-27-04-2010.

14

Emergence of ULFA

A Challenge to Peace Process

Manju Singh

The United Liberation Front of Assam (ULFA) is a separatist group in Assam, among many other such groups in North East India. It seeks to establish a sovereign state of Assam. The Government of India banned the organization in 1990 and classified it as a terrorist group, while the U.S. State Department lists it under 'other groups of concern'.

ULFA was formed on April 7, 1979 by Bhimkanta Buragohain, Arbindo Rajkhowa, Anup Chetia, Pradip Gogoi, Bhadreshwar Gohain and Paresh Barua at Rang Ghar, the 17th century amphitheatre of the Ahom Royalty in Sibsagar to establish a 'Sovereign Socialist Assam' through an armed struggle.

ULFA According to Government of India

The Government of India has classified it as a terrorist organization and has banned it under the Unlawful Activities (Prevention) Act in 1990. The Government of India accuses ULFA of maintaining links with the Inter Services Intelligence (ISI) of Pakistan and Directorate General of Forces Intelligence (DGFI) of Bangladesh are waging a proxy war on their behalf against India. The outlawed group is said to be looking to China for shelter following mounting pressure from both Myanmar and Bangladesh which in turn are pressured by India.

ULFA According to Itself

The ULFA is a revolutionary political organization engaged in a liberation struggle against state terrorism by India for the establishment of a sovereign independent Assam. It does not consider itself a secessionist organization as it claims that Assam was never a part of India. It claims that among the various problems that the people of Assam are confronting, the problem of National identity is the most basic and therefore, it seeks to represent independent minded struggling people irrespective of race, tribe, caste, religion and nationality. The ULFA has laid down certain qualifications for those seeking its membership.

Qualifications for Membership of ULFA

Clause 1: He must be a permanent resident of Assam. However, the volunteers from any other country will be recognized conditionally.

Clause 2: He must have the firm determination to wage armed struggle till the successful conclusion of national liberation struggle.

Clause 3: He must have mental fitness. Membership may be provided to the physically handicapped even regarding their integrity.

Clause 4: He must have capacity to maintain secrecy.

Clause 5: He must submit totally to the Constitution of the party for the interest of the emancipation of Assam.

Clause 6: He must be above the age of 18 years. It may be changed with time.

Clause 7: Any person addicted to porn book/magazine, cinema and songs would be disqualified.

Clause 8: He mustn't take any intoxicating material.

Clause 9: A person shall be disqualified for membership if he is involved in anti-social activities.

Clause 10: Every member of the party must be ready for any task and he/she must be whole time worker.

Clause 11: He must comply with the responsibility of any appointment at any place heartily and without protest after receiving the membership.[1]

ULFA Leadership

ULFA, essentially a secessionist outfit, termed Constitution of India as 'a tool for colonial exploitation of Assam' and demanded right of self-determination. All this obviously had influenced the thinking and philosophy of the ULFA leadership whose profile is as follows.[2]

High Command

	Name		Designation
1.	Arbindo Rajkhowa	—	Chairman
2.	Paresh Barua	—	Commander-in-Chief
3.	Anup Chetia	—	Secretary General
4.	Manoj Hazarika	—	Vice Chairman
5.	Pradip Gogoi	—	Vice Chairman
6.	Raju Barua	—	Dy. Commander-in-Chief
7.	Sashadhar Choudhary	—	Foreign Secretary
8.	C. Hazarika	—	Finance Secretary

Senior Officers

	Name		Designation
1.	Mithinga Daimary	—	Publicity Secretary (Relieved of his charge in mid-2000 Paresh Barua personally handling the media).
2.	Ashantha Baghphukan	—	Organizing Secretary (He was ULFA's Senior most leader in Bhutan who rose to become organizing secretary in 1999. He took over the post after the arrest of Pradeep Gogoi).
3.	Pranati Deka	—	Cultural Secretary (In jail since September 1997).
4.	Babu Sarma	—	Chief Medical Officer, ULFA-A units in Bhutan.

Middle Level Officers

	Name		Designation
1.	Dhrishti Rajkhowa	—	Appointment unknown
2.	Tapan Barua	—	Commander, ULFA's 28th Battalion.
3.	Captain Lohit Deuri	—	General Staff Office GHQ, ULFA, Bhutan (Surrendered).

Major Factors Responsible for the Growth and Working of this Terrorist Outfit

Initially ULFA did not have much influence but gradually it became very popular with the villagers, the middle class, students and academicians. There were many reasons for its growth which can be enumerated as[3]:

1. Firstly, ULFA workers had introduced many welfare works at village and society level. They solved many village level disputes and pushed forward projects like village roads, flood bandhs and village lights, etc. They became modern day Robin Hoods. Slowly they began to expand their influence in the districts of Barpeta, Nagaon, Kamrup, Sonitpur and Nalbari of lower Assam. During the highly unpopular elections of 1983, ULFA got an opportunity to propagate their views and establish their organization with the backing of many powerful politicians as well as senior government functionaries in the administration as well as the police. The elections took place at the cost of thousands of innocent lives. It had great psychological impact on the common people of Assam. This gave an opportunity to the extremist elements to propagate their views that the Indian State machinery could get away with such large scale state violence to defeat the popular boycott of elections, primarily because resistance to it was peaceful and that results would have been different if the people resisting the Government move were also armed. This argument found acceptance within sizeable sections of the younger generation and enabled ULFA to secure a large number of recruits and also to garner substantial public support.
2. After the Assam accord in 1985, the elections to the state assembly took place in which Asam Gan Parishad (AGP) came to power which was sympathetic to ULFA. During its reign the outfit made massive fund collection and recruitment. Thus the AGP Government contributed significantly to the subsequent growth of ULFA.
3. Thirdly, extortion served as an effective means to serve the purpose of funds collection. Funds were collected from the local traders by giving them threat over the phone. The higher echelons of the business world like the tea industry were easy prey particularly when a sympathetic political party was in power. In

the initial stages of its growth, ULFA's extortion served dual purpose of collecting the funds and earning the good will of the public. This was achieved by targeting only those individuals and groups who were known to have amassed wealth by corrupt and illegal means. ULFA collected huge amount of funds and earned a Robin Hood like image. This state of affairs was transformed at a later stage when, in their quest for funds, even innocent and honest people were targeted resulting in the organization losing its image as a group of revolutionaries who could do no wrong in the eyes of a large section of the people. The most well known instance of the exposure of the outfit as a ruthless and not so innocent one was the abduction and brutal killing of Sanjay Ghosh, a social activist.

4. The alienation of a large proportion of the state's populace from the rest of India played a great role in helping the ULFA to expand its influence. This alienation was result of various factors, including the geographical location of the region: the inept handling of even the genuine demands and aspirations of the people of the region by an insensitive and, by and large, ill-informed establishment at the national level etc. Assam produces, more than 400 million kg of tea with a turnover of Rs.20 billion. However, the headquarters of all the tea companies are located outside the state and, hence it is believed by all sections of the people that Assam has been deprived of the benefits of a larger share of taxes paid by the industry, and also denied business opportunities for local people in the supply and servicing requirements of this huge industry. This had always been a sore point with the local populace, and the ULFA cadres harped on this, among other issues, to buttress their argument on discrimination against Assam and the Assamese by the big business lobby assisted by the Union and State Governments. Similar was feeling of deprivation and discrimination in the matter of oil industry. The oil wells in Assam produce five million tonnes of crude oil but the first refinery to process this crude oil was set up in Barauni in Bihar. It was only after a popular movement that a small refinery was set up at Guwahati and later a second at Numaligarh, as a result of the agreement reached with the AASU in the settlement of the anti-foreigners agitation. These and similar instances created a feeling that Assam gets even its legitimate dues only after agitations and sacrifice of

valuable lives. What better fertile ground could any extremists set-up hope for, to propagate their theory that India and Indians had never considered Assam as a part of the nation, and were only interested in exploiting the rich natural resources of the state.

5. The next major contributory factor for the growth and operational success of the outfit were certain geographical features. The region has border with four foreign countries: China, Myanmar, Bangladesh and Bhutan, among these Bangladesh and Bhutan served as safe heaven for the ULFA, providing excellent training and operational bases. It was very easy for them to hit their targets in many of the lower Assam districts from their bases in Bhutan and escape back to their camps there. This was a very major tactical advantage to them and a disadvantage to the security forces.
6. The next contributory factor was unemployment and lack of development of the region.

Spread of ULFA and Foreign Hand

Once ULFA was born and commenced its operations to destabilize the state and declared war on the so called State-machinery it was but natural that foreign powers inimical to India, to extend assistance to them. The Inter Services Intelligence (ISI), Pakistan's external intelligence agency is known to have helped ULFA in a big way, particularly in matters of training camps located in Bangladesh, in the procurement of arms and ammunition and in arranging training and indoctrination to selected cadres in Pakistan and Afganistan. The ISI of Pakistan along with DGFI of Bangladesh had undertaken important operations in Assam in order to divert the Indian Military to their region from their primary role in Kashmir. This conspiracy had come to light in recent years especially after the arrest of ISI sponsored agents in the heart of Assam's Capital.[4] At one point of time ULFA was known to have been in touch with the Srilankan Liberation Tigers of Tamil Eelam (LTTE), but the extent of link, if any, is not clear. As far as Bangladesh is concerned, in addition to allowing its soil to be used for ULFA's camps and hideouts, its Directorate of General Forces Intelligence (DGFI) also rendered help to this outfit.

The case of Bhutan is on a different footing. The General headquarters, the Council of Headquarters and security-cum-training camps of ULFA are known to be located in Bhutan. The dense hilly jungles of Bhutan adjoining Assam have been extensively and very effectively used by the insurgents to launch successful forays into Assam from their camps there. ULFA activities inside Bhutan had risen dramatically since 1995 after their safe heavens in Bangladesh came under attack by the then Bangladesh Government.

ULFA had camps located in the forests of southern Bhutan and the Samdruk Dzonkha area and it was at one such camp where the ISI trained ULFA.

Growth of ULFA into a Violent Movement

The ULFA remained relatively dormant for some years after its formation in 1979. After the Assam accord of 1985, the ULFA nurtured the idea of forming a violent underground movement and liberating the state of Assam from the clutches of India.

There had been speculations on the All Assam Students Union (AASU) and ULFA relationship, some felt that ULFA had watched the AASU movement from close angles and learnt some lessons in organizing and conducting such movements.

The 1983 assembly polls were excessively violent because they were held in the wake of the boycott call by AASU, since it was alleged that the electoral rolls prepared in 1979 contained names of over 4 million aliens who, if allowed to participate in polls, would vitiate their sanctity. AASU deemed the Saikia Government that came into power as a result of these, as illegitimate. It was during these unpopular elections and the tenure of Saikia Government (1983-85) that ULFA rose to power and made significant in roads into the body politic of Assam. After the Assam accord in 1985 the Assam Gana Parishad came to power and Prafulla Kumar Mahanta became the Chief Minister of Assam. ULFA had infiltered some departments of the Mahanta Government. Mahanta did not act even when he knew that the ULFA activities were harming his Government.[5]

Operation Bajarang

Alarmed at the large scale kidnapping for ransom, extortion and looting of banks, murders of hostages, complete breakdown of the State Police Machinery, the Central Government dismissed the AGP Government headed by Prafulla Kumar Mahanta and imposed President's Rule on November 27th, 1990. The same day ULFA was declared "unlawful" under the Unlawful Activities (Prevention) Act of 1967. The army crackdown known as "Operation Bajrang" began from the 28th November, 1990. The operation Bajrang moved on, under Lieutenant General Ajai Singh of the Western Command against the militants in Upper Assam. But so strong was the intelligence of the militants that they received timely information to take precautionary measures before the arrival of the troops. The Army's raid went into deserted camp, but they got sufficient intelligence for future operations. They also found mass graves amidst jungles near Lakhimpur as concrete evidence of ULFA's brutalities. This caused a wave of disgust in the usually peace loving people of Assam. The common man was also feeling the punch of extortion and strong arm tactics of militants. The High Command of ULFA started shifting camps as the Army's presence increased and they eventually shifted most of their camps to Bangladesh. This phase of the operation resulted in the capture of about 500 militants most of whom were lower level cadres and informants with some low grade weapons.

In the Assembly elections of 1991 with the backing of the Muslims, Bengalis and some tribals, Congress party won the majority and Hiteshwar Saikia once again formed the Government. ULFA became active during his term of office and indulged itself into several sabotages and killings. They started kidnapping personnels from oil and tea industry both for money and release of ULFA detainees. They kidnapped fourteen executives of the Oil and Natural Gas Commission (ONGC) including Soviet Engineer Gritchenko Sergoi. The ULFA bargained that hostage would be released if twenty-four of its cadre were freed from prison. Sergoi was killed as he could not be subdued by threats or physical intimidation. The failure of the negotiations over the hostage issue and the killing of ONGC officials, Sergoi and later T.S. Raju sparked off nation-wide protests. Oil Engineers went on strike and refused to work unless their friends were released and security ensured. The Centre and Saikia's government had to abandon the search for a negotiated settlement and planned Operation Rhino.[6]

Operation Rhino

Operation Rhino rolled on in September 1991 with greater secrecy. This operation had immediate success and resulted in capture of some top leaders of ULFA. ULFA's dream was shattered with the arrest and shooting of its Deputy Commander in Chief Hirak Jyoti Mahanta. This was the story of ULFA during the first decade of its existence.[7]

SULFA and the Process of Peace

Surrendered ULFA came to be known as SULFA (Surrendered United Liberation Front of Assam). The phenomenon of surrender by ULFA ultras started during the tenure of Hiteshwar Saikia Government during 1991-96. Hiteshwar Saikia succeeded in creating fractions within ULFA with Saikia announcing amnesty in March 1992, Sunil Nath, ULFA's publicity chief led over 3,500 youth over ground. Later outfit's Deputy Commander in Chief and Foreign Secretary also surfaced to swell the ranks of the surrendered ULFA, popularly known as SULFA. It was a great success and there was no reason to deny the credit for it to Saikia. By the end of 1995, 4860 ultras had surrendered and they were given many incentives.[8]

Following the loss of its cadres, the ULFA rewrote its Constitution to re-energize itself. Its leadership reiterated its demand for an independent Assam outside the Union of India in October 1993. After re-working philosophy and rejuvenating its cadres, it started working from its sanctuaries in Bangladesh and understandably became even bolder in its depredations. It was in this period that ULFA created and revealed its image of Robin Hood, robbing the rich to help the poor. The image, action and ideology gained its popularity for some time. But it started losing people's respect and sympathy when its cadres launched on a course of mindless violence since May 1996 onwards. It suffered further decline when a popular social activists like Sanjoy Ghosh was killed. Towards the end of 1990s, its image stood shattered for several reasons:[9]

1. The Robin Hood was dead
2. Youth's enthusiasm to joint ULFA flagged
3. Lack of funds
4. Lavish style of living enjoyed by its leaders
5. The success of C1 operations by the Security Forces
6. The leadership decided on an expedient short-cut. Discarding their ideology and ideals, they launched vicious attacks on minorities to divide the Assamese.

As for the SULFA (Surrendered ULFA) cadres it was said that they were an intelligence asset in the initial stages: Then came the time when they were a serious concern to civil and military authorities, becoming a law unto themselves. They indulged in looting, extortion and even killing to settle personal scores, all made possible since they had been allowed to retain their arms for reasons of personal security. But the things became really dangerous with the ULFA-SULFA clashes, which were not unexpected as SULFA was the main source of information on their former colleagues.[10]

The ISI and ULFA

On 6th April, 2000, the then Chief Minister of Assam, Prafulla Kumar Mahanta, in the State Assembly presented the comprehensive report of ISI threat on Assam. According to the sixteen page report the activities of the ISI were mainly in the following areas:[11]

1. Promoting indiscriminate violence in the State by providing active support to the local militant outfits.
2. Creating new militant outfits along ethnic and communal lines by instigating ethnic and religious groups.
3. Supplying explosives and sophisticated arms to various terrorist groups.
4. Causing sabotage of oil pipelines and other installations, communication lines, railways and roads.
5. Promoting fundamentalism and militancy among local Muslim youth by misleading them in the name of *Jehad.*
6. Promoting communal tensions between Hindu and Muslim citizens by way of false and highly inflammatory propaganda.

Intelligence reports indicated that the ISI had sought to smuggle sixty kilograms of RDX into Assam. This was attempted in the month of August 1999 when the ISI decided to unleash "Operation Tehsad" in North-East India. The motivation was to destroy the oil industry and surface transport. The ISI gave ULFA the first installment of the explosives with which they could begin their operations—four explosions took place in three days on rail tracks and trains.

The ISI had also organized training for the ULFA cadres in association with the Directorate General of Field Intelligence of Bangladesh (DGFI). A retired Bangladesh Army Officer Brig. Joimullah Khan Choudhary, supervised the training. There was also evidence to suggest that the ISI had activated the border areas in Nepal for relocation of some of the militant camps, especially after the presence in Bhutan had become a problem. The ULFA alone with the NDFB had reportedly already set up camps in Jhapa Tapegung and Panchthar in Eastern Nepal.

The Pakistani misadventure in Kargil brought out into the open

ULFA-ISI nexus. According to the Indian army operating in Assam, the ULFA was involved in passing the information of troops' movements, to and from Assam, to the ISI. The ULFA was also allegedly pressurized by the ISI to make anti-Indian statements primarily supporting the Liberation of Kashmir.

It had also been reported that the genocide perpetrated by the ULFA during the closing months of 2000, when they began to systematically target Hindi speaking Assamese, was planned by the ISI. Indeed, intelligence reports had suggested that members of Bangladesh based Jamaat-e-Islami's student wing, the Islamic Chatra Shibir, operated along with the ULFA to perpetrate the acts of terror.

The ISI had clearly won the "Upper Assam Restraint" round, and the ULFA was completely under the control of the Pakistani Intelligence Agency and would not hesitate to perpetrate acts of terror which it would have not even considered in the past. Indeed, the ULFA, which had earlier taken extra precautions not to inflict harm on innocent civilians, seemed to have thrown caution to the winds, when it hurled a grenade in Guwahati on the day of the Assamese New Year.

ULFA and Bangladesh

Bangladesh along with Myanmar is a country that had housed the ULFA's training and liaison camps as well as its safe houses. Moreover, it was in the cities of Dhaka and Chittagong that the leaders of ULFA used to reside. Also most arms consignments dispatched to the ULFA from the Orient were conducted through Bangladesh. The ULFA more over seemed to have a working relationship with the Bangladesh. Some leaders of Bangladesh were reported to have publicly called the ULFA as well as other North-East Militant Groups as freedom Fighters.[12] Bangladesh has allowed its aid to be used for ULFA camps and hideouts. Intelligence reports also indicate that there were as many as 155 militant camps in Bangladesh which used to train and house militants from North East India.

The Indian Ministry of Home Affairs, some years ago, published a booklet called 'Bleeding Assam' and stated that the leaders of the ULFA were running lucrative business in Bangladesh and were living a life of luxury. The ISI-DGFI nexus kept some important ULFA leaders under constant protection, as they feared that they might leave Bangladesh in order to return India and surrender. DGFI rendered all help to this outfit ULFA.

The ULFA's geo-political compulsion, its connection with the ISI, the organization's paraphernalia in Bangladesh and indeed, the entire process by which it has abdicated its ideology, have, therefore, only expedited the fundamentalist agenda which is being engineered in Assam. Although, it may be said that the ground was already fertile for the growth of Islamic movements in Assam as a result of not only the illegal influx into the state from Bangladesh but also because of the dynamics that given birth to Islamic fundamentalism of the day (especially after 11th September 2001). The fact of the matter is that a strong ethnic movement such as the ULFA would have stood in the way of the fundamentalist progress had it not reneged on its founding principles.

ULFA-Burma-Bhutan

There was an interesting offshoot to the active phase of the ULFA and Burmese relations. From their Burmese base, ULFA had through the good offices of NSCN (I-M), established a number of safe houses and liaison offices in Thailand, essentially for arms procurement. Senior ULFA leaders frequently visited Changmai (hottest arms market for illegal arms trade then and even today) to augment their arsenal from the Khmer Rouge elements operating on the Ranong Coast and Bangkok to rest in the five-star resorts.

As a result of joint operations and improved economic relations with Myanmar since 2000, ULFA came under pressure to move out of Burma.

Later Reports talked of nearly all leaders shifting to their Bhutan camps. Bhutan Government, however, had talked to the ULFA leadership to move out, as a result of the Indian insistence, but so far majority of ULFA cadres were confined in their Bhutanese sanctuaries. No doubt Thimpu was putting pressure on ULFA and Bodo outfits to vacate their soil. But this was easier said than done. Some observers felt the Royal Bhutanese Army did not have the fire powers and the logistics to force the ULFA and NDFB out of their base in Bhutan. It did not seem keen to seek help from India. It was also possible that Thimpu had some genuine difficulties. The economy of many villages in Southern Bhutan still revolve around the militant camps at places like Kalikhola and Noglang. Moreover, the ULFA cadres had been good guests, under instruction never to be high-handed towards the locals. Moreover, ULFA had nowhere to go. It seemed inevitable that ULFA-Bhutan problem will have to await the solution of ULFA-India problem.

All this notwithstanding, Bhutanese Army finally acted in December 2003 and smashed all the ULFA and NDFB camps in three weeks.

ULFA Setting up Bases in Nepal

Intelligence called from various sources disclosed ULFA setting up five camps in Nepal in the areas under the Maosist leader Pushpa Kumar Dahal, likely existing in the districts of Bara, Dang etc. Paresh Barua's trusted aide Rana Deuri from Darrang districts, was incharge of these Nepal camps, housing about 150 cadres. Deuri was close to the CPI, which had for the past few years figured in the ULFA's 'Golden Triangle' plan for the movement of the cadres between Bhutan, Bangladesh and Nepal. The ouster of the ULFA set-up in Bhutan following Operation "All Clear" in December 2003 necessitated these camps, which might not be exclusive to ULFA, but possibly shared with the Maoists. In any case analysts had long suspected an ULFA-Maoist nexus.

The report of ULFA shifting base from other adjoining countries came at a time when some intellectuals were trying to bring ULFA to the negotiations table at New Delhi.

Ethnic Cleansing

The most worrying aspect of October 2000 killings was that it was for the first time that ULFA had resorted to targeting unarmed civilians of a particular community. It had followed the foot-steps of the Kashmiri terrorists who had cleansed the valley of the Kashmiri Pandits. This was the start of the Ethnic cleansing in Assam.

It is to be noted that Ethnic killings started in Assam (Karbi Anglong District) by the United People Democratic Solitary (UPDS) and Dima Halam Daegah (DHD) militants six months before the ULFA resorted to in October 2000. The Hindi-speakers continued to be targeted periodically in the two hill districts of Assam till September 2000 when unidentified gunmen killed relatives of two senior UPDS militants. But the very next month, ULFA picked up where the UPDS had left, mowing down 15 Biharis in two incidents on 22nd October, 2000. That is how ULFA launched a new course which is still continuing.

Various theories were going on about the real culprits behind these killings. A "Senior Minister" said he had heard Central Intelligence Agency was behind it all, to get the Governor's rule imposed in Assam. The AGP and Congress blamed each other, for being "Allies of ULFA". Prafulla Mahanta said the Congress was helping the ULFA to destabilize his Government, aimed at winning the Assembly elections barely six months away (which were due in May 2001). Mahanta claimed to have documentary proof and wanted Congress barred from contesting the elections while BJP blamed both these parties. ULFA's objective was to have Governor's rule imposed in Assam which would afford a free hand to SULFA whose unchecked excesses would alienate the people and give an opportunity to ULFA to try and win back people's faith that it had lost during the past few years, especially after its support to Pakistan during the 1999 Kargil War.[13]

The ULFA movement, which was rooted to ethnic chauvinism also set a pattern for a number of ethnic groups in Assam to demand secession from Assam or India. Prominent among such groups include BODO Security Force (BSF), National Democratic Front for Bodoland (NDFB), Bodo Liberation Tigers (BLT), United Peoples Democratic Solidarity (UPDS), Dimasa National Security Force (DNSF), Dima Halun Daoga (DHD), Muslim United Liberation Tigers of Assam (MULTA), Kamtapur Liberation Organization (KLO), United Tribal Nationalist Liberation Front (UTNLF), Hmar People Council (HPC), Rabha National Security Force (RNSF), Tiwa National Revolutionary Force (TNRF), Bengali Tiger Force (BLT), Adivasi Security Force (ASF), Peoples United Liberation Front (PULF), Gorkha Tiger Force etc.

Infiltration from Bangladesh

The ULFA was supposed to protect Assamese identity from the threat of demographic invasion from Bangladesh, which still continues. The joint operation of both Bangladesh and Pakistan for Islamic expansionism in Assam through infiltration caused an alarming rate of growth in Muslim population of Assam.

According to 1991 Census figures, while four districts of Assam had Muslim majority, the other five districts had Muslim population varying from 32.74 per cent to 49.17 per cent. "Although the 2001 Religious census was not declared, an independent analysis that was conducted seems to show that there has been a sizeable growth in population among Muslims in Assam. The districtwise figures as per 1991 Census are:

Muslim Population

District		
Dhubari	–	70.45
Goalpara	–	50.80
Barpeta	–	50.07
Hailakandi	–	54.79

Bongaigaon	–	32.74
Morigaon	–	45.31
Nagaon	–	47.19
Karimganj	–	49.17
Cachar	–	34.49

The 1991 Census figures in Assam showed the increase of Muslim population from 24.56 per cent in 1971 to 28.53 per cent in 1991. If the decadal growth of Muslim population in Assam is taken into consideration it might have increased to over 31 per cent. Contrary to the growth rate of Muslim population in the state, its Hindu population decreased from 72.51 per cent in 1971 to 67.13 per cent in 1991. Decrease rate of about 5 per cent in 20 years against 4 per cent growth of Muslims might have reduced the Hindu population to about 62 per cent. Since, the indigenous people of State were mostly Hindus such trend in the growth of Muslim populations, if allowed to continue, a day is not very far when Assamese identity will turn into Muslim Identity. Assam under Islamic subjugation would then become another Kashmir.

Report on Illegal Migration into Assam as submitted to the President of India by the Governor, Lt.Gen. (Retd.) S.K. Sinha in 1998 warned that "if the present trends are not arrested, the indigenous people of Assam would be reduced to a minority and there may, in course of time, be a demand for the merger of Muslim dominated bordering districts with Bangladesh".[14]

A report "worked out by the group of Ministers headed by the Union Home Minister in 2001 noted that more than 15 million illegal immigrants have entered India over the last five decades."[15]

The Ministry of Home Affairs, Government of India in a booklet titled 'ULFA Alienated' with a sub-title 'Bleeding Assam (1999)'—condemned ULFA as a "most treasonous unit in the North-East". Highlighting the statements of its top leaders as an attempt to stab its own people on their back, it remarked: "Jaichand was a patriot compared to ULFA". It also quoted Chandra Prasad Saikia, President, Assam Sahitya Sabha saying, "No Assamese, even in the remotest part of the State will help Pakistan and support ULFA's support to it. The ULFA does not represent Assamese, they represent only themselves." Arbinda Rajkhowa, Chairman of ULFA was quoted saying, "India has been occupying Assam illegally like Kashmir, which was never an integral part of India."

Present Status of ULFA

ULFA is reportedly commanding three active armed battalions and is in possession of sophisticated weapons. It is running training camps in neighbouring countries with the help of ISI and other insurgent groups. In the last quarter of 2004 Government of Bhutan took a tough stand against ULFA. The king of Bhutan personally commanded his army and demolished all the ULFA camps from his territory. Even though ULFA lost its credibility to a great extent due to 'lumpenisation' of its cadres and killing of innocent civilians, it continues its militancy in the state in association of other terrorist groups and is still a force to reckon with.

The separatist violence of ULFA has shed the blood of thousands of people including innocent civilians during last twenty-five years but instead of reducing the danger against which it has been fighting, it has only aggravated it. It has now joined hands with the same forces, which are responsible for adding to the plight of Assamese. Its compromise with Bangladesh and Pakistan in encouraging Islamic militancy and abatement to Illegal migration, therefore, eroded its popularity to a great extent but ethnic Assamese are still not ready to fully disown it. Underlying sympathy for ULFA among the ethnic Assamese are still the unresolved key issues and its main strength.[16]

The Union Government made several efforts to make contacts with the ULFA leaders but nothing fruitful came out. The Centre extended ban on ULFA on February 7, 2003 under the Unlawful Activities Prevention Act, 1967 for two years. ULFA was declared an Unlawful Organization on 27th November, 1996 and the ban had been extended every two years ever since. The U.S. State Department in its 2004 country report on terrorism released on 28th April, 2005, added ULFA to the Other Selected Terrorist Organizations (OSTO) list.

Peace Efforts Made by the Government

From early 2004, noted Assamese writer and Gyanpeeth Awardee Indira Mamoni Goswami had been active in bringing ULFA and New Delhi to the negotiating table. On 15th November, 2004 she submitted a petition to the Prime Minister's special adviser M.K. Narayanan. She told the press that Prime Minister agreed to her suggestion to initiate the process to open dialogue with ULFA by January 2005.

On September 8, 2005, the ULFA appointed an eleven-member delegation 'Peoples Consultative Group' (PCG) to hold negotiations with the Indian Government. The group put forward six demands as conditions for talks, including the demand for a sovereign and independent Assam. The Union Government accepted most of the conditions, considering the ground realities, but the contentious issue of sovereignty remained unresolved.

Two rounds of negotiations were held between the PCG and the Union Government without any tangible results. Both parties agreed to hold the third round of talks after the results of the assembly elections. A sense of mistrust prevailed between both sides during the crucial phase of talks, as the ULFA did not abjure violence even after repeated appeals.

Many observers and analysts contend that the ULFA's decision to enter the peace process stems from two factors. First, 'Operation Flush Out' by the Royal Bhutan Army in 2003 deprived the ULFA of a safe heaven. Secondly, there are divisions within the Organization over the question of sovereignty. This resulted in the surrender of a large numbers of the ULFA's cadres, including many of its top leaders and activists, to the army. Besides, the ULFA's declining popularity and support within Assam has also forced it to enter the peace process. The group has lost considerable ground among the masses because of its continual resort to violence.

The economy of Assam has been shattered during the last 26 years and no significant development work has been accomplished. Political parties and civil society organizations are also pressurizing the ULFA to negotiate with the Union Government. Gyanpeeth Awardee, Dr. Mamoni Raisom Goswami and two other influential organizations, the All Assam Students' Union (AASU) and the Assam Jatiyatabadi Yuba Chatra Parishad (AJYCP), are playing leading roles in bringing the ULFA to the negotiating table.

ULFA conveyed its willingness to hold talks with the Union Government, thus granting another opportunity to end the insurgency in Assam. The PCG, mainly appointed by the ULFA, is largely drawn from civil society organizations. Some of its members are known to be sympathizers of the ULFA. The members are Arup Borbora (lawyer), Lachit Bordoloi, Mukul Mahanta (engineer), Ajit Bhuyan (editor), Haider Hussain (editor, *Asomiya Pratidin*), Brajen Gogoi (doctor), Dilip Patgiri (adviser to the Asom Jatiyatabadi Yuba Chatra Parishad), Diganta Konwar (journalist), and Hiranya Saikia (sports organizer). Goswami is the chief interlocutor and she is assisted by Reboti Phukan, a former footballer and childhood friend of the ULFA commander-in-chief, Paresh Barua.[17]

Principal Parties' Position

The ULFA advanced six major demands for resolving the problem in Assam. They are:

- Demand to end, or suspend, army operations against its cadres,
- Release of its top leader captured by the security forces,
- Information about those cadres captured during 'Operation Flush Out' in Bhutan in 2003,
- Third Party mediation for peace talks,
- Holding talks in World forum like the United Nations (UN), and
- Demand for a sovereign and independent Assam.

The ULFA has repeatedly insisted on the issue of a sovereign and independent Assam and has instructed the PCG to make this demand the lifeline of the peace talks. The demand to end or suspend army operations against the ULFA cadres also sparked controversy.

The ULFA has, so far, faced three major army operations; Operation Bajrang and Rhino in 1991-92, and 'Operation Flush Out' conducted by the Bhutan Royal Army in 2003. The ULFA's backbone seems to have broken after these assaults, and the withdrawal of army operations may lead to the regrouping of the ULFA.

The release of its top five central committee members: Vice Chairman Pradeep Gogoi, Publicity Secretary Mithinga Daimary, Ramu Mech, Arpan Saikia, and founder adviser Bhimkanta Buragohain is one of its demands. Buragohain has, however, passed away.

Other demands include information about missing cadres, particularly Abhijit Deka, Prakash Gogoi, Ashanta Baghphukan, Bening Rabha and Nilu Chakravarthy. They went missing during Bhutan's operations. The ULFA's demands such as holding talks under auspices of world forum like the UN, or with third party mediation has softened. Nevertheless, it has threatened to indulge in violence unless its demand for sovereignty is endorsed.

The Union Government has elucidated that any peace negotiations with the ULFA is possible only if the organization softens its stand on the sovereignty demand. After the first round of talks on 25th October, 2005, India's National Security adviser, M.K. Narayanan, disclosed the Union Government's decision to discuss all contentious issues regarding the state's peace and development. The Government reiterated its willingness to talk to all insurgent groups if they adjure violence and urged the ULFA to do the same. The Union Government illustrated its eagerness to suspend counter-insurgency operations and also expressed willingness to release some of the ULFA's top leaders for creating a conducive atmosphere for talks. However, the Union Government has categorically stated that sovereignty is non negotiable. On 1st April, 2006, India's Prime Minister, Dr. Manmohan Singh, in an election rally in Assam ruled out any understanding, or negotiations, with the ULFA on sovereignty. Singh revealed that all the demands advanced by the ULFA are not subject to negotiation.

The State Government also took measures to initiate direct negotiations with the ULFA. The Assam Government announced an offer of safe passage on 7th January, 2006 for a span of 14 days, hence allowing the ULFA cadres to meet their family members, with prior intimation to the concerned authorities. However, the ULFA expressed its unwillingness to avail such offers by calling it a political gimmick. Such an offer is not exceptional; in 1991, the state government made a similar offer to the ULFA'S top leaders to meet the then Prime Minister P.V. Narasimha Rao. Again, in 1999, the AGP Government proposed a 10-day safe passage, when around 250 militants responded. However, some of them apparently did not go back as they surrendered to the authorities. The Union Government remained firm, and rather inflexible, on the ULFA's core demand of sovereignty and stressed the need to solve this issue within the purview of the Constitution.[18]

First Round of Talks

On 25th October, 2005, the PCG and the Indian Government held their first round of talks, thus raising hopes of ending the insurgency movement. The talks, however, received a jolt in the initial stages when the army launched an operation in the Dibru-Saikhowa National Park in upper Assam's Tinsukia district. During the operation, code-named "Operation Balwan", two ULFA camps were destroyed and five of its top leaders were killed. The first round of talks was meant to prepare the ground for a formal bilateral declaration of ceasefire, and then to facilitate direct talks with the ULFA at later stage. M.K. Narayanan led the government's team, and Assam's Chief Minister, and other senior officials, also attended. Dr. Manmohan Singh articulated his willingness to discuss all issues concerning the state, but insisted on solving it within the Constitutional framework.

The PCG has appealed to the government to restrain army operations. The Union Government acquiesced to this request. Nevertheless, the Union government instructed the security forces to remain vigilant against any possible attacks. The first round of talks addressed many issues, aiming to bring ULFA to the negotiating table. The ULFA expressed its satisfaction with the PCG's move to raise the issue of 'sovereignty' during the talks. According to the ULFA, it is the first organization to take up the issue of sovereignty with the Union Government.

In an editorial of its mouthpiece '*Swadhinta*' (Freedom), the group said, "25th October was a red-letter day in the history of the northeast as, on this day, the issue of sovereignty was raised by the group through the PCG." However, the ULFA was not pleased with the ongoing army operations and reiterated its demand to halt these operations. Even Indira Goswami expressed concern about army operations and urged the government to stop it.

Second Round of Talks

The beginning of the second round of talks was marked by three complications: Violence unleashed by the ULFA prior to Republic Day in January 2006, the ULFA-AASU spat on the issue of sovereignty and the Union Government's decision to invite five members from the PCG to the second round of talks.

As a result, the ULFA asserted its unwillingness to negotiate with the Union government, and expressed its willingness to hold talks in an international forum like the UN. It expressed doubt over the sincerity of the Indian government, in its decision to invite five members, though the PCG attended the second round in full strength. These talks were held on 7th February, 2006. M.K. Narayanan, ESL Narasimhan, Union Home Secretary V.K. Duggal, other senior officials of the PMO, and the Home Ministry attended the talks.

Three main issues that were discussed include: suspension of army operations, release of the ULFA's central committee members, and the information about missing cadres during Bhutan's operation. The discussion helped both parties to resolve some differences. The Union Government's statement stated that it agreed to demands like suspending army operations and releasing the ULFA's detainees. Narayanan stressed on the need to work out modalities before suspending army operations. Furthermore, the Union government agreed to release some of the detainees in consultation with the state government. Both sides also agreed to hold another round of talks before commencing direct talks with the ULFA. No doubt, the talks helped resolve some difficulties, but the contentious issue of sovereignty continued to be the sore point.

Violence/Extortion by ULFA

The peace parleys between the ULFA-nominated PCG and the Union Government did not stop the ULFA's reign of violence. The ULFA perpetrated several attacks before the Republic Day Celebrations, thus derailing the peace process.

The ULFA resorted to sporadic acts of violence such as blowing up of oil pipelines, hurling grenades at the Guwahati Refinery, boycotting of the Republic Day Celebrations on 26th January, 2006, bombing of the high security Republic Day Venue—Judges Field at Guwahati, etc. These attacks resulted in the death of three people and wounded more than 31. On 22nd January, 2006, ULFA carried out at least ten attacks on vital installations like oil installations, and gas pipelines, at Chetiapathar, under Chabua police station, and Bokulia Chariali under Duliajan police station. This severely crippled the supply of crude oil and natural gas in the state and the North Eastern Electric Power Corporation (NEEPCO) was forced to temporarily shutdown. The supply of gas to Assam Gas Company Limited (AGCL) was also disrupted when ULFA triggered an explosion in the main gas supplying pipeline to the plant. It has become a tendency for ULFA to engage in such type of violence on important national days, such as Republic Day and Independence Day.

These subversive activities have been explained by the PCG as natural reactions to the Indian Government's delaying tactics in holding the second round of talks. The PCG justified its statement by arguing that the group has not declared any ceasefire and therefore, such violence is not unexpected. On 6th February, 2006, Assam's Minister of State for Home Affairs, Rockybul Hussain, issued a statement stating that, "70 subversive incidents took place and public property worth Rs. 95,70,300 was damaged. Four army personnel and 24 people were killed, including civilians and militants. In fact, the ULFA's violent activities have been more systematic," he added. Since the inception of the peace talks, the ULFA has served two extortion notes. First, it imposed a Rs.500 crore extortion demand to the Oil and Natural Gas Corporation (ONGC) in the first week of January 2006, when the oil major was planning to invest Rs. 33 billion in exploration and other activities in Assam. The ULFA's extortion demand created ripples of fear and uncertainty among the 5,000

ONGC employees serving in Assam. A majority of ONGC's workers are engaged in field operations in isolated and difficult terrain. Hence, they become soft targets for kidnapping and shooting.

The ULFA issued another extortion demand of Rs.25 lakh to an independent candidate in the assembly election, Bijoy Krishna Nath. Such extortion bids by the ULFA led to a drying up of the inflow of capital in the state. Investments have been low and the foreign technical experts are reluctant to take up projects in Assam. These acts of violence, and extortion bids, raised serious doubts in the minds of the peacemakers regarding the real motives of the ULFA, and a sense of untrustworthiness prevailed.

Civil Society Organisations' Intervention and Parleys with Centre

Civil society organizations have been accused of overtly promoting and supporting the ULFA. Human rights organizations such as the 'Manab Adhikar Sangram Samiti' (MASS) and The People's Committee for Peace Initiatives in Assam (PCPIA) have been accused of being sympathizers of the ULFA. As a result, the ULFA enjoys the confidence and the credibility of such organizations. Therefore, the neutrality of these organizations is repeatedly questioned by the government. The PCPIA, described as a conglomeration of 21 organizations, adopted a resolution in Guwahati on 30th January, 2006, demanding a justice oriented solution without compromising the dignity of Assam and demanded the restoration of sovereignty of the ULFA. In essence, the organization called for a plebiscite on the contentious issue of sovereignty and the right to self-determination. Importantly, the rally was addressed by many leading public figures and intellectuals, including Indira Goswami. The resolutions adopted in the rally appealed to the Union Government to expedite the peace process, suspend army operations, and include sovereignty in the agenda of talks. Genuine civil society groups need to take the front seat in developing an atmosphere for peace and stability in their respective states. Civil society organization in Assam must take the initiative in developing an atmosphere for peace rather than supporting the ULFA's cause.

Indira Goswami was not the only one working to see the talks between ULFA and New Delhi becoming a reality. There was another curious group working for the same aim. A platform of ULFA sympathizers named People's Committee for Peace Initiative (PCPI) was formed for the purpose. The PCPI convened a conclave on 22nd March, 2007 to revive

Assam Peace Talks. ULFA Chairman Arbindo Rajkhowa on 29th March, 2007 rejected Assam Chief Minister Tarun Gogoi's offer for unconditional talks and threatened to step up violence by suicide bombers. In a hard hitting statement he ruled out the possibility of budging from their demand of sovereignty.

In May 2007 ULFA militants shot dead six unidentified Hindi speaking people in various areas of Dibrugarh and Sibsagar districts. The ethnic cleansing kept on continuing. Police sources said that the ULFA had reportedly threatened villagers of dire consequences if they did not intensity the agitation against the security forces for killing innocent civilians in upper Assam. The public had raised their voice in upper Assam against the ULFA due to its continuing strike against innocent civilians. The Assam Police Intelligence Chief said that the ULFA used young boys as its frontline strike force.

Police sources revealed that ISI had been providing explosive to the ULFA to carry out subversive activities in public places. The ULFA triggered off 32 blasts in different parts of Assam while the police managed to recover 66 bombs.

The Union Minister of State for Home, Sriprakash Jaiswal said, "There are intelligence reports that ULFA camps are not only running, but also being nourished in Bangladesh." He informed that India had asked and is continuously putting pressure on the Bangladesh Government to keep watch and contain the activities of the ULFA but accused it as "reluctant or weak to co-operate" with India in taking action against them.

The Union Government had set three conditions to resume the stalled peace initiative with the ULFA. These included a direct communication from the outfit's top leadership indicating their willingness to talk with the government, the presence of emissaries of the either side in the talks and to facilitate meetings with the detained leaders in jail along with the safe passage to sweeten the deal. M.K. Narayan, the National Security Adviser, conveyed these conditions to Indira Goswami, the chief mediator of ULFA. Indira Goswami led a delegation of the 'Nagrik Shanti Manch' to Prime Minister Dr. Manmohan Singh on June 11 to discuss the restarting of peace talks with the ULFA but nothing concrete came out. In October 2008 there were serial blasts in which 77 persons were killed and 300 injured in 13 simultaneous blasts in Assam capital Dispur and adjoining city of Guwahati and three districts Kokrajhar, Barpeta and Bongaigaon. The investigating agencies found that the Bangladesh based HUJI had provided the expertise to ULFA and NDFB as none of them has the technology to explode such devastating bombs.

ULFA was launched a fund raising drive in which it was sending extortion letters to the businessmen and ONGC employees of the town. ULFA had changed its extortion strategy. Instead of issuing written extortion notes, the outfit was demanding a huge amount of cash from the businessmen by sending SMS through mobile phones.

In December 2008 the army launched an operation in Sibsagar to liberate upper Assam from the clutches of the outfit.

Assam Government announced a monetary package to rehabilitate and sustain the pro-peace ULFA, the cease-fire group. The package would be funded from both the Central and the State Government funds in the initial phase so that time was not wasted in getting clearance. The group had asked for INR 3,000 for an unmarried cadre and INR 5,000 for a married cadre. The Centre gave a consolidated stipend of INR 2,000 per month to a cadre in the cease fire period. Pro-peace leaders Mrinal Hazarika and Jiten Dutta welcomed this decision and termed it as positive.

In 2009, ULFA militants triggered serial bomb blasts in three different areas of Guwahati city, 5 persons were killed and 80 injured. These blasts were triggered hours before the scheduled arrival of Union Home Minister P. Chidambaram. "From *prima facie* evidences collected from thc spot, it appears to be the handiwork of suspected ULFA militants," said ASP of Police of Guwahati City, Debojit Deori. D.G. of Police, G.M. Srivastav told *The Hindu*—"The ULFA wanted to demonstrate its presence ahead of Chidambaram's visit."

The pro-talks group for the ULFA had reportedly given up the demand for sovereignty. In a press meet held at the designated camp at Kakopathar, the pro-talk group leader Mrinal Hazarika said they would now sit for talks with the Government within the framework of the Constitution of India.

The pro-talks faction of the ULFA raised a demand for "full autonomy" to Assam within the framework of the Constitution of India after it detached itself from the ULFA's demand for restoration of "Assam's sovereignty". The president of the pro-talks faction Mrinal Hazarika and two senior leaders, Prabal Meog and Jiten Dutta informed that the faction had submitted an 18 point charter of demands to the Assam C.M. Tarun Gogoi on February 19, 2009 for solution of the insurgency problem in Assam through negotiation. He further added that Gogoi had assured them to send the memorandum to the Prime Minister for consideration by the Central Government. Those political parties who were going to highlight these demands in the coming Lok Sabha polls would receive moral support from them.

Militant outfits like the ULFA and KLO were reportedly on an extortion drive in different villages of Dhubri District. These outfits were demanding INR 50,000 to INR 500,000 from middle class businessmen and servicemen residing in various villages in Dhubri District.

On 30th March, 2009, *Assam Tribune* reported that a group of Islamist militants had entered upper Assam with the help of local militants, to create disturbance in the parliamentary election scheduled to be held in April 2009.

53 militants surrendered before the Army in Tinsukia District. The blast occurred in Lalmati area, where the Union External Affairs Minister Pranab Mukherjee was supposed to address a public gathering as a part of ruling Congress party's election campaign. Senior S.P. of Police said, "From the *prima facie* evidence, it appears to be the handwork of the banned ULFA."

On 6th April, 2009, 10 persons were killed and about 59 others injured in four explosions carried out by suspected ULFA. D.G. of Assam Police, G.M. Srivastav said—"This is the handiwork of ULFA boys ahead of the outfit's Raising day."

On 27th April, 2009, suspected ULFA militants shot dead a pro-talk cadre, Hitesh Rabha in Goalpara District. The pro-talks ULFA leader, Robin Gogoi was earlier shot dead by suspected ULFA militants in the Tinsukia District. This was the second major attack by suspected ULFA militants on the pro-talks group within a month. Pro-talk leader Maradona Russell held ULFA 'Commander-in-Chief' Paresh Barua and 'Chairman' Arbindo Rajkhowa responsible for the killings. He warned that his group would not remain a silent spectator to the killing of its members.

On 6th November, 2009 ULFA's Foreign Secretary Sashdhar Choudhary and Finance Secretary Chitraban Hazarika were arrested by Border Security Force near Agartala.[19] ULFA chairman Arbindo Rajkhowa has been arrested by Bangladesh security forces from somewhere near Dhaka and handed over to India.

Along with him, National Liberation Front of Tripura (NLFT) chairman Biswmohan Dev Verma was also arrested and it came within a fortnight of the arrest of ULFA 'foreign secretary' Chitrabon Hazarika and 'finance secretary' Sashadhar Chaudhury.[20] They were presented before the court and the police handcuffed them. In the court they declared that they would not surrender and nothing short of sovereignty would be discussed. The handful of United Liberation Front of Asom supporters, who raised slogans in support of Arabindo Rajkhowa when he was produced in court, and the anger of the outfit's chairman at being handcuffed, cuts little ice with the common people of the state.

"Rajkhowa said he will not participate in talks in handcuffs. Hasn't he realised that he is no special person in the eyes of the law? After engineering the killing of thousands of people for 30 years, does he expect to be brought back with gold bangles and a garland?" asked college lecturer Farooq Ahmed of Barpeta district sarcastically.

ULFA's Commander-in-chief Paresh Borua who is still at large has ruled out any talks with the Indian Government unless the government agrees to include sovereignty in the agenda of talks.

By humiliating the ULFA top leadership with handcuffs and forcing them to accept the peace process at gunpoint, the Centre has shut the doors permanently. This new tough handling will send negative and positive angles to militants.

ULFA has indulged in violence, terror and bomb blasts for nearly 30 years and with Rajkhowa's arrest by the Bangladeshi security agencies, it seems that the endgame has begun for the terror outfit. Is Rajkhowa finally giving in and has he run out of options? Reacting to Rajkhowa's arrest and his desire to engage in peace talks Assam Chief Minister Tarun Gogoi said that the picture was not yet very clear. "I am not in the dark, nor in the clear picture. I am in between," said Gogoi while addressing a press conference in Guwahati.

Conclusion

ULFA was born like a cub to protect its territory from the poachers of Bangladesh. Ironically, it jumped into the circus ring of Islamic expansionists jointly managed by Pakistan and Bangladesh, which occasionally release and command it only for creating devastating disorder in Assam. It wants secession from India without realizing the ground reality that how the various ethnic groups, who hardly have anything in common with ethnic Assamese, would react if the State is separated from India. Will it again seek help from ISI or other agencies inimical to India for maintaining its hegemony over them? Or will it prefer to become their colony?

In view of the changing historical reality of the country, ULFA's dream for political destiny of Assam being separate from India, which disappeared following the reconstitution of its colonial geography on the eve of partition—may not come true. Perhaps only the people of Assam could convince the ULFA leaders to join the national political current and save the aggravated crisis of their identity from the threat of Islamisation and socio-economic degeneration of their motherland. The flip side is that the Government of India is not paying required attention to the North East. Instead of looking at problems from the vote bank politics, there is need to understand the genuine grievances of the Assamese and redress the past wrongs. Assam may be geographically too far away but the Assamese are great people with a sense of history and belonging to proud cultural milieu. They need understanding and respect.

If the ULFA were to rethink on its demand for sovereignty and the Union Government about suspending army operations in the State, then peace is possible. Furthermore, the ULFA must be sincere and respond positively to a negotiated political settlement. The vicious terror that the ULFA has unleashed is being perceived as self-serving and it has lost considerable support from the masses. The process of peace can be expected only when direct talks are held and ceasefire prevails in the State.

Notes

1. www.google.com/ulfa site.
2. *Ibid.*
3. K. Hrishikeshan, 'Assam's Agony: The ULFA and Obstacles to conflict resolution', published in *Faultlines*, Vol. XII, Delhi, 2002, pp. 23-30.
4. *Hindustan Times*, 18.1.2001, p. 5.
5. Col. Ved Prakash, *Terrorism in India's North East: A Gathering Storm*, Kalpaz Publications, Delhi, 2008, pp. 193-195.
6. Lt. General N.S. Narhari, *Security Threats to North East India: The Socio-Ethnic Tensions*, Manas Publications, New Delhi, 2002, pp. 69-70.
7. *Ibid.*, p. 70.
8. Col. Ved Prakash, *Terrorism in India's North East: A Gathering Storm*, Kalpaz Publications, Delhi, 2008, pp. 195-198.
9. *Ibid.*, p. 209.
10. *Ibid.*, p. 210.
11. Jaideep Saikia, *Terror and Islamist Militancy in North East India*, Vision Books, New Delhi, 2002, p.75.
12. *Ibid.*, p. 81.
13. Col. Ved Prakash, *Terrorism in India's North East: A Gathering Storm*, Kalpaz Publications, Delhi, 2008, pp. 223-225.
14. Dipankarson Gupta, Sudhir Kumar Singh, *Insurgency in North East India, The Role of Bangladesh,* Authors Press, Delhi, 2004, p. 98.

15. *Ibid.*
16. See Sanjib Baruah, *India against itself*, Oxford University Press, New 1999.
17. D.P. Kumar, *Challenge to Indias Unity*, B.R. Publishing Corporation, Delhi, 1990.
18. See H.M. Barch, *Encyclopaedia of North East India*, Mittal Publications, 2001.
19. *North East Sun*, December 2009, p. 10.
20. *Ibid.*

15

Corporate Responsibility Towards Environment in India

An Overview

Roopa Sharma

It is well-known that India's rapid growth and urbanisation has brought it among the ten most industrialised nations of the world. India produces almost everything that it consumes: food, clothing, household consumer goods, fertilizers and petroleum products, coal and steel, heavy electrical machinery and machine tools, locomotives and other railway equipment, motor vehicles and ships. However, India has 18 per cent of the world's population, 18 per cent of the world's cattle population but 2½ per cent of the world's area. These factors pose a huge challenge in balancing its economic growth with conserving its meagre natural resources. This chapter studies how well is India's corporate and industrial sector meeting this challenge through CSR and environmental compliance. Corporate Social Responsibility (CSR) is basically a concept whereby companies decide voluntarily to take responsibility for the impact of their activities on society, communities, customers, employees, shareholders and the environment in all aspects of their operations.

In India the issue of Corporate Social Responsibility (CSR) relates to a business unit providing safety for workers at workplace and giving them medical benefits and creating other welfare schemes in areas like education and employment. If experts are to be believed, corporate social responsibility is still in its nascent stage in India. It is misunderstood for charity by a large number of Indian companies. Environment disclosures of our companies are largely driven by the need to gain legitimacy for their acts of depredations.

We do not have to go far to seek the reason for this. The regulatory framework governing corporate disclosure in India includes the

Companies Act 1956 and the Securities and Exchange Board of India (Amendment) Act 2002. The Companies Act mandates the preparation of annual accounts of companies in accordance with the Accounting Standards issued by the Institute of Chartered Accountants of India (ICAI) However, there is no requirement under either the Indian Companies Act or Accounting Standards (ASs) to disclose environmental information.

The Securities and Exchange Board of India is the supervising body over the 23 stock exchanges in the country. Each of them has different listing requirements, concerning issued and subscribed equity capital. However, there is no requirement from these stock exchanges to disclose environmental information. Left off the hook, our industrial units go about undeterred in spewing out their smoke and effluents into the country's skies and waters. The chapter studies this issue in four parts. Part I unfolds CSR in India, part II examines with environmental compliance status of Indian industries, part III evaluates with economic incentives and policy initiatives by the government to address the issue of pollution with special reference to the new CSR clause 135 and part IV reveals with local initiatives and movements against industrial pollution.

PART I: CORPORATE SOCIAL AND ENVIRONMENTAL RESPONSIBILITY IN INDIA

Rapid industrialisation in the fifties and the sixties made India self-reliant on one hand but it was always accompanied by destruction, spoilage and degradation of the environs that our industries operated in. Their wanton use of natural resources accompanied with their abuse in the form of polluting water and air and degradation of land led to the genesis of expecting responsible behaviour from such units. The concept of CSR was coined in the western world during the early 1970s to describe the enterprise owners' responsibility beyond wealth generation for their shareholders.

However, in India, the concept took root in the real sense of the word in the 90s when much-needed economic reforms were introduced in the country, which resulted in significant changes in State and market relations ushering in the era of globalization and economic liberalization in India[1]. The major impact of these economic reforms has been the entry and the presence of transnational corporations (TNC) in the country. Some of these TNCs had highly developed corporate social responsibility initiatives based on the stakeholder participation model ushered in the 90s, the era of globalisation. The success and effectiveness of these TNCs in tapping international markets had a 'rub-off' effect on Indian enterprises, looking to fly higher as they benefitted from liberalisation factor behind the development of the concept of CSR in India was as Indian businesses started competing in the developed markets of Europe, America and the Far East they had to comply with entry level norms like certification for responsible corporate practices like ISO 14000, SA 8000, AA 100[2] as well as compliance codes formulated by OECD and UN Global Compact[3] of 2000 in order to be classified as global enterprises[4]. This meant that they had to adopt new corporate social responsibility standards having greater public private partnerships, multi-stakeholder initiatives and more civil society organizations becoming part of CSR arrangements.

Apart from these changes, India experienced the trickledown effects of the 1972 UN Conference on Human Environment held at Stockholm followed by the UN Conference on Environment and Development held at Rio de Janeiro in June 1992, both of which India had participated in[5]. The world witnessed settlement of transnational environment disputes from the "Polluter Pays" principle and the genesis of the principles of sustainable development and trans generational justice from the "sick utilitario principle" (do not harm the other person's property just as you would like to peaceably enjoy yours) at these Conferences. Yet, it was the Bhopal gas disaster of 1983 that showed India what corporate callousness could result in[6].

Then came the Earth Summit and the Kyoto Protocol followed by international concern on GHG emissions and Carbon footprint. Globalisation has resulted in the proliferation of new laws and regulations that direct business activities to address diverse social problems. Resultantly over the last decade the slot of Corporate Social Responsibility has risen steadily higher in India.

However, the Indian mindset continues to equate Corporate Social Responsibility with philanthropy or charity. Welfare programmes or initiatives like setting up of primary schools, hospitals or women's health centres for the immediate benefit of the company's workers continue to be introduced not as a duty or a responsibility but as a form of charity that is supposed to indicate the virtues of the company or the organization. It is merely considered a policy that should be implemented in business operations rather thar giving importance to social good.[7] Such acts are more in line with the Legitimacy Theory of corporate behaviour[8] which posits that firms try to behave in a way that society wants them to behave.

It lays down that the organisation must appear to consider the rights of the public at large, not merely those of the investors.

- This philanthropy-based model that most of our companies has embraced has several problems.
- The corporation does not commit its resources fully behind such a project and often confines itself to one-time or periodical financial grants[9].
- Since it is an act of charity, the corporation does not feel the need for community participation in the designing or management of such initiatives and people participation, if any, is restricted to limited implementation aspects reducing the efficiency and effectiveness of corporate social responsibility measures at the ground level.
- A company's community development approach is based on the argument that it needs to "give something back to society" lacks transparency and specific standards.
- Community development approaches often amount to little more than window-dressing and their cost must be compared to cost of mitigations of violations of social and environmental standards within companies."[10]

A Dutch initiative has made a striking finding vis-à-vis Indian Companies that of the three aspects of CSR, namely, social, economic and environmental, Indian companies' CSR initiatives have largely revolved around the social and economic aspects[11].

The practice of public disclosure of CSR in our companies: A study undertaken in 2011 on public disclosures on CR performance made by the top 100 listed companies by revenue points out that "Only 31 out of the top100 companies are publicly reporting on their CR performance of which only 25 per cent have systems to measure, monitor and report on such issues. Thus, about one third (31) of top 100 companies in India report on CR performance"[12].

Sustainability Corporate Responsibility Reporting: Too is at a very nascent stage in India. Sustainability report is the disclosure on the social, economic and environmental impact of a company upon its surroundings. The reasons behind environmental disclosures of Indian companies have been given as "Strengthening reputation and brand" and "Ethical considerations" according to the above study.[13]

These studies also reveal that Corporate Environmental

Responsibility is largely carried out as an image building exercise by our companies without any core commitment to sustainability principles etc. It continues to be an eyewash in the form of planting trees somewhere or putting a waste water treatment plant another place.

The beginning of environmental reporting in India: Early 1990's, marked the beginning of environmental reporting by a few heavily polluting industries. Environmental disclosure practices of India corporate have been studied by a number of people. Some studies have relied upon Annual Reports of Companies as published on their websites and justifiably so as the Indian Companies Act, 1956 makes it mandatory for companies to prepare their annual reports[14].

A survey by D.P. Malarvizhi[15] in 2008: was conducted by going through the official websites of top 24 Indian companies (listed in stock exchange) as per *Economic Times* ranking of 500 Indian companies, January 2007. It says.

> "Companies are experiencing growing demands from a variety of fronts to disclose their environmental performance. Increasingly, such information is being published in a user-friendly format on the Internet. Indian companies do not include quantitative disclosure on their environmental initiatives. Many companies limit themselves to descriptive information without disclosing the amount of operating expenses and environmental investments made in a financial year.
>
> Thirty-three per cent of companies (8 of the top 24 in the sample) in the sample, report on their environmental initiatives in purely descriptive terms. Companies merely state that it had undertaken investment projects related to environmental protection activities or that it has invested in eco-compatible projects. Some briefly describe even the type of the process undertaken and the foreseen results in terms of emissions reduction and/or energy consumption."

A very comprehensive study[16] relating to the **Annual Reports (2003-04)** of a sample of 38 top Indian companies as listed on *www.indiainfoline.com* (on 31/12/2003) has been reproduced here.

Characteristics of environmental information disclosed: As shown in Table 15.1, out of 38 only 19 companies have disclosed environmental information within their annual reports. Of these, companies in the 'oil and gas' sector provide the maximum information concerning the

Table 15.1

Environmental disclosure of sector 1 companies on websites	*Number of companies in sample*	*Number of companies not disclosing*
Oil & Gas	6	—
Diversified[17]	3	—
Pharmaceutical	4	2
Manufacturing	14	3
Technology	8	7
Media and entertainment	1	1
Services	2	2
Total	29	19

environment, followed by 'manufacturing' firms. This can be justified by the fact that there is a high chance that companies belonging to these two sectors highly interfere with the environment.

None of the 19 companies have disclosed 'bad news.' This may be due to the fact that they had no such news to disclose. Another reason may be that they were reluctant to disclose their environmental 'bad' news to the users of annual reports. This is consistent with the expectation of Ahmed and Sulaiman (2004)[18] as 'bad' news may damage public reputation. Most of the 'good news' comprises of obtaining award(s) and/or compliance with external standard(s).

In a survey based on 1997-98 annual reports of Indian companies carried out by *Business Today* 1998, it was said that disclosures of environmental, energy and social issues were "still limited to little more than a sentence or two each in the annual reports.[19] Each of the above surveys point at the negligible number of Indian companies and industries that take sustainable issues seriously even though they make the top brass.

This brings us to the other important issue, namely, the extent of environmental compliance in the Indian industrial sector as mandated by India's environmental regime.

PART II: ENVIRONMENTAL COMPLIANCE STATUS, INDIA

India is experiencing rapid economic growth of about 6.4 per cent annually over the last two decades, which is placing significant pressure on the environment. While it is estimated that 75 per cent of the wastewater generated is from municipal sources, industrial waste from large and medium-sized plants contributes to over 50 per cent of the total pollution loads. The accompanying graphs reveal that—

- Ambient particulate matter in India is five times the level in USA (while China's are seven times the U.S. level) See Fig. 15.1, Panel A[20].
- Water pollution concentration in India is higher than both the US and China.

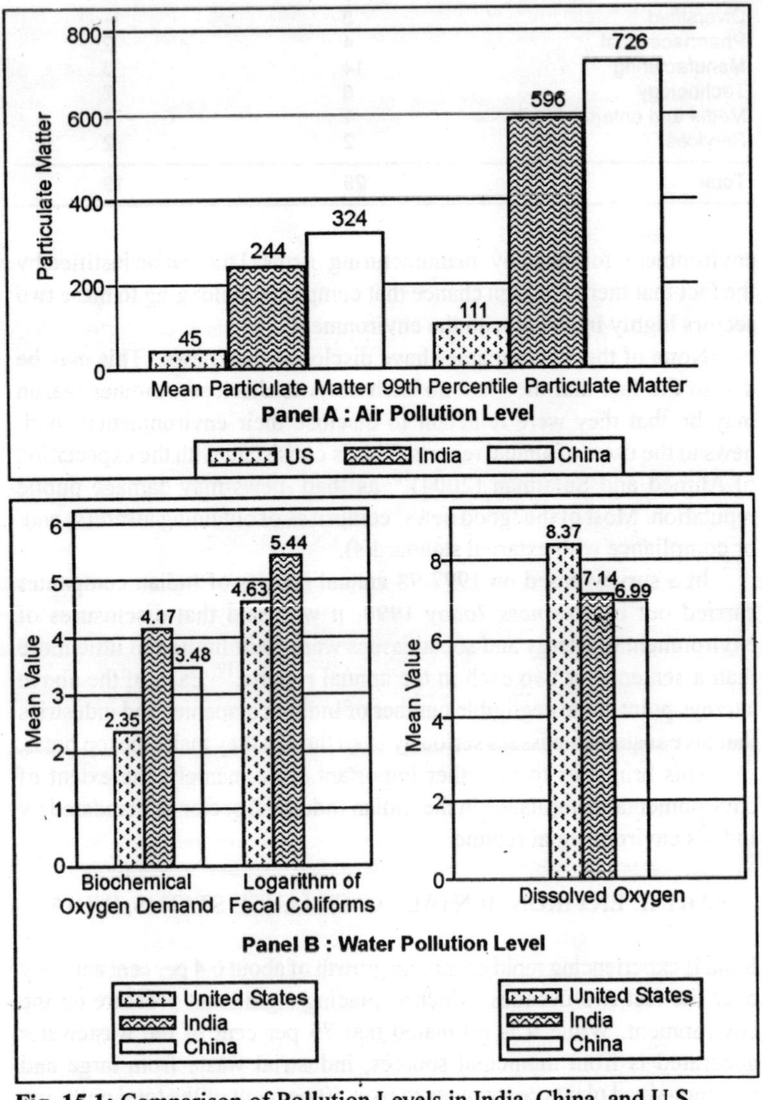

Fig. 15.1: Comparison of Pollution Levels in India, China, and U.S.

A 1995 World Bank study conservatively estimated India's annual environmental damage at $9.7 billion, or 4.5 per cent of gross domestic product. Of this, $7 billion was due to air and water pollution.[21] These show that India though is experiencing economic growth of around 6.5 per cent annually but it is at that stage of development where growth trumps environmental concern.

India's rivers and streams suffer from high levels of pollution from waste generated primarily from industrial processes and municipal activities. Water pollution concentration in India is higher than that of the US and China.

To address these environmental challenges in coordination with the State Governments, the Central Government has identified and targeted 17 highly polluting industries[22] and 24 environmental problem areas spread over different states comprising largely of Small and Medium industrial clusters[23]. The chemical and engineering industries are at the top of this list, since they are the major contributors to air, water, and waste pollution. These industries include integrated iron and steel plants, non-ferrous metallurgical units, pharmaceutical and petrochemical complexes, fertilizers and pesticide plants, thermal power plants, textiles, pulp and paper, tanneries and chloralkali units.[24] They emit large amounts of nitrogen, sulphur and carbon oxides into the air. Emissions of lead, arsenic and chromium, from iron and steel industries, are extremely toxic. Waste disposal from such industries causes extensive water and soil contamination too. Extraction of raw materials causes large-scale surface disturbance and erosion. To make matters worse, it is not the large scale industries alone that cause heavy pollution. There are over 4.5 million small to medium size industries (SMEs) and over 2000 industrial estates/ clusters in India compared to over 7500 large-scale industries.

Though the SMEs account for over 40 per cent of the industrial output in value terms from the organised and unorganised manufacturing sectors in India, according to the Confederation of Indian Industries (CII)[25], it is estimated that the pollution generated by them is more than their share of industrial production. In fact, many of these are highly polluting. According to the MOEF, SMEs are responsible for an estimated 70 per cent of the total industrial pollution load nationwide. The effluents of these units be it treated or untreated are discharged by them in nearby water bodies, municipal drains, on to the road, into wells, polluting groundwater as well as the natural water sources. Due to inadequate facilities for discharging the industrial effluents, stagnant pools built up in the vicinity of the industrial areas. These stagnating effluents percolate into drains and pollute the groundwater. Small-scale industry in general is of significant economic importance in India. This is due to the large number of units, their wide geographical spread and generally labour intensive technologies. The small scale industry is a major employer and is credited with providing local employment opportunities, due to their lower capital requirements. The government offers a number of incentives for the growth and promotion of these industries extending facilities like soft loans and infrastructure for the industrialists.

However, 'end-of-pipe' technologies, such as on-site pre-treatment facilities, require high capital investment, financial costs, and specialised technical skills. Lack of access to these inputs as well as finances to fund them, creates a disincentive framework for many SMEs. This situation provides opportunities for both rent-seeking and/or direct defaulting of pollution control parameters. An observation is worthy to note here. "*In fact, a number of large- and medium-sized industries in the region covered by the Ganga Action Plan do not have adequate effluent treatment facilities. Most of these defaulting industries are sugar mills, distilleries, leather processing industries, and thermal power stations. Most major industries have treatment facilities for industrial effluents. But this is not the case with small-scale industries, which cannot afford enormous investments in pollution control equipment as their profit margin is very slender*".[26]

The environmental management problems for small scale industries are more severe due to a variety of reasons, including:

- *Obsolete, Inefficient Production Process:* The small industry sector in India has traditionally enjoyed considerable subsidies and protection as employment generating units for the local youth. This has meant that entrepreneurs have little incentives to modernise their operations. Besides most of them thrive on little capital. Accordingly, these industries are often more polluting per unit of output than many of their larger, technologically more up-to-date counterparts.
- *Difficulties in Obtaining Financing for Modernisation:* Agencies like the World Bank, OECD, Bilateral Aid etc. that give funds to finance Pollution Prevention and Control measures prefer large companies.
- *Human Resource Constraints:* Generally, large firms use either in-house environmental managers or local consulting firms to help them improve environmental performance; these approaches are beyond the means of smaller firms.

- *Lack of Access to Information:* Many larger industrial firms have relatively good access to information on pollution prevention and control technologies available worldwide. Smaller firms usually have very limited, if any, access to such information.
- *Lack of will:* Another problem is the relatively small amount of time that a small entrepreneur has on a single issue relating to supply of pollution control equipments, its finance and its replace ability or reparability. Small scale units are unable to pay the salaries to attract chemical engineers with appropriate skills, which are already in short supply in the Indian market. This reduces their ability to apply new technology.

Legal Enforcement Authority

In India the pollution control regime is purely of Command and Control (CAC) type. State Pollution Control Boards (SPCB) are India's primary pollution control enforcers. They prescribe discharge standards and inspect equipment, industrial plants, and manufacturing processes and penalise industry violations in their respective states. Under the Water Act,1974, the Air Act,1981 and the Environment Protection Act,1986, the pollution control boards have the authority to issue and revoke consents to operate, require self-monitoring and reporting, conduct sampling, inspect facilities, require corrective action and prescribe compliance schedules. In practice, only large and medium-sized facilities have the required permits. There are many reasons for this. Many SPCBs are severely understaffed and face financial crunch. The vacancy ratio is as high as 65 per cent at the SPCB of Karnataka, 54 per cent in Punjab, 46 per cent in Goa, and 43 per cent in Andhra Pradesh (Planning Commission, 2001-02).

Often SPCBs hire contract employees (e.g., in Manipur, Sikkim, Kerala, Madhya Pradesh) who do not get standard civil service benefits and, therefore, have low work motivation.

Due to the very large number of industrial units operating in some states, it is physically not possible for the inspectors to visit each and every facility in an year and re- issue or cancel valid Consents to Operate[27].

Most Small-scale Industries Operate without any Consents

The SPCBs provide incentives to industry to set up on-site Effluent Treatment Plants (ETP) or Common Effluent Treatment Plants (CETP) for clusters of Small Scale industries. According to prescribed policy, all industrial effluent is required to be treated by CETPs before being released into a water body. The ***enforcement powers*** include emergency measures of disconnecting water or power supply and facility closure, which are widely used in some states. However, their effectiveness is limited. They often lack the technical capacity to monitor hazardous wastes. Moreover, they must rely on time-consuming judicial remedies to close down polluting industries. Poor enforcement is also due to political interference in India, corruption is pervasive.

Consent to Establish. All polluting facilities are legally required to obtain from the respective SPCB a consent (permission) to establish (CTE) and a Consent To Operate (CTO), under the Water (Prevention and Control of Pollution) Act,1974 and the Air Act 1981 (amended in 1987). **Consent to Operate** refers to a permission that an industrial unit must obtain in order to operate for discharge of wastes and emissions into water and air. Upon verification of compliance with these conditions, a CTO is issued with emission and effluent limits.

Under the environmental laws, every industrial unit is supposed to keep air emissions and water quality within the regulatory limits. The requirements for granting this permission (usually the consent to operate is annual) are that the unit does not exceed the quoted quantities and that adequate measures are taken to ensure compliance with pollution standards. All this is laid down as part of green clearance, but compliance as well as monitoring is lax. It is common practice for SPCB officials to give official notice of a forthcoming control visit to units. It is, therefore, possible to alter the operations so that compliance is ensured. In some cases, (larger) units have end-of-pipe treatment, which is only switched on or used when a visit is expected.

As far as compliance is concerned, most boards claim that a majority of industries are complying with the standards. However, compliance is defined quite uniquely in India: Industries having pollution control equipment are considered to be in compliance with standards! The data on actual compliance status based on monitoring and inspection is not compiled by most Boards[28]. The State Pollution Control Boards mostly go by data submitted by polluters themselves.Besides, environmental consents can be obtained by corrupt practices given the financial crunch most of the Boards are operating under.

As a solution to this problem, the High Court of Gujarat had mandated a system of third-party pollution audits of industrial units in 1996. Under this system, the granting of consent is based on an environmental audit by a third party. External auditors are engaged to take periodic readings of key water and air pollution parameters. However, since the auditors are paid directly by the companies and there are no incentives for correct auditing. Similarly, industrial units that do not have any control equipment or treatment facilities continue to function. This is because in India, non-compliance is cheaper than meeting standards. There are also no deterrent mechanisms such as fines or penalties that could be imposed on non-complying industries. In order to fine a defaulting industry, the board has to initiate a long-drawn out process of filing a case in court of law. The court is entitled to impose punishments ranging from imprisonment of 18 months to six years, in addition to a fine. Pursuing cases through trial and appellate courts, however, has proven to be an ineffective enforcement response, since courts are overburdened, procedures are cumbersome, and resources of state boards are overstretched.

There is often a huge backlog of environmental cases as these are not a priority for the courts. The effect of the described illegal influencing measures is that industrialists have been able to keep the private costs of production below the social costs of production[29], which is one of the reasons the Indian industry is competitive in relation to industrialised countries where externalities are increasingly being internalised[30].

India likely to become a Pollution Haven

According to the Pollution Haven Hypothesis,[31] it is predicted that India may end up becoming a Pollution haven because of its lax environmental laws and reporting procedure. It should be mentioned that a polluting activity in a high-income country normally faces higher regulatory costs than its counterpart in a developing country. Under these circumstances the pollution intensive industries will have a natural tendency to migrate to countries with weaker environmental regulations.[32] It is well known that the Government of India is trying to increase Foreign Direct Investment (FDI) to US$ 50 billion within five years from 2008. A huge investment can be expected in chemicals, pesticides, textiles etc. Besides India is considered an attractive destination for investment by foreign companies due to its cheap labour. The Pollution Haven Hypothesis (PHH) predicts that as rich developed countries tighten their grip on environmental pollution, they move their manufacturing to countries where regulation is lax and investment is welcomed due to their poverty.

PART III: ECONOMIC INCENTIVES AND POLICY INITIATIVES BY THE GOVERNMENT

Principal economic instruments include rebate on the water cess, bank guarantees, subsidies for pollution control equipment, and other fiscal incentives.

Monetary incentives on pollution abatement equipments are provided by the Central and the State Governments for their installation in the form of subsidies. The Common Effluent Treatment Plant (CETP) subsidy scheme is undertaken by the MOEF to enable clusters of small-scale industries to establish or upgrade CETPs. The Central and State Governments subsidize each 25 per cent of total project costs for CETP and common hazardous waste incinerators.

Rebate on the Water Cess

The Water Cess is calculated on the basis of water consumed by industry/ local authority for specified purposes. The Water Cess will be levied and collected from all the industries with water consumption of more than 10 cubic meter per day provided they are not generating hazardous waste. The cess rate is specified by the Government and it varies for industry from 0.5 Rs/m^3 to 3 Rs/m^3 depending on the purpose of water use and the presence of biodegradable or toxic pollutants in the eventual effluent. Industries that comply with effluent standards, are connected to a wastewater treatment plant, and do not consume water in excess of the prescribed limit are entitled to a 25 per cent rebate in the water cess. The rebate scheme thereby encourages compliance.

Public-Private Partnerships (PPP). Through economic incentives, both the Central and State Governments are promoting Public-Private Partnerships (PPPs) for the development of infrastructure for environmental services. For example, in Gujarat 10 per cent of the total investment of USD 1,644 million for controlling pollution has come through a public-private partnership. CETPs, TSDF, and conveyance pipelines for treated wastewater disposal into deep sea are eligible for a 25 per cent state subsidy.

Other Incentive Initiatives. Some states are introducing initiatives to encourage good environmental behaviour through packages of economic and regulatory incentives. For example, the Gujarat PCB provides incentives to industries implementing Environmental Management Systems (EMS) by issuing them consents on a priority basis and of longer validity (six years), providing 25 per cent rebates in water cess and 50 per cent discounts on fees for environmental audits (*see* Section 3.3). Some states have even tried to make ISO 14001 certification a precondition for consent renewal for the 17 most polluting categories of industries.

ISO Certification. Ministry of Micro Small and Medium Enterprises provides incentive to those small scale/ ancillary undertaking who have acquired ISO 9000/ISO 14001/HACCP certifications by order dated 28th October, 2002. Upto 31st March 2009, 18778 Micro and Small units have been benefited from the scheme. Table below shows the prevalence of the most important certificates in the area of CSR. While the ISO 14000 standard of environmental management is widely applied in India other certifications are of far less importance.

Year of acquiring ISO 14000 Certificate	*No. of Indian Companies*
1995	1
1996	2
1997	28
1998	40
1999	111
2000	257
2001	400
2002	605

All the above incentives are not very effective though in achieving results on environmental degradation due to lax implementation, and a number of factors relating to CPCB and SPCBs as mentioned above.

Policy Initiatives: Over the past several years, India has been updating its corporate law and legal framework to increase transparency, accountability, and align with international business standards. The primary focus of these efforts has been the revision of the Companies Act of 1956. The issue of CSR has benefitted from our thrust upon the above-mentioned goals. For instance, The Ministry of Corporate Affairs had released Voluntary Guidelines on CSR in 2009 as the first step towards acknowledging the concept of Business Responsibilities. Keeping in view the feedback from stakeholders, it was decided to revise and mandate the same in 2011, with a more comprehensive set of guidelines that encompassed social, environmental and economical responsibilities of businesses[33]. The same were incorporated in the Companies Bill 2011. Companies did not take kindly to the proposed Bill and are seeking to nullify it to voluntary spending and not mandatory spending. It was in

2013 that India, set itself apart from other Asian countries by codifying Corporate Social Responsibility (CSR) spending for targeted companies *via* Section 135 of the Companies Act, 2013.[34] Section 135 (the "CSR Clause") requires some companies (read big and rich) to spend a prescribed formula-based amount on CSR for the applicable fiscal year, report on these activities, or explain why they failed to spend, in the annual board report.

Section 135 of the new Act applies to qualifying companies only and lays down that,

- Every Company with net worth of Rs. 500 crore[35] or more, or turnover of Rs. 1,000 crore or more or a net profit of Rs. 5 crore (about U.S. $900,000) or more during any financial year to constitute a Corporate Social Responsibility Committee or Board committee consisting of three or more directors of which at least one has to be an independent director; and
- Ensure that the company spends, in every financial year, at least 2 per cent (the 2% formula) of the average net profits it made during the three immediately preceding financial years, in pursuance of its Corporate Social Responsibility Policy. A qualifying company that fails to spend the required amount will have to explain that failure in the report of the board of directors. The CSR activities may comprise any number of activities listed in Schedule VII of the Companies Bill (outlined below). Another requirement is that companies are to give preference to local area of operation for CSR spending.

Fines and/or Imprisonment for Failure to Comply and Report

While a company is not subject to liability for failing to spend on CSR under the 2 per cent Formula, a company and its officers are subject to liability for not explaining such a failure in the report of the board of directors. Failure to explain is punishable by a fine on the company of not less than 50,000 rupees (about US $900) and up to 25 lakh rupees (about US $46,000). Further, officers who default on the reporting provision could be subject to up to three years in prison and/or fines of not less than 50,000 rupees (about US $900) and as high as 5 lakh rupees (about US $9,200).

Permissible CSR Activities

The CSR Clause leaves it to the discretion of the company's board to determine the exact manner in which the CSR amounts are spent. However, Schedule VII of the Companies Bill requires the CSR policy created by the CSR committee involve at least one of the following focus areas:

1. Eradicating extreme hunger and poverty;
2. Promotion of education;
3. Promoting gender equality and empowering women;
4. Reducing child mortality and improving maternal health;
5. Combating [HIV], [AIDS], malaria and other diseases;
6. Ensuring environmental sustainability;
7. Employment-enhancing vocational skills;
8. Social business projects;
9. Contribution to the Prime Minister's National Relief Fund or any other fund set up by the Central Government or the State Governments for socio-economic development, and relief and funds for the welfare of the Scheduled Castes, the Scheduled Tribes, Other Backward Classes, minorities and women; and
10. Such other matters as may be prescribed.[36]

Likely Outcomes of the CSR Clause

The CSR Clause will only apply to some of the over 800,000 companies in India, including over 8,000 publicly listed companies and multinational companies. The accounting firm Ernst & Young estimates that the law would cover over 2,500 companies in India and generate over US$ 2 billion of CSR spending in local communities.[37] With the new legislation, India would possibly become the first country to have CSR spending through a statutory provision[38]. The Bill is set to make independent directors more accountable. Ill equipped that our companies are with the nuances of CSR reporting and performing it is easy to assume that companies are not expected to do CSR on their own. They have to outsource it to implementing agencies. The Non-Governmental Organisations (NGOs) are likely to benefit once the companies bill is passed. But then they have to be empanelled by the company. With the passage of the bill, the trusts of the companies will also be placed under scrutiny to check whether they are being used for the purpose they are created. If the law is passed, it is likely to create a huge demand for people specialising in CSR. "There is likely to be a demand of nearly one lakh people once the law is passed."[39] CSR has for the first time been recognized in the Company Law. It will encourage companies who had previously never thought about this space at all to give serious thoughts to it.

This will also ensure a gradual shift from the traditional charity model to a more strategic CSR model that fits in with the long term objectives of the company. This mandate is also likely to promote innovation of new business solutions as part of CSR. Companies are good at finding new opportunities and solutions. If they can focus their creativity and finance on finding products that can make profits and provide a social good then progress will accelerate.

However, there are some weaknesses in the clause still. For instance, —CSR does not have a clear definition given by the Government, although there are nine principles where areas like development, human rights and inclusive growth have been highlighted. The definition will be central to how companies approach this clause. If CSR is tied to philanthropy it will limit Indian CSR to writing cheques for good causes with little effect on core business performance. If it is too wide it will be an open door for Green Wash and Creative Accounting. The new Companies Bill needs clear guidelines and rules on how to calculate the mandatory two per cent CSR spending. CSR should be as much (if not more) about how companies make their money rather than how they spend it. If a company fails to meet the desired standard; it may get away by providing the reason. Such a statement may, in practice, defeat the very purpose of clause 135.[40]

PART IV: LOCAL INITIATIVES AND MOVEMENTS AGAINST INDUSTRIAL POLLUTION

This part of the chapter studies the importance of the participation of the local communities in environmental decision-making to safeguard their resources and to influence industries to stem their pollution. India has witnessed a wide range of people's movements against environmental depredations caused by Public sector undertakings and private enterprises.[41]

Unlike in Western countries, environmental movements in India emerge only when the immediate livelihoods are directly affected[42] Murty *et al.* (1999) reported the results of a survey of a number of industrial estates and an All-India Survey of large-scale water polluting factories providing evidence of local community pressure resulting in the industries complying with standards. For example, the recent case of Orissa High Court[43] culminating in the rejection of Vedanta resources' plans for the six-fold expansion of the Lanjigarh aluminium refinery. This victory for environment was brought about mainly by the protests of the tribals against the residue of the aluminum refining process that includes highly toxic alkaline chemicals and radioactive materials threatening the health and lives of thousands of people.

Similarly in Raigad district of Maharashtra, a coal thermal power plant got scrapped due to locals 'protests in 2011. In the same year in Wardha district local movements encouraged by an NGO successfully won a court hearing against Lanco company against their corrupt environmental practices. The company in connivance with the State Pollution Control Board manipulated the minutes of the public hearing (a mandatory exercise to determine the support for the industrial project). The judges revealed that basic public hearing norms were violated and those who opposed the project were beaten by the company's hired goons.

The case of Patancheru, one of the most polluted industrial area in Medak district of Andhra Pradesh also shows how the local people organised protests against the District Administration as effluents seeped into the groundwater causing many to fall ill and many cattle deaths ultimately winning handsome compensation against the offending company, etc. Local opposition to the pollution started in 1986 when about 3,000 villagers marched to the Chief Minister's office after suffering large-scale crop losses and health damages due to contamination and the pollution of nearby river. In 1989, about 5,000 people held a demonstration before the state assembly, demanding an end to industrial pollution. In the same years farmers blocked the highway running through Pattancheru for two days. The villagers also filed court cases by jointly sharing the cost with contributions of Rs. 200 per household. This legal action through the collective effort of the people ultimately forced the factories in the industrial estate to have a CETP for complying with water pollution standards. Similar experiences are reported from many other industrial estates like the Plachimada Gram Panchayat[44] standing up against Coca Cola Ltd. ending up in cancelling the licences of the MNC or the Tiruppur farmers case[45] the Forests' Rights case,[46] highlight informal regulation by local communities resulting in factories complying with standards. The ongoing struggle of Jharkhand tribals against the proposed 12,000 acres steel plant to be put up by Arcelor Mittal is another instance of refusing to allow corporates to degrade or spoil an area with their effluents. In the wake of the 73rd Amendment to the Constituition of 1992, many village panchayats have shown sustainable solutions by effective monitoring of their environs like the Kerela coastal panchayats and in Haryana.

More than anything else, the main advantage in involving the local people is the justification of their cause, since they will not hesitate volunteering to safeguard their own survival, and the relative ease in achieving victory for the environment. The regulation of industrial discharge can be accomplished far better with the help of local bodies than MINAS or the SPCBs etc. To achieve this, the local council of the areas affected by these effluent discharges can be empowered to collect samples randomly of effluents and send it for analysis to a public funded laboratory.

CONCLUSION

In the current times when India has increased FDI manyfold with a number of companies vying to set up manufacturing units in India and the liberal approach of the government in issuing clearances for industrial units all over, a multi-pronged strategy involving better CSR accountability, insisting upon greater accountability in annual audits and Director's reports, better equipped Pollution Control Boards complete with laboratories, qualified staff recruited on the contracts of regular salaries and manageable workloads, Economic Instruments of Pollution Control (MBIs) offering greater subsidies on filtering and effluent treatment equipment, and most important of all, the empowerment of local communities would work towards sustainability of India's environment. Otherwise the future of many little, assetless, powerless Indians is likely to be vitiated by our poisoned common resources that are a lifeline for them.

Notes and References

1. Prior to the 80s there was extensive state regulation of businesses under Prime Minister, Mrs. Gandhi's License Regulations which refer to the heavy regulation of economic activity in India through various methods like quotas, permits, permissions and licenses.
2. These are international standards that certify a company on its EMS or Environment Management System. These have proved to enhance the image of the company in developed countries.
3. The Global Compact is a framework for businesses that are committed to

aligning their business operations and strategies with ten universally accepted principles that postulate that companies should embrace, support and enact, a set of core values in the areas of human rights, labour standards, the environment and anti-corruption. As the world's largest, global corporate citizenship initiative, the Global Compact is first and foremost concerned with exhibiting and building the social legitimacy of business and markets.

4. These are international standards that certify a company on its EMS or Environment Management System. These have proved to enhance the image of the company in developed countries. ISO 14001 is often a requirement for doing business in Europe and Asia. In India, about 1500 companies have been certified for ISO 14001. BIS (Bureau of Indian Standards) is the nodal agency for ISO 14000 certification, but it is not a mandatory regulation
5. At the Rio de Janeiro Earth Summit of 1992, for the first time environmental issues were put on the world table. Till Rio 1992, environment was considered a local or national issue. But science and fears of a changing climate altered all that. Emission limits were needed for all industrialised countries. For this, global rules were essential and global cooperation imperative. The contemporary multi-stakeholder CSR agenda took off around this time. At that time only a few global brand-name corporations, often reacting defensively to civil society pressures, introduced new concepts and selected improvements in environmental management systems and eco-efficiency, and some accepted codes of conduct (Utting, 2005, 2). The stakeholder participation model was ushered in this conference.
6. In December 1983 the US based Union Carbide company that made fertilisers in its Bhopal unit leaked tonnes of methyl iso cyanide gas resulting in the death of more than 3000 people and maiming of many more.
7. Emerging trends in CSR: Perspectives and experiences from post liberalised India by Sudip Mahapatra and Kumar Visalakh, NALSAR, Hyderabad.
8. Dowling, J. and Pfeffer, J. (1975). Organisational Legitimacy: Social Values and Organisational Behaviour. *Pacific Sociological Review*, 18(1), 122-136.
9. See supra footnote 7.
10. Tatjana Chahoud *et al.* Corporate Social and Environmental Responsibility in India—Assessing the UN Global Compact's Role, Bonn 2007 German Development Institute D.I.E.
11. CSR in India, CREM Report. Amsterdam, 2004.
12. KPMG Corporate Responsibility Survey 2011 by KPMG Global Climate Change and Sustainability Services (GCCSS).
13. *Ibid.*

14. Researches around the world show that annual reports are the most favoured channel of disclosure, since annual reports are qualified, verifiable disclosures with high credibility. Under the Indian Companies Act, 1956 Companies are required to file Balance Sheet, Profit & Loss Account along with Directors' Report and Auditors Report and Annual Return, separately, with the Registrar of Companies, in each calendar year.
15. "Corporate environmental reporting on the internet" an insight into Indian practices". By D.P. Malarvizhi, Sangeeta Yadav., 2008.
16. The rhetoric of Environmental Reporting: The case of India. Mir and Chatterjee, *Managerial Auditing Journal*, 23(6), 609-629.
17. Diversified' sector includes companies operating in more than one area encompassing FMCG, hotels, paperboards and packaging, agribusiness, home and personal care products, food and beverages, childcare, cooking, pet care and wellness. 'Technology' sector includes companies in telecom services or other Information Technology (IT) services. 'Services' sector includes companies in transport services.
18. Environmental disclosures of Malaysian property development companies, *Social Responsibility Journal*, Vol. 9, ISS: 2, pp. 241-258.
19. Environmental Disclosures in Annual Reports by Sunil Arora, Garima Kapoor, *Environment Management Practices*, 2007.
20. Rajaram, T. Das, A.; Water pollution by industrial effluents in India: Discharge scenarios and case for participatory ecosystem specific local regulation *Futures,* Volume 40, Issue 1, February 2008, pp. 56-69.
21. Quenching that growing thirst, Gem Paul, TOI, 20.3.2008.
22. All these fall in the Red category. Industries are categorized on the basis of their pollution potential in three broad categories *viz*. Red, Orange and Green. "Red" represents highly polluting industries e.g. chlor alkali, iron and steel, aluminium smelter, dyes, pesticides 'Orange' represents moderately polluting industries like hotels and restaurants, automobile repair, mirrors, soap and 'Green' represents marginally polluting units like *atta chakkies*, apparel making, ice cream, etc.
23. In August 2009, the government had identified 24 critically-polluted areas in the country. These industrial clusters are Angul Talcher in Orissa, Ankleshwar in Gujarat, Bhadravati in Karnataka, Chembur in Maharashtra, Dhanbad in Jharkhand, Digboi in Assam, Durgapur in West Bengal, Greater Cochin, Howrah, Jodhpur, Korba, Manali, Govindgarh, Najafgarh (Delhi), Nagda, North Arcot, Pali, Parwanoo, Singrauli, Tarapur, Vapi, Visakhapatnam and Vellore. This endeavour was carried out in 2009 pursuant to the area based approach to environmental regulation through different CPCB and SPCB programmes.
24. Major polluting industries are subject to a special regime of inspection from the SPCBs and are subject to the water cess.

25. The Confederation of Indian Industries and FICCI are India's largest industry and business employers.
26. *The Economist*, 17.3.2008, Varanasi.
27. OECD 2006. Environmental Compliance and Enforcement in India: Rapid Assessment. Jointly produced by OECD and the Secretariat of the Asian Environmental Compliance and Enforcement Network (AECEN) under the OECD Programme of Environmental Co-operation with Asia. *http://www.oecd.org/dataoecd/39/27/37838061.pdf*
28. "Turnaround Reform Agenda For India's Environmental Regulators" Centre for Science and Environment, 2009.
29. Improving the environmental performance of small scale industries in the South, by Clancy and Lakmakker, Netherlands.
30. Social costs of production include the costs to society as a whole. Environmental degradation (externality) is a cost to society. If no private costs are made to prevent or abate this effect, the private costs of production (internalities) lay below the social costs. Thus the industry has been able to prevent the internalisation of externalities.
31. The haven hypothesis (or pollution haven effect) posits that jurisdictions with weak environmental regulations—'pollution havens'—will attract pollution polluting industries relocating from more stringent locales. This principle says that a company would want to locate its production unit in a country with the lowest environmental standards.
32. Copeland and Taylor (1995) in "Globalization and Environment: Can *Pollution Haven Hypothesis* alone explain the impact of Globalization on Environment?" by Soumyananda Dinda in *www.isid.ac.in/~planning/Soumyananda.pdf* accessed on 8th of July.
33. In 2009, the government made it mandatory for all public sector oil companies to spend 2 per cent of their net profits on corporate social responsibility. In case of public sector companies earning a profit of Rs. 500 crore and above, CSR spending should be between 0.5 to 2 per cent of the net profit. It would be mandatory for corporates to disclose to shareholders whether they have made a contribution of 2 per cent of net profit toward corporate social responsibility activities.
34. http://www.kordant.com/assets/2-Percent-India-CSR-Report.pdf
35. Equivalent of US $ 90 million.
36. Charles Ostertag Companies Getting Ready For 'The CSR Clause' In India, GIVE2ASIA 05/06/2013 .
37. Ernst & Young, "Understanding Companies Bill 2012,"February 2013. http://www.ey.com
38. Rule Soon to Raise CSR Spending by Rs. 27,000 cr. Thursday, March 7th, 2013 | Filed under What is CSR | Posted by: indiacsr.
39. *New Indian Express* 12/8/13.
40. August 12, 2013 by 4th wheelBlog. http://the4thwheel.com/Blog/companiesbill2011/

41. Examples are Silent Valley Movement in Kerela, Chipko Movement in Uttar Pradesh, Aapiko Movement in Karnataka, *Narmada Bachao Andolan* in Central India, Gandhamardhan Movement in Odisha, Sardar Sarvor Project in Central India, the movement against Tehri Dam in Uttar Pradesh, the movement against Konkan Railway Projects in Maharashtra, the movement against vehicular as well as industrial pollution in Delhi etc., which aimed at halting environmental degradation or bringing about environmental restoration or regeneration or sustainable use of natural resources.
42. (Guha, 1991; Kothari, 2001; Krishna, 1996) *Source*: www.icec.ac.in 'People's participation in environment protection: A case study of Patancheru by Geetanjoy Sahu accessed on 13.3.13.
43. Prafulla Samantra *vs*. MoEF, Delhi HC 2009.
44. Permatty Grama Panchayat *vs*. Hindustan Coca Cola Pvt. Ltd, High Court of Kerala 2003.
45. Jan 2011, Mad HC leading to the closure of over 700 dyeing units in Tamil Nadu.
46. TN Godavarman Thirumulpad *vs*. Union of India SC 2007.

Index